A Place at the Altar

A Place at the Altar

PRIESTESSES IN REPUBLICAN ROME

Meghan J. DiLuzio

PRINCETON UNIVERSITY PRESS
Princeton and Oxford

Library of Congress Cataloging-in-Publication Data

Names: DiLuzio, Meghan J., 1981– author.
Title: A place at the altar : priestesses in Republican Rome / Meghan J. DiLuzio.
Description: Princeton : Princeton University Press, 2016. | Includes bibliographical
references and index.
Identifiers: LCCN 2015047927 | ISBN 9780691169576 (hardcover : alk. paper)
Subjects: LCSH: Women priests—Rome. | Rome—Religion. | Rome—Religious
life and customs.
Classification: LCC BL815.W66 D55 2016 | DDC 292.6/1—dc23 LC record available
at https://lccn.loc.gov/2015047927

British Library Cataloging-in-Publication Data is available

This book has been composed in Minion Pro and Copperplate Gothic Std

Printed on acid-free paper. ∞

Printed in the United States of America

1 3 5 7 9 10 8 6 4 2

FOR MY PARENTS

CONTENTS

ILLUSTRATIONS

ACKNOWLEDGMENTS

I owe a special debt to Harriet Flower, who supervised the dissertation from which this book developed. She was (and continues to be) an example to me, an ideal adviser, offering guidance and unfailing encouragement at every stage. I also owe much to the insight and enthusiasm of my readers, Denis Feeney and Michael Flower, and to the support of the faculty and my fellow graduate students in the Department of Classics at Princeton University. I first began thinking about Roman priestesses in a seminar cotaught by Michael Flower and John Gager during my first semester at Princeton. John Gager also presided over the Religion and Culture workshop at the Center for the Study of Religion, which helped to fund my final year of graduate study. I am grateful to him and to the other fellows for their comments on what eventually became chapters 1 and 4 of this book.

I have exceptionally fine colleagues and students in the Department of Classics at Baylor University. My life has been immeasurably enriched by the five years I have spent in their company. I am grateful to Simon Burris and Julia Dyson Hejduk, who read and commented on various portions of the manuscript, offering many helpful suggestions for improvement. Lee Ann Riccardi, who provided advice on chapter 5, has been more than generous as a mentor since my days at The College of New Jersey, where I was fortunate enough to learn from other great teachers, including John Karras and David Pollio. I would also like to thank the audiences and individuals who have listened to and commented upon various aspects of this work over the years. I am particularly grateful to Jörg Rüpke for discussing the project with me at an early stage, to the late Carin Green for guidance as I began the revision process, and to Katariina Mustakallio for supplying inspiration and advice as the book was nearing completion. Molly Lindner graciously shared her work in advance of publication. I am also grateful to the anonymous readers for Princeton University Press, who provided me with many useful comments. Any remaining faults and errors are strictly my own.

My research in Italy was initially made possible with funding from the Department of Classics and the Program in the Ancient World at Princeton University and subsequently through grants from the Department of Classics and the College of Arts and Sciences at Baylor University. For permission to visit and photograph various objects and monuments in Rome, I am indebted to the

Soprintendenza and especially to Carlotta Caruso, Orietta Rossini, and Maurizio Rullo. I am also grateful to Filippo Merola, director of the Museo Correale di Terranova in Sorrento, and to the staff of the Greece and Rome department at the British Museum in London for their assistance and permission to study and photograph objects in their collections.

I completed the final revisions to this book during a leave generously supported by Baylor University and a fellowship from the Volkswagen Foundation. I am grateful to Volkhard Krech, director of the Käte Hamburger Kolleg at the Ruhr-Universität Bochum, where I spent a happy and intellectually engaging year as a visiting research fellow, and to Alexandra Cuffel and Adam Knobler for their friendship and support, both in Bochum and in Ewing.

I am grateful to Rob Tempio and Sara Lerner of Princeton University Press for their help in turning my manuscript into a book, and to David Rollow for his careful copyediting. My former student Amy Welch drew figure 5.14. Material from chapters 1 and 6 was published in *Gods, Objects, and Ritual Practice in Ancient Mediterranean Religion*, edited by Sandra Blakely (Bristol: Lockwood Press, 2016). I wish to thank the publisher for permission to reprint it here.

My family has offered patience (often more than I deserved) and encouragement through all the years of writing. I am especially grateful to my parents, Richard and Barbara Gandy, to whom I dedicate this book. My deepest debt of gratitude is to my husband and colleague, Joseph DiLuzio, whose love and wisdom have improved every moment and every page.

ABBREVIATIONS

Ancient sources are abbreviated according to the conventions in the *Oxford Classical Dictionary*. All translations are my own unless otherwise noted.

BNP   *Brill's New Pauly: Encyclopaedia of the Ancient World*, 15 vols. (Leiden, 2002–2010).

CAH²   *The Cambridge Ancient History*², 14 vols. (Cambridge, 1970–2000).

CCCA   M. J. Vermaseren, *Corpus Cultus Cybelae Attidisque*, 7 vols., *Études Préliminaires aux Religions Orientales dans l'empire Romain*, 50 (Leiden, 1977–1989).

CIL   *Corpus Inscriptionum Latinarum* (Berlin, 1893–).

ILLRP   A. Degrassi, *Inscriptiones Latinae Liberae Rei Publicae*, 2 vols. (Florence, 1957–1963).

ILS   H. Dessau, *Inscriptiones Latinae Selectae*², 5 vols. (Berlin, 1954–1955).

InscrIt   *Inscriptiones Italiae* (Rome, 1931–).

LTUR   E. M. Steinby, ed., *Lexicon Topographicum Urbis Romae*, 6 vols. (Rome, 1993–2000).

MRR   T.R.S. Broughton, *Magistrates of the Roman Republic*, 3 vols. (New York, 1951–1986).

OLD   P.G.W. Glare, *Oxford Latin Dictionary* (Oxford, 1982).

RE   *Paulys Real-encyclopädie der classischen Altertumswissenschaft* (Stuttgart, 1894–1967).

RRC   M. H. Crawford, *Roman Republican Coinage*, 2 vols. (Cambridge, 1974).

ThesCRA *Thesaurus Cultus et Rituum Antiquorum*, 8 vols. (Basel, 2004–2014).

TLL   *Thesaurus Linguae Latinae* (Leipzig, 1900–).

A Place at the Altar

Introduction

Exegi monumentum aere perennius
regalique situ pyramidum altius,
quod non imber edax, non Aquilo impotens
possit diruere aut innumerabilis
annorum series et fuga temporum.
non omnis moriar, multaque pars mei
vitabit Libitinam: usque ego postera
crescam laude recens, dum Capitolium
scandet cum tacita virgine pontifex.

I have completed a monument more enduring than bronze,
higher than the royal structure of the pyramids, which neither
devouring rain nor the wild north wind can ever destroy, nor the
innumerable succession of the years, nor the flight of time. I shall
not wholly die, and a great part of me will escape Libitina. I shall
continue to grow, fresh with the praise of posterity, as long as the
pontifex climbs the Capitol beside the silent virgin.

—Horace *Carmina* 3.30.1–9

In the epilogue to his first collection of odes, the Augustan poet Horace links
his vision of poetic immortality to the ritual activity of the Vestal Virgins. His
metaphorical *monumentum* may be loftier than the pyramids, but his poetry
will find readers only as long as Rome remains standing —only as long, that is,
as *pontifices* and Vestals continue to sacrifice to the gods on the Capitol. Few
modern scholars would quarrel with the idea that the Vestals, like the Capitol
itself, served as a potent symbol of Rome and the permanence of its empire. But
what of their female colleagues, the numerous women who held official positions within the public religious system during the period of the Republic? The
ancient evidence suggests that these priestesses also had a considerable presence in the life of the community. It is unfortunate, therefore, that they remain
not only silent, but also nearly invisible in many modern accounts of Roman
religion. This book aims to restore Rome's priestesses to their proper place in
the religious landscape. It argues that priestesses performed a wide range of

ritual activities, and that they did so in an official capacity, and on behalf of the Roman people. Ultimately, it proposes a new interpretation of Roman religion, one that emphasizes a reliance upon cooperation among various priestly figures, both male and female, to maintain Rome's relationship with her gods (*pax deorum*).

Despite copious evidence to the contrary, historians of Roman religion have generally supposed that women, with the exception of the Vestal Virgins, were excluded from official priestly service at Rome.[1] For many years, a general lack of interest in women and their roles in Roman society reinforced this assumption.[2] Even after pioneering studies of women's ritual activities began to appear in the middle of the twentieth century, scholars continued to construe priesthood as an exclusively male activity.[3] Olivier de Cazanove even argued that Roman women suffered from "sacrificial incapacity" (*incapacité sacrificielle*)— that is, exclusion from sacrifice, including especially animal sacrifice, and its related activities.[4] John Scheid concurred, asserting in one influential essay, "The cult and the priestly powers were, above all, men's business, on both the public and the private levels. The priestly act, celebrated in the name of a community, could not be entrusted to a woman, considered incapable of representing anyone but herself."[5]

De Cazanove and Scheid classified women who performed priestly roles as "exceptions" to this rule.[6] The priestesses of Ceres and Magna Mater, so they argued, officiated in naturalized "foreign" cults without undermining the principle of female sacrificial incapacity. Native Roman priestesses, on the other hand, were described as intruders crossing into "male" territory either as "adjuncts of their husbands," like the *flaminica Dialis* (priestess of Jupiter) and the *regina sacrorum* (queen of the sacred rites), or, in the case of the Vestal Virgins,

[1] In his entry on "priests (Greek and Roman)" in the fourth edition of *The Oxford Classical Dictionary*, for instance, North (2012: 1209) writes, "In Rome . . . priests are (with the exception of the Vestal Virgins) males, formed into colleges or brotherhoods." Other recent accounts of Roman priesthood support this assertion either explicitly or implicitly (see, for example, Szemler 1972: 6–8; Beard 1990; Scheid 1993 (French original Scheid 1992a); Estienne 2005a; Porte 2007), as do the popular handbooks (North 1989: 619; Beard, North, and Price 1998: 71, 296–297; North 2000: 19; Scheid 2003: 131; Warrior 2006: 42). For a more inclusive view of priestly service in the city of Rome, see Edlund-Berry 1994; Richlin 1997 (= Richlin 2014: 197–240); Böhm 2003; Schultz 2006b: 69–81, 140–142; Flemming 2007; Rüpke 2007b: 223–228, 2008 (German original Rüpke 2005); Rives 2013: 141–142. For priestesses elsewhere in the Latin west, see further below.
[2] In Wissowa's (1912: 501–523) discussion of the pontifical college, for instance, the *flaminica Dialis* (priestess of Jupiter) merits only a few brief references (1912: 502, n. 7, 506, 507, 516, n. 117) despite appearing in Latin citations elsewhere in the text (1912: 516, n. 115, 517, n. 125). The question of her husband's dependence upon her status as *flaminica* (on which see chapter 1) is never raised.
[3] Important early studies include Le Bonniec 1958; Gagé 1963; Guizzi 1968. For an overview of historical trends in the study of women's roles in Roman religion, see Schultz 2006b: 2–3; Tzanetou 2007; Holland 2012b: 204–206, 213; Colantoni 2012: 272–273; Richlin 2014: 28–33.
[4] De Cazanove 1987. Earlier work (Piccaluga 1964; Gras 1983) had focused only on women's supposed exclusion from handling sacrificial wine (see further below).
[5] Scheid 1993: 57. See also Scheid 1992c (French original Scheid 1991), 2003. As Colantoni (2012: 273) has noted, Scheid's work "has served as a lightning rod of sorts," attracting critical comment from Staples 1998: 5–8; Schultz 2006b: 6–7, 131–137; Flemming 2007; Hemelrijk 2009; Richlin 2014: 28–29.
[6] De Cazanove 1987: 168–169; Scheid 1993: 57.

as "honorary men."[7] Relying upon the work of Mary Beard, whose landmark article "The Sexual Status of Vestal Virgins" suggested that Vestal identity was constituted by a combination of matronal, virginal, and male elements, Scheid argued that the most prominent exceptions to the rule of sacrificial incapacity were in fact "ambiguous" and, for this reason, "allowed to wield some of the religious powers traditionally reserved for men."[8]

The view that women were excluded from official public cult became generally accepted. In recent years, however, a number of important studies have challenged specific aspects of this general picture, including the theory of female sacrificial incapacity.[9] Celia Schultz, Rebecca Flemming, and Emily Hemelrijk have argued persuasively not only that earlier scholars had ignored abundant counterevidence proving women's sacrificial capacity, but also that their arguments had been built upon a misreading of their antiquarian sources.[10] One example is the well-known ritual formula that appears in the title of de Cazanove's article:

> exesto, extra esto. sic enim lictor in quibusdam sacris clamitabat: hostis, vinctus, mulier, virgo exesto; scilicet interesse prohibebatur. (Festus (Paulus) 72L)

> Exesto: "be away!" For thus the *lictor* used to shout during certain sacred rites, "foreigner, prisoner, woman, virgin, be away," clearly prohibiting them from being present.

Although de Cazanove and Scheid interpret this passage as evidence for women's exclusion from all public sacrifices, the text clearly states that they were prohibited from attending only "certain sacred rites" (*quibusdam sacris*).[11] Rather than confirming a general ban on female participation in sacrificial rituals, the formula suggests that women were normally present and, therefore, had to be actively excluded with a shout of "*exesto.*"[12]

The passages thought to confirm an interdiction on women's handling of important sacrificial materials such as wine, grain, and meat are equally unpersuasive. The ancient prohibition on women's consumption of undiluted wine (*temetum*), for instance, is widely reported in the written sources.[13] It is always,

---

[7] Scheid 1993: 57. The phrase "Vestal virgins, honorary men" appears in the index of Hopkins 1983.
[8] Scheid 1992c: 384.
[9] See, for example, Spaeth 1996; Staples 1998; Schultz 2006b; Takács 2008.
[10] Schultz 2006b: 131–137; Flemming 2007; Hemelrijk 2009. See also Gaspar 2012: 132–136; Rives 2013. Recent work on sacrifice in classical Greece has also challenged the orthodox view (expressed most forcefully by Detienne 1989) that Greek women were excluded from animal sacrifice (see especially Osborne 1993; Dillon 2002: 131–135; Connelly 2007: 179–190).
[11] De Cazanove 1987: 167–168; Scheid 1992c: 379.
[12] Compare Cic. *Leg.* 2.21, which prohibits women from performing nocturnal sacrifices, with the exception of those performed according to religious custom (*rite*) and on behalf of the people (*pro populo*).
[13] See, for example, Cic. *Rep.* 4.6; Dion. Hal. *Ant. Rom.* 2.25.6; Val. Max. 2.1.5, 6.3.9; Pliny *H.N.* 14.89–90; Gell. *N.A.* 10.23.1–5; Plut. *Num.* 3.5, *Quaest. Rom.* 6 = Mor. 265b–e; Serv. ad *Aen.* 1.737. For a discussion of this evidence as it relates to the theory of female sacrificial incapacity, see especially Schultz 2006b: 132–134; Flemming 2007: 92–97; Hemelrijk 2009: 257.

however, situated within a domestic context and usually associated with fears of adultery and the safety of the household storeroom, over which the matron was supposed to keep watch. Women are described as handling or drinking wine in ritual settings, and we should not assume that a restriction tied to daily life, one explicitly concerned with enforcing matronal temperance and chastity, applied to the religious sphere as well.[14] In fact, the late antique commentator Servius rejects such a view when he reports that in ancient times (*apud maiores nostros*), women refrained from drinking wine "except on certain days and for the sake of the sacred rites" (*nisi sacrorum causa certis diebus*, ad *Aen.* 1.737). Women regularly drank wine on religious occasions and, during later periods, at other times as well.

Similar criticisms may be leveled against another passage cited in support of female sacrificial incapacity: "Why, in ancient times, were wives not allowed to grind grain or cook?" (Διὰ τί τὰς γυναῖκας οὔτ' ἀλεῖν εἴων οὔτ' ὀψοποιεῖν τὸ παλαιόν, Plut. *Quaest. Rom.* 85 = *Mor.* 286f). De Cazanove and Scheid interpret this text as a religious rule excluding women from animal sacrifice and its related processes, including the preparation of *mola salsa*, the salted grain used to consecrate sacrificial victims.[15] In his answer to the question, however, Plutarch places the restriction firmly within a domestic setting and interprets it as a concession granted by the Romans to their Sabine wives.[16] Both the privilege and its etiology are presented as curiosities of the legendary past. In fact, the ancient sources routinely associate women with the production and storage of food products, including those necessary for public and private rituals.[17]

There is ample evidence, moreover, that women could communicate with the gods through sacrifice. The Vestal Virgins offered a sow at the December rites of Bona Dea.[18] The *flaminica Dialis* sacrificed a ram to Jupiter on the market days (*nundinae*).[19] Like the male *pontifices* and *flamines*, the *flaminicae* and the Vestals were permitted to use the *secespita*, a type of sacrificial knife.[20] On the Kalends, the first day of every month, the *regina sacrorum* sacrificed a sow or a sheep to Juno.[21] According to Cicero, the *sacerdos Cereris* performed rites (*sacra facere*) on behalf of the Roman people, perhaps including the sacrifice of a pig.[22] The *saliae virgines* (Salian Virgins) performed a sacrifice (*sacrificium*

---

[14] Ov. *Fast.* 3.523–542; Plut. *Quaest. Rom.* 20 = *Mor.* 268d–e; Macrob. *Sat.* 1.12.25; Festus (Paulus) 455L.

[15] De Cazanove 1987: 162–168; Scheid 1992c: 380. See also Versnel 1993: 266.

[16] See also Plut. *Rom.* 15.4, 19.7, with Schultz 2006b: 132, 134; Flemming 2007: 91–92; Hemelrijk 2009: 256.

[17] See especially chapters 1 and 6.

[18] Cic. *Har. resp.* 12, 37, *Att.* 1.13.3, with chapter 6.

[19] Macrob. *Sat.* 1.16.30, with chapter 1.

[20] Serv. ad *Aen.* 4.262, with chapter 1.

[21] Macrob. *Sat.* 1.15.19, with chapter 2.

[22] Cic. *Balb.* 55, with chapter 3.

facere) while dressed in military garb.[23] A priestess known as the *damiatrix* offered a sacrifice (*sacrificium facere*) to the goddess Damia.[24]

Laywomen are recorded as officiants as well. Cato enjoins the *vilica*, the slave
housekeeper on his country estate, to supplicate (*supplicare*) the *Lares*, the deities of the hearth.[25] In 207 BC, Rome's *matronae* (married women) sacrificed
to Juno Regina, apparently without the assistance of a priest or magistrate.[26]
Women who had been married only once (*matronae univirae*) had the right
of sacrificing (*ius sacrificandi*) in the cults of Pudicitia (Sexual Virtue).[27] An
armita was a virgin who sacrificed (*sacrificans*) with the fold of her *toga* thrown
over her shoulder, while the *simpulatrix* was a woman devoted to divine matters (*rebus divinis*) who took her name from the *simpulum*, a ladle used to pour
wine at sacrifices.[28] The number and variety of these examples argue forcefully
against a formal rule of female "sacrificial incapacity," even if women enjoyed
fewer opportunities to preside over animal sacrifices than men.[29] The Romans
welcomed women at the republican altar.

The question of women's subordination to male authority in the ritual sphere
is less easily settled. It indeed seems that married priestesses like the *flaminica Dialis* and the *regina sacrorum* were subject to the authority of their priestly spouses,
though not to the extent implied by Scheid's characterization of them as "adjuncts
of their husbands."[30] Other priestesses were more independent. The administration of cults under female control seems to have been left to the women themselves, particularly where men were actively excluded. Such self-government was
naturally an "internal autonomy" that relied upon the continued consent of the
people and the senate—that is, of Roman men.[31] But priestesses were not the only
public officials whose activities were circumscribed by a higher authority. The
augur, for instance, whose most important duty was to interpret signs from the
gods (*auspicia*), was subordinate to the authority of the senate and the magistrates.[32] He could act only at their request or, in the case of the inauguration of a
priest, at the behest of the *pontifex maximus*, the chief of the pontifical college.
The *pontifex maximus*, moreover, could impose a fine (*multa*) on any member
of his college, restrict a colleague's ability to leave the city, and even compel a
private citizen to take up a priestly office against his will.[33] As we shall see, the

[23] Festus 439L, with chapter 3.
[24] Festus (Paulus) 60L, with chapter 3.
[25] Cato *Agr.* 143.2.
[26] Livy 27.37.8–10, with Schultz 2006b: 34–37.
[27] Livy 10.23.9.
[28] Festus (Paulus) 4 (*armita*), 455L (*simpulatrix*).
[29] For the likelihood that women sacrificed less frequently than men, see Hemelrijk 2009: 264; Rives
2013: 142–144.
[30] Scheid 1993: 57.
[31] As stressed by Mæhle 2008: 67–68.
[32] North 1986: 257; Beard 1990: 36; Briquel 2003.
[33] See, for example, Cic. *Phil.* 11.18; Livy 27.8.4–10, 37.51.1–7, 40.42.8–11; Val. Max. 1.1.2; Livy *Per.*
19, with Wissowa 1912: 510–513; Beard, North and Price 1998: 106–108.

subordination experienced by female priests was qualitatively different from that experienced by male priests, but subordination in and of itself is no reason to exclude them from the scholarly conversation.

Another problematic issue in the study of Roman priestesses has been the assertion that women's religious activities were "marginal" and "deviant," restricted to the household or to "suburban sanctuaries and the temples of foreign gods."[34] The tendency to downplay the formal significance of women's rituals owes much, in my view, to the assumption of a gendered division between public and private.[35] The Romans, however, did not define the public sphere in quite the way scholars have supposed.[36] Rituals described as marginal in modern scholarship—those concerning so-called private matters such as chastity, marriage, fertility, childbirth, and the nurture of children—were fully integrated into the formal structures of civic life. The festival calendar is crowded with such rites.[37] What is more, a consciousness that women's cult activity ensured the survival of the state pervades the written sources. When the Greek rites of Ceres were interrupted following the Roman defeat at Cannae in 216 BC, for instance, the senate ordered Rome's *matronae* to limit their mourning period to thirty days "in order to prevent any other public or private rites from being abandoned for the same reason" (*ne ob eandem causam alia quoque sacra publica aut privata desererentur*, Livy 22.56.3).[38] Threats to the community were not limited to the battlefield. Women's worship addressed the perils of agricultural failure, famine, disease, and infant mortality. Like the military establishment, it could not be permitted to lapse.[39]

Women also participated in cults with a more obvious martial or political focus, including those long regarded as male-dominated.[40] Juno Sospita and Juno Regina, for instance, took an interest in political matters and exercised considerable authority over the fate of the Roman people.[41] The cult of Fortuna Muliebris and the "Festival of the Handmaidens" on the Nonae Capratinae (July 7) were thought to commemorate the heroism of women whose actions had saved the city from destruction.[42] Rome's *matronae* regularly participated

---

[34] Scheid 1992c: 377. For a critique of this view, see especially Staples 1998: 5–6; Schultz 2006b: 20–45.

[35] For a discussion of how the trope of "separate spheres" has influenced the study of Greco-Roman antiquity, see Golden and Toohey 2003: 3–4, 15. More generally, see Kelly 1984: 1–18; Nelson 1990; Clark 2004: 230–231.

[36] For a general discussion, see Wallace-Hadrill 1996.

[37] Boëls-Janssen 1993: 469–477; Takács 2008: 25–59; Richlin 2014: 228–230.

[38] Under normal circumstances, women remained in mourning for ten months (Ov. *Fast.* 1.35, 3.134; Plut. *Num.* 12.2; Cass. Dio 56.43.1).

[39] Though demographic evidence for the Roman world is limited, scholars generally agree that as many as thirty percent of newborns died before their first birthday and nearly half before age ten (Saller 1994: 23–25). Crop failure is likewise difficult to quantify. At the very least, we can be certain that the annual harvest yield varied considerably under Mediterranean conditions (Prudent. *C. Symm.* 2.997–1000, with Erdkamp 2005: 51–53). Human and agricultural fertility were serious concerns on both an individual and a communal level.

[40] See especially Dorcey 1989; Schultz 2000, 2006b: 22–45.

[41] Hänninen 1999a, 1999b; Schultz 2006a, 2006b: 22–28, 33–37.

[42] See chapter 3 (Fortuna Muliebris); Green 2010 (Nonae Capratinae).

in public expiatory rites in times of civic or military crisis.[43] The Vestals guarded the eternal flame of Vesta and the *pignora imperii*, the "pledges of empire" that guaranteed Roman hegemony, while the *saliae* offered a sacrifice for the success of Rome's military operations.[44]

More often than not, these rituals enforced an expectation of *castitas* (chastity) and *pudicitia* (sexual virtue). The Vestals and the *saliae* were virgins and only *matronae univirae* were permitted to worship Fortuna Muliebris. Other cults, including those of Pudicitia and Venus Verticordia (Heart-Turner), who was credited with the power to turn "the minds of virgins and women from lust to sexual virtue" (*virginum mulierumque mens a libidine ad pudicitiam*, Val. Max. 8.15.12), were even more explicit in their cultivation of these virtues.[45] It is striking, however, that cults associated with *castitas* and *pudicitia* often received special attention in times of great national crisis.[46] Venus Verticordia, for instance, was introduced at Rome during the Second Punic War (218 BC–201 BC), and received a temple following a notorious case of unchastity within the Vestal order at the end of the second century BC.[47] In the Roman mind, female virtue was implicated in guaranteeing the wellbeing of the civic community, not just the integrity of individual households.[48]

The interdependence of the religious system, in which every public cult contributed to the maintenance of the *pax deorum*, makes it difficult to argue that rituals involving women were "marginal" to the interests of the state. In fact, the ancient sources suggest that finances, rather than gender, played a more prominent role in distinguishing between the *sacra publica*, the public rites in the city of Rome and its immediate environs, and rituals observed privately (*sacra privata*):[49]

> publica sacra, quae publico sumptu pro populo fiunt, quaeque pro montibus, pagis, curis, sacellis: at privata, quae pro singulis hominibus, familiis, gentibus fiunt. (Festus 284L)

> Public rites are those that are performed at public expense on behalf of the people (*populus*), and also those that are performed on behalf of the hills (*montes*), rural districts (*pagi*), divisions of the people (*curiae*), and shrines. Private rites, on the other hand, are those that are performed on behalf of individuals, households, or clans (*gentes*).

According to the definition offered here, the Roman *sacra publica* fell into two groups. The first contained rites performed by priests and magistrates on behalf

---

[43] See especially Schultz 2006b: 28–37.
[44] See chapters 6 (Vestals) and 3 (*saliae*).
[45] Langlands 2006: 47–51, 59.
[46] Langlands 2006: 57.
[47] Val. Max. 8.15.12; Plin. *H.N.* 7.120; Ov. *Fast.* 4.157–160; Obseq. 37.
[48] For the civic import of *pudicitia*, see Langlands 2006: 49–50.
[49] As Rüpke (2006: 22) has written concerning the *lex Ursonensis*, "the financing of the cult is the leitmotif that holds together the whole passage on religion."

of the *populus*, that is, the entire citizenry of Rome. These rites fulfilled the community's obligations toward its gods and were financed by the state, either from the public treasury or with income generated from land set aside for the upkeep of a specific cult or priesthood.[50]

The second category of *sacra publica* comprised a group of rites performed on behalf of various divisions of the city and citizenry of Rome.[51] These include the Septimontium, a festival celebrated by the residents of the seven hills (*septem montes*); the Paganalia, a festival observed by rural villages (*pagi*); the rites of the *curiae* (ancient divisions of the Roman people); and the Argei festival, which involved twenty-seven shrines located throughout the city. These rituals were publicly financed as well, though in some cases with funds maintained by the group involved, rather than from the treasury of the Roman people.[52] Private rites (*privata*), on the other hand, included those performed on behalf of individuals, households, and clans and funded by private resources.

This method of distinguishing between public and private rites has important implications for our understanding of women's roles in Roman religion, particularly their role as public priestesses. A ritual performed for the benefit of the Roman people was classified as public and funded by the public treasury, regardless of the gender of the officiant. Even more fundamentally, since the Romans did not distinguish between "sacred" and "secular," but rather regarded ritual activity as a natural function of the civic community, it follows that priestesses who held leadership positions were essential to public life at Rome.[53] Far from delimiting an area of exclusion or marginalization from the public realm, ritual practice granted women a vital role in the community, particularly on festival days when they offered sacrifices, prayed to the gods, or performed other rituals in the presence of their fellow citizens.[54]

While we should not go so far as to posit a view of Roman religion that assigns full religious equality to men and women, a new model is clearly in order. Beard herself laid the groundwork for a different approach in an "affectionate critique" of her earlier work, arguing in "Re-reading (Vestal) Virginity" that gender categories are not "objective, cultural 'givens.'"[55] By applying unproblematized labels (virginal, matronal, and male) to various aspects of Vestal identity, Beard's earlier work had failed to account for the socially contingent nature of identity markers such as sacrificial capacity, which worked to express

---

[50]Dion. Hal. *Ant. Rom.* 2.75.3; App. *Mithr.* 22; Festus 204L; Symmachus *Ep.* 1.68; Oros. 5.18.27 with Beard 1998: 86–89; Rüpke 2007b: 21–22.

[51]Rüpke 2007b: 24.

[52]For publicly funded rites in the *curiae* and on the Oppian Hill, see (respectively) Dion. Hal. *Ant. Rom.* 2.23.1; *CIL* 6.32455, with chapter 2.

[53]As North (1990a: 52) stresses, "There was no 'Church' to the Roman 'State'—just the Republic (*res publica*)."

[54]Scholars working on classical Greece have come to similar conclusions about the significance of women's participation in civic cult (see, for example, Blundell 1995: 163; Blundell and Williamson 1998; Dillon 2002; Goff 2004; Connelly 2007; Parca and Tzanetou 2007; Kaltsas and Shapiro 2008).

[55]Beard 1995: 169.

gender only in conjunction with other factors such as biological sex, physical health, age, civic status, wealth, and ethnicity.[56] In fact, the ritual sphere was an important space for the formation of socially appropriate gender identities.[57] Through the communal performance of ritual, men and women, both as ritual actors and as spectators, internalized and publicly affirmed the values that were thought to hold the community together, including ideas about proper womanly behavior and the relation between the sexes. "Put simply," as Beard has written, "the Vestals constructed Roman gender, as much as gender (and its ambiguities) constructed the Vestals."[58]

The process by which priestly officials reinscribed gender norms was almost entirely implicit and unspoken. Occasionally, however, it receives comment, as when Cicero writes that other women (*mulieres*) may look to the Vestals for evidence "that the nature of women permits complete chastity" (*naturam feminarum omnem castitatem pati*, Cic. *Leg.* 2.29). Invoking the rhetoric of exemplarity, Cicero situates Vestal virginity within a familiar discourse about the regulation of female sexuality.[59] The *flaminica Dialis*, on the other hand, served as a template for a wider range of womanly virtues, including especially fidelity in marriage. According to Festus, Roman brides wore the *flammeum*, the *flaminica*'s signature orange-yellow veil, as a good omen (*ominis boni causa*, 79L) because she was not permitted to divorce her husband. Throughout the republican period, moreover, the *flamen* and *flaminica Dialis* were required to marry by *confarreatio*, an archaic ritual that placed the *flaminica* under her husband's control (*manus*) and granted her the legal standing of a daughter (*in filiae loco*).[60] When they approached the altar of Jupiter, they affirmed a social hierarchy based upon the subordination of women to men.

The gender norms of Roman society, however, could countenance both a husband's absolute legal authority over his wife and her active role in civic cult. The *flaminica Dialis* was not a passive tool, like the *apex* (the *flamen*'s distinctive hat) or the sacrificial knife.[61] She was a public priestess with her own agency and a well-defined ritual program.[62] As we have seen, her obligations included

---

[56] Throughout this book, the term "gender" is used to differentiate biological sex from the construction of gender identities through socialization (e.g., dressing a child in pink or blue) and the organization of the relation between the sexes (e.g., the confinement of women to the house). Scott 1986 remains a classic discussion of scholarly views on the concept of "gender." For an overview of its impact on the study of Greco-Roman antiquity and on that of religion, see (respectively) Foxhall 2013: 1–23; Clark 2004.

[57] For a broader discussion of this phenomenon, see especially Lincoln 1981; Bell 1997: 210–252.

[58] Beard 1995: 170.

[59] As Levine (1995: 104) has observed, priestesses were "set apart by the community as living icons of Roman ideals." For similar observations about the moral exemplarity of priests and priestesses, see also Dion. Hal. *Ant. Rom.* 8.38.1; Cancik-Lindemaier 1996b: 143; Mustakallio 2010: 15–16; Gallia 2014: 235–237.

[60] See chapter 1.

[61] Schultz 2006b: 81.

[62] Festus (Paulus) 82L, with chapter 1. The dynamic between women's subjection and their agency has been a crucial issue in feminist scholarship from Lerner's classic *The Creation of Patriarchy* (1986) to Levin-Richardson's (2013) recent analysis of sexual graffiti in Pompeii. As Hollywood (2004: 246–247)

regular blood sacrifices in the *regia*, the official headquarters of the *pontifex maximus* in the Forum Romanum.[63] The presence of priestesses in the Forum (and on the Capitol) naturalized women's active participation in public life and reinscribed a wide range of ideal female behaviors, including even animal sacrifice.

It must be conceded that the priestesses in this book were, for the most part, elite citizen women. Slaves make an appearance as support personnel, and some freedwomen held priestly offices in the cults of Bona Dea and Magna Mater. The most important positions, however, were accessible only to elites. It is not at all clear, moreover, that Roman women saw themselves as a unified interest group.[64] Elite *matronae*, for example, likely considered themselves not in solidarity with, but rather in opposition to married women of lower status in some contexts, and against slave women and prostitutes in others. Distinctions between different groups of women were regularly dramatized through ritual. At the Matralia in early June, freeborn *matronae univirae* asserted their superiority over slave women by inviting a slave into the temple of Mater Matuta and then driving her out with slaps and insults.[65] The ritual sphere granted some women considerable authority, but that authority could be used to enforce hierarchical divisions based on civic status and sexual access to the body.[66]

A focus on gender leads to a fuller understanding of the nature of Roman priesthood, one that better accounts for the remarkable diversity of public priests in republican Rome.[67] Perhaps most significantly, it reveals that the Romans employed a surprisingly egalitarian approach to managing the community's relations with the divine. At a basic level, both men and women could sacrifice and address the gods on behalf of the Roman people. Differentiation occurred at the level of the individual office, but priesthood itself was a fundamentally cooperative endeavor. The joint funerary monument of Licinia Flavilla and Sex. Adgennius Macrinus, which records the wife's service as a *flaminica* in the imperial cult at Nimes and the husband's position as *pontifex*, neatly illustrates this point.[68] As Amy Richlin has stressed in her analysis of this epitaph and others like it, "Women who were priestesses would have been very likely to have male kin who held priesthoods, and probably perceived religious activity as something men and women had in common, not something that separated them."[69]

---

has written, "the very conditions that bring about subordination are also the source of agency (however limited or constrained that agency might be in particular situations of subordination—even at times to the point of effacing agency entirely)." The cult of Pudicitia, for instance, placed the burden for cultivating *pudicitia* on married women, allowing them to take ownership of their sexuality, even as it worked to inculcate communally sanctioned attitudes about the regulation of women's sexual behavior (as argued by Langlands 2006: 47).

[63] Macrob. *Sat.* 1.16.30, with chapter 1.
[64] Cooper 1996: 113.
[65] Plut. *Quaest. Rom.* 16 = *Mor.* 267d, *Cam.* 5.2, with Richlin 2014: 230–232.
[66] Richlin 2014: 10, 197–240.
[67] For a discussion of the unusual variety of priesthoods at Rome, see Beard 1990: 19–25.
[68] *CIL* 12.3175 (= Rüpke 2007b: 224, fig. 22).
[69] Richlin 2014: 213.

The Sources

The evidence explored in this book comes from a wide variety of male-authored texts, each with its own artistic and didactic aims. The interpretation of these fragmentary and often tendentious sources is not without difficulty. As Christopher Smith has rightly emphasized, "the evidence we have for Roman religion is often ancient interpretation—indeed Roman religion sometimes seems as if it is interpretation, not a transcendent reality which we struggle to grasp or recreate, but a series of ancient readings of [the] reality of the world."[70] Women's ritual activities, particularly sex-segregated rituals, are especially liable to distortion in male-authored texts, where negative stereotypes about women abound.[71] The rhetorical use of gender can obscure our view of antiquity. We must contend, moreover, with the fact that nearly all surviving accounts of religion in republican Rome date to the imperial period. Can we be confident that the priestesses in this book really did the things that the ancient sources claim they did?

Many of the texts cited in this study are scholarly in form—that is, they are "writings meant to preserve or elucidate Roman cultural memory in non-narrative, non-mimetic form, with a commitment to the truth."[72] While they belong to a range of technical genres, they share, to varying degrees, content characterized by modern scholars as "antiquarian."[73] Antiquarianism emerged together with historiography in the second century BC and shared with it an interest in Rome's past. Eschewing the literary pretention and chronological structure of historiography, antiquarians preferred the systematic discussion of individual topics and specific details in learned monographs based on what they believed to be the facts of the matter.[74] Antiquarian writing could cover almost any subject, though it generally focused on the habits and institutions of the Roman people.[75]

Ancient scholarship was tralatitious, as modern scholars rightly emphasize, with each author "taking over and passing on the accumulated learning of the last."[76] The works of the late republican and Augustan antiquarians in particular were virtually canonized by later authors, with the result that the tradition remained heavily weighted towards these periods well into late antiquity.[77]

---

[70] Smith 2000: 136. See also Feeney 1998, 2004.

[71] Consider, for example, Juvenal's account of the December rites of Bona Dea (*Sat.* 6.314–341, with Lyons 2007; Šterbenc Erker 2013: 52–53) or the popular stereotype of women's fascination with "foreign" cults (Beard, North, and Price 1998: 299–300). For a more general discussion of the difficulties inherent in recovering information about women's rituals, see Beard 1995; Fantham 2002; Clark 2004; Schultz 2006b: 6–7; Kraemer 2011, especially 5–11; Richlin 2014: 204–205.

[72] Kaster 2010: 492.

[73] On Roman antiquarian writing, see especially Rawson 1972, 1985: 233–249; Maslakov 1983 (with a focus on late antiquity); Stevenson 1993, 2004.

[74] For the development of systematic organization in Latin prose, see Rawson 1978.

[75] Stevenson 2004: 141–151. See, for example, Cicero's (*Acad.* 1.9) summary of Varro's antiquarian writings.

[76] Wallace-Hadrill 1983: 42. See also Stevenson 2004: 125–127.

[77] Stevenson 1993: 20–23; Kaster 2010: 501–502.

In many ways, the tendency to reproduce earlier research reflects one of the aims of antiquarian writing: to serve as a reference for readers in search of information about a single topic.[78] Antiquarianism, in this respect, was a generous, open-handed discipline, willing to facilitate the work of the historians, poets, jurists, and grammarians who visited its storehouse of well-organized facts.[79] As a result, our knowledge of antiquarian scholarship derives almost entirely from citations in texts that cannot reasonably be described as antiquarian in form or function.

Quoting from earlier writings was a common method of research in the ancient world, yet it is worth remembering that someone conducted the initial inquiry.[80] While we must not pretend that ancient scholars operated like modern historians, we should not underrate their work either. The antiquarians often demonstrate a sophisticated ability to collect and synthesize material from a variety of sources, including literary texts, official documents, laws, monuments, and inscriptions.[81] Research on Rome's religious institutions presumably proceeded from oral tradition as well as from the study of religious jurisprudence (the *ius sacrum*), the ritual calendar (*fasti*), and the written records (*commentarii*) maintained by various public priests.[82] These *commentarii* did not provide detailed ritual scripts, but they did contain prayers, liturgical reports (e.g., "a ram offered to Jupiter on the Ides"), and collections of rules, "defined and redefined or commented on by the priests at public or private request" (e.g., "the *flamen Dialis* is not permitted to ride a horse").[83] The sources available to the antiquarian were rich and varied, particularly when supplemented by personal observation.[84]

The great polymath and author M. Terentius Varro (116–27 BC) necessarily occupies a prominent place in any discussion of Roman antiquarianism.[85] Widely acknowledged as the most learned of the Romans, he wrote over seventy different works covering almost every imaginable area of scholarship.[86] Only the *Res rusticae* (*On Agriculture*) and six books of the *De lingua latina* (*On the Latin Language*) are extant, along with fragments preserved by later authors. Of

---

[78] Gell. *N.A.* pr. 12, with Stevenson 1993: 288; Kaster 2010: 497.

[79] Kaster 2010: 497. Many antiquarian works were clearly designed as reference works complete with indexes and content lists (Stevenson 2004: 127–130).

[80] For the research methods of the Roman antiquarian, see Stevenson 1993: 127–185, 2004: 124–141, especially 134–138.

[81] Stevenson 1993: 140–146, 291.

[82] For an assessment of the ancient evidence for priestly writing and the oral transmission of knowledge in Roman religion, see especially Beard 1998; North 1998; Rüpke 2004; Scheid 2006; Rüpke 2008: 24–38, all with sound critiques of earlier scholarship.

[83] Scheid 1992b: 122, 2006: 19. For the inscribed records of the *fratres arvales* (Arval Brothers), which may or may not be entirely representative of other priestly *commentarii*, see the new edition by Scheid 1998.

[84] On the role of autopsy in antiquarian research, see Stevenson 2004: 138.

[85] For an updated biography and a list of works, see Sallman 2010.

[86] Cic. *Brut.* 205 (*vir ingenio praestans omnique doctrina*); Quint. *Inst.* 10.1.95 (*vir Romanorum eruditissimus*); Aug. *Civ. Dei* 19.22 (*doctissimus Romanorum*).

particular relevance to the present study are books five and six of the *De lingua latina*, which provide etymologies for Latin words of time and place and recycle much antiquarian learning from his famous *Antiquitates rerum humanarum et divinarum* (*Divine and Human Antiquities*), which survives only in the quotations of later authors.

The grammarian M. Verrius Flaccus (ca. 55 BC–ca. AD 20), who flourished during the principate of Augustus, was the next generation's leading scholar.[87] His *De verborum significatu* (*On the Meaning of Words*), a Latin lexicon in forty books, included numerous quotations from early Latin authors and a wealth of antiquarian material.[88] Innovative in its organizational scheme (Verrius may have been the first author to arrange his text in rough alphabetical order), the content generally reproduced the works of late republican scholars.[89] The original has not survived, but an abridged version is partially preserved in the mid-imperial lexicon of Sex. Pompeius Festus (later second century AD).[90] Roughly five hundred years later, a Carolingian scholar known as Paul the Deacon (ca. AD 720–799) produced a condensed version of Festus, omitting, unfortunately, many entries related to Roman religion and editing glosses he found too obscure for his audience at Charlemagne's court.[91] His epitome survives in its entirety. Together, Festus and Paul provide a crucial link, albeit in fragmentary and abbreviated form, to the antiquarian tradition of the first century BC.

C. Plinius Secundus (AD 23/24–79), better known as Pliny the Elder, and the Greek author Plutarch of Chaeronea (ca. AD 45–before 125) are also important sources for the study of Roman priestesses.[92] Neither author was an antiquarian, though both incorporate much relevant material in their works. Later in the second century AD, Aulus Gellius (ca. 125 AD–after 170) compiled his *Noctes Atticae* (*Attic Nights*), a miscellany in twenty books based on

[87] Suet. *Gramm.* 17.1–3, with Kaster 1995: 190–6.

[88] For the *De verborum significatu* and its survival in later epitomes, see especially the essays in Glinister and Woods 2007. Scholarly activity unquestionably provided an intellectual framework for the restoration (or appropriation) of ancient traditions after the instability of the civil wars (North 1986: 253–254; Gordon 1990: 191; Wallace-Hadrill 1998; Frier 1999: 37, 199). Verrius incorporated major events in the career of Augustus into his *Fasti Praenestini*, an annotated festival calendar displayed in the Forum of Praeneste (for the surviving fragments, see *CIL* I², pp. 230–239 = *InscrIt* 13.2.17). But there are also indications that scholarship could be used as a form of resistance. Labeo's love of liberty (*libertas*) reportedly led him to consider no action legal unless his research into Roman antiquity (*Romanis antiquitatibus*) assured him that it had been sanctioned in the past (Gell. *N.A.* 13.12.2, with Stevenson 1993: 69). In fact, he refused the consulship offered to him by Augustus (Pompon. *Dig.* 1.2.2.47). For a more nuanced view of antiquarian scholarship under Augustus, see Stevenson 2004: 120–121; Glinister 2007: 24–32.

[89] For a discussion of Verrius' sources, see Glinister 2007; Lhommé 2007; North 2007.

[90] The text of Festus survives in the Codex Festi Farnesianus, a mutilated and fire-damaged manuscript from the second half of the eleventh century now in Naples (Bibl. Naz. IV.A.3). The Farnesianus contains about half of the original, beginning in the middle of the letter "M" and trailing off near the end of the letter "V." Although Festus occasionally criticizes Verrius or adds quotations from Lucan (AD 39–65) and Martial (ca. AD 40–102/4), the majority of his material derives from Verrius' original (Glinister 2007: 11–12).

[91] For Paul and his epitome, see Woods 2007.

[92] Pliny (*H.N.* pr. 17) claims to have read about two thousand volumes from one hundred different authors. For a discussion of Plutarch's sources, see Rose 1924: 11–45.

notes and excerpts collected in the course of several decades of wide reading.[93] Unlike Plutarch, Gellius generally cites his sources by name. His chapter on the Vestal order, for instance, relies heavily upon a pair of Augustan jurists— M. Antistius Labeo (d. before AD 22), author of both a treatise *De iure pontifico* (*On Pontifical Law*) and a commentary on the Twelve Tables, and C. Ateius Capito (cos. suff. AD 5).[94] For the cult formula spoken by the *pontifex maximus* when he ritually "seized" a new Vestal during a ceremony known as the *captio*, Gellius cites an unnamed work by a certain Fabius Pictor, perhaps a *pontifex* or *flamen* active during the middle of the second century BC.[95] He closes the chapter by quoting the memoirs of L. Cornelius Sulla (cos. 88, 80 BC) and an oration of M. Porcius Cato (cens. 184 BC) in order to contradict the view held by many that the term "to be taken" (*capi*) ought to be used only of a Vestal.[96] As a whole, the chapter suggests careful research, either by Gellius himself or an unacknowledged intermediary.

Even further removed from the period of the Republic is the late antique grammarian Servius (fl. late fourth–early fifth century AD), author of an important commentary on the poems of Vergil.[97] Many hold that this work is based on an earlier fourth-century AD commentary by Aelius Donatus (b. ca. AD 310). A longer text, commonly known as Servius Auctus, is understood to be the work of an anonymous compiler of the seventh century AD, who (as the name suggests) expanded his copy of Servius with additional material from the Servian source commentary not included by Servius himself.[98] The commentary, particularly in its longer form, is a significant source for Roman religion.[99] Most relevant to the present study is a group of notes identifying allusions to Aeneas and Dido as the *flamen* and *flaminica Dialis*.[100] When Vergil describes

---

[93] Gell. *N.A.* pr. 1–5. On Gellius and his antiquarian sources, see especially Stevenson 2004; Holford-Strevens 2005: 65–80, 2015 (with an emphasis on Varro). For his value as a "citing authority," see also Cornell 2013: 69–73.

[94] Gell. *N.A.* 1.12.1, 1.12.8, with Stevenson 1993: 68–73.

[95] Gell. *N.A.* 1.12.14. The identity of this Fabius Pictor is uncertain. The quotation of a Latin cult formula argues against the annalist Q. Fabius Pictor (b. ca. 270 BC), who wrote in Greek (Cornell 2013: 229, n. 7). Q. Fabius Maximus Servilianus (cos. 142 BC) is known to have written a history and often assumed to have written a work on pontifical law (see Cornell 2013: 229 for the details), but is nowhere associated with the cognomen Pictor. Cicero, on the other hand, records a Ser. Fabius Pictor as a legal scholar and an expert in antiquities (*antiquitatis bene peritus, Brut.* 81). This may be the same Fabius Pictor cited by Nonius (518.34–37M) as the author of a work on the pontifical law and by Varro (*apud* Non. 223.17M) as the author of a *commentarius*, which indicates that he was writing as a priest (Münzer *RE* Fabius 128; Rüpke 2008: 677, No. 1600, n. 6). Rüpke (2008: 677, No. 1600, n. 5) has thus proposed Ser. Fabius Pictor (ca. 190–after 149 BC) as the source for the ritual formula quoted by Gellius and suggested, more tentatively, that he may have served as *flamen Quirinalis* in the middle of the second century BC.

[96] Gell. *N.A.* 1.12.16–17.

[97] For the date and identity of Servius, see Kaster 1988: 356–359.

[98] For the relationship between the longer and the shorter forms, see Goold 1970: 102–122. The longer text is also known as Servius Danielis, DServius, or DS after its first editor, P. Daniel. The non-Servian material it preserves is printed in italics in the edition of Thilo and Hagen (1881–1902).

[99] Servius contains fewer notes on cultural and religious matters than Servius Auctus (Kaster 1980: 256–257; Cameron 2011: 572, 575).

[100] This is the most common manifestation of the "Aeneas as priest" theory (see Serv. ad *Aen.* 1.706, with Starr 1997: 65).

Dido climbing her "high pyre" (*altos . . . rogos*, 4.645–646), for instance, the Servius Auctus commentator claims that she is committing a ritual error (*piaculum*), since the *flaminica* was not allowed to climb more than three stairs (unless they were so-called Greek stairs, which were evidently constructed in such a way as to prevent anyone from catching a glimpse of her ankles).[101] While we may reject the interpretation of Dido as a *flaminica*, we need not discard the commentator's testimony about the rules governing the historical priestess as well.[102] Like their midimperial predecessors, the grammarians of late antiquity copied freely from earlier sources.[103] In sum, the Servian commentary constitutes an important repository of antiquarian learning stretching back to the republican period.[104]

Even more clearly than the exegetical tradition represented by Servius, the *Saturnalia* of Macrobius Ambrosius Theodosius (praef. praet. AD 430) highlights the antiquarian tastes of late antique scholars and their respect (*verecundia*) for the past.[105] Set during the Saturnalia (December 17–19) in about AD 383, the dialogue purports to describe a gathering of Roman nobles and learned men whose wide-ranging conversation "promises an accumulation of things worth knowing" (*noscendorum congeriem pollicetur*, pr. 4). Few Romanists would disagree that Macrobius provides a treasure trove of antiquarian material about various topics, including the Roman calendar and pontifical and augural law, his sources often quoted, though generally not by name.[106] As Alan Cameron has recently argued, "There can be little doubt that the work of Verrius and the jurists is the ultimate source, via intermediaries like Gellius and Festus, of most references to cult practices in Macrobius and the late antique commentators."[107]

Antiquarian writing shaped less obviously scholarly works as well, including the etiological elegies of Propertius (first century BC) and Ovid (43 BC–AD 17).[108] Ovid's *Fasti*, a playful meditation on the Roman festival calendar and its transformation under Augustus, is unthinkable apart from a thriving antiquarian tradition. The poet adopts a mock-scholarly persona throughout, and his method of "research" includes the consultation of ancient books (*annalibus priscis*, 1.7,

---

[101] Serv. Auct. ad *Aen.* 4.646.
[102] The allegorical interpretation of Aeneas as *flamen* was not universally accepted even in antiquity (see Serv. ad *Aen.* 9.298; Serv. Auct. ad *Aen.* 1.706, 4.262, with Starr 1997: 63–64).
[103] Lloyd 1961; Kaster 1980: 256–258. In fact, the note on Dido's pyre may depend upon Gellius (*N.A.* 10.15.29), who describes an identical taboo (*caerimonia*) restricting the *flaminica*'s ability to climb stairs.
[104] Late antique grammarians did occasionally misunderstand or misrepresent Roman ritual (Cameron 2011: 604–606). In order to defend the theory that Aeneas is "everywhere" (*ubique, ad Aen.* 4.103) depicted as a *flamen*, even after the deaths of Creusa and Dido, for instance, the Servius Auctus commentator must argue that the *flamen Dialis* was permitted to remarry following the death of the *flaminica* (ad *Aen.* 4.29), a claim that directly contradicts the evidence of Gellius and Plutarch (see chapter 1).
[105] For the date and identity of Macrobius, see Cameron 1966.
[106] For a general overview of Macrobius' sources, see Wessner 1928: 182–196.
[107] Cameron 2011: 578. It is striking that aside from Homer and Vergil, Macrobius mentions no author as frequently as he does Varro (Stevenson 1993: 112).
[108] Miller 1982, especially 401–407.

4.11) as well as autopsy and conversations with priests and lay practitioners.[109] Ovid is often maligned as a source for Roman ritual, but his poem is not uninformed.[110] What is perhaps even more important, his exegesis and "rituals in ink" provide an imaginative vision of ritual practice that is worthy of attention in its own right.[111] When the narrator asks the *flaminica Dialis* to recommend an auspicious day for his daughter's wedding, both the question and her answer, complete with its antiquarian digression on the taboos she observes when marriage ought to be avoided, invite the reader to reflect upon her role in public cult and to imagine her as a repository of ritual knowledge.[112] Who better to help choose a propitious time for a wedding than the priestess whose veil would hide the blushes of the bride?

The antiquarian evidence, whatever its limitations, receives support from a modicum of material evidence as well as from other written sources of the late republic and early principate—Cato's *De agri cultura* (*On Agriculture*), the speeches and dialogues of Cicero, and Livy's history. Almost entirely lacking for the city of Rome itself, epigraphic evidence from Italy and the Latin west suggests that the practice of assigning official priestly roles to women was common and widespread, and that these offices were integral to the self-perception of the women who held them.[113] Admittedly, the state of the evidence prevents us from gaining the kind of detailed view of women's religious activities that we would like. There are some priestesses about whom we know almost nothing apart from their titles. Even so, we may acknowledge their existence and situate them within a larger narrative of women's priestly service at Rome. Indeed, this expansion is one of the primary benefits of a comprehensive approach: it allows us to compare evidence related to various offices and to identify potential patterns of organization and conduct. Despite the difficulties and shortcomings outlined above, the evidence suggests that Rome was a city populated with numerous female religious officials. When taken together, these texts enable us to redraw the boundaries of priesthood in ancient Rome.

---

[109] Miller 1982: 402–403.

[110] As Scheid (1992b: 129) has written, "Ovid is neither ignorant, wrong nor merely descriptive: he is only clever and subtle."

[111] Beard 2004: 125–126. See also Scheid 1992b: 122–129.

[112] Ov. *Fast.* 6. 219–234, with chapter 1.

[113] For the dearth of epigraphic evidence from republican Rome, see Schultz 2006b: 49, 70–71. On the epigraphic material (mostly imperial in date) from Italy and the Roman west, see especially Spickermann 1994; Ward 1998; Zimmermann and Frei-Stolba 1998; Hemelrijk 2005, 2006; Schultz 2006b: 69–79; Hemelrijk 2007; Gaspar 2012; Richlin 2014: 207–218, 233–238.

CHAPTER ONE

The *Flamen* and *Flaminica Dialis*

In the midst of the notorious Sullan proscriptions in late 82 BC, Rome's new dictator L. Cornelius Sulla (cos. 88, 80 BC) ordered a young C. Julius Caesar (cos. 59 BC) to divorce his wife, Cornelia, the daughter of Sulla's bitter enemy, L. Cornelius Cinna (cos. 86, 85, 84 BC). Caesar refused the demand and was promptly added to the list of the proscribed.[1] He fled Rome, took refuge in Sabine territory, was discovered and arrested by Sulla's henchmen, but managed to escape by bribing his captors.[2] Even though Sulla eventually granted his fellow patrician a pardon, Caesar remained in a self-imposed exile until the dictator's death in 78 BC.[3] Roman historians have generally focused on the political implications of Caesar's decision not to divorce Cornelia.[4] In the civil wars that rocked the decade of the eighties BC, Caesar presumably sympathized with the allies of his uncle Marius and his father-in-law Cinna. His refusal to renounce his affiliation with the Cinnan faction can be read as a sharp, if somewhat foolhardy, rebuke of Sulla and his new regime.

Without diminishing the political implications of this episode, we should consider the possibility that Caesar denied the dictator's request for religious reasons as well. Evidence suggests that he had been serving as *flamen Dialis* since 84 BC at the latest.[5] The *flamonium Diale* was a prestigious priesthood dedicated to Jupiter and open only to patricians married by a ritual known as *confarreatio*.[6] The occupant of this office was bound by a number of cumbersome social and religious sanctions, including one that was directly related to Caesar's situation in 82 BC. The marriage of a *flamen*, Aulus Gellius tells us, could not lawfully be dissolved except by death (*matrimonium flaminis nisi*

---

[1] Vell. Pat. 2.41.2; Plut. *Caes.* 1.1–3. Not every scholar agrees that Caesar was actually proscribed, but the evidence strongly suggests that he was. His patrimony and Cornelia's dowry were seized, he was arrested (and escaped only by means of a bribe), and he received an official pardon from Sulla. For a full discussion, see Ridley 2000: 220, with further bibliography.

[2] Cic. *Lig.* 32; Suet. *Iul.* 1.2.

[3] According to Suetonius (*Iul.* 1.2), Sulla was finally persuaded to relent through the intercession of the Vestals (see chapter 7 for further discussion).

[4] Ridley (2000: 220–226) summarizes the various explanations that have been offered.

[5] Vell. Pat. 2.43.1; Suet. *Iul.* 1.1; Badian 1961, 1990, 2009; Sumner 1973; Rüpke 2008: 734–735, No. 2003. Many scholars have argued that Caesar was appointed as *flamen Dialis* but never fully inaugurated. For this view, see especially Taylor 1941; Leone 1976; Liou-Gille 1999.

[6] For the *flamen Dialis*, his qualifications, and his obligations, see Vanggaard 1988; Marco Simòn 1996.

morte dirimi ius non est, N.A. 10.15.23).[7] If Caesar had renounced Cornelia, he would have forfeited his position as *flamen Dialis* as well.

Caesar's dilemma illuminates a central, defining feature of the priesthood under consideration in this chapter. The *flamen Dialis* was not permitted to divorce his wife. But *why* was divorce prohibited? It was not primarily a legal or even a moral issue; the Romans regarded divorce as improper and even irresponsible, but it was never strictly forbidden and occurred often enough among the elite.[8] The answer to this fundamental question lies instead in the sophisticated and characteristically Roman structure of the priesthood. A *flamen* could not dissolve his marriage because the flaminate of Jupiter did not belong to him alone, but to his wife the *flaminica* as well.

As I show in this chapter, the *flamen* and *flaminica Dialis* served the gods together as priest and priestess of Jupiter. Until fairly recently, however, modern scholars have either denied or heavily qualified the official priestly status of the *flaminica Dialis*, describing her instead as the Roman equivalent of the pastor's wife.[9] This analogy is inappropriate in light of the ancient evidence for her status and religious activities. Though modern ministry wives are expected to fulfill a wide variety of informal roles within their religious communities, they lack a title or official status within the religious hierarchy. Sociologists tend to describe this phenomenon, in which a wife gains vicarious achievement through her husband's professional position, as a "two-person single career."[10] The flaminate, on the other hand, was closer to the "coordinated career" model, or what is sometimes known as the "two-body problem" in academic circles.[11] The *flaminica* was the wife of a priest and a priestess in her own right, a dual role that is aptly captured by an excerpt from Paul the Deacon's epitome of the lexicon of Festus:

> flammeo vestimento flaminica utebatur, id est Dialis uxor et Iovis sacerdos, cui telum fulminis eodem erat colore. (82L)

---

[7] See also Plut. *Quaest. Rom.* 50 = *Mor.* 276d–e.

[8] On Roman attitudes towards divorce, see Treggiari 1991: 471–473, 1996a.

[9] See, for example, Wissowa 1912: 503–508, especially 506; Latte 1960: 402–404; Pötscher 1968; Dumézil 1970: 576, 580; Scheid 1992c: 384, 401–403. Even Boëls-Janssen, who has written three detailed articles on the religious status of the *flaminica Dialis* (Boels 1973; Boëls-Janssen 1989, 1991), ultimately concludes that her role within the flaminate was restricted to promoting personal and civic fertility. The work of Schultz (2006b: 79–81) has been particularly instrumental in reshaping scholarly opinions of the official status of the *flaminica Dialis*. For a more positive approach, see also Vanggaard 1988: 30–32; Van Haeperen 2002: 81, 364, 367, 377; Böhm 2003: 82–83; Flemming 2007; Takács 2008: 114; Holland 2012b. Readers with Finnish may also wish to consult Mustonen 2010.

[10] For the concept of the "two-person single career," see Papanek 1973; Schwartz 2006: 2–3, with further bibliography. Schwartz in particular explores the working of this phenomenon within the religious sphere in her study of American rebbetzins, wives who work in partnership with their rabbinic husbands to serve their congregations.

[11] Butler and Paisley (1980) define the "coordinated career couple" as two people pursuing careers in the same field who are, therefore, colleagues as well as partners. The coordinated career couple is a special type of the more familiar "dual-career couple" (see Rapoport and Rapoport 1969). Admittedly, the coordinated career couple is an imperfect metaphor for the *flamen* and *flaminica Dialis*: unlike most universities, Rome always hired both spouses.

The *flammeum* was a garment used by the *flaminica*, that is, the wife of the *flamen Dialis* and the *sacerdos* of Jove, whose thunderbolt was the same color.

In this passage, Paul explains that the *flaminica*, whose veil mimicked the hue of Jupiter's lightning bolt, was not only the wife (*uxor*) of the *flamen Dialis*, but also the priestess (*sacerdos*) of Jove.

The flaminate of Jupiter was a joint priesthood shared by a husband and a wife and as such it requires an entirely different interpretive model from the one traditionally applied to male priests at Rome. It is the aim of this chapter, therefore, to reconstruct the *flaminica's* ritual activities and to establish a new framework for understanding them. The ancient evidence, though often intractable, demonstrates that the *flaminica Dialis* was a religious official in her own right with her own role, both in separate rituals that she was responsible for independently and in rituals that she shared with her husband the *flamen*. A fresh consideration of household religion at Rome and the role of women within domestic cult also suggests, moreover, that joint priesthoods like the flaminate were the product of a characteristically Roman preference for cooperation between men and women in the practice of public and private religion. The religious realm not only allowed women to exercise an unusual degree of autonomy, but actually required them to do so on behalf of their households and, in the case of elite priestesses like the *flaminica Dialis*, on behalf of the community as a whole.

Ritual practice constituted Roman women as agents.[12] At the same time, however, it reinforced the proper gendered identities to which they were expected to conform. The *flaminica Dialis* may have had her own title and official role within public cult, but she was still subordinate to her husband. The final section of the chapter explores this tension, analyzing how the flaminate participated in the social and historical construction of gender categories and gender ideologies.

Becoming the *Flamen* and *Flaminica Dialis*

During the historical period, the *pontifex maximus* chose a new *flamen Dialis* from a list of three nominees that had been prepared in advance by the members of the pontifical college.[13] Before making his selection, the *pontifex maximus* presumably scrutinized each candidate's qualifications in order to ensure that he and his wife were fit to serve. The *flamen*, like his fellow *flamines maiores* and the *rex sacrorum* (king of the sacred rites), was required to be a patrician and the

---

[12] See the introduction.
[13] Tac. *Ann.* 4.16.2, with Van Haeperen 2002: 99–100.

child of a confarreate marriage.[14] Above all, however, the *flamen* and *flaminica* themselves had to be living in a marriage concluded by the rite of *confarreatio*.[15] The ceremony took its name from the cake of *far* (emmer wheat) that was offered to Jupiter Farreus and then shared by the bride and groom. The antiquarians tell us that this sacrifice created *manus* (the controlling hand). In Roman law, the term *manus* expressed a relationship between a husband and wife based on the power of the former over the latter.[16] A woman who entered *manus* left the *patria potestas* (paternal power) of her *paterfamilias* (male head of the household) and entered the legal authority of her new husband.[17] She became a member of his kinship group and was granted the same legal rights as a daughter.[18]

For the *flaminica Dialis*, the religious implications of marriage by *confarreatio* may have been even more significant than the legal consequences. A woman married with *manus* was a member of her husband's religious community and a full participant in his family rites (*sacra familiaria*). The transfer of a new wife's allegiance from her natal cult to that of her husband's family began on her wedding day. During the procession to the groom's house (*domum deductio*), the bride offered a coin at the local compital shrine announcing her presence to the *Lares compitales* and indicating her intention to join the local religious community of which her husband was already a member.[19] When she arrived at her new home, she placed a coin for the *Lares familiares* on the hearth and offered prayers to the household *genius*.[20] The creation of *manus*, therefore, ensured that the *flamen* and *flaminica Dialis* belonged to the same community of worshippers in every sphere of religious activity.

Though the popularity of *confarreatio* waned during the late Republic, it remained a requirement for the *flamen* and *flaminica Dialis* well into the imperial period. The insistence on this form of marriage may have been connected to the religious consequences of *manus*. Consider, for example, Tiberius' quandary in AD 23, when he was unable to find three candidates for the flaminate of Jupiter who had been born into a confarreate marriage. According to Tacitus, the *princeps* and *pontifex maximus* complained that many families had abandoned *confarreatio* due to negligence (*incuria*) and a desire to avoid the difficulties in-

---

[14] Gai. *Inst.* 1.112; Serv. Auct. ad *Aen.* 4.646. For the *rex sacrorum* and the remaining *flamines maiores*, see chapter 2.

[15] Tac. *Ann.* 4.16.2; Gai. *Inst.* 1.112; Serv. Auct. ad *Aen.* 4.646. For a general discussion of *confarreatio*, see Corbett 1930; Treggiari 1991: 21–24; Linderski 2005.

[16] See Gardner 1986: 11–14; Treggiari 1991: 16–32.

[17] Gell. *N.A.* 18.6.9; Serv. Auct. ad *Aen.* 11.476.

[18] Gell. *N.A.* 18.6.9. In fact, Gaius (*Inst.* 2.139) uses the legal term *in filiae loco* (in the situation of a daughter) to describe the consequences of *manus*. Like a man's children who were in his *potestatas*, a wife in *manus* had no property of her own before her husband's death (Cic. *Top.* 23, with Corbett 1930: 110; Treggiari 1991: 29). It should be noted, however, that a husband's disciplinary power over a wife in *manus* was more restricted than that over his children (Gardner 1986: 11; Treggiari 1991: 30).

[19] Non. 852L.

[20] Non. 852L; Arn. *Nat.* 2.67; Boëls-Janssen 1993: 254; Schultz 2006b: 127; Hersch 2010: 176–177, 278–279; Johansson 2010: 138–140.

herent in the ceremony itself.[21] What is perhaps even more important, however, he claimed that the legal consequences of *confarreatio*, namely the fact that a woman married in this way came into the legal authority of her husband, were unpopular.

Tiberius eventually inaugurated Cornelius Lentulus Maluginensis, the son of the previous *flamen Dialis*.[22] In order to rectify the untenable situation he had faced, however, Tiberius asked the senate to redefine the legal consequences of the rite of *confarreatio*:

> igitur tractatis religionibus placitum instituto flaminum nihil demutari: sed lata lex qua flaminica Dialis sacrorum causa in potestate viri, cetera promisco feminarum iure ageret. (Tac. *Ann.* 4.16.3)

> It was decided, therefore, when the question of impediments had been examined, that nothing be altered in the established practice of the *flamines*; but a law was passed whereby the *flaminica Dialis* should be in the legal power (*potestas*) of her husband for the purpose of the sacred rites (*sacra*), but should enjoy the usual legal standing of women in other matters.

By granting the *flaminica Dialis* a legal standing commensurate with that of her married peers, Tiberius and the senate were able to retain confarreate marriage as a precondition for entrance to the flaminate of Jupiter.[23] The ritual import of the mandate remained untouched: she came into the legal authority (*in potestate*) of her husband for the sake of the sacred rites alone (*sacrorum causa*).

A prospective *flaminica* had to be a *univira* (one-man woman), that is, she could not have been married to another man before she wed the *flamen*.[24] She was not, however, required to be a patrician by birth, presumably because *confarreatio* created *manus*.[25] A woman who entered *manus* transferred herself from her natal family to the family of her new husband, becoming a member of his kinship group for religious purposes with the same legal rights as a

---

[21] Tac. Ann. 4.16.2.

[22] Tac. *Ann.* 4.16.4, with Rüpke 2008: 638, No. 1348.

[23] Gaius (*Inst.* 1.136) dates the provision to 11 BC, which suggests that Tacitus may have transposed to AD 23 a debate that took place over thirty years earlier, when Augustus inaugurated Ser. Cornelius Lentulus Maluginensis (Rüpke 2008: 638, No. 1349). Regardless of the precise date, it is clear that the legal standing of the *flaminica Dialis* was altered during the early principate.

[24] Jer. *Ep.* 123.56; Serv. Auct. ad *Aen.* 4.29. For the significance of her status as a *univira*, see further below.

[25] For the creation of *manus* by *confarreatio*, see Gai. *Inst.* 1.108–110; Gardner 1986: 11–14; Treggiari 1991: 16–32. While it has been argued that *confarreatio* was restricted to patrician men and patrician women (see, for example, Taylor 1941: 116–117), there is clear evidence that plebeian women were marrying patrician men by *confarreatio* by at least the middle of the second century BC (as argued forcefully by Linderski 2005: 228–229). We know the names of only two *flaminicae maiores*, both *flaminicae* of Mars, from the republican period and both belonged to unquestionably plebeian families (Livy *Per.* 48; Val. Max. 6.3.8; Macrob. *Sat.* 3.13.11). Since the *flamen Martialis* was required to be married by *confarreatio*, we must conclude that patrician men and plebeian women were permitted to celebrate this rite.

daughter.[26] Simply put, a plebeian woman who came into her husband's *manus* through marriage by *confarreatio* became a member of his patrician family.[27] The social status of a prospective *flaminica*'s natal family was of little significance; only her relationship to the prospective *flamen* mattered.

Once he had made his decision, the *pontifex maximus* ritually "seized" his chosen candidate in a ceremony known as the *captio* and oversaw his inauguration in the *comitia calata* (convoked assembly), a nonvoting assembly that met on the Capitoline Hill.[28] The central rites of the *inauguratio* (inauguration) were performed by an *augur*, who asked for Jupiter's approval of the candidate and, provided the correct signs were observed, declared the *flamen* fully inaugurated.[29] Although the ancient sources are silent on the matter, the *flaminica Dialis* presumably participated in the inauguration ceremony as well.[30] The *inauguratio* was the crucial moment when the candidate, up to this point an average Roman citizen, became a *flamen* with all the attendant privileges and responsibilities. His wife and fellow priest would have undergone a simultaneous change in status, and may even have been officially inaugurated alongside her husband. Both the prohibition against divorce and the provision requiring the *flamen* to abdicate his position if the *flaminica* predeceased him suggest that the couple was regarded as a unified entity, rather than as two individual priests. A new *flamen Dialis*, in other words, could not be installed in office without his *flaminica*.

At the very least, it appears that *flamines* and *flaminicae* celebrated their elevation to religious office together. Publicia, the wife of L. Cornelius Lentulus Niger (pr. ca. 61 BC), was present at a sumptuous banquet in honor of his inauguration as *flamen Martialis* (priest of Mars) and is explicitly described as the new *flaminica*.[31] Lentulus and Publicia had both undergone a change in status and, quite appropriately, are identified by their flaminical titles.[32] The celebration, which was attended by the *flaminica*'s mother and four Vestals, her

---

[26] Gell. *N.A.* 18.6.9; Gardner 1986: 11–14; Treggiari 1991: 16–32.

[27] As suggested by Rüpke 2012a: 190. The legal evidence is borne out by the story of Verginia, who was excluded by patrician *matronae* from the worship of Pudicitia Patricia (Patrician Chastity) on the grounds that she had married outside the patriciate (*e patribus enupsisset*, Livy 10.23.4) when she became the wife of the plebeian consul L. Volumnius Flamma Violens (cos. 307, 296 BC). In response to this slight, Verginia founded a shrine to Pudicitia Plebeia (Plebeian Chastity) in her home and invited the plebeian *matronae* to worship there with her (Livy 10.23.3–10, with the detailed notes in Oakley 1997: 247–250; Festus 270L; Mæhle 2008). This etiological narrative may be a late fabrication, but it makes sense only if we accept that women assumed the social status of their husbands after marriage. Although Livy's Verginia appeals to her birth into the patrician Verginii, it is clear that her marriage to Volumnius had fundamentally changed her social status.

[28] For the *captio*, see Livy 27.8.5; Gell. *N.A.* 1.12.15–16; Gladigow 1972: 369; Bätz 2012: 68–69. For the *inauguratio*, see Gell. *N.A.* 15.27.1.

[29] For the inauguration of religious officials by augurs, see Cic. *Brut.* 1, *Phil.* 2.110; Macrob. *Sat.* 3.13.11; Catalano 1960: 220–246; Linderski 1986: 2215–2222.

[30] Van Haeperen 2002: 101.

[31] Macrob. *Sat.* 3.13.10–11, quoted below.

[32] Although Wissowa (1912: 506, n. 33) claims that Publicia was not present in her official capacity as *flaminica* but rather as the matron of the house, I cannot understand his reasoning.

new colleagues in the extended pontifical college, belonged to Publicia as well as to her husband. Macrobius, who offers the vignette as an example of late republican excess, quotes from the digest of the *pontifex maximus* Q. Caecilius Metellus Pius (cos. 80 BC), an authoritative source and a guest at the banquet in question. This glimpse of life in the pontifical college is unparalleled in extant literary sources, but there were undoubtedly many other occasions like it, where new *flamines* and *flaminicae* publicly commemorated an important transition in their shared life.

Serving the Gods Together

Following the *inauguratio* and the celebratory banquet, the *flamen* and *flaminica Dialis* began a life of joint religious service.[33] Plutarch emphasizes the cooperative nature of the priesthood:

> Διὰ τί ὁ ἱερεὺς τοῦ Διός ἀποθανούσης αὐτῷ τῆς γυναικός ἀπετίθετο τὴν ἀρχήν, ὡς Ἀτήιος ἱστόρηκε; πότερον ὅτι τοῦ μὴ λαβόντος ὁ λαβὼν εἶτ' ἀποβαλὼν γυναῖκα γαμετὴν ἀτυχέστερος; ὁ μὲν γὰρ τοῦ γεγαμηκότος οἶκος τέλειος, ὁ δὲ τοῦ γήμαντος εἶτ' ἀποβαλόντος οὐκ ἀτελὴς μόνον ἀλλὰ καὶ πεπηρωμένος· ἢ συνιερᾶται μὲν ἡ γυνὴ τῷ ἀνδρί, ὡς καὶ πολλὰ τῶν ἱερῶν οὐκ ἔστι δρᾶσαι μὴ γαμετῆς συμπαρούσης . . . (*Quaest. Rom.* 50 = *Mor.* 276d)

Why did the priest of Zeus [i.e., the *flamen Dialis*] resign his office when his wife died, as Ateius has recorded?[34] Is it because a man who has taken a wife and then lost his spouse is more unfortunate than one who has not married? For the household of a married man is complete, but that of a man who, having taken a wife, then loses her is not only incomplete, but also incapacitated. Or is it because the wife participates in her husband's sacred ministry, since there are many sacred rites (*hiera*) that he cannot perform without the assistance of his wife?

Following the format he adopts throughout the *Quaestiones*, Plutarch offers two alternative answers to the question he has raised. The first emphasizes the stigma attached to a widower, whom Plutarch regards as more unfortunate (ἀτυχέστερος) than a man who has never married, since his household is incomplete (οὐκ ἀτελὴς) and no longer self-sufficient. The second suggestion, which is very likely the one that Plutarch finds most compelling, focuses instead on the nature of the institution: the *flamen* resigned his office because his

---

[33] Boels (1973) provides a detailed discussion of the *flaminica*'s religious activities, but tends to overemphasize her role as a fertility talisman.

[34] The jurist C. Capito Ateius (cos. suff. AD 5) is known to have authored a work on the pontifical law (*ius pontificum*).

priesthood was incomplete without her.[35] The *flaminica* served alongside her husband, assisting him with his ritual obligations and performing others on her own in her capacity as the priestess of Jupiter. The range of duties belonging to the flaminate required its occupants always to act in concert. The *flamen* and *flaminica Dialis* complemented one another, and as a result, their partnership was greater than the sum of its parts.[36]

Indeed, later in the same passage, Plutarch notes, "one might wonder less at this [i.e., the *flamen*'s resignation] if he observes also that the death of one of the censors compelled the other to resign his office" (ἥττον δ' ἄν τις τοῦτο θαυμάσειε προσιστορήσας ὅτι καὶ τῶν τιμητῶν θατέρου τελευτήσαντος ἔδει καὶ τὸν ἕτερον πεπαῦσθαι τῆς ἀρχῆς, *Quaest. Rom.* 50 = *Mor.* 276e).[37] Despite the myriad differences between the censorship and the flaminate, these offices shared one important regulation. Neither a censor nor a *flamen* could continue in office after the death of his colleague. This point of correspondence underscores the fundamentally cooperative nature of the flaminate and the official character of the *flaminica*'s position within the religious system.

Later still, Plutarch suggests, with some hesitation, that the *flaminica Dialis* was regarded as the priestess of Juno (ἱερὰν τῆς Ἥρας εἶναι δοκοῦσαν, *Quaest. Rom.* 86 = *Mor.* 285a), thereby establishing a symmetrical relationship between the priestly couple and the divine couple they served. Following the Greek model, Roman myth made Juno the wife of Jupiter. In cult, however, she was mainly an independent figure, despite her association with Jupiter and Minerva in the Capitoline triad.[38] It is possible (and perhaps even likely) that the *flaminica Dialis* performed rituals in honor of Juno. Most extant sources, however, emphasize her role as the priestess of Jupiter, and it is in these sources that we must seek clues about her religious activities.

As the priest and priestess of the chief deity of the Roman state, the role of the *flamen* and *flaminica Dialis* in public religion was vital. For this reason, special rules, considered more fully below, kept the couple in the city at all times. Unlike the *pontifices* or augurs, who could act in the place of a colleague when necessary, the *flamen* and *flaminica* performed a ritual program unique to their priesthood. They were essentially fulltime religious professionals. Indeed, according to Aulus Gellius, the *flamen* celebrated religious rites on a daily basis (*cotidie feriatus, N.A.* 10.15.16). Regulations requiring him to wear his

---

[35] As Russell (1973: 45) has noted, when Plutarch presents alternative explanations in his *Quaestiones*, "the most favoured solution usually comes last." Although Russell derives this practice from Aristotle, Plutarch may have been influenced by Varro as well (Macrob. *Sat.* 3.4.3, with Stevenson 2004: 139–141).

[36] As observed by Mustakallio 2010: 16. Previous scholarship tends to stress the fact that the *flaminica*'s marital status was the only justification for her priestly role, ignoring the equally significant fact that it was the only justification for the *flamen*'s priestly status as well (see, for example, Boels 1973; Scheid 1992c: 384, 401–403).

[37] Two former consuls were chosen as censors every five years and granted the responsibility not only of taking the census and enrolling men in the army, but also of regulating the morals of their fellow citizens (Cic. *Leg.* 3.7).

[38] As Fowler (1895) rightly points out in his discussion of this text.

apex at all times and to keep a box of sacrificial cakes near his bed suggest that he was ready for action at every moment.[39]

Some of these daily rites may have taken place at the Temple of Jupiter on the Capitol. Others were celebrated in the *flaminia,* the house of the flaminical couple.[40] A brief entry in Paul's epitome of Festus reveals that the *flamen* performed certain sacrifices at a table known as an *adsidela,* so named because he officiated there while seated.[41] The flaminical hearth was also a place of some significance in public cult. The written sources tell us that fire was taken from it for use at sacrificial rites, perhaps all those over which the *flamen* or *flaminica* presided.[42] As the female head of household was responsible for the care and maintenance of the domestic hearth, we should probably assume that the *flaminica* tended the sacred fire on the hearth in the *flaminia.* She may even have supervised the transfer of this flame in a portable hearth (*focus* or *foculus*) to the altar of Jupiter.[43]

The *flaminia* was an important religious space within a network of mainly archaic cults. Festus even goes so far as to call the house an *aedes,* a term generally reserved for temples and houses of the gods.[44] It may have been an official residence set aside for the priest of Jupiter and his cult, like the public house of the *pontifex maximus* in the Forum Romanum.[45] During the New Year's festivities on March 1, the previous year's laurel garlands were removed from the *flaminia* and replaced with fresh branches.[46] The *regia,* the Temple of Vesta, the curial buildings, and the houses of the other *flamines* received new decorations as well and the flame on the hearth of Vesta was kindled afresh to mark the beginning of the new year. These religious buildings belong to a very ancient layer of Roman cult. As we shall see in the coming chapters, they were also united by the presence of priestesses within their walls.

In addition to observing these daily rituals, the *flamen Dialis* sacrificed a ram to Jupiter on the Ides of every month.[47] He also played a central role in the celebration of several annual public festivals, including the feast day of Fides on October 1, the Lupercalia in February, and the twin Vinalia, a pair of wine festivals held in honor of Jupiter on April 23 and August 19.[48] The *flaminica* likely accompanied the *flamen Dialis* on most occasions and may often have

---

[39] Gell. *N.A.* 10.15.17 (*apex*), 10.15.14 (box of sacrificial cakes).

[40] For the *flaminia,* see Gell. *N.A.* 10.15.7; Festus 79L; Serv. Auct. ad *Aen.* 2.57, 8.363; Palombi 1995a.

[41] Festus (Paulus) 18L. Servius may have had the *adsidelia* in mind when he remarked that the *flamen* never sat before an empty table (*mensa inanis,* ad *Aen.* 1.706).

[42] Gell. *N.A.* 10.15.7; Festus (Paulus) 94L.

[43] Roman sacrifices generally began with the offering of incense and wine on the fire in a portable hearth that was placed beside the main altar (Serv. Auct. ad *Aen.* 3.134; Wissowa 1912: 417; Scheid 2007: 264).

[44] Festus 79L.

[45] When a fire in the Basilica Aemilia spread to the Temple of Vesta in 14 BC, the Vestals carried the sacred objects to the house of the *flamen Dialis* on the Palatine (Cass. Dio 54.24.2).

[46] Ov. *Fast.* 3.135–140; Macrob. *Sat.* 1.12.6. See also chapter 6.

[47] Ov. *Fast.* 2.587–588; Festus 93L, 372L; Macrob. *Sat.* 1.15.16.

[48] Varro *Ling.* 6.16 (Vinalia); Livy 1.21.4 (Fides); Ov. *Fast.* 2.282 (Lupercalia).

played an important role. We know, for instance, that both the *flamen* and the *flaminica* attended the ceremony at the bridge during the Argei festival in early May.[49] While the ancient sources focus primarily on the *flamen*, Roman authors may have taken the *flaminica*'s attendance for granted, making it difficult for us to appreciate the full range of her religious activities. What little evidence we do possess suggests that the *flaminica* was an active ritual agent with a highly visible role in public cult.

We may begin to sketch a picture of the *flaminica*'s role on festival days through an analysis of her ritual implements. According to Aulus Gellius, the *flaminica* wore a twig (*surculus*) from a fruitful tree (*arbor felix*) in her mantle.[50] Gellius may have in mind the *arculum*, which a gloss in the Servius Auctus commentary on Vergil's *Aeneid* describes as a pomegranate branch bent into the form of a crown (*corona*, 4.137) and tied together with a white woolen tie. Both the *flaminica Dialis* and the *regina sacrorum* wore this crown when they offered sacrifices.[51] The pomegranate symbolized abundance and fertility in the ancient world.[52] The *arculum*, therefore, may have evoked the fecundity embodied by all married couples in Roman society, including priestly couples like the *flamen* and *flaminica Dialis* and the *rex* and *regina sacrorum*.[53] According to Festus, however, this crown also served a practical function:

> arculum appellabant circulum, quem capiti inponebant ad sustinenda commodius vasa quae ad sacra publica capite portabantur. (15L)

> They gave the name *arculum* to that circle that they placed on their head in order to support more conveniently the vessels that they carried on their heads to the public sacrifices.

This description suggests that the *arculum* functioned like the cushion that basket-bearers employed to support their burdens as they marched in religious processions. If the *flaminica*'s ritual headgear served the practical purpose proposed in the lexicon of Festus, this suggests that her role was often supportive, though not without significance. The *flaminica* may even have used the *arculum* to carry fruit or grain offerings to sacrifices over which her husband the *flamen* presided. Admittedly, Verrius or his epitomator may have misunderstood the purpose of the *flaminica*'s wreath. The author of the Servius Auctus commentary simply reports that the *regina sacrorum* wore the *arculum* at certain sacrifices (*in sacrificiis certis*), while the *flaminica* wore it whenever she

---

[49] See below.

[50] Gell. *N.A.* 10.15.28. The term *arbor felix* usually refers to a fruitful tree, as opposed to an *arbor infelix*, which did not produce any edible fruit (André 1964). Boels (1973: 83) suggests that the "fruitful" branch of the *flaminica*'s wreath symbolized her role as a guarantor of civic fertility.

[51] Festus 101L; Serv. Auct. ad *Aen.* 4.137.

[52] Despite its significance in myth and ritual, medical writers, and perhaps many individual women as well, were also aware of the pomegranate's potential as a contraceptive and abortifacient (see Riddle 1992: 25–26).

[53] Boels 1973: 83–86; Flory 1996: 63.

sacrificed (*omni sacrificatione*, ad *Aen.* 4.137). Perhaps the *arculum* was simply an element of the *flaminica*'s ritual costume, discussed more fully below.[54]

Other sources reveal that the *flaminica* presided over certain sacrifices independently. We hear, for instance, that she employed a type of sacrificial knife known as the *secespita*:

> secespita autem est culter oblongus, ferreus, manubrio eburneo, rotundo, solido, vincto ad capulum argento auroque, fixo clavis aeneis, quo flamines, flaminicae, virgines pontificesque ad sacrificia utuntur eaque iam sacra est. (Serv. ad *Aen.* 4.262)

> The *secespita* is an oblong knife made of iron with a rounded ivory handle fastened to the hilt with silver and gold and fixed with bronze nails. The *flamines*, *flaminicae*, Vestals, and *pontifices* use it for sacrifices, and it is itself a sacred thing.[55]

The *flaminica*'s right to use this implement is significant, as it further undermines the consensus that Roman women were prohibited from offering blood sacrifices.[56] After a preliminary offering of incense and wine, the presiding official at a Roman sacrifice sprinkled the victim with *mola salsa*, poured a little wine on its forehead, and ran the knife along its back.[57] This series of gestures, known collectively as the *immolatio*, consecrated the victim to the deity meant to receive the offering. Once the *immolatio* had been completed, the celebrant ordered professional ritual slaughterers (*victimarii*) to kill and butcher the animal. Elite Roman priests did not get their hands dirty; the hard work of sacrifice fell to public slaves. The man or woman who held the *secespita*, however, was the official in charge and the most important human figure present at the rite. Possession of a *secespita*, therefore, confirms that the *flaminica* presided over sacrificial rites in her capacity as the priestess of Jove.

We know of at least two occasions when the *flaminica* probably employed her instrument of sacrifice. According to Macrobius, she was required to perform an expiatory sacrifice whenever she heard thunder (*flaminica quotiens tonitrua audisset, feriata erat donec placasset deos*, *Sat.* 1.16.8). Citing the second-century AD historian Granius Licinianus, Macrobius also reports that she sacrificed a ram to Jupiter in the *regia* on the *nundinae* (market days), which occurred every eight days (*flaminica omnibus nundinis in regia Iovi arietem soleat immolare*, *Sat.* 1.16.30).[58] This rite presumably guaranteed the *flaminica*

---

[54] Indeed, it is difficult to reconcile Festus' description of the *arculum*'s function with evidence for the *flaminica*'s high *tutulus* hairstyle, discussed below.

[55] See also Festus 472L; Festus (Paulus) 473L; Siebert 1999: 75–79. Both Festus and Servius cite the Augustan jurist M. Antistius Labeo (d. before AD 22) as the source of their nearly identical definitions.

[56] See the introduction.

[57] For a description of a "typical" Roman sacrifice, see Scullard 1981: 24; Beard, North and Price 1998: 36–37; Scheid 2007.

[58] For the Romans, who counted inclusively, the *nundinae* occurred every ninth day. So Ovid writes, "there is also the day that always returns on a rotation of nine" (*est quoque qui nono semper ab orbe redit*,

significant prestige within the civic community, even though no more than a handful of priests could have witnessed the sacrifice proper.[59] Markets were an essential feature of life in ancient cities, marking the rhythm of time and providing regular opportunities for farmers and craftsmen to exchange their goods.[60] In Rome, the *nundinae* were also an occasion for political activity. According to the first-century BC historian P. Rutilius Rufus, the Romans held assemblies of the people (*comitia*) on the *nundinae* so that laws could be promulgated and so that candidates for office could canvass before a larger crowd (*frequentiore populo*, Macrob. *Sat.* 1.16.34–35).[61] Like the *nundinae* themselves, the *flaminica*'s sacrifice may have had a multifunctional character, addressing Jupiter as the chief deity of the civic community and seeking his approval for the economic and political activities that would take place throughout the day.

Regardless of its precise function, the location leaves little doubt that the sacrifice was a public rite (*publicum sacrum*) made on behalf of the Roman people (*pro populo*). The *regia*, meaning "royal house," was actually a *fanum* (shrine).[62] It stood in the Forum and was the site of some of the most ancient rituals in the city. The college of pontiffs held official meetings there and stored their records in its archive. A shrine (*sacrarium*) of Mars within its precinct held the shields and spear of the god of war, which generals rattled before setting off on campaign.[63] The *rex* and *regina sacrorum* offered sacrifices to Janus and Juno respectively.[64] The mysterious group of priestesses known as the *saliae virgines* (Salian Virgins) also sacrificed while dressed in military garb in the presence of a *pontifex maximus*.[65] The Vestal Virgins and the *pontifex maximus* performed secret rites in the shrine of Ops Consiva, a goddess of the harvest.[66] In this ancient building with its varied cultic associations, the *flaminica Dialis* sacrificed a ram to Jupiter every eight days. Even the *regia*, a vital religious center in the heart of the Forum, thoroughly integrated the activities of male and female priests.

Fast. 1.54). For the debate over whether or not the *flaminica*'s sacrifice indicates that the *nundinae* were sacred to Jupiter (*feriae Iovis*, Macrob. *Sat.* 1.16.30), see Michels 1967: 103–106; Rüpke 2011: 32–34, 59–63; Ker 2010: 362–365.

[59] Rüpke (2011: 33), for example, stresses that the "public" did not witness the sacrifice because the *regia* was accessible only to a small number of priests.

[60] For the economic and social significance of the *nundinae*, see MacMullen 1970; Shaw 1981; de Ligt 1993; Frayn 1993; Ker 2010.

[61] For political activity on the *nundinae*, see also Livy 7.15.13; Dion. Hal. *Ant. Rom.* 7.58.3; Michels 1967: 103–106; Ker 2010: 362–363, 366–367. At some point, perhaps in the *lex Hortensia* of 287 BC, assemblies (*comitia*) and gatherings of the people (*contiones*) were prohibited on market days (as suggested by Michels 1967: 105–106). The term *trinundinum*, the minimum number of days between the promulgation (*promulgatio*) of a law and its adoption by an assembly of the people (Cic. *Dom.* 41, *Phil.* 5.7; Schol. Bob. 140St.), may indicate that legislation was posted for three consecutive market days (so Lintott 1965) and thus that the *nundinae* retained some political functions in the later Republic, but this is not certain.

[62] Festus 346–348L, with Scott 1999.

[63] Serv. ad *Aen.* 7.603.

[64] Varro *Ling.* 3.12; Ov. *Fast.* 1.318; Macrob. *Sat.* 1.15.19, with chapter 2.

[65] Festus (Paulus) 419L, with chapter 3.

[66] Varro *Ling.* 6.21; Festus 354L, with chapter 6.

It is more difficult to determine a precise context for the third ritual implement with which the *flaminica* is associated. Near the beginning of the second book of the *Fasti*, Ovid claims to have seen the *flaminica* asking for *"februa"* and receiving a twig of pine in return (*ipse ego flaminicam poscentem februa vidi; / februa poscenti pinea virga data est*, 27–28). Though Ovid does not reveal who gave the *flaminica* her pine twig, he does provide an explanation of its purpose. The term *februa*, he tells us, describes "anything with which our bodies are purified" (*quodcumque est quo corpora nostra piantur*, 29). Indeed, *februa* could take a variety of forms. Ovid includes under this heading wool (*lanas*, 21), salted grain (*torrida cum mica farra*, 24), the strips of leather with which the Luperci "purify the earth" (*solum lustrant*, 32), and the leaves cut from a "pure tree" (*arbore pura*, 25) that priests wear on their "chaste brows" (*casta tempora*, 26). Some commentators have suggested that the *flaminica* placed the pine twig in her *arculum*.[67] As we have seen, however, other sources specify that this wreath was made from a pomegranate branch.[68] Matthew Robinson has recently proposed that she used the pine branch to sprinkle water at rites of purification.[69] This is an attractive suggestion, particularly in light of compelling evidence associating the *flaminica* with some of the most important purification rituals in the festival calendar.

During certain purificatory rites, the *flaminica Dialis* was prohibited from combing or adorning her hair and presumably from wearing her *flammeum* as well. These restrictions were rooted in the ritual calendar and may be related to the fact that the festival days on which the *flaminica* left her hair unkempt coincided with days on which marriage was prohibited or considered inauspicious. Ovid, for instance, warns young women to avoid marriage in March on the days when the *salii* moved (*movere*) and purified (*lustratio*) the holy shields (*ancilia*) of Mars. "On these days too," he points outs, "the belted wife of the *apex*-wearing *flamen Dialis* must have her hair uncombed" (*his etiam coniunx apicati cincta Dialis / lucibus impexas debet habere comas, Fast.* 3.393–398).

The *flaminica* also left her hair uncombed and unadorned during the rites of the Argei.[70] This festival began with a procession to the twenty-seven Argei shrines on March 16 and 17 and culminated on the Ides of May with a ceremony at the Pons Sublicius, during which the Vestals threw twenty-seven rush dolls into the Tiber. According to Plutarch, the Romans avoided marriage during May as well. He offers several explanations for this taboo, including one related to the nature of the Argei rite:

ἢ ὅτι τῷ μηνὶ τούτῳ τὸν μέγιστον ποιοῦνται τῶν καθαρμῶν, νῦν μὲν εἴδωλα ῥιπτοῦντες ἀπὸ τῆς γεφύρας εἰς τὸν ποταμὸν πάλαι δ'ἀνθρώπους;

---

[67] Frazer (1929) and Le Bonniec (1969) ad loc.
[68] See above.
[69] Robinson 2011: 76.
[70] Plut. *Quaest. Rom.* 86 = *Mor.* 285a; Gell. *N.A.* 10.15.30. For the rites of the Argei, see also chapter 6.

διὸ καὶ τὴν Φλαμινίκαν, ἱερὰν τῆς Ἥρας εἶναι δοκοῦσαν, νενόμισται σκυθρωπάζειν, μήτε λουομένην τηνικαῦτα μήτε κοσμουμένην. (*Quaest. Rom.* 86 = *Mor.* 285a)

Or is it because in this month they observe their most important purificatory rite, during which they now throw images [i.e., rush dolls] into the river from the bridge, but formerly human beings? And for this reason it is customary for the *flaminica*, who is reputed to be devoted to Juno, to maintain a sad countenance, neither bathing nor adorning herself at this time.[71]

Plutarch suggests that the *flaminica* appeared at the bridge ceremony unwashed and unadorned on account of the somber character of the rite, which had once involved, and still evoked, human sacrifice. Perhaps even more relevant, however, is his notice that the Argei festival was the most important purificatory rite in the ritual calendar and, therefore, functionally similar to the lustration of the *ancilia* in March. The *flaminica*'s unkempt appearance appears to have been related to the nature of these purification rites, which were incompatible with weddings.

A third example tends to confirm an association between the desire to avoid marriage during important purification rites and the appearance of the *flaminica*. The festival days surrounding the Vestalia, which culminated in a ritual purification of the *aedes Vestae* (Temple of Vesta), were regarded as *nefasti* (unfit for public business) and *religiosi* (sacred).[72] In Ovid's *Fasti*, the *flaminica Dialis* advises the poet not to give his daughter in marriage during this period, which ran from June 7 to 15:

> donec ab Iliaca placidus purgamina Vesta
>   detulerit flavis in mare Thybris aquis,
> non mihi detonso crinem depectere buxo,
>   non ungues ferro subsecuisse licet,
> non tetigisse virum, quamvis Iovis ille sacerdos,
>   quamvis perpetua sit mihi lege datus.
> tu quoque ne propera: melius tua filia nubet
>   ignea cum pura Vesta nitebit humo." (6.227–234)

Until the tranquil Tiber with its yellow waters has carried down to the sea the filth (*purgamina*) from Ilian Vesta, I am not permitted to comb my hair with shaped boxwood, or to have cut my nails with iron, or to have touched my husband, even though he is the priest of Jupiter, even though he has been given to me by a permanent law. You, too, be in no hurry; your daughter will marry better when fiery Vesta shines on a pure floor.

---

[71] For the suggestion that the *flaminica* was the priestess of Juno, see above.
[72] Festus 296L.

This depiction of the *flaminica* as a repository of religious knowledge related to women's lives is striking, to say the least, and certainly very plausible, even if we doubt the reality of the conversation as Ovid records it.[73] In the lines preceding this passage, Ovid claims to have asked the *flaminica* to tell him what days were suitable for weddings and which days should be avoided. She responds that the first part of June is an inauspicious time to wed, citing the fact that she is not permitted to comb her hair or cut her nails until the purification of Vesta's temple is complete. These prohibitions are similar to the ones that she observed in March and May. In this passage, however, the *flaminica* provides another highly significant piece of information: she was not permitted to touch her husband until the *nefas* period had ended.

This final prohibition brings into sharper focus the connection between purification festivals, the actions and appearance of the *flaminica Dialis*, and the suspension of weddings. The *flamen* and *flaminica* were required to abstain from sexual relations during important purificatory rites, perhaps because they participated in these rituals and were expected to be ritually pure themselves. The desire to avoid marriage during the same period, however, may indicate that the prohibition was more widely applicable than Ovid's *flaminica* suggests. In either case, the *flaminica*'s appearance on these days might be best understood as an outward sign that she was observing the interdiction against sexual relations with her husband. Given the ideological and practical significance of the marital relationship within the flaminate, the *flaminica* assumed what can best be described as an attitude of mourning during periods when ritual abstinence was required.[74]

While the ancient sources do not specifically mention the *flammeum* in the context of these purification rites, their focus on the *flaminica*'s uncombed and unadorned hair, which would have been hidden by the veil, suggests that she appeared without her signature attribute. As a symbol of good fortune and fidelity in marriage, the *flammeum* would have seemed particularly incongruous during periods when weddings were prohibited. In fact, when the city was small, the *flaminica*'s unusual appearance might have served as a signal to other women, warning them to avoid marriage until the purification ceremonies had been completed.

In addition to these regularly recurring rituals and sacrifices, the *flaminica Dialis* may have been present at marriages concluded by *confarreatio*. This ceremony, performed in the presence of at least ten witnesses and formalized by "certain and sacred words" (*certis et sollemnibus verbis*, Gai. *Inst.* 1.112), took its name from the cake of *far* that was offered to Jupiter Farreus and then shared by the bride and groom. According to the written sources, the *flamen Dialis*

---

[73] Hersch 2010: 283. In reporting a conversation with a specialist, Miller (1982: 403–404) suggests that Ovid is adapting a motif from Callimachus' *Aitia*, an important model for the *Fasti*.
[74] As noted by Littlewood 2006: 72.

and the *pontifex maximus* officiated at this rite, joining the bride and groom through an offering of grain and *mola salsa*. The *flaminica* likely attended as well. She may even have served as the *pronuba* (attendant of the bride). In modern scholarship, the *pronuba* is associated most clearly with the so-called *dextrarum iunctio*, the joining of the couple's hands.[75] She may also have prepared the wedding torches, decorated the bridal bed, and offered advice to the young bride. The ancient sources stress that the woman who performed this office had to be a *univira*, but they do not say that she had to be a member of the family.[76] The *flaminica Dialis*, in other words, may have been qualified to serve as *pronuba* at every confarreate marriage performed in the city of Rome. Even if she did not fulfill this role, her presence at the ceremony surely added to its gravity and religious character. If the *flammeum*, the *flaminica's* brightly colored veil, could bring good fortune to a bride on her wedding day, how much more so could the presence of the priestess herself?[77]

Ritual Prohibitions

The religious life of the *flamen* and *flaminica Dialis* was not shaped by their ritual obligations alone. In fact, the *flamen* may be best known for the bewildering list of *"caerimoniae"* (ritual prohibitions) that regulated his dress, diet, behavior, and even his interactions with his wife the *flaminica*.[78] According to Aulus Gellius, "The ritual prohibitions of the *flaminica Dialis* are nearly the same, and they say that she observes others separately" *(eaedem ferme caerimoniae sunt flaminicae Dialis; alias seorsum aiunt observitare, N.A. 10.15.26–27).* The fact that the *flaminica* observed ritual prohibitions as well adds additional support to the notion that she shared fully in the flaminate. These prohibitions were uniquely obtrusive. With the possible exception of the Vestals, whose perpetual virginity and fulltime service at the hearth of Vesta dictated many of the paramaters of their personal lives, no other Roman priest or priestess was hedged about by such onerous restrictions. It was, for instance, a ritual fault for either the *flamen* or the *flaminica* to be out of the city for a single night.[79] They were also forbidden to mount a horse or to see an army drawn up outside of the *pomerium*, the ritual boundary of the city.[80] In contrast to most elite priests, who were able to enjoy a full military and political career in conjunction with their religious office, the priestly couple that served Jupiter led a truly religious

---

[75] For a full discussion of the literary and artistic evidence for the *pronuba*, see Hersch 2010: 190–212.
[76] Festus 282L; Festus (Paulus) 283L; Tert. *Cast.* 13.1.6; Serv. Auct. ad *Aen.* 4.166.
[77] Festus 79L, quoted below.
[78] Detailed modern discussions of these prohibitions include Pötscher 1968; Boels 1973; Vanggaard 1988: 88–104; Marco Simón 1996: 77–139.
[79] Livy 5.52.
[80] Gell. *N.A.* 10.15.3–4; Plin. *H.N.* 28.146; Plut. *Quaest. Rom.* 40 = *Mor.* 274d; Festus 71L; Festus (Paulus) 295L.

existence. Their ritual program was crucial to the continued wellbeing of the Roman state, and the prohibitions associated with their priesthood provided a safeguard against the possibility that this program should lapse.

Aulus Gellius, a Latin author and grammarian of the second century AD, is perhaps our best source for the *flamen* and *flaminica Dialis*.[81] According to his own citations, Gellius based his extended discussion of the priesthood on material in books about the public priests (*in libris qui de sacerdotibus publicis compositi sunt*, 10.15.1) and the work of Fabius Pictor, either the famous annalist Q. Fabius Pictor (b. ca. 270 BC), who wrote in Greek, or the author of a work on the pontifical law (*ius pontificum*) active in the middle of the second century BC.[82] Much of his description presumably reflects the state of the flaminate during this period. Despite its inherent conservatism, however, Roman religion was not a static system. As is his custom elsewhere in the *Noctes Atticae*, Gellius supplements his republican material with a notice that some requirements had been relaxed or remitted entirely over time.[83] For instance, a pontifical decree preserved by the first-century AD jurist Masurius Sabinus ruled that the *flamen* might take off his *apex* at home (*sub tecto*, Gell. *N.A.* 10.15.17). Tacitus also reports that during the principate of Augustus, the *pontifices* decided that a *flamen* suffering from a serious illness might be absent from the city for more than two nights, provided it was not on days of public sacrifice (*diebus publici sacrificii*, *Ann.* 3.71) and not more than twice in the same year. What I have sketched below, therefore, is not a snapshot of a single moment in time, but rather a composite picture of the office as it was understood during the Republic and early principate.

Regulations Governing the Marriage of the *Flamen* and *Flaminica Dialis*

The various taboos and regulations attested for the *flamen* and *flaminica Dialis* fall into several broad categories. Not surprisingly, the first category concerns the integrity and stability of their marriage. As noted above, they were not permitted to divorce and the *flamen* was compelled to resign the priesthood if the *flaminica* died in office.[84] The logic behind these two conditions is fairly transparent. The flaminate of Jupiter required the service of both husband and wife in order to function properly. What was even more important, their union as a married couple and as a pair of priests was regarded as exclusive and inimitable. Neither the *flamen* nor the *flaminica* could be replaced once their inauguration had occurred. The *flamen*'s marriage, Gellius stresses, could not be dissolved except by death (*matrimonium flaminis nisi morte dirimi ius non est*, *N.A.* 10.15.23).

---

[81] Gell. *N.A.* 10.15.1–32.
[82] Although Palmer (1972: 341) identifies this Pictor with the annalist, see the introduction for the suggestion that he is an antiquarian of the second century BC.
[83] For examples, see Stevenson 1993: 145.
[84] Gell. *N.A.* 10.15.22–3; Plut. *Quaest. Rom.* 50 = *Mor.* 276d–e.

There were even regulations regarding the *flamen* and *flaminica*'s marital bed. The feet of this bed were smeared with a thin layer of clay (*luto tenui*, Gell. *N.A.* 10.15.14). No other person was permitted to sleep in the bed, and the *flamen* and *flaminica* were not permitted to sleep away from it for three nights consecutively (*trinoctium*).[85] This stipulation may be connected to the practice of *trinoctium*, whereby a wife could circumvent the creation of *manus* through *usus* (continuous possession) by absenting herself from her husband's home for three consecutive nights each year.[86] The *flaminica* entered her husband's *manus* through *confarreatio*, or more specifically, through the sacrifice of a cake of *far* to Jupiter Farreus. It seems unlikely, therefore, that the *flamen*'s legal authority over his wife could have been broken by *trinoctium*. Even so, the prohibition against either spouse spending more than three nights away from the marriage bed may have been modeled on the practice.[87] Its effect was to further emphasize the marital bond between a *flamen* and his *flaminica*, which formed the basis of their priesthood.

Regulations Governing the Ritual Purity of the *Flamen* and *Flaminica Dialis*

Other prohibitions ensured that the *flamen* and *flaminica* remained ritually pure and able to fulfill their daily religious obligations. Contact with death was prohibited with particular care.[88] In the ancient world, a person in mourning (*funestus*) or one who had been in close contact with a corpse was prohibited from sacrificing for a period of time because the pollution of death was believed to be offensive to the gods.[89] For this reason, priests like the *flamen* and *flaminica Dialis* were subject to stringent restrictions regarding contact with death in order to ensure that they would be able to carry out their ritual duties without interruption.[90] They were not permitted to touch a corpse, to approach a tomb, or even to hear the sound of funerary flutes.[91] The *flaminica* was prohibited from wearing *calcei morticini*, shoes made from the skin of an animal that had died of natural causes (*sua sponte*, Serv. ad *Aen.* 4.518); only an animal that had been slaughtered (*occisus*) or sacrificed (*immolatus*) was free from mournful associations (*funestus*, Festus 152L). Death is inevitable, of course, and it would have been unreasonable to prevent a *flamen* and *flaminica* from mourning the death of a close friend or relative. Gellius notes, in fact, that

---

[85] Gell. *N.A.* 10.15.14.
[86] Cic. *Flacc.* 34, 84; Gell. *N.A.* 3.2.12–13; Gai. *Inst.* 1.111; Treggiari 1991: 18–21.
[87] Pötscher 1968: 229; Boels 1973: 79. Alternatively, Albanese (1969) has suggested that the absence of three nights would have interrupted Jupiter's *potestas* over the flamen and therefore invalidated his priesthood.
[88] See especially Marco Simón 1996: 126–134.
[89] See, for example, Serv. ad *Aen.* 11.2, with Lindsay 2000.
[90] Lindsay 2000: 154–157.
[91] Gell. *N.A.* 10.15.24; Cic. *Tusc.* 1.16; Festus (Paulus) 82L.

the *flamen* was permitted to attend a funeral, though he may have been required to abstain from performing his ritual functions until he had been purified.[92]

The *flamen* and *flaminica* were also forbidden to touch, see, or refer to yeast, raw meat, goats, dogs, ivy, or beans.[93] While the objects on this list were not inherently polluting in an everyday context, they evidently threatened the ritual purity of the *flamen* and his wife. Beans, for example, were a staple of the ancient diet. In Roman society, however, they were also associated with death; Festus relates the taboo to the fact that beans were offered to the spirits of the dead at the Lemuria and the Parentalia.[94] Plutarch suggests that goats were off limits on account of their reputation for lasciviousness while dogs were unsuitable companions due to their belligerence and their association with Hecate and the crossroads.[95] In spite of the explicit prohibition, however, the well-attested presence of guard dogs at the Temple of Jupiter on the Capitoline would in fact have made it impossible for the *flamen* and *flaminica Dialis* to avoid encountering one now and then.[96]

The prohibition against yeast has parallels in the ancient Near East, where leavened dough was considered a profane substance.[97] Plutarch connects this proscription with the one banning raw meat, and explains both within the context of death pollution. Raw meat and fermented flour, Plutarch insists, are in a similar intermediary state, "for neither is it a living creature nor has it yet become a cooked food" (οὔτε γάρ ἐστι ζῷον οὔτ᾽ ὄψον ἤδη γέγονεν, Plut. *Quaest. Rom.* 110 = *Mor.* 290a). While raw meat was considered repulsive because it resembled an open wound (ἑλκώδη), yeast was actually regarded as an agent of corruption and putrefaction that could spoil the flour if left unchecked. Cooked meat and leavened bread were not prohibited because these were finished products ready for consumption.

The taboo against handling raw meat and unleavened bread would have made it impossible for the *flaminica Dialis* to prepare a meal for her family. Presumably this did not present much of a challenge, however, since elite Roman households relied upon slaves to do their cooking. It is more difficult to reconcile these food prohibitions with the *flamen*'s and *flaminica*'s known ritual responsibilities. How, for example, could they avoid seeing or referring to raw meat when they presided over an animal sacrifice? The ancient sources avoid addressing this tension, and we can only assume that the flesh of a consecrated sacrificial victim was exempt from the taboo.

---

[92] Gell. *N.A.* 10.15.25. Huet (2015: 146) suggests (plausibly, I think) that a screen was placed between the *flamen* and the corpse.
[93] Gell. *N.A.* 10.15.12; Plin. *H.N.* 18.119; Plut. *Quaest. Rom.* 109–111 = *Mor.* 289f–290d; Festus (Paulus) 72L; Serv. Auct. ad *Aen.* 2.57.
[94] Festus 77L.
[95] Plut. *Quaest. Rom.* 111 = *Mor.* 290a–d.
[96] Livy 3.29.9, 5.47.2–4; Dion. Hal. *Ant. Rom.* 13.7.3; Gell. *N.A.* 6.1.6; Plut. *Cam.* 27.2.
[97] Vanggaard 1988: 95.

Regulations Against "Binding" the *Flamen* and *Flaminica Dialis*

A third category reveals that the *flamen* and *flaminica* had to remain free from physical and social constraints. The *flamen* was forbidden from swearing an oath, Plutarch suggests, because the gods would not accept his prayers and sacrifices if he perjured himself.[98] Modern scholars, on the other hand, compare the prohibition to others stipulating that the *flamen* and *flaminica* could not be bound, either literally or figuratively, nor could they be associated with anything that symbolized bondage.[99] They could not touch ivy or pass under an arbor of vines, have a knot on their clothing, or wear a ring unless it was hollow and perforated.[100] Only a free person was permitted to cut their hair.[101] If a person in bonds entered the *flaminia*, he had to be loosed and the bonds drawn up through the hole in the roof over the *impluvium* (the pool of water in the center of the *atrium*).[102] Similarly, if anyone on his way to be flogged fell at the *flamen*'s feet as a suppliant, it was considered a *piaculum* (ritual fault) to flog the man on that day.[103] The *flamen* was also released from *patria potestas* upon entrance to his priesthood. Like the swearing of an oath, *patria potestas* would have subjected him to social and religious bonds that were evidently incompatible with his position as *flamen Dialis*.[104] The *flaminica*, of course, remained subject to her husband's *manus*, for reasons we shall explore more fully below. The *flamen* and *flaminica*, it seems, could be constrained only by the regulations associated with their priesthood.

Dressing the Part

In most societies, both ancient and modern, clothing and other adornment serve to communicate and reinforce social status and gender roles.[105] This was especially true in ancient Rome, where costume was carefully prescribed in a variety of civic and ritual contexts. The *flamen* wore at all times the *albogalerus*, a close-fitting cap made from the hide of an animal sacrificed to Jupiter.[106] Fas-

---

[98] Plut. *Quaest. Rom.* 44 = *Mor.* 275c–d. See also Gell. *N.A.* 10.15.5, 31; Livy 31.50.7; Cass. Dio 59.13.1; Festus 226L; Festus (Paulus) 92L.

[99] See, for example, Guizzi 1968: 184–185; Vanggaard 1988: 96–97; Saquete 2000: 108; Forsythe 2005: 137.

[100] Gell. *N.A.* 10.15.13 (vines); 10.15.9 (knot); 10.15.6 (ring).

[101] Gell. *N.A.* 10.15.11.

[102] Gell. *N.A.* 10.15.8; Serv. Auct. ad *Aen.* 2.57.

[103] Gell. *N.A.* 10.15.10. According to Plutarch, the *flamen Dialis* was a "living and sacred statue" (ἔμψυχον καὶ ἱερὸν ἄγαλμα, *Quaest. Rom.* 111 = *Mor.* 290c) who functioned like an altar or a sanctuary.

[104] Tac. *Ann.* 4.16; Gai. *Inst.* 3.114; Ulp. 10.5. The Vestal Virgins were also exempt from *patria potestas* (see chapter 4).

[105] Important studies of Roman clothing include Bonfante-Warren 1973; Sensi 1980–1981; Sebesta and Bonfante 1994; Croom 2002; Cleland, Harlow and Llewellyn-Jones 2005; Edmondson and Keith 2008; Olson 2008; Harlow 2012.

[106] Gell. *N.A.* 10.15.32; Festus 9L; Siebert 1999: 122–125, 127.

tened to the top of this cap was the *apex*, a long, narrow spike made of olivewood (*virgula oleagina*, Festus 9L).[107] His senatorial shoes (*calcei*) signified his membership in Rome's social and political elite, while his purple-striped *toga praetexta* asserted his priestly status.[108] When sacrificing, the *flamen* also wore a wool cloak known as the *laena*.[109] The *flaminica* was required to spin and weave, with her own hands, her own as well as her husband's ritual garments.[110] With the aid of her *secespita*, the sacrificial knife discussed above, she began weaving the *laena* immediately after the *inauguratio*.[111] This unusual practice reveals a significant ritual dimension to what was otherwise a quintessentially domestic task. The *laena*, moreover, had to be made entirely of wool, a fabric that was valued for its purity and apotropaic qualities.[112] In fact, a *flaminica* once committed a serious *piaculum* by carelessly employing a linen thread as sewing material for her husband's cloak.[113] The *flamen's* priestly costume not only differentiated him from ordinary citizens, but also guaranteed his ritual purity when he approached the altar.

The costume of the *flaminica Dialis* likewise articulated her status as the priestess of Jupiter and as an ideal *matrona* (married woman). During the republican period, freeborn *matronae* belonged to a loosely defined social group known as the *ordo matronarum*.[114] They were clearly differentiated from other women by various *insignia* (symbols of rank), including a garment known as the *stola*. Indeed, Paul the Deacon defines the *matronae* as "those who had the right to wear *stolae*" (*quibus stolas habendi ius erat*, 112L). This long, slip-like dress with over-the-shoulder straps was worn over the tunic and belted under the breast.[115] In addition to communicating social status, it preserved

[107] See also Festus 17, 21L; Serv. Auct. ad *Aen.* 8.664, 10.270; Isid. *Orig.* 7.12.17, 19.30.5.

[108] Livy 27.8.4–10; Plut. *Quaest. Rom.* 113 = *Mor.* 291b–c. Praetextate garments took a variety of forms. Curule magistrates, the augurs, the *pontifex maximus*, the *flamines*, and various other priestly officials wore the *toga praetexta* (Livy 1.8.3; Pliny *H.N.* 8.195, 9.136; Festus 430L). The Vestal Virgins wore a praetextate veil known as the *suffibulum* when they sacrificed (Varro *Ling.* 6.21; Festus (Paulus) 475L), and the *victimarii* who assisted at public sacrifices wore the *limus*, a long rectangular skirt with a praetextate border (Serv. ad *Aen.* 12.120). In addition to communicating the wearer's status, the border on a praetextate garment served important apotropaic and ritual functions. The color purple was associated with blood, which symbolized life and was used in many ancient cultures to ward off evil forces. For this reason, children wore the *toga praetexta* until adulthood (Cic. *Lael.* 33). Praetextate garments also proactively guarded against ritual pollution. According to Festus (282L), "praetextate speech" (*praetextus sermo*) was speech devoid of obscenity. Those who wore praetextate garments were forbidden to use obscene language, and the purple border warned those nearby to refrain from polluting words, gestures, or activities, particularly those associated with sexuality. For a discussion of praetextate garments and their ritual significance, see Sebesta 2005.

[109] Suet. *Frag.* 167; Pley 1911; Bonfante-Warren 1973: 394–295, 607–609.

[110] Serv. Auct. ad *Aen.* 4.262, 12.120.

[111] Serv. Auct. ad *Aen.* 4.262. The *flaminica* likely employed the *secespita* in place of the *spatha* (weaving sword), a long, flat wooden tool that was used to push the weft threads upwards in order to create a tighter weave (Wild 1970: 67).

[112] Serv. Auct. ad *Aen.* 4.263, 12.120; Pley 1911; Sebesta 1994a: 47.

[113] Serv. Auct. ad *Aen.* 12.120.

[114] For the term, see Val. Max. 5.2.1. For the privileges and duties associated with elite *matronae*, see Gagé 1963: especially 100–153; Hallett 1989: 3–61, 211–262; Dixon 1998; Richlin 2014: 218–224.

[115] For a detailed discussion of the literary and visual evidence for the *stola*, see Sebesta 1994a; Croom 2002: 75–78; Olson 2008: 27–33. The ancient sources do not state explicitly that the *flaminica* wore the *stola*, but Ovid does describe her as the belted (*cincta*, *Fast.* 3.393) wife of the *flamen Dialis*.

a *matrona*'s modesty and indicated that she was a woman to whom respect should be shown.[116] The *flaminica* was required to guard her modesty with particular care; she could never gird her dress above her knees and she was prohibited from climbing a ladder consisting of more than three steps, except the so-called Greek stairs (*scala Graecae*), which, as previously mentioned, were constructed in such a way that they would not expose her feet or ankles to those standing below.[117]

Other elements of the *flaminica*'s dress and adornment had a more explicit ritual function, including, perhaps, her *tutulus* hairstyle.[118] Varro and Festus indicate that this coiffure was reserved for *flaminicae* and *matresfamilias*, that is, legally wedded wives of *patresfamilias*.[119] It was achieved by coiling the hair on the crown of the head and binding it in place with purple ribbons (*vittae*).[120] Varro likens the resulting conical shaped bun to a *meta* (turning post).[121] The hairstyle may have had an apotropaic quality, warding off evil influences and unfavorable omens as the *flaminica* performed her ritual obligations. Varro, for instance, suggests that it was called a *tutulus* either because it protected (*tuendi*) the hair or because the highest place in the city, the citadel, was called the safest (*tutissimum*, *Ling.* 7.44). That the *albogalerus* of the *flamen* was also described as a *tutulus* tends to confirm the ritual significance of the *tutulus* hairstyle.[122] Like the city of Rome, the priestess had to be unassailable.

It is generally held that the *tutulus* was abandoned by ordinary women as early as the first quarter of the fifth century BC.[123] While this scenario explains the absence of the hairstyle in surviving portraits, it may underestimate the extent to which the *tutulus* survived in the ritual sphere. Both Varro and Fes-

---

[116] Sebesta 1997: 535; Olson 2008: 27. *Matronae* could not be moved aside to make way for magistrates on the street (Festus 142L) or touched by an official serving a summons (Val. Max. 2.1.5); the *stola* must have warned officials and other pedestrians about a woman's status.

[117] Gell. *N.A.* 10.15.29; Serv. Auct. ad *Aen.* 4.518, 646, with Sebesta 1997: 537.

[118] Varro *Ling.* 7.44; Festus 484L; Festus (Paulus) 485L. Recent discussions of the *tutulus* hairstyle include Bonfante-Warren 1973: 596, 614; Sebesta 1994a: 49; Siebert 1995; Bonfante 2003: 75–76; Olson 2008: 39–40.

[119] According to Paul's epitome of Festus (112L), a woman could not be called a *materfamilias* until her husband became a *paterfamilias*, that is, until his father died and he became the head of his household. Other sources claim that only a wife married with *manus* rightly held the title *materfamilias* (Cic. *Top.* 14; Gell. 18.6.9; Serv. Auct. ad *Aen.* 11.476; *Tit. Ulp.* 22.14; Treggiari 1991: 28, 34–35).

[120] Festus 484L: *tutulum vocari aiunt flaminicarum capitis ornamentum, quod fiat vitta purpurea innexa crinibus, et exstructum in altitudinem.* (They say that the hairstyle of the *flaminicae* is called the *tutulus*. It is created by fastening purple ribbons to the hair and piling it up high). Stephens (2013, February 9) has suggested that a portrait head from the mid-first-century BC now in the Musei Capitolini (Inv. No. 172) may depict the tutulus hairstyle. While the subject of this portrait is shown wearing a high bun on the crown of her head, no *vittae* are visible.

[121] Varro *Ling.* 7.44.

[122] Festus 484–486L; Serv. Auct. ad *Aen.* 2.683. In fact, Helbig (1880: 515) suggested that the *tutulus* hairstyle also originated as a type of hat while Schilling (1954: 44) maintained that the *tutulus* was a hat even during the historical period.

[123] Bonfante-Warren (1973, followed by Sebesta 1994a: 49–50; La Follette 1994: 57–60; Olson 2008: 40) suggests that the *tutulus* survived as the *seni crines*, the six-tressed coiffure of the Vestals and the Roman bride, but there is no evidence that these two hairstyles were ever identical (as noted by Fantham 2008: 167; Hersch 2010: 78–79). See also Boëls-Janssen 1989: 130.

tus tell us that the hairstyle was worn by *matresfamilias*, and it is difficult to believe that they are reporting information that had been out of date since the early fifth century BC.[124] Other Augustan sources may also refer to the hairstyle, though admittedly not by name. Tibullus and Ovid, for instance, say that chaste matrons wore *vittae* as an emblem of their modesty (*insigne pudoris*, Ov. *Ars am.* 1.31).[125] It is unlikely, however, that these ribbons formed a part of the matron's daily costume.[126] Livia, the wife of the first emperor Augustus, is shown wearing *vittae* only when she is depicted as a priestess.[127] Like the *infula* (priestly headband), woolen *vittae*, particularly when worn in combination with the *tutulus*, may have developed a special ritual function, marking the wearer as a chaste and pure ritual agent.[128] It is possible, therefore, that when matrons participated in the various rituals assigned to the *ordo matronarum*, they wore their hair bound up with *vittae* as a symbol of their privileged status. The *flaminica Dialis*, on the other hand, arranged her hair in the *tutulus* every day because she celebrated religious rites continually.

Over her *tutulus*, the *flaminica* wore the *rica*, "a square, purple garment with a fringed border that the *flaminicae* used to wear in place of a small mantle" (*vestimentum quadratum, fimbriatum, purpureum, quo flaminicae pro palliolo utebantur*, Festus (Paulus) 369L).[129] Freeborn citizen virgins with both father and mother living wove this small veil from fresh, white wool and dyed it with a deep blue pigment (*caeruleo colore*, Festus (Paulus) 369L).[130] According to Varro, the *rica* took its name from the fact that in the Roman rite, women veiled their heads when they made sacrifices (*quod Romano ritu sacrificium feminae cum faciunt, capita velant*, *Ling.* 5.130). While this etymology is undoubtedly mistaken, it does suggest that the *rica* was a ritual veil used by women to cover their heads when they sacrificed. As we have already seen, wool was an important ritual fabric valued for its purity and for its apotropaic qualities. Festus and Paul the Deacon describe the *rica* of the *flaminica* as purple (*purpureum*), which implies that it was also decorated with a purple border (*praetextatum*). Praetextate garments were worn by a variety of priestly officials and, like wool clothing, were thought to turn away evil influences and unfavorable omens. Gellius tells us that the *flaminica* wore a twig from a fruitful tree (*arbor felix*, *N.A.* 10.15.27) in her *rica*. Most scholars agree that this twig was the *arculum*, a pomegranate wreath that the *flaminica* "had to use at all the sacrifices" (*omni sacrificatione uti debebat, Aen.*

---

[124] It may be significant that Varro uses the present tense to describe the hairstyle (*habent*) and the imperfect tense to refer to its name (*dicebantur, Ling.* 7.44).

[125] Ov. *Ars am.* 3.483, *Rem.* 386, *Pont.* 3.3.51–52; Tib. 1.6.67, with Sebesta 1994a: 49, 1997: 535; Wood 1999: 159, n. 47; Fantham 2008; Olson 2008: 36–38.

[126] As argued by Sebesta 1994a: 49; Sebesta 1997: 535; Sensi 1980–1981; Torelli 1984: 72.

[127] Wood 1999: 116.

[128] For the *infula*, see Festus (Paulus) 100L, with chapter 5.

[129] Rather confusingly, Festus (342L) elsewhere cites Granius for a definition of the *rica* as a small mantle (*palliolum*) worn by the *flaminica* in place of the *vitta*. Recent discussions of the *rica* include Freier 1963; Boëls-Janssen 1989: 128–132; Flemming 2007: 104–106.

[130] Festus (Paulus) 369L, with Prescendi 2010: 81.

4.137). All of the evidence thus points to the conclusion that the *rica* was a ritual veil.

The most distinctive element of the *flaminica*'s costume was undoubtedly her brightly colored *flammeum*.[131] She shared this large, diaphanous veil with the Roman bride, a point to which we shall return. The *flammeum*'s most arresting feature was its color. Pliny the Elder reports that the hue was reserved exclusively for brides, and the existence of a guild of fabric dyers known as the *flammarii* (Pl. *Aul.* 510) or *flammeari* (Festus 79L) likewise suggests that the color was unique.[132] Unfortunately, however, the written sources offer conflicting descriptions of the *flammeum*'s key attribute. Gellius simply says that the *flaminica* covered herself with a dyed garment (*venenato operitur*, *N.A.* 10.15.27).[133] An anonymous fourth-century AD scholiast on Juvenal claims that the *flammeum* was blood red (*sanguineum*) in order to conceal the blushes of the bride.[134] Catullus, Lucan, and Pliny the Elder, on the other hand, describe the bridal veil as yellow (*luteum*).[135] Pliny elsewhere uses *luteum* as a substantive to refer to an egg yolk, which suggests that the *flammeum* was actually a deep orange-yellow color.[136] This is more or less consistent with the description found in Paul's epitome of Festus, since a lightning bolt (*telum fulminis*, 82L) could appear as a flash of yellow or orange.

The visual evidence tends to confirm that the *flammeum* was yellow in color. A wall painting from the Villa Imperiale at Pompeii shows a bride seated on a bridal couch wearing a gauzy yellow veil. Scholars have also identified elements of the bridal costume in the famous middle first century BC fresco from the Villa of the Mysteries at Pompeii. The woman shown seated on an ivory couch to the left of the entrance wears a deep yellow mantle with a purple border. The presence of various bridal elements, including the betrothal ring and the marriage contract, indicate that she is a bride and her yellow veil the *flammeum*. Finally, in the so-called *Aldobrandini Wedding* from an Augustan house in Rome, the same yellow color is used for the shoes of the central female figure as well

---

[131] Festus 79L; Festus (Paulus) 82L. Recent discussions of the *flammeum* include Boëls-Janssen 1989: 119–121; La Follette 1994: 55–56; Staples 1998: 146–147; Croom 2002: 112; Olson 2008: 21–25; Hersch 2010: 94–105.

[132] Pliny *H.N.* 21.46.

[133] See also Serv. Auct. ad *Aen.* 4.137. The verb *venenare* usually means, "to poison," which led Schilling (1954: 44) to suggest that the *flaminica*'s veil had a magical quality. As Boëls-Janssen (1989: 126) stresses, however, *venenare* can also mean "to dye" (see, for example, Verg. *Geor.* 2.465; Hor. *Ep.* 2.207; Festus 516L). While Boëls-Janssen (1989: 121–128) argues that the *venenatum* was a separate, purple veil that the *flaminica* wore in place of the *flammeum* on ritual occasions, I would suggest instead that Gellius and Servius are simply describing the *flammeum*. That Servius is commenting on Dido's purple robe (*Sidoniam . . . chlamydem*, 4.137) when he mentions the *venenatum* of the *flaminica* is not decisive, since his attempts to prove that Vergil "everywhere" (*ubique*, 4.262) shows Dido and Aeneas as the *flamen* and *flaminica Dialis* are often forced.

[134] Schol. ad Juv. 2.225. Some modern scholars, presumably following this gloss, have also described the *flammeum* as red (see, for instance, Rossbach 1853: 279, 285; Beard 1980: 15, n. 24; Sensi 1980–1981: 73–74; Torelli 1984: 33).

[135] Catull. 61.8–10, 68.133; Luc. 2.360–364; Plin. *H.N.* 21.46.

[136] Pliny *H.N.* 10.148, with Hersch 2010: 96–98.

as for the mattress and a veil, presumably the *flammeum*, which lies on the bed beside her.[137]

What was the significance of this distinctive color? A gloss in an ancient commentary on Lucan's *Pharsalia* suggests, albeit tentatively, that the *flammeum* imitated the color of fire (*flammei coloris*, 2.360).[138] Modern scholars have been eager to connect the veil to the flame of the hearth, since the bride would have tended this fire in her new home.[139] Along similar lines, Nicole Boëls-Janssen cites the myths surrounding the conceptions of Romulus and Servius Tullius—their mothers were said to have conceived by a spark from the hearth—in support of her argument that each aspect of the *flaminica*'s dress and ritual role was designed to promote civic fecundity.[140]

Judith Sebesta, on the other hand, suggests that the dye for the *flammeum* was produced from the *crocus sativus*, the saffron crocus.[141] In ancient Greece, female garments dyed with the stigmas of saffron crocuses included the wedding veil and the *krokotos*, which prepubescent girls wore at the Arkteia, a kind of initiation rite presided over by Artemis at Brauron.[142] The use of this color to mark important female rites of passage may be related to the medicinal functions of the saffron crocus; it can be used to induce and ease menstruation, to promote high birth weights, and even in higher doses to induce abortion, thus affording women some control over their reproductive cycles.[143] It is tempting to attribute a similar significance to the Roman bridal veil.[144] The written sources generally describe the *flammeum* as yellow (*luteum*), rather than saffron-colored (*croceum*), but the two shades may have been closely related.[145] Paul's epitome of Festus, on the other hand, connects the color to Jupiter's lightning and implies that the *flammeum* was interpreted primarily as a sign of the *flaminica*'s priestly status. These possibilities are not mutually exclusive, of course, since the *flaminica* was both an ideal wife and a priestess.

The written sources indicate that the *flammeum* completely enveloped the wearer's head and face (*caput involverat flammeo*, Petr. *Satyr.* 26.1) in order to

---

[137] Catullus (61.160) reports that the bride's shoes were the same color as her veil. Long understood as a wedding scene, the *Aldobrandini Wedding* has recently been reinterpreted either as a representation of the myth of Phaedra and Hippolytus (Müller 1994) or as a depiction of the myth of Alcestis and Admetus (Kilpatrick 2002). Accepting either one of these new interpretations does not diminish the relevance of the painting since the central figure, whether Phaedra or Alcestis, appears to be dressed as a Roman bride (Olson 2008: 25).

[138] The term *flammeum* is related to *flamma*, the Latin word for flame (*TLL* s.v. *flammeus*).

[139] Boels 1973: 81; La Follette 1994: 56, 62, n. 15; Sebesta 1997: 540, n. 33.

[140] Boels 1973: 81; Boëls-Janssen 1989: 120.

[141] Sebesta 1997: 540, n. 33, followed by Olson 2008: 22.

[142] Rehak 2002: 42, with further bibliography.

[143] Riddle 1992: 85; Rehak 2002: 48–50.

[144] Olson (2008: 22), for instance, writes that the color "was peculiarly appropriate for bridal accoutrements: it was linked to the woman's social and biological role in ancient society, achieved through marriage and childbearing."

[145] André 1949: 157; Clarke, J. 2003: 73. Ovid refers to the veil of Hymenaeus, the god of marriage, as saffron-colored (*multo splendida palla croco*, *Her.* 21.162).

shield her modesty (*tectura pudorem*, Luc. 2.360).[146] As Karen Hersch stresses, the plot of Plautus' *Casina*, in which a male slave dressed as a bride is mistaken for a young girl, implies that brides were typically heavily veiled.[147] The *flammeum* may, however, have been made of thin and gauzy fabric. Lucan, at least, calls it a lightweight garment (*leviter . . . velarunt*, 2.360–361), and Seneca describes it as thin (*flammeo tenui*, Oct. 702). Given the difficulties inherent in depicting transparent fabric in stone, most relief sculptures render the *flammeum* as an opaque veil covering the bride's hair and forehead with the back and sides reaching almost to her feet.[148] Regardless of the precise weight of the fabric, the *flammeum* offered the *flaminica* an unusual degree of protection from the public gaze. It shielded her modesty and demonstrated her respectability. At the same time, however, the amount of brightly colored material enveloping her must have made an impressive visual impact, drawing the eye of the observer toward her whenever she appeared in public. She would have been instantly recognizable as the priestess of Jupiter veiled in the color of Jupiter's lightning.

A Complete Priesthood

The evidence clearly shows that the *flaminica Dialis* occupied a legitimate and official position within the public religious system. As a duly appointed priestess, she could not be summarily dismissed by the *flamen*, even on the orders of a dictator. Nor could the *flamen* continue in office after her death. As we have seen, Plutarch probes the reasons behind this second provision in his fiftieth *Roman Question*, first contemplating the grief of a widower and his incomplete household before positing a more concrete explanation.[149] The *flamen Dialis*, Plutarch suggests, resigned his office "because the wife participates in her husband's sacred ministry (since there are many ceremonies that he cannot perform without her assistance)." The ancient evidence considered above confirms that the *flaminica* was an indispensible member of the priesthood that she shared with her husband. The flaminate of Jupiter could function only when the *flamen* and the *flaminica* worked together.

The existence of a cooperative priesthood is not unique in and of itself. Many of Rome's most important religious offices, including the pontificate and the augurate, were based on a collegial model. There are, however, important differences between the flaminate and other cooperative offices. While the priesthood of Jupiter required the service of a mixed-gender pair, the major religious colleges were always filled by officials of the same gender. Familial

---

[146] See also Lucr. 2.361–362; Mart. 12.42.3; Festus 174L.
[147] Hersch 2010: 99.
[148] Croom 2002: 112; Olson 2008: 21.
[149] Plut. *Quaest. Rom.* 50 = *Mor.* 276d–e, quoted above.

ties were explicitly prohibited by a rule that only one member of a family could serve in a particular college at any given time.[150] Furthermore, the occupants of these single-sex multiperson offices generally shared the same degree of religious competence with their colleagues. Each member of the college of augurs, for example, possessed equal authority to interpret the auspices or to inaugurate a new priest.

In contrast to this essentially egalitarian model of priestly service, the ritual competencies of a pair of married priests were by no means identical. The *flamen* and *flaminica Dialis* may have been colleagues, but the *flaminica* could not replace her husband at the Lupercalia, nor could the *flamen* sacrifice a ram to Jupiter on the market days. Each spouse had specific and well-defined functions within the priesthood they shared. Even the titulature of the flaminate expressed the special relationship between a *flamen* and his *flaminica*. The term *flaminica* derives from the noun *flamen* and means "of or belonging to a *flamen*."[151] Even more significantly, the titles *flamen* and *flaminica* did not mean "priest" and "priestess" in a general sense. Throughout the republican period, these titles were reserved for the members of priestly couples serving in a joint office. The *pontifices*, whose wives did not exercise independent priestly authority, were not called *flamines*, nor were the Vestal Virgins titled *flaminicae*. The flaminate was a distinctive religious office requiring the cooperative efforts of a husband and a wife.

A strict division of labor along gender lines is characteristic of the Roman ritual system more generally. Sacred rites had to be celebrated at the correct time, in the correct place, according to the correct procedure, and by the correct person. The appropriate form of a sacrifice or the gender of its celebrant depended upon that ritual's precise social and religious context. The gendered nature of ritual practice is clearly articulated by Dionysius of Halicarnassus:

> Ἐπεὶ δὲ καὶ διὰ γυναικῶν ἔδει τινὰ ἱερὰ συντελεῖσθαι καὶ διὰ παίδων ἀμφιθαλῶν ἕτερα, ἵνα καὶ ταῦτα γένηται κατὰ τὸ κράτιστον, τάς τε γυναῖκας ἔταξε τῶν ἱερέων τοῖς ἑαυτῶν ἀνδράσι συνιερᾶσθαι, καὶ εἴ τι μὴ θέμις ἦν ὑπ' ἀνδρῶν ὀργιάζεσθαι κατὰ νόμον τὸν ἐπιχώριον, ταύτας ἐπιτελεῖν καὶ παῖδας αὐτῶν τὰ καθήκοντα λειτουργεῖν. (*Ant. Rom.* 2.22.1)[152]

> And because some sacred rites (*hiera*) had to be performed by women and others by children whose fathers and mothers were living, in order that these also might be fulfilled to the greatest advantage, he [i.e., Romulus] ordered that the wives of the priests should join in performing the rites along with their husbands, and that their wives should carry out

---

[150] For the *lex Domitia*, see North 1990b.
[151] *OLD* s.v. "*flaminica*."
[152] Plutarch (*Quaest. Rom.* 50 = *Mor.* 276d) uses the same verb (συνιεράομαι) to describe the activities of the *flaminica Dialis*.

whichever rites could not lawfully be celebrated by a man according to the native custom, and that their children should perform rituals proper to them as well.

There were, Dionysius tells us, certain rites which men were forbidden to celebrate. For this reason, he explains, Romulus established priestly couples in the thirty *curiae* (ancient divisions of the Roman people), who together performed the rites assigned to men as well as those assigned to women.

The rituals associated with the cult of Jupiter also required the service of a priestly couple. In keeping with traditional Roman gender roles, the *flamen* generally took the lead while his wife provided assistance. Plutarch, however, emphasizes the cooperative nature of the flaminate by drawing attention to the fact that the couple worked together: the *flamen*, he says, could not fulfill his sacred obligations without the *flaminica*. The flaminate of Jupiter was a "complete" priesthood only when the *flamen* and *flaminica* served the gods together.

Serving the Household Gods Together

The joint priesthood of Jupiter did not spring to life in a vacuum. As we shall see in chapter 2, Rome boasted numerous priestly couples serving in various capacities. The gender-coded complementarity of the flaminate, moreover, closely replicated the structures of ritual practice in the elite household. I would argue that it is important to think of the two as related phenomena.[153] In many ways, the organization of the family unit, its internal power dynamics, and its ritual forms represented a microcosm of the *res publica*. As Varro observed in his now fragmentary *Antiquitates rerum divinarum*, "individual families ought to worship the gods as the state does, communally" (*etenim ut deos colere debet communitus civitas, sic singulae familiae debemus, apud* Non. 510M). This is not to say that Roman civic religion had its origin in the household, as has sometimes been argued, but rather that domestic and civic ritual participated in the same culture and, even more importantly for our purposes, were shaped by the same discourses of gender and gender relations.[154] This point has not, in my opinion, received adequate attention from modern scholars.

The Roman household was a unit with many and varied ritual responsibilities, and while the *paterfamilias* supervised most of this activity, the women, children, and slaves of the house regularly took part.[155] Numerous ancient

---

[153] Scheid (2005d: 129–160, especially 129–130) has argued that private and public rites at Rome participated in the same "*culture religieuse*" and should, therefore, be understood in relation to one another.

[154] The Vestal order, for instance, is sometimes imagined as having arisen out of the royal household, where the virgin daughters of the king tended the hearth (see chapter 4).

[155] For the role of women in domestic cult, see especially Boëls-Janssen 1993: 253–271; Schultz 2006b: 121–137. For the role of children, see Néraudau 1984: 226–31; Harlow and Laurence 2002: 37; Mantle

sources testify to the communal and collective dimension of worship in the private realm, and not just at births, marriages, and funerals, where women naturally performed a range of important ritual functions. According to Dionysius of Halicarnassus, Romulus had established a law whereby "a woman joined to her husband by a sacred marriage is a partner in all of his possessions and religious rites" (γυναῖκα γαμετὴν τὴν κατὰ γάμους ἱεροὺς συνελθοῦσαν ἀνδρὶ κοινωνὸν ἁπάντων εἶναι χρημάτων τε καὶ ἱερῶν, *Ant. Rom.* 2.25.2). The Christian author Prudentius, on the other hand, describes the indoctrination of pagan children, who were taught from an early age to worship the household gods not by their fathers, but rather by their mothers, whom they watch "pale-faced in prayer" before the household shrine (*spectarat matremque illic pallere precantem, Contra Symm.* 1.207).[156]

Modern scholars, however, have long quoted Cato the Elder's injunction to the *vilica*, the slave housekeeper on a country estate, as evidence for women's marginalization within the ritual sphere.[157] In his second-century BC treatise on estate management, Cato writes:

> rem divinam ni faciat neve mandet, qui pro ea faciat, iniussu domini aut dominae. scito dominum pro tota familia rem divinam facere. (*Agr.* 143.1)

> She [i.e., the *vilica*] must not perform a religious ritual or engage another to perform it for her without the orders of the master or the mistress. Let her understand that the master performs religious rituals for the whole household.

What has not always been noticed, however, is the fact that Cato grants both the master (*dominus*) and the mistress (*domina*) authority to assign ritual tasks to the *vilica*.[158] He describes some of these duties in the very next sentence:

> focum purum circumversum cotidie, priusquam cubitum eat, habeat. Kalendis, Idibus, Nonis, festus dies cum erit, coronam in focum indat, per eosdemque dies lari familiari pro copia supplicet. (*Agr.* 143.2)

> Let her [i.e., the *vilica*] keep the hearth clean and swept every night before she goes to bed. On the Kalends, Ides, and Nones, and whenever a feast day comes, let her hang a garland over the hearth, and on those same days make offerings to the *Lares familiares* as circumstances allow.

According to Cato, the *vilica* cared for the hearth on a daily basis and decorated it on festival days. Even more importantly, she was required to supplicate the

---

2002: 100–102; Prescendi 2010; Vuolanto 2012. On household religion more generally, see also Orr 1978; Foss 1997; Bodel and Olyan 2008; Giacobello 2008; Dolansky 2011a, 2011b; Johansson 2011.

[156] Fathers, of course, did play an important role in the transmission of ritual knowledge, in particular to their sons. For a discussion of religious education within the household, see Prescendi 2010.

[157] See, for example, Versnel 1992: 31.

[158] As stressed by Richlin 2014: 206.

Lares familiares, the guardian deities who resided at the hearth.[159] Cato's use of the verb *supplicare* (to make offerings) suggests that the *vilica* prayed and offered a small sacrifice of grain or wine.[160] It is difficult to argue, I think, that these obligations were marginal or insignificant. The landowner (or the *vilicus* in his absence) may have been the head of the household, but neither he nor his agent could fulfill their ritual roles without the assistance of their wives.

Freeborn wives and daughters worshipped or assisted in the worship of the *Lares* as well. In Plautus' *Rudens*, a comedy written about a half a century before Cato's *De agricultura*, the protagonist Daemones orders his wife to prepare an offering so that he may sacrifice to the *Lares familiares* in thanks for the return of their long lost daughter, Palaestra.[161] Similarly, in the prologue of the *Aulularia*, the *Lar* explains that he has revealed a treasure to Euclio for the sake of the miser's daughter, Phaedria, who, "with daily offerings of incense, or wine, or something, prays to me constantly and gives me garlands" (*mihi cottidie /aut ture aut vino aut aliqui semper supplicat, / dat mihi coronas*, 23–25). Like Cato's *vilica*, Phaedria prays to the *Lar* and offers him small gifts. Together, these texts reveal that the women of the household, both slave and free, participated in the worship of the *Lares* during the republican period.

Visual evidence from Pompeii supports the notion that women were involved in the cult of the *Lares* as well. The *lararium* in the kitchen of the House of Sutoria Primigenia depicts the entire *familia* attending a sacrifice at a small round altar.[162] The largest figures are the *Lares*, who frame the scene. Next in size are the figures of the *paterfamilias* and his wife. Both appear veiled (*capite velato*), which confirms that they are in the act of sacrificing. The thirteen persons to the right of the couple likely represent their children and slaves. The elaborate composition of this scene and its communal focus distinguish it from standard *lararium* paintings, which usually include only the *genius* and the *Lares*.

Literary evidence, however, suggests that the crowd depicted at the altar in the House of Sutoria Primigenia was more typical than the image of the solitary *genius* in the shrine of the House of the Vettii. The whole family, including children and slaves, fulfilled clearly defined sacred obligations both in the course of daily practice and on special occasions. A Roman matron was responsible for tending the domestic hearth, the seat of Vesta and the *Lar familiaris*, and the *penus* (storeroom), which was guarded by the *Penates*. With the assistance of her daughters, she ground the *far* necessary for the daily grain offering and ensured that the *penus* was well supplied with incense and wine.[163]

---

[159] For the *Lares*, see especially Foss 1997: 197–198.

[160] For typical offerings to the *Lares*, see Plaut. *Aul.* 23–25; Tib. 1.10.21–24; Hor. *Carm.* 3.23.3–4; Juv. 9.137–138.

[161] Plaut. *Rud.* 1206–1207.

[162] Fröhlich 1991: 178–179; Clarke, J.R. 2003: 75–78; Giacobello 2008: 156–158, Cat. No. 28. Compare the *lararium* from the House of Julius Polybius, which depicts the *genius* and *iuno* (female *genius*) together (Giacobello 2008: 216–217, Cat. No. 113).

[163] For the grinding of *far*, see Cato *Agr.* 143.3; Plin. *H.N.* 18.107. For the provision of incense and wine, see Gell. *N.A.* 4.1.7, 20, with Schultz 2006b: 127. This is not to say, of course, that wealthy *matronae*

Women also performed ritual tasks on festival days of significance to the family as a domestic or agricultural unit.[164] In the second book of the *Fasti*, Ovid imagines a charming scene in which each member of a rural family participates in the celebration of the Terminalia, a festival in honor of Terminus, the god of boundary stones (*termini*):

> ara fit: huc ignem curto fert rustica testo
>   sumptum de tepidis ipsa colona focis.
> ligna senex minuit concisaque construit arte,
>   et solida ramos figere pugnat humo;
> tum sicco primas inritat cortice flammas;
>   stat puer et manibus lata canistra tenet.
> inde ubi ter fruges medios immisit in ignes,
>   porrigit incisos filia parva favos. (645–652)

> An altar is set up. To it a rustic woman herself carries, on a broken potsherd, a flame taken from the warm hearth. The old man splits the firewood, arranges the pieces expertly, and struggles to fix the branches in the solid ground. Then he kindles the first flames with dry bark. The boy stands by and holds the wide baskets in his hands. When he has thrown grain from these into the fire three times, the little daughter offers cut honeycombs.

Ovid's description allows us to see how various ritual obligations might be divided among members of the family.[165] The *rustica* brings the flame from the hearth for the sacrifice while her son and daughter place the offerings on the altar.[166] The patterns of ritual practice in the household provided structure and meaning to a family's relationship with the gods and with one another. Each member had a place in the family, and each fulfilled a specific role in worshipping the household gods. The domestic religious community, in other words, was only "complete" when husband and wife served the gods together. Reading public and domestic ritual practice alongside one another helps to illuminate crucial similarities, and allows us to better understand the logic of the ritual system as a whole. In both spheres of activity, cooperation between men and women was essential.

Serving as *Exempla*

The priesthood of Jupiter reflected the fact that both the *paterfamilias* and the *materfamilias* took part in domestic worship. In public and in private, the ritual obligations assigned to men and women complemented and completed one another.

---

spent much time laboring over these tasks. As Foss (1997) has demonstrated, for example, many household *lararia* from Pompeii are located in the kitchen quarters, where the slave members of the family must have performed the majority of the required rituals.

[164] See especially Dolansky 2011b, 2011c.

[165] See also Hor. *Ep.* 2.1.139–144; Tibullus 1.10.20–24.

[166] See also Plaut. *Rud.* 1206–1207, discussed above.

At the same time, given their prominence in the public sphere, the *flamen* and *flaminica Dialis* reinforced this cooperative model by serving as a template for the ideal married couple (and their household) in a variety of ritual contexts.[167]

Marriage was the lynchpin of the *flamen* and *flaminica*'s exemplarity. As we have seen, the pair had to be married by *confarreatio*. The creation of *manus*, a consequence of the marriage ceremony, bound the *flamen* and *flaminica* together as an indivisible pair. Their relationship was uniquely "complete" and could not be reproduced within the context of single-sex priestly colleges. The existence of *manus* also established a clear hierarchy of power within the marriage and the flaminate. Like the religious community in the household, the *flamen* and *flaminica* served alongside one another and in a particular relationship to one another. As they performed their ritual obligations on a daily, monthly, and yearly basis, the *flamen* and *flaminica Dialis* served as *exempla* by placing the values associated with *manus* marriage on public display.

Since marriage was above all an institution for the production of legitimate children, the flaminate also presented an image of the ideal Roman family.[168] On one level, their union may have symbolized (or even guaranteed) the fertility of the entire Roman community.[169] As we have seen, the *arculum* worn by the *flaminica* was made from a pomegranate twig, a symbol of fertility throughout the ancient Mediterranean.[170] Aulus Gellius even uses the botanical term *surculus* to describe the *arculum*, which indicates that the twig was still green and living and, therefore, had within it the power of reproduction.[171] The pomegranate wreath worn by the *flaminica*, in other words, represented the fecundity of the ideal *matrona* and may even have inspired the wreath of flowers worn by brides on their wedding day.[172]

It seems likely, moreover, that the children of the *flamen* and *flaminica Dialis* assisted their parents with their ritual obligations. There is some precedent for this hypothesis. Dionysius of Halicarnassus, as we have seen, notes that curial priests were assisted by their wives and children.[173] The antiquarians tell us only that the *flaminius camillus* and the *flaminia sacerdotula*, young children who assisted the *flamen* and *flaminica* respectively, had to have both father and mother living throughout their period of service.[174] The children of the *flamen* and *flaminica Di-*

---

[167] As suggested by Mustakallio 2010: 15–16. See also the introduction.

[168] For the procreative function of marriage, see Cic. *Off.* 1.54, *Fin.* 5.65; Gell. *N.A.* 1.6.2; Treggiari 1991: 5–13, 205–228; Dixon 1992: 67–68; Dolansky 2011c, especially 199–200.

[169] For the notion that the union of the *flamen* and *flaminica Dialis* might guarantee the fertility of the Roman people (as, for example, the fire on the hearth of Vesta was thought to assure the continued safety of the Roman state) see especially Pötscher 1968; Boels 1973.

[170] Boels 1973: 83–86; Flory 1996: 63.

[171] Gell. *N.A.* 10.15.27.

[172] For the bridal wreath, see Olson 2008: 24.

[173] Dion. Hal. *Ant. Rom.* 2.22.1, quoted above.

[174] Festus (Paulus) 82L. Macrobius (*Sat.* 3.8.6–7) also mentions young attendants, but not the requirement that they be *patrimi et matrimi*. According to Varro (*Ling.* 5.130), *sacerdotulae* wore a special headband known as a *capital*.

alis necessarily fit this criterion, and we may be justified in suspecting that they assisted their parents when circumstances permitted.[175] The image of an entire family serving a public cult together is striking, though hardly surprising given the centrality of the family in Roman society. Roman marriage brought men and women together to form families, and those families performed religious rituals at the domestic hearth and on the public stage as well.

Additional effort was expended to guarantee that the *flaminica* embodied the virtues of the ideal *matrona*. She was responsible, as we have seen, for weaving her own and her husband's ritual garments. Like all *matronae*, she was expected to be a skilled woolworker (*lanifica*), a term that functions as a by-word for feminine virtue in Roman literary and epigraphic sources.[176] One of the most famous examples, the second-century BC epitaph of Claudia, praises her affection for her family and concludes, "she kept her house, she worked wool" (*domum servavit, lanam fecit, CIL* 6.15346). The *flaminica* may also have trained the *flaminia sacerdotula*, perhaps her own daughter, to spin the wool for the *rica*, the small veil that she wore under her *flammeum* when she sacrificed.[177]

The *flaminica Dialis* was also an exemplary *univira*, a *matrona* who had known only one husband.[178] She was required to be a virgin when she wed the *flamen* and may have been expected to remain faithful to him after his death as well. Women who had been married only once had a privileged role in Roman religion; the cults of Mater Matuta, Pudicitia (Sexual Virtue), and Fortuna Muliebris (Feminine Fortune) were restricted to *univirae*.[179] The ideal that a woman should marry only once in her life, even if she had been widowed at an early age, appears frequently in Latin literature and funerary inscriptions as well.[180] Valerius Maximus describes an ancient custom of bestowing a crown of *pudicitia* upon *matronae* who refused to remarry.[181] Even Catullus once remarked, "to live content with one husband is the glory of highest glories for brides" (*uiro contentam uiuere solo, / nuptarum laus ex laudibus eximiis*, 111.1–2). The locus classicus for the image of the *univira*, however, is Dido's promise to remain faithful to Sychaeus in the fourth book of Vergil's *Aeneid*:

ille meos, primus qui me sibi iunxit, amores
abstulit; ille habeat secum servetque sepulcro. (28–29)

---

[175] As suggested by Boels 1973: 80; Mantle 2002: 93–94.

[176] For the language of wool working in funerary inscriptions, see especially Lefkowitz 1983; Lattimore 1962: 295–300.

[177] See further above.

[178] For the *univira*, see Treggiari 1991: 233–236; Böels-Janssen 1996; Williams 1958; Lightman and Zeisel 1977; Langlands 2006: 47–48, 61–64.

[179] Livy 10.23.3–10; Val. Max. 2.1.3, with Böels-Janssen 1996. For the cult of Fortuna Muliebris, see also chapter 3.

[180] For the epigraphic evidence, see especially Forbis 1990.

[181] Val. Max. 2.1.3, with Langlands 2006: 61–64.

That man who first joined me to himself has taken away my love; let him keep it with him, and guard it in the grave!

Although Dido ultimately fails to keep her pledge, the episode illustrates Roman attitudes toward marriage and conjugal fidelity. Several centuries later, this very passage prompted the author of the Servius Auctus commentary to cite the example of the *flaminica Dialis*. "In accordance with the religious sanctions of the ancients," he writes, "the *flaminica* is permitted to have only one husband" (*caerimoniis veterum flaminicam nisi unum virium habere non licet*, ad *Aen.* 4.29).[182] A Roman reader would have understood the logic behind explaining Dido's pledge to Sychaeus through an appeal to the *flaminica Dialis*: she was universally acknowledged as an exemplar of one-man-womanhood.

The costume of the *flaminica Dialis* reveals how her status as an exemplary *univira* worked on a visual level.[183] As discussed above, we can be confident that the *flaminica* wore the *stola*, a special overdress reserved exclusively for married women. This long garment symbolized the *pudicitia* and moral probity expected of the *matrona* who wore it.[184] More than a dress, the *stola* helped to define a group of women based on social status and reinforced an expectation of moral conduct. When she appeared in public in her *stola*, the *flaminica* re-affirmed that she belonged to the *ordo matronarum* and that she upheld the virtues associated with this group.

Even more significant in this context is the *flaminica*'s distinctive yellow veil. According to Festus, Roman brides wore the *flammeum* as a good omen, be-cause the *flaminica* was not permitted to divorce her husband (*flammeo amici-tur nubens ominis boni causa, quod eo assidue utebatur flaminica, id est flaminis uxor, cui non licebat facere divortium*, 79L). But the *flammeum* was more than a talisman against divorce. It was a pledge that the bride would give her husband no justifiable cause for separation by remaining chaste, modest, and faithful. When a young bride veiled herself with the *flammeum*, the *flaminica*'s signature attribute, she made a public commitment to emulate the precedent set by this ideal *univira*.

The adaptation of an element of the *flaminica*'s ritual costume from a public to a private ritual context is highly significant. It suggests that religious officials served an important function in Roman society quite apart from the perfor-mance of specific sacred obligations. The parameters of the *flaminica*'s public role not only shaped her own experience of religious service, but also articu-lated a version of ideal femininity to the community as a whole. The *flaminica Dialis* was a living monument whose costume and ritual program continually inscribed into the public consciousness the qualities most prized in a Roman

---

[182] For the presentation of Aeneas and Dido as the *flamen* and *flaminica Dialis* in the Servius Auctus commentary, see Starr 1997.
[183] Levine 1995: 104.
[184] See also chapter 5.

matrona, including modesty, chastity, and fidelity to her husband. Her primary audience, the freeborn married woman, was encouraged to begin emulating these virtues on her wedding day, when she put on the *flammeum* and made an offering to the *Lares* at her new husband's hearth.

Conclusion

The flaminate of Jupiter was a joint priesthood shared by the *flamen Dialis* and his wife, the *flaminica Dialis*. I have argued in this chapter that the ancient evidence challenges our traditional framework for understanding priestly service at Rome. Religious offices (and officials) were far from homogeneous. While the collegial model certainly predominated, many priesthoods required the joint service of a married couple. In addition to the *flamen* and *flaminica Dialis*, this category of priesthood also included the *rex* and *regina sacrorum*, the fifteen *flamines* and *flaminicae* who served at the level of citywide cult and performed rites *pro populo*, married couples who represented each of the thirty *curiae*, and perhaps even priestly couples serving communities associated with the seven hills as well. Roman religion is not known for its theological or institutional coherence, but the two-person religious office filled by a married couple does appear to offer one example of consistency across overlapping religious communities.

The sophisticated structure of the flaminate also yields important insight into the ways in which Roman religion reflected and reinforced the religious roles of men and women in the family. Household and civic cult shared a single religious culture in which the cooperation of men, women and children was essential for the performance of ritual activities. Ritual roles were determined by gender, and there was clearly a hierarchy at work in defining family members in relation to one another. Nonetheless, it was the variety of their roles and the cooperation required among them that characterized ritual practice in the private and public spheres. Many Romans, therefore, likely viewed joint priesthoods such as the flaminate of Jupiter as the natural state of affairs. After all, married couples could be found serving the gods together at public altars and in almost every house in the city.

CHAPTER TWO

Priestly Couples

This chapter argues that priestly couples had a larger role in the Roman ritual system than modern scholars have realized. The *rex sacrorum* and the *flamen Martialis* certainly shared their offices with the *regina sacrorum* and the *flaminica Martialis* respectively. It seems very likely that the wives of the thirteen remaining *flamines* were *flaminicae* as well. These priests performed public rituals (*sacra publica*) on behalf of the Roman people (*pro populo*). There is secure evidence, moreover, that priestly couples served smaller religious communities within the city, including those of the thirty *curiae* (*pro curiis*), ancient divisions of the Roman people, and perhaps of the seven hills as well (*pro montibus*). The married couple was a widespread and pervasive model of priestly service at Rome.[1]

As I argue in chapter 1, priestly couples are best understood in relation to the patterns of worship in the household, where husbands and wives fulfilled complementary religious roles. Priestly couples exemplified traditionally asymmetrical gender constructions and relationships. It is clear, however, that the structure of Roman society included a robust ritual role for both sexes. Wives and priestesses offered sacrifices at domestic hearths and public altars because the religious system was thought to function properly only when men and women served their gods together. It is regrettable, therefore, that we know so little about the priestesses under consideration in this chapter. In the absence of detailed evidence for their ritual obligations, I have chosen to provide an overview of the priesthoods that they shared with their husbands. This approach provides a context within which we may imagine their ritual activities and allows us to better appreciate the degree to which religious service at Rome was a cooperative endeavor.

Flamines and *Flaminicae*

According to the Romans, the title *flamen* described a priest who served the cult of an individual Roman god.[2] Tradition held that Rome's second king, Numa

---

[1] Although priests and priestesses of the imperial cult were known as *flamines* and *flaminicae* respectively, they were not, as a rule, married couples and are not included in this chapter. Rather than copying the Roman flaminate exactly, towns in Italy and the western provinces adopted individual features of this priesthood, including its priestly titles, in order to enhance the dignity of the new imperial cult. For the *flaminicae* of the imperial cult, see especially Hemelrijk 2005, 2006, 2007.

[2] Cic. *Rep.* 2.26. The most detailed discussion of the *flamines* remains Vanggaard 1988.

Pompilius, had appointed the first *flamines* on the advice of his wife, the nymph Egeria.[3] Modern scholars generally agree that these priesthoods were among the oldest ones at Rome. The number fifteen, which has achieved canonical status in modern scholarship, is found only in the lexicon of Festus.[4] The number of *flamines* (and of *flaminicae* as well) may have been higher (or lower) during the archaic period. *Flamines* were distinguished one from another by a cognomen derived from the name of the deity whose cult they superintended.[5] Only thirteen titles are specifically attested: *Dialis* (Jupiter), *Martialis* (Mars), *Quirinalis* (Quirinus), *Carmentalis* (Carmenta), *Cerialis* (Ceres), *Falacer* (Falacer), *Floralis* (Flora), *Furrinalis* (Furrina), *Palatualis* (Palatua), *Pomonalis* (Pomona), *Portunalis* (Portunus), *Volcanalis* (Vulcan), and *Volturnalis* (Volturnus).[6] Festus implies that there was a strict hierarchy of precedence within this group based upon the relative rank (*dignatio*) of the deity concerned.[7] The *flamen Dialis* naturally ranked first in the hierarchy followed by the *flamen Martialis* and the *flamen Quirinalis*.[8] These three formed a subset of *flamines* and were regarded as *maiores* (greater). The remaining *flamines* were classified as *minores* (lesser).

It is generally held that the gods served by the *flamines* constituted an early version of the Roman pantheon.[9] The classification of the *flamines Dialis*, *Martialis*, and *Quirinalis* as *maiores* could even indicate that Jupiter, Mars, and Quirinus formed an archaic triad that was only later supplanted by the Capitoline triad of Jupiter, Juno and Minerva.[10] We know too little about early Roman religion to be certain. By the late Republic, however, some of the deities had become so obscure that antiquarian writers were no longer sure of their function. Varro reports that in his day, even the name of the goddess Furrina was barely known:

> Furrinalia <a> Furrina, quod ei deae feriae publicae dies is; cuius deae honos apud antiquos. Nam et ei sacra instituta annua et flamen attributus: nunc vix nomen notum paucis. (*Ling.* 6.19)

---

[3] Varro *Ling.* 7.45; Cic. *Rep.* 2.26; Livy 1.19.5, 20.23.

[4] Festus 144L.

[5] Varro *Ling.* 5.84.

[6] Given the diversity in the extant list, it is difficult to speculate about the deities served by the two unattested *flamines*. Based on a late second century AD epitaph from Numidian Cuicul recording a *sacerdos Neptunalis* (*ILS* 9489), Rüpke (2008: 523, No. 572) has suggested that one may have been a *flamen Neptunalis* (the title "*sacerdos*" eventually replaced the title "*flamen*" for priests outside of the imperial cult). Elsewhere, however, Rüpke (2007: 225) suggests that the remaining flaminical *cognomina* may have been *Virbialis* and *Lucularis*.

[7] Festus 144L. See also Festus 198L; Festus (Paulus) 145L.

[8] The three *flamines maiores* are frequently mentioned together and almost invariably appear in the same order (the only exception is Festus 292L). It has been argued (see, for example, Wissowa 1912: 504) that six of the *flamines minores* are listed in order of precedence in a quotation from Ennius at Varro *Ling.* 7.45. As Vanggaard (1988: 28) points out, however, Ennius may have rearranged the order to fit the meter.

[9] See, most recently, Marco Simón 1996: 45–46; Lipka 2009: 57.

[10] As suggested by Wissowa 1912: 23.

The Furrinalia is named from Furrina, because this day is a public holiday (*feriae publicae*) for this goddess. Honor was paid to her among the ancients, for they even instituted an annual sacrifice for her and assigned to her a *flamen*, but now her name is scarcely known and only by a few.

Had the cult of Furrina lapsed entirely by the late first century BC? Varro implies that it had not, but it is difficult to imagine that the Romans continued to celebrate a festival in honor of a goddess whose name was familiar only to a handful of antiquarians. Perhaps Varro exaggerates the extent of Furrina's obscurity. At the very least, we are left with the distinct impression that the religious systems of the archaic and historical periods differed significantly from one another. The obscurity of Furrina's name and cult underscores how religious practices evolved in response to the changing nature of Roman society.[11] Deities of central importance in early Rome faded into obscurity or were gradually replaced, for reasons completely unknown to us, by gods whose cults served similar functions. All of this makes it difficult to assemble a coherent picture of the *flamines* as a group.

It is likewise impossible to disentangle the genuinely early flaminical priesthoods from those instituted at a later date. While it seems likely that many of the rituals performed by the *flamines* were very ancient, others clearly were not. The republican poet Ennius claims that Numa established the *flamen Floralis*, but there is some evidence that this priesthood was first instituted much later, perhaps in response to the growth of the cult of Flora following the foundation of a new temple in the Circus Maximus and the institution of the Floralia in about 240 BC.[12] A coin minted in 57 BC indicates that an ancestor of the otherwise unknown moneyer C. Servilius was the first *flamen Floralis*.[13] If the ancestor is M. Servilius Pulex Geminus (cos. 202 BC), as Jörg Rüpke has suggested, then the coin minted by his descendant reveals that not all of the *flamonia* were instituted at a very early date.[14] At least one of these priesthoods very likely dates to the later third century BC, which indicates that the process of establishing the group of fifteen *flamines* known to Festus was more fluid than has generally been suspected.

The distinction between the *flamines maiores* and the *flamines minores* appears to have been related to the social status of the priests in each category, as well as to the relative status of their respective deities.[15] A number of ancient

---

[11] Forsythe 2005: 137. On the question of change in Roman religion, see especially Rüpke 2012c.

[12] Ennius *apud* Varro *Ling.* 7.45. For the foundation of the Temple of Flora in the Circus Maximus and the institution of the Floralia on the recommendation of the Sibylline Books, see Vell. Pat. 1.14.8; Tac. *Ann.* 2.49; Papi 1995.

[13] *RRC* 423/1. The obverse of the coin shows a head of Flora and the legend FLORAL PRIMVS, which Crawford (*RRC* 423/1) resolves as "*(flamen) Floralis primus*" (first *flamen Floralis*).

[14] For the identification of Geminus as the unnamed *flamen Floralis*, see Rüpke 2008: 892, No. 3069. This interpretation assumes that Ennius (239–169 BC), who was writing within living memory of the first Floralia, deliberately disguised the novelty of the office by attributing its foundation to Numa.

[15] Mitchell (2005: 140–141) suggests that the greater and lesser *flamonia* were associated with the *maiores* and *minores gentes* (greater and lesser clans) respectively. Too little, however, is known about the *maiores* and *minores gentes* and their relationship to the priesthoods for certainty.

sources indicate that the three greater flaminical priesthoods were open only to patrician candidates, that is, to the descendants of the *patres*, the heads of the great Roman families who constituted the senate of Romulus.[16] The patriciate, later expanded to include other important families, formed a hereditary nobility by the beginning of the Republic and monopolized entry to most priesthoods, magistracies, and the senate until the end of the so-called struggle of the orders in the early third century BC.[17] Families that did not belong to the patriciate were defined as plebeian. The plebeians secured admission to the consulship in 366 BC and membership in the great priestly colleges of the augurs and *pontifices* through the *lex Ogulnia* of 300 BC.[18] This process led to the emergence of a new nobility composed of both patricians and plebeians, and the distinction between the two orders gradually disappeared outside of the religious sphere.

That the *flamines maiores* were always of patrician status is confirmed by prosopographical evidence; every known *flamen maior* was the member of a family of undisputed patrician standing.[19] The *flamines minores*, on the other hand, may have been drawn from among the plebeians throughout the historical period.[20] The only known *flamen minor* from the period of the Republic is the plebeian M. Popillius Laenas (cos. 359, 356, 354 (?), 350, 348 BC), who served as *flamen Carmentalis* in the middle of the fourth century BC.[21] In fact, there is no indication in the ancient sources that the patrician elite had ever contested the right of plebeians to hold the lesser flaminical priesthoods. Patrician control over major public priesthoods was evidently not as monolithic as the historical tradition suggests; plebeians were serving as *flamines minores* by the middle of the fourth century BC at the latest and may have been doing so for many years.

The *Flamines* and *Flaminicae Maiores*

The religious and social import of the distinction between the patrician *flamines maiores* and the predominately plebeian *flamines minores* is obscure, particularly because the historical development of the two groups is poorly understood. As noted above, the Roman tradition assumes that the *flamines* of Jupiter, Mars and

---

[16] For the patrician status of the *flamines maiores*, see Cic. *Dom.* 37–38; Livy 6.41.9; Tac. *Ann.* 4.16; Festus (Paulus) 137L. For the *patres* and the senate of Romulus, see Cic. *Rep.* 2.23; Livy 1.8.7; Dion. *Ant. Rom.* 2.8.3; Plut. *Rom.* 13.2.

[17] For the addition of new families to the patriciate, see Cic. *Rep.* 2.35; Livy 1.35.6; Dion. Hal. *Ant. Rom.* 3.67.1; Tac. *Ann.* 11.25.2. The formation of the patriciate is a complex and vexed issue. For a detailed discussion of the topic, see Mitchell 1990. For the struggle of the orders, see also the essays in Raaflaub 2005.

[18] For the *leges Liciniae Sextiae* and the admission of plebeians to the consulship, see Livy 6.34.5–42. For the *lex Ogulnia* and the admission of plebeians to the major priestly colleges, see Livy 10.6.3–9.2.

[19] Vanggaard 1988: 47. See also the lists and biographies in Rüpke 2008.

[20] Mommsen 1864–1879: 1, 78; Vanggaard 1988: 47–49.

[21] Admittedly, it is difficult to confirm any hypothesis about the social status of *flamines minores* on the basis of a single career, particularly one as exceptional as that of Laenas. It must be noted in this context that we hear of a plebeian *rex sacrorum* from the middle of the third century BC, despite the fact that this office was formally closed to plebeians throughout the republican period (Livy 27.6.16, 36.5; Rüpke 2008: 787–788, No. 2368).

Quirinus were "greater" because these three gods possessed the greatest *dignatio*. We might speculate that the patricians monopolized these priesthoods for their prestige and allowed plebeians access to offices associated with the cults of less important deities, but this is no more than a guess.

We can say with certainty that the three greater *flamonia* shared a number of important characteristics. They were members of the extended pontifical college, a body that included the *pontifices*, the *rex sacrorum*, and the Vestal Virgins. The *flaminicae* and the *regina sacrorum* were likely full members as well.[22] All three *flamines maiores* were required to be patricians born of confarreate marriages and had to be living in a marriage concluded by the same rite.[23] Like the *flamen Dialis*, the *flamen Martialis* and the *flamen Quirinalis* were inaugurated by an *augur*, presumably in the *comitia calata* (convoked assembly), which met on the Capitol under the presidency of the *pontifex maximus*.[24] They served for life, though a *flamen Martialis* or a *flamen Quirinalis* presumably had to give up his office after the death of his wife. The three *flamines maiores* shared some ritual obligations as well. On the foundation day of the Temple of Fides (Faith), they rode to the Capitol in a covered carriage (*curru arcuato*) with their right hands wrapped to the fingers in a white cloth.[25]

We do not know whether or not the *flamen Martialis* and the *flamen Quirinalis* were originally subject to the same ritual regulations that governed the lives of the *flamen* and *flaminica Dialis*.[26] Aulus Gellius does not mention these priests in his detailed discussion of flaminical taboos (*caerimoniae*). Even so, some of the restrictions clearly applied to the *flamen Martialis* and the *flamen Quirinalis* at least initially, including the prohibition against leaving Rome. Over the course of the second century BC, however, this rule was gradually relaxed as individual *flamines* sought to renegotiate their public role, sometimes in conflict with the *pontifex maximus*.[27] By the first century BC, these priests were free to pursue traditional political careers and even to leave the city to govern a province or to lead an army on campaign. Only the *flamen Dialis*, whose ritual program included daily sacrifices, was bound to the city until well into the imperial period.[28]

---

[22] For the composition of the *collegium pontificum*, see Festus 198–200L; Wissowa 1912: 501; Van Haeperen 2002: 80–84; Rüpke 2008: 43.

[23] Cic. *Dom.* 38; Tac. *Ann.* 4.16; Festus (Paulus) 137L, with chapter 1. Some scholars have even suggested that *confarreatio* was created *ex nihilo* by the patricians, perhaps during the middle of the fifth century BC, in order to limit access to the greater *flamonia* (Noailles 1936; Koschaker 1937). For a discussion and critique of this theory, see Linderski 2005: 224–225.

[24] Macrob. *Sat.* 3.13.10; Gell. *N.A.* 15.27.1.

[25] Livy 1.21.4.

[26] See chapter 1.

[27] During the First Punic War, for example, the *pontifex maximus* prevented the *flamen Martialis* A. Postumius Albinus (cos. 242 BC) from leaving the city to take part in a decisive battle (Val. Max. 1.1.2), while in 131 BC, the consul P. Licinius Crassus Mucianus used his status as *pontifex maximus* to strip his colleague, the *flamen Martialis* L. Valerius Flaccus, of his military command (Cic. *Phil.* 11.18).

[28] In AD 22, the *flamen Dialis* argued that he ought to have the same right to govern a province as the *flamen Martialis* and the *flamen Quirinalis* (Tac. *Ann.* 3.58). Tiberius thought differently.

The *Flamen* and *Flaminica Martialis*

Was the wife of the *flamen Martialis* a priestess as well? The ancient evidence suggests that she was. The occurrence of the designation *flaminica Dialis* in several Latin sources suggests that there was a need to distinguish between more than one priestess who bore the same title.[29] A pontifical text quoted by Macrobius confirms this hypothesis. The passage describes an elaborate banquet held in 69 BC in honor of the inauguration of L. Cornelius Lentulus Niger (pr. ca. 61 BC) as *flamen Martialis*. The guest list included a number of distinguished magistrates and male priests as well as four Vestals, the new *flamen's* mother-in-law and his wife, Publicia, who is designated as the *flaminica*: "On the third dining couch were the Vestals Popilia, Perpennia, Licinia, and Arruntia, and Lentulus' wife, the *flaminica* Publicia, and Sempronia, his mother-in-law (*in tertio triclinio Popilia Perpennia Licinia Arruntia virgines Vestales et ipsius uxor Publicia flaminica et Sempronia socrus eius*, *Sat.* 3.13.11). Macrobius gives as the source of this quotation the fourth volume of the pontifical records of Q. Caecilius Metellus Pius (cos. 80 BC), *pontifex maximus* for over thirty years and a trustworthy witness to the veracity of Publicia's title.[30] The wife of the *flamen Martialis* was a priestess known as the *flaminica Martialis*.

Unfortunately, the religious activities of the *flamen* and *flaminica Martialis* are poorly understood. Like the *flamen Dialis*, the *flamen Martialis* may have presided over sacrifices while seated at an *adsidela*.[31] Valerius Maximus tells us that the he was responsible for certain rituals in honor of Mars (*caerimoniae Martis*, 1.1.2). During the historical period, Mars was connected primarily with war and with a series of festivals marking the beginning of the fighting season in March, including the processions of the *salii*.[32] His temple stood outside of the *pomerium* near the Porta Capena and was the site of *suovetaurilia*—that is, the sacrifice of a pig (*sus*), sheep (*ovis*), and bull (*taurus*)—marking the census and the purification of the army (*lustratio exercitus*) or navy (*lustratio classis*).[33] It was also the starting point for the annual parade of equestrian youth on July 15 (*transvectio equitum*).[34] The right-hand horse of the victorious team at the October Horse was apparently sacrificed to Mars.[35] Some of these rites, and perhaps others performed in the shrine of Mars in the *regia*, where the *ancilia* (shields) and *hastae* (spears) of the war god were kept, probably formed part of the *flamen's* ritual program.

---

[29] See, for example, Tac. *Ann.* 4.16; Gell. *N.A.* 10.15.26.

[30] Macrob. *Sat.* 3.13.10.

[31] At least this is one way to interpret the plural forms in Paul's epitome of Festus: *adsidelae mensae vocantur, ad quas sedentes flamines sacra faciunt* (tables at which *flamines* offer sacrifices while seated are called *adsidelae*, 18L).

[32] For the *salii*, see chapter 3.

[33] Cic. *Div.* 1.102; Dion. Hal. *Ant. Rom.* 4.22.1; App. *B Civ.* 5.96.

[34] Livy 9.46.15; *Vir.* 3.32.2.

[35] Festus 190L.

Possession of a priestly title suggests that the *flaminica Martialis* had ritual responsibilities as well.[36] None are explicitly attested in the ancient sources, but this should come as no surprise. The ancient tradition scarcely mentions the obligations of the *flamen Martialis*, let alone those of his wife. If her position was analogous to that of the *flaminica Dialis*, and it seems fair to assume that it was, then she presumably had a special costume and her own ritual program. According to the author of the Servius Auctus commentary on the *Aeneid*, the "*flaminicae*" employed the *secespita*, the ritual knife associated especially with the members of the pontifical college.[37] Admittedly the plural form is not conclusive, but it does raise the possibility that the *flaminica Martialis* presided over sacrifices in her capacity as a public priestess.

Although we know virtually nothing about the rights and obligations of the *flaminica Martialis*, we do possess brief biographical notices about two women who held this office. As we have seen, Publicia, the wife of Lentulus Niger, is recorded as the *flaminica* of Mars in an account of a banquet in honor of her husband's inauguration as *flamen*. A second Publicia served as *flaminica Martialis* from 168 BC until her death in 154 BC.[38] In this year, Publicia and another woman, Licinia, were accused of poisoning their husbands, L. Postumius Albinus (cos. 154 BC) and Claudius Asellus. They were released after an initial inquiry (*de veneficiis quaesitum*, Livy *Per.* 48) and strangled to death by a decision of their kinsmen (*propinquorum decreto*, Val. Max. 6.3.8). The episode is a curious one. The fourth-century AD author Julius Obsequens, whose *Book of Prodigies* was based on Livy's history, implies that Albinus became ill (*aeger*) and died because he had set out for his province, despite the fact that "he did not find a head on the liver of a very large number of victims" (*in plurimis victimis caput in iocinere non invenit*, 17), a sure sign that he did not have divine approval for his departure.[39] Was the accusation of poisoning an attempt to divert attention from a minor religious crisis?[40] It is regrettable that Livy's version of events has not survived. In any case, the family evidently weathered the scandal: the couple's son, L. Postumius Albinus, was inaugurated as *flamen Martialis* in about 110 BC.[41]

---

[36] Rüpke 2008: 861, No. 2853. Wissowa (1912: 506, n. 5), on the other hand, argued that the *flaminica Martialis* did not have any cultic responsibilities.

[37] Serv. Auct. ad *Aen.* 4.262.

[38] Livy *Per.* 48 (where the name is given as Publilia); Val. Max. 6.3.8; Rüpke 2008: 861, No. 2853. For the inauguration of her husband, L. Postumius Albinus (cos. 154 BC), see Livy 45.15.10; Rüpke 2008: 856, No. 2820.

[39] Whether or not it was *fas* (permitted) for the *flamen Martialis* to leave the city on campaign was still an open question in this period (see above).

[40] For Roman *matronae* (married women) accused of poisoning their husbands during times of social crisis, see also Livy 8.18, 39.8–19, 39.41, 40.37, 40.43; Val. Max. 2.5.3; Pailler 1987.

[41] Cic. *Brut.* 135, with Rüpke 2008: 855, No. 2819. In 131 BC, the younger Albinus minted a coin depicting the goddess Roma on the obverse with an *apex* (the cap of a *flamen*) behind her head and the god Mars riding in a chariot on the reverse (*RRC* 252/1). This coin has been understood as an allusion to his father's flaminate and perhaps even as evidence that Albinus wished to lay claim to the priesthood, occupied after his father's death by L. Valerius Flaccus (cos. 131 BC), on the basis of heredity (Rüpke

The *Flamen* and *Flaminica Quirinalis*

Although the title *flaminica Quirinalis* is not specifically attested in the ancient sources, there are good reasons to assume that the wife of the *flamen* of
Quirinus was also a priest. The three *flamines maiores* shared a number of obligations, as we have seen, and it stands to reason that all three served jointly
with their wives as well. Very little, however, is known about the priesthood, its
activities, or the god it served.[42] Ovid mentions a *dies natalis* (foundation day) of a
Temple of Quirinus on June 29.[43] This is presumably the Temple of Quirinus that
stood on the Quirinal Hill near the sanctuaries of several Sabine deities.[44] Titus
Tatius and his Sabines had supposedly settled on the Quirinal, and Varro reports
that Quirinus himself was a Sabine god.[45] The Romans, moreover, identified an
etymological link between Quirinus and *Quirites*, the official term for the citizenry of Rome after the unification of the Sabine and Roman communities.[46] His
original range of functions may have included agricultural and military concerns,
but the primary focus of his attention was on the early political community.[47]

During the historical period, Quirinus was also associated with the deified Romulus.[48] That there was a *heroon* (shrine) of Romulus-Quirinus near
the *comitium* (assembly place) in the Forum Romanum reinforces the notion
that this god presided over the political activities of the archaic community.[49]
In later periods, the Quirinalia on February 17 may have focused on the deified Romulus, at least if we believe Ovid's etiology in the *Fasti*.[50] While little is
known about the rites involved, the *flamen* and *flaminica Quirinalis* may have
presided.[51] The relationship between Quirinus and Romulus may also explain
why we hear that on December 23, the *flamen Quirinalis* and the *pontifices* offered a sacrifice to the dead (*parentatio*) at the grave of the elusive Acca Larentia.[52] According to one version of her mythical biography, she was the wife of
Faustulus and the foster mother of Romulus and Remus.[53]

At least one of the *flamen*'s ritual obligations addressed the perils of the
agricultural cycle. At the Robigalia on April 25, he sacrificed a sheep and a

---

2008: 855, No. 2819). Indeed, the flaminate of Mars may have been regarded as something of a family
tradition among the Postumii Albini: A. Postumius Albinus (cos. 242 BC) served as *flamen Martialis* in
the third century BC (Livy *Per.* 19; Val. Max. 1.1.2; Rüpke 2008: 855, No. 2817).

[42] As Gordon and Reynolds (2003: 264) point out, not a single votive to Quirinus is known from
Rome, making it even more difficult to assess the content and character of his cult.

[43] Ov. *Fast.* 6.795.

[44] Ziolkowski 1992: 139–144; Coarelli 1999b; Curti 2000.

[45] Varro *Ling.* 5.74.

[46] Festus 304L.

[47] Livy 5.52.7; Dion. Hal. *Ant. Rom.* 2.48.2; Festus 238L; Forsythe 2005: 137; Smith 2006: 201.

[48] Porte 1981; Jocelyn 1989; Doubordieu 2008.

[49] Curti 2000: 88–89.

[50] Varro *Ling.* 6.13; Ov. *Fast.* 2.475.

[51] Rüpke 2011: 74.

[52] Gell. *N.A.* 7.7.7; Plut. *Rom.* 4.3; Macrob. *Sat.* 1.10.15.

[53] Plut. *Rom.* 4.3; Macrob. *Sat.* 1.10.17.

dog in the grove of Robigus at the fifth milestone on the *via Claudia*.[54] Ovid tells us that this sacrifice protected the grain crops from mildew (*robigo*). The Consualia on August 21 has also been understood as an agricultural festival designed to protect the newly stored harvest.[55] This public festival (*feriae publicae*, Varro *Ling.* 6.20) began with the uncovering of the underground altar of Consus, which stood at the first turning post (*meta*) in the Circus Maximus. Horses and mules—the Romans used both animals to tread grain on threshing floors—were garlanded with flowers and given a day of rest, and there were organized races, both of individual animals and of teams yoked to chariots. Varro tells us that the games (*ludi*) were organized "by the priests" (*ab sacerdotibus,* *Ling.* 6.20), by which he presumably means the *pontifices*.[56]

According to the early Christian author Tertullian, the *flamen Quirinalis* and the "virgins" (*virgines*), perhaps the Vestal Virgins, offered a sacrifice at the underground altar:

> et nunc ara Conso illi in circo demersa est ad primas metas sub terra cum inscriptione eiusmodi: CONSUS CONSILIO MARS DUELLO LARES COILLO POTENTES. sacrificant apud eam nonis Iuliis sacerdotes publici, XII. Kalend. Septembres flamen Quirinalis et virgines. (*Spect.* 5.7)

> Even now there is an altar to that Consus buried underground in the Circus at the first turning post with an inscription to this effect: "Mighty are Consus in counsel, Mars in war, the Lares in the house's interior." The public priests (*sacerdotes publici*) sacrifice on it on the Nones of July, the *flamen Quirinalis* and the virgins on the twelfth day before the Kalends of September.

Modern historians (rightly, I think) maintain that the inscription is not genuinely archaic.[57] Even so, Tertullian's information about the sacrifice itself may be correct. Dionysius of Halicarnassus, who emphasizes that the festival continued in his own day, mentions sacrifices and offerings as well, though unfortunately without specifying the gender or identity of the officiant.[58]

The name Consus is usually derived from the verb *condere* ("to hide," or "to store") and, for this reason, it is assumed that Consus and the Consualia ensured the protection of the newly stored grain crop.[59] In principle, it would not

---

[54] *InscrIt* 13.2 (*fast. Praen.* April 25). Ovid (*Fast.* 4.901–942), however, says that he witnessed the festival on his return from Nomentum, which suggests that the rites were celebrated on the *via Nomentana*.

[55] For Consus and the Consualia, see Cic. *Rep.* 2.7; Varro *Ling.* 6.20, *ARD* 140 Cardauns; Livy 1.9.6; Dion. Hal. *Ant. Rom.* 1.33.2, 2.30.1–31.3; Ov. *Fast.* 3.199; Tac. *Ann.* 12.24; Plut. *Quaest. Rom.* 48 = Mor. 276c, *Rom.* 15.5; Tert. *Spect.* 5.5–7, 8.6; August. *Civ. Dei* 2.17; Serv. ad *Aen.* 8.636; Lydus *Mag.* 1.30; Festus (Paulus) 36, 135L. For the identification of Consus as a harvest deity, see Fowler 1899: 207–208; Wissowa 1912: 201–203; Latte 1960: 72; Scullard 1981: 177–178; Humphrey 1986: 62–63; Tramonti 1989; Scholz 1993; Dumézil 1996: 1.156–158, 267–268; Bernstein 1997; Wildfang 2001: 246–247; Scheid 2005b; Wildfang 2006: 28–30; Takács 2008: 54–56.

[56] Bernstein 1997: 417.

[57] Bernstein 1997: 441, with further bibliography.

[58] Dion. Hal. *Ant. Rom.* 2.31.2.

[59] Lydus *Mag.* 1.30. For an overview of the orthodox position, see Bernstein 1997: 418–422. For alternative etymologies, see Noonan 1990; Keaney 1991: 207–208.

be surprising to find in the Roman pantheon a deity whose sphere of influence included the protection of stored provisions.[60] Losses to mildew and infestation were evidently considerable, and the amount of space devoted to advice on the construction and maintenance of granaries in agricultural treatises indicates that the task of preserving stored crops was a difficult one.[61] The Consualia, on this reading, addressed a real source of anxiety in the life of the Roman farmer and his wife, who managed the household *penus*. Even after Rome became a sophisticated urban center, the preservation of the food supply remained a pressing issue both for the community as a whole and for individual families.

Other scholars have challenged this traditional interpretation of Consus and the Consualia. André Piganiol, for instance, identified Consus as a chthonic deity who mediated between the underworld and the world of the living.[62] Most recently, Carin Green has stressed that the Circus Maximus was set in the *vallis Murcia*, a swampy valley between the Palatine and the Aventine hills that was prone to periodic flooding until the late nineteenth century.[63] In fact, the *spina*, the elongated barrier between the turning posts, covered a stream running through the valley to the Tiber. The Romans, Green concludes, were "unlikely ever to have had a ritual in which they stored grain in an underground altar in an area of regular flooding, on or beside a running brook."[64] A reconsideration of the ancient evidence is clearly in order.

As Lawrence Richardson has emphasized, the altar of Consus sat not only at the turning post of the Circus Maximus, but also at the point where the *pomerium*, the sacred boundary of the city of Rome, turned toward the Forum after running across the *vallis Murcia* from the Forum Boarium (Cattle Market).[65] Perhaps, as Richardson and Green argue, the location of the altar reveals the god's character and function.[66] If Consus was a boundary deity, this could explain why the Vestals, who had a unique relationship with the *pomerium*, offered sacrifices to him at the Consualia.[67]

Most ancient sources, on the other hand, identify Consus as a god of counsel (*consilium*) and connect the Consualia to the rape of the Sabine women.[68] In this

---

[60] Compare the *Penates,* who guarded the provisions stored in the household *penus* (Gell. *N.A.* 4.1.1–23).

[61] See, for example, Varro *Rust.* 1.57.2; Colum. *Rust.* 1.9.10; Plin. *H.N.* 18.301; White 1970: 189, 196–197.

[62] Piganiol 1923: 1–14. See also Rossetto 1993.

[63] Green 2009: 66.

[64] Green 2009: 67. See also Holland 1961: 46.

[65] Richardson 1992: 100, s.v. "Consus," followed by Green 2009, 2010. The ancient source for the line of the *pomerium* is Tac. *Ann.* 12.24.

[66] Richardson 2002: 100, s.v. "Consus"; Green 2009, 2010.

[67] The Vestals were granted burial within the *pomerium* and credited with the ability to root runaway slaves to the spot, provided they had not yet crossed the sacred boundary of the city (see chapter 4).

[68] For Consus as a god of secret counsels, see Varro *ARD* 140 Cardauns; Dion. Hal. *Ant. Rom.* 2.31.3; Tert. *Spect.* 5.8; August. *Civ. Dei* 4.11; Serv. ad *Aen.* 8.636; Festus (Paulus) 36L. For the connection between the Consualia and the Sabine women, see Cic. *Rep.* 2.7; Varro *Ling.* 6.20; Verg. *Aen.* 8.636; Livy 1.9.6; Dion. Hal. *Ant. Rom.* 1.33.2; Ov. *Fast.* 3.199; Strabo 5.3.2; Plut. *Rom.* 15.5; Tert. *Spect.* 5.5; August. *Civ. Dei* 2.17; Serv. ad *Aen.* 8.636. The story also appears on the Basilica Aemilia frieze, where

familiar tale, a shortage of women prompts Romulus to seek wives for his citizens from among the neighboring communities. When his peaceful overtures are rejected, he concocts a plan to seize brides by force, vowing to institute an annual festival in honor of Consus should his plan succeed. Having invited his neighbors to the first Consualia, Romulus instructs the Romans to abduct as many Sabine maidens as they can lay their hands on. Reconciled to their fate by flattery and the promise of marriage and motherhood, the women consent to the arrangement.

In the imagination of the late Republican antiquarians, the Consualia commemorated the formation of Rome's first families and celebrated the god who had counseled Romulus to adopt this unorthodox plan.[69] It is unclear when this popular etiology gained currency, or how it is related to the identification of Consus with Equestrian Neptune.[70] Given the assimilation of Romulus with Quirinus, however, it is hardly surprising that the *flamen Quirinalis* played a role at a festival that came to be associated with an important event in the first king's reign.[71] Perhaps, in this case, Tertullian's *virgines* were not Vestals, but rather marriageable citizen virgins who ritually reenacted the reconciliation between Romulus and the Sabine maidens. Their sacrifice may have been added to the Consualia only after the myth of the Sabines began to acquire a central role in shaping Roman identity.[72] This scenario fits plausibly with evidence for the development of other Roman festivals during the republican period.[73] As legends about the figure of Romulus-Quirinus took shape, the ritual program of the *flamen Quirnalis* (and of his *flaminica*, if she existed) may have been altered in other ways that we are unable to trace in the extant sources.

The *Flamines* and *Flaminicae*(?) *Minores*

The written sources are nearly silent on the subject of the *flamines minores*. There were undoubtedly regulations governing their selection, but no discussion of the question has survived. New *flamines minores* may have been chosen by the *pontifex maximus* and perhaps inaugurated in the *comitia calata* as well.[74] It is almost certain, on the other hand, that they were not subject to the ritual

---

representations of the festival frame scenes of Romans carrying off Sabine women (Albertson 1990: 807–808, with further bibliography).

[69] For a discussion of the relationship between the myth of the Sabine women and the foundation of the Consualia, see especially Lambrechts 1946; Bremmer 1987a; Bernstein 1997; Green 2009: 74. Although Bernstein (1997: 445) cautions that the tradition may never have acquired official validity, the inscription quoted by Tertullian (*Spect.* 5.7) suggests that the identification of Consus as a god of counsel (*consilium*) extended beyond the literary sources.

[70] For the identification of Consus with Neptune, see Livy 1.9.6; Dion. Hal. *Ant. Rom.* 1.33.2, 2.30.1–31.3; Strabo 5.3.2; Plut. *Quaest. Rom.* 48 = Mor. 276c; Tert. *Spect.* 5.5–7; Serv. ad *Aen.* 8.636.

[71] Compare his role at the sacrifice to Acca Larentia (see above).

[72] The myth of Romulus as the founder of Rome was well established by the beginning of the third century BC. For a discussion of the evidence, see especially Cornell 1975.

[73] For a discussion of the relationship between ritual, myth (ancient "exegesis"), and the formation of Roman identity in the late Republic, see especially Beard 1987.

[74] Most scholars maintain that the *flamines minores* were not inaugurated (see, for example, Mommsen 1887–1888: 2, 26; Vanggaard 1988: 56; Van Haeperen 2002: 304).

taboos that regulated the behavior of the *flamen* and *flaminica Dialis*. Presumably they were not required to marry by *confarreatio*, since this ritual appears to have been reserved for patrician men, and it is equally unlikely that they were forbidden to ride a horse or required to abstain from seeing or touching yeast, raw meat, goats, or dogs.

The example of Popillius Laenas, who served as *flamen Carmentalis* in the first half of the fourth century BC, shows that *flamines minores* were free to pursue ordinary political careers and even to leave the city on campaign.[75] Laenas was elected aedile and held the consulship five times, earning a triumph in 350 BC for a victory over the Gauls.[76] Of course we should bear in mind that a five-time consul and *vir triumphalis* may not be a typical Republican *flamen minor*. Nonetheless, his career suggests that members of the plebeian elite could utilize the lesser *flamonia* as a means to augment their social status and visibility within the community at a time when options for religious service were more limited than they would become after 300 BC.

It is possible, perhaps even probable, that the wives of the *flamines minores* were *flaminicae* as well, though this hypothesis cannot be confirmed on the basis of our fragmentary evidence.[77] As we have seen, the flaminate of Jupiter required the participation of both the *flamen* and his wife in order to be considered fully "complete." The *flaminica Dialis* served alongside her husband, assisting him with his ritual obligations and performing rites independently in her capacity as priestess of Jupiter. The strength of their joint priesthood was its reliance on the cooperative efforts of the *flamen* and the *flaminica*. If the remaining *flamonia* resembled the priesthood of Jupiter in any way, and their shared priestly title suggests that they did, then it stands to reason that these offices were filled by priestly couples as well. During the archaic period, when the deities worshipped by the *flamines minores* were presumably central to civic religion, the impression created by women's priestly service may have been even more pronounced than it was in later periods.

The *Rex* and *Regina Sacrorum*

The *rex* and *regina sacrorum* (king and queen of the sacred rites) served in a joint office that invites comparison with the flaminical priesthoods and confirms the prevalence of this model of priestly service in early Rome.[78] Romans

---

[75] Rüpke 2008: 853, No. 2807.

[76] For the aedileship of Laenas, see Livy 7.2.3. For the five consulships and the triumph, see Livy 7.12.1–4, 17.1, 18.10, 23.1–24.9, 25.1. Cicero (*Brut.* 56) notes that during his first consulship in 359 BC, he interrupted a public sacrifice over which he was presiding in order to halt a plebeian revolt. It is unclear, however, whether he was presiding over the sacrifice in his capacity as consul or *flamen Carmentalis*.

[77] Against this suggestion, see, for example, Wissowa 1912: 506, n. 5; Boels 1973: 77; Vanggaard 1988: 30–31.

[78] Some ancient sources refer to the *rex sacrorum* as the *rex sacrificolus* (see, for example, Varro *Ling.* 6.31; Livy 2.2.1) or simply as the *rex* (see, for example, Varro *Ling.* 6.12). Detailed studies of the *rex sacrorum* are difficult, though see the useful discussion in North 1989: 61–65.

in the late Republic believed that the first *rex* and *regina sacrorum* had been appointed to take over the ritual duties of the king and queen following the expulsion of the Tarquins at the end of the sixth century BC, an event that was supposedly commemorated during the Regifugium on February 24, when the *rex sacrorum* sacrificed in the *comitium* before fleeing the Forum.[79] The *rex* and *regina sacrorum* did perform certain sacrifices in the *regia*, a sacred complex in the Forum that was regarded in later periods as the residence of the legendary king Numa Pompilius.[80] Other evidence, including the fact that the *rex sacrorum* was explicitly prohibited from holding political office and from obtaining membership in the senate throughout the republican period, likewise suggests that the priesthood was the product of a division of the religious and political powers once held by the Roman king.[81] Indeed, Livy claims that the *rex sacrorum* was placed under the authority of the *pontifex maximus* in order to prevent him from threatening the liberty (*libertas*) of the new Republic.[82]

While many scholars agree that there may have been a historical relationship between the kingship and the Republican *rex sacrorum*, it is impossible to determine how much continuity there may have been from the regal period to the early Republic, primarily because we know nothing certain about the religious responsibilities of the king or queen. According to the Roman etiology, the *rex* and *regina sacrorum* shared their priesthood because the office had its origin in the royal household, where the king and queen presumably performed their ritual functions jointly. More recently, however, a number of scholars have suggested that the priesthood actually predated the institution of the Republic.[83] In this scenario, the Romans appointed a priestly couple not to replace the royal couple after the expulsion of the last king, but rather to complement their functions during the period of the monarchy. Unfortunately, neither theory can be confirmed on the basis of our fragmentary evidence.

The *rex sacrorum*, and presumably the *regina sacrorum* as well, belonged to the extended pontifical college, although they did not occupy a prominent position in the hierarchy. Like the *flamines maiores*, the *rex sacrorum* was selected by the *pontifex maximus* and inaugurated in the *comitia calata*.[84] The priesthood was officially restricted to members of the patriciate throughout the republican period.[85] The *rex sacrorum*, moreover, was required to be born of

---

[79] Ov. *Fast.* 2.685–852; Plut. *Quaest. Rom.* 63 = Mor. 279c–d; and Aus. ad *Ecl.* 23.13 (p. 102 Green).

[80] For the *regia* as the house of Numa, see Ov. *Fast.* 6.263; Tac. *Ann.* 15.41; Plut. *Num.* 14; Cass. Dio fr. 1.6.2; Festus 346–348, 439L.

[81] Livy 40.42.8.

[82] Livy 2.2.1. See also Dion. Hal. *Ant. Rom.* 4.74.4.

[83] Cornell 1995: 232–236; Bendlin 2008; Smith 2006: 260; Rüpke 2012c: 21.

[84] Gell. *N.A.* 15.27.1; Livy 40.42.8, with Van Haeperen 2002: 99–101.

[85] Cic. *Dom.* 38; Livy 6.41.9. We know of at least one plebeian *rex sacrorum* from the republican period, M. Marcius, who may have been inaugurated in the middle of the third century BC (Livy 27.6.16, 36.5; Rüpke 2008: 787–788, No. 2368). It seems likely that the *cognomen* "Rex," adopted by some Marcii beginning in the early second century BC, was meant to advertise this man's tenure in office.

a confarreate marriage and had to be married by the same rite.[86] The *regina sacrorum* consequently entered her husband's *manus* and became a full member of his household with the legal status of a daughter and a role in his *sacra familiaria* (household rites). The *rex* and *regina sacrorum* lived in a public house situated in the Forum, Rome's civic and religious center, where they may have performed rituals on a regular basis, just as the *flamen* and *flaminica Dialis* celebrated daily rites in the *flaminia*.[87]

Despite the *rex sacrorum*'s relative insignificance during the late republican period, we are comparatively well informed about his ritual program. He sacrificed a ram to Janus in the *regia* on January 9 during the *dies Agonales*.[88] The significance of this festival is unclear. Ovid implies that the ram was offered to Janus (*Ianus agonali luce piandus erit, Fast.* 1.318), to whom the month of January was sacred. For this reason, some modern scholars have argued that the *rex sacrorum* was the priest of Janus, a conjecture that is not well supported by the ancient evidence.[89] He also participated in the Consualia on December 15, but his role at this festival is quite uncertain.[90]

The *rex sacrorum*'s most important ritual obligations were related to the regulation of the lunar calendar, which suggests that he wielded considerable power in early Rome.[91] On the Kalends, he performed a sacrifice in the *curia Calabra* with the assistance of a *pontifex minor* (a pontifical scribe), who called on Juno Covella five or seven times to signify the number of days until the observance of the Nones.[92] The *rex sacrorum* then convened an assembly of the people in order to inform them of the date in a similar manner.[93] The *regina sacrorum* sacrificed a pig or a sheep to Juno in the *regia* on the same day.[94]

The rituals on the Kalends prepared for the Nones, when the *rex sacrorum* announced the *feriae* (festival days) to be celebrated during the month.[95] He may have proclaimed the names and dates of the feasts and no more, though Macrobius suggests that he provided "reasons" (*causas*) and ritual instructions as well (*quid esset . . . faciendum, Sat.* 1.15.12). While it is unlikely that the announcement contained mythological material, the *rex sacrorum* may have provided simple instructions along the lines of "come wearing a wreath," or "bring

---

[86] Gai. *Inst.* 1.112.

[87] Festus 372L.

[88] Varro *Ling.* 6.12; Festus 9L; *InscrIt* 13.2.393.

[89] See, for example, Wissowa 1912: 504, 515; Holland 1961: 133, 265; Szemler 1978: 343; Porte 2007.

[90] *InscrIt* 13.2.136 (*fast. Praen.* December 15). The conclusions of Lambrechts 1946 are highly speculative.

[91] For the Roman calendar, see Michels 1967; Feeney 2007; Rüpke 2011. For the role of the *rex sacrorum* in regulating the calendar, see especially Rüpke 2011: 24–27, 76–78, 80–81, 83, 111–119.

[92] *InscrIt* 13.2.111 (*fast. Praen.* January 1); Serv. Auct. ad *Aen.* 8.654; Michels 1967: 20; Rüpke 2011: 24–25. The *pontifex minor* determined the number of days until the Nones by observing the moon prior to the sacrifice.

[93] *InscrIt* 13.2.11 (*fast. Praen.* January 1); Serv. Auct. ad *Aen.* 8.654; Macrob. *Sat.* 1.15.9–12.

[94] Macrob. *Sat.* 1.15.19. See further below.

[95] Varro *Ling.* 6.13, 28; Macrob. *Sat.* 1.15.12, with Rüpke 2011: 25–26.

wine with you."[96] Even after the introduction of a calendar with fixed months, the *rex sacrorum* continued to issue his proclamation, which suggests that the information he provided was more substantial than what could be found in the published *fasti* (festival calendars).[97]

Rituals are also recorded for March 24 and May 24 with the calendar symbol Q.R.C.F., which may be resolved as *Quando Rex Comitiavit Fas*.[98] While the details are uncertain, it seems that the *rex* performed a sacrifice in the *comitium* and then announced the end of the two-and-a-half day *nefas* period surrounding the Tubilustrium on March 23 and May 23, a festival for the purification of ritual trumpets (*tubae*).[99] In March, this ritual took place on the final day of the Quinquatrus, a five-day festival in honor of Mars that marked the beginning of the campaign season.[100] The trumpets have thus been identified as those used to call the army to assembly.[101] Jörg Rüpke, however, has suggested that the Q.R.C.F. sacrifice may have been performed on a monthly basis in early Rome and should thus be understood as another of the *rex sacrorum*'s calendar-related responsibilities.[102]

Finally, during the Regifugium on February 24, the *rex sacrorum* sacrificed in the *comitium* before fleeing the Forum.[103] Despite the popular Roman etiology, this ritual likely dramatized the end of the year rather than the expulsion of the Tarquins.[104] Every second year, or more irregularly, when the cycle of intercalation began to unravel, the *rex sacrorum* sacrificed and then announced the insertion of an intercalary month in order to rectify the difference between the solar year and the lunar months.[105] The Regifugium may even have provided the context for a ritual recorded by Servius, during which the Vestals approached the *rex* and asked, "Are you on the alert, king? Be alert!" (*vigilasne rex? vigila!*, ad *Aen.* 10.228). After all, keeping time was important business.

The significance of the *rex sacrorum*'s ritual program should not be underestimated. Prior to the introduction of a fixed solar calendar, the Roman community depended upon the *rex sacrorum* and his assistant, the *pontifex minor*, to establish the date of the Nones and on that day to announce the religious festivals to be celebrated during the month. The *rex sacrorum*, in other words,

---

[96] Michels 1967: 136; Rüpke 2011: 26.

[97] It is unclear when the transition from a calendar with true lunar months to a calendar with standardized months took place. Some ancient sources allude to adjustments made to the calendar by the *decemviri* in the middle of the fifth century BC (Cic. *Att.* 6.1.8; Ov. *Fast.* 2.47–51; Macrob. *Sat.* 1.13.21, with Michels 1967: 119–144). Macrobius (*Sat.* 1.15.9, with Rüpke 2011: 39–40), however, dates the transition to the reforms of Cn. Flavius (aed. 304 BC), who first published the *fasti* near the end of the fourth century BC. For a detailed discussion of the issues involved, see Rüpke 2011: 38–67.

[98] *InscrIt.* 13.2.430, 461 (*fast. Praen.* March 24, May 24); Varro *Ling.* 6.31; Festus 311L. For the Q.R.C.F. days, see especially Rüpke 2011: 26–30.

[99] Varro *Ling.* 6.31; Festus 310, 311, 346L. Days marked as *nefas* on the calendar were those on which public business was forbidden.

[100] Varro *Ling.* 6.14; Festus 480L.

[101] Scullard 1981: 94–95.

[102] Rüpke 2011: 28–29.

[103] Ov. *Fast.* 2.685–852; Plut. *Quaest. Rom.* 63 = Mor. 279c-d; and Aus. ad *Ecl.* 23.13 (p. 102 Green).

[104] Rüpke 2011: 76.

[105] For the system of intercalation and the *rex sacrorum*'s role within it, see Rüpke 2011: 68–86.

controlled the organization of social time, including not only the days on which feasts were celebrated, but also the days on which it was permissible (*fas*) to conduct public business. In early Rome, much of the rural population presumably crowded into the city to hear his monthly proclamations. The *rex sacrorum*'s responsibility for announcing the intercalary month at the Regifugium in February must also have contributed to his prominence within the community. As Rüpke has remarked, intercalation created the impression that the *rex sacrorum* had "control over time."[106] It is not surprising, therefore, that he was prohibited from accumulating political power.[107]

The *regina sacrorum* had a ritual program of her own as well. In his lengthy discussion of the Roman calendar, Macrobius reveals that she offered a sacrifice to Juno in the *regia* on the Kalends:

> Romae quoque Kalendis omnibus, praeter quod pontifex minor in curia Calabra rem divinam Iunoni facit, etiam regina sacrorum, id est regis uxor, porcam vel agnam in regia Iunoni immolat. (*Sat.* 1.15.19)

> At Rome too, on every Kalends not only does the *pontifex minor* make an offering to Juno in the *curia Calabra*, but the *regina sacrorum*, that is, the wife of the *rex* [i.e. the *rex sacrorum*], sacrifices a sow or a ewe to Juno in the *regia*.

This sacrifice clearly complemented the rituals performed by the *rex sacrorum* and the *pontifex minor* at the *curia Calabra*. As we have seen, their activities established the date of the Nones, which in turn determined the length of the month. The *regina sacrorum*'s parallel sacrifice to Juno presumably contributed to their efforts to help the moon along as it waxed towards this important date. The fact that she performed this ritual inside of the *regia* and away from public view does not diminish its relevance to the delicate operation of keeping time in early Rome. The *rex* and *regina sacrorum* worked in tandem on the Kalends; the *rex* sacrificed before a public assembly on the Capitol while his wife sacrificed in the *regia*, the traditional house of the Roman king and one of the most important sanctuaries in the city. Their religious roles were not identical, but both were vital.

The *regina sacrorum*'s sacrifice on the Kalends was almost certainly not her only ritual obligation. The author of the Servius Auctus commentary on Vergil's *Aeneid* claims that she wore the *arculum*, a ritual crown made from a pomegranate twig, at "certain sacrifices" (*sacrificiis certis*, 4.137). The plural forms surely indicate that she presided over, or at least attended, multiple religious rites during the course of the year.[108] She may, for example, have performed parallel

---

[106] Rüpke 2011: 80.

[107] Over time, as the *pontifices* acquired more control over the process of intercalation, they were able to manipulate the system for their own financial or political aims (Rüpke 2011: 68–86).

[108] For the *arculum*, see chapter 1. Festus calls the crown the *inarculum* and stresses that the *regina* (presumably the *regina sacrorum*) wore it while sacrificing (*sacrificans*, 101L).

sacrifices on the Regifugium and the Q.R.C.F. days, just as she did on the Kalends. Unfortunately, however, the *regina sacrorum* appears as a rather flat figure in the ancient sources, which demonstrate little interest in the priesthood that she shared with her husband. The *rex* and *regina sacrorum* became increasingly obscure figures over the course of the republican period as the *pontifices* assumed greater control over the regulation of the calendar. While they continued to perform their ritual obligations, many Romans undoubtedly ceased to take notice. Even so, there remained at Rome well into the imperial period an important priesthood filled by a priestly couple.

Priestly Couples in the Roman *Curiae*

Thus far we have concentrated on priestly couples that performed public rites (*sacra publica*) on behalf of the whole community (*pro populo*). There were also, however, priestly couples assigned to the public rites performed on behalf of the *curiae* (*pro curis*), ancient divisions of the Roman people. Like all *sacra publica*, curial rituals were paid from the public treasury (ἐκ τοῦ δημοσίου, Dion. Hal. *Ant. Rom.* 2.23.1). The *curiae* and their priests were thus part of civic cult, operating at a different level of social organization than the *flamines* and *flaminicae* and the *rex* and *regina sacrorum*, but no less integral to the business of fulfilling the community's ritual obligations to its gods.

Our most important source for the curial couples, and for curial religion in general, is the Greek historian Dionysius of Halicarnassus, who devotes nearly three chapters of his *Antiquitates Romanae* to the subject.[109] Dionysius cites his own autopsy and the *Antiquitates* of Varro as sources for this detailed discussion.[110] Much in his account reflects what Christopher Smith calls the historian's "imaginative vision" of how ancient Roman institutions worked.[111] Like many ancient authors, Dionysius stitched together fragments of a complex and often contradictory tradition in order to present a coherent historical narrative. Dionysius also engages in a fair amount of comparative history. His tendency to view the *curiae* through the lens of the Greek phratry may have led him to misunderstand much of what he observed or to overemphasizes similarities between the two institutions at the expense of uniquely Roman features.[112] Modern historians must acknowledge that parts of his description may bear only a passing resemblance to historical reality.[113] We can be confident, however, that the priestly couples were not the product of Dionysius' zeal for comparative history: the

---

[109] For a discussion of Dionysius and his interest in the *curiae*, see Smith 2006: 192–198, 347–355.
[110] Dion. Hal. *Ant. Rom.* 2.21.2.
[111] Smith 2006: 192.
[112] See, for example, Dion. Hal. *Ant. Rom.* 2.23.2.
[113] See especially Smith 2006: 197–198.

Greeks excluded women from serving the phratries in an official capacity.[114] The curial priesthood belongs to a distinctively Roman tradition.

The origins and initial organizational principles of the *curiae* are essentially irrecoverable.[115] The Romans attributed their creation to Romulus, who reportedly divided the population of his fledgling state into three tribes, and each tribe into ten *curiae*.[116] The dominant tradition held that he named the *curiae* for prominent Sabine women in recognition of their efforts to reconcile their fathers and husbands.[117] Membership was not restricted to patricians or to members of certain *gentes* (clans), as has sometimes been argued, but included the entire citizen body, the *Quirites*, making association with a *curia* at least notionally mandatory for all Romans.[118]

Evidence suggests that the *curiae* were organized at an early date for administrative and political purposes.[119] Together, they constituted the *comitia curiata* (assembly of the *curiae*), traditionally regarded as the oldest of the three Roman voting assemblies.[120] By the late Republic, the *comitia curiata* had a mostly formal function, having lost most of its powers to the *comitia centuriata* (centuriate assembly) and the *comitia tributa* (tribal assembly). It does not necessarily follow, however, that the curiate organization itself had become meaningless. Individual *curiae* maintained an identity, and one focus of this identity was their common cult activities. Indeed, Dionysius claims to have witnessed the celebration of communal feasts on festival days and gives the impression that religious activity in the *curiae* continued undiminished in his own day.[121]

Dionysius tells us that the rituals associated with the *curiae* were under the direction of sixty priests known as *curiones*.[122] These priests were supervised by a *curio maximus* and may have formed a college along the lines of the major priestly colleges.[123] Dionysius also reveals that the wives of the curial priests served alongside their husbands in an official capacity:

Ἐπεὶ δὲ καὶ διὰ γυναικῶν ἔδει τινὰ ἱερὰ συντελεῖσθαι καὶ διὰ παίδων
ἀμφιθαλῶν ἕτερα, ἵνα καὶ ταῦτα γένηται κατὰ τὸ κράτιστον, τάς τε
γυναῖκας ἔταξε τῶν ἱερέων τοῖς ἑαυτῶν ἀνδράσι συνιερᾶσθαι, καὶ εἴ τι

[114] For the religious activities of the phratries, see Lambert 1993: 225–236.
[115] For a detailed discussion of the *curiae* with further bibliography, see Smith 2006: 184–234.
[116] Cic. *Rep.* 2.14; Livy 1.13.6; Dion. Hal. *Ant. Rom.* 2.7; Plut. *Rom.* 14; *Dig.* 1.2.2.2 (Pomponius).
[117] This folk etiology may stem from the fact that one of the *curiae* was called "Rapta" (Palmer 1970: 76). Six other curial names are attested in the ancient sources: Foriensis, Veliensis, Velitia, Acculeia, Faucia, and Titia. An eighth, Tifata, is sometimes proposed but its authenticity is doubtful (Palmer 1970: 77–78; Smith 2006: 188).
[118] For the *curiae* as groups of *gentes*, see Mommsen 1887–1888: 3, 89–94; Carandini 1997. For a critique of this view, see Cornell 1995: 114–118; Smith 2006: 198–202, 211–212.
[119] They may also have had a military function, but this is less certain (Smith 2006: 201).
[120] Dion. Hal. *Ant. Rom.* 2.14.3. On the *comitia curiata*, see also Botsford 1909: 196–199; Taylor 1966: 3–6, passim; Smith 2006: 210–225.
[121] Dion Hal. *Ant. Rom.* 2.23.2–5.
[122] Dion. Hal. *Ant. Rom.* 2.21.2, 2.21.3.
[123] Festus 113L.

μὴ θέμις ἦν ὑπ' ἀνδρῶν ὀργιάζεσθαι κατὰ νόμον τὸν ἐπιχώριον, ταύτας ἐπιτελεῖν καὶ παῖδας αὐτῶν τὰ καθήκοντα λειτουργεῖν. (*Ant. Rom.* 2.22.1)

And because some sacred rites (*hiera*) had to be performed by women and others by children whose fathers and mothers were living, in order that these also might be fulfilled to the greatest advantage, he [i.e., Romulus] ordered that the wives of the priests should join in performing the rites along with their husbands, and that their wives should carry out whichever rites could not lawfully be celebrated by a man according to the native custom, and that their children should perform rituals proper to them as well.

This priesthood clearly resembles the flaminate and the office of the *rex* and *regina sacrorum*. Indeed, Paul the Deacon reports that the curial priests were known as *curiales flamines* (*flamines* of the *curiae*).[124] It is curious that modern scholars have almost universally ignored the wives of the curial *flamines*, who may have used the title "*flaminicae*."[125] In what follows, I consider the curial priesthood as a joint office along the lines of the flaminate and the office of the *rex* and *regina sacrorum*. Although there is very little direct evidence in the ancient sources for the wives of the *curiones* and their responsibilities, it is possible to construct a reasonably full context for their service by reconsidering the evidence for religious activity in the *curiae*.

According to Dionysius, each *curia* appointed (ἀποδείκνυσθαι, *Ant. Rom.* 2.21.3) their own *curiones*, presumably selecting a new priest from among their *curiales* (members of a *curia*). He does not distinguish between the two *curiones* in any way, which suggests that the criteria for selection to this priesthood applied equally to both officials. Only men over the age of fifty in possession of considerable wealth who had no physical blemishes were eligible. Dionysius discusses these qualifications as well as the benefits of holding the curial priesthood in the following passage:

ἀλλ' ἐξ ἑκάστης φράτρας ἐνομοθέτησεν ἀποδείκνυσθαι δύο τοὺς ὑπὲρ πεντήκοντα ἔτη γεγονότας τοὺς γένει τε προύχοντας τῶν ἄλλων καὶ ἀρετῇ διαφόρους καὶ χρημάτων περιουσίαν ἔχοντας ἀρκοῦσαν καὶ

---

[124] Festus 56L: *curiales flamines curiarum sacerdotes* (the *curiales flamines* were the priests of the *curiae*). Rüpke (2008: 11) has suggested that *flamen* is the "technically more exact" title, even though *curio* is more common in the literary and epigraphic sources. The curial *flamines* may have been distinguished from one another by *cognomina* derived from the name of the *curia* that they represented or by the name of the *curia*'s special deity (Palmer 1970: 118). Against this interpretation, see Scheid and Granino Cecere 1999: 91, n. 51.

[125] The wives of the *curiones* receive no mention in modern discussions of the *curiae* (see, for example, Kübler 1901b; Estienne 2005b; Smith 2006; Rüpke 2008), or of women's religious activities (see, for example, Scheid 1992c; Schultz 2006b; Takács 2008; Holland 2012b). Only Palmer (1970: 80) acknowledges their responsibility "to attend to purely female rites," though he stops short of assigning them full priestly status.

μηδὲν ἡλαττωμένους τῶν περὶ τὸ σῶμα· τούτους δὲ οὐκ εἰς ὡρισμένον τινὰ χρόνον τὰς ἔταξεν τιμὰς ἔχειν, ἀλλὰ διὰ παντὸς τοῦ βίου, στρατειῶν μὲν ἀπολελυμένους διὰ τὴν ἡλικίαν, τῶν δὲ κατὰ τὴν πόλιν ὀχληρῶν διὰ τὸν νόμον. (*Ant. Rom.* 2.21.3)

But he [i.e., Romulus] established a law that two men over fifty years of age, of outstanding birth and distinguished merit, in possession of a sufficient fortune, and without any bodily defects should be chosen from each *curia*, and that they should hold these honors not for any fixed period of time, but for life, having been released from military service by their age and from obligations toward the city by the law.

Dionysius predictably focuses on the selection criteria applied to the *curiones*, though some of the provisions, such as the requirement that they be free from bodily defects, presumably pertained to their wives as well.[126] Other conditions provide indirect information about the female members of the curial priesthood, particularly those related to the couple's social and financial status.

Dionysius reports, for instance, that each *curia* selected two men distinguished for their birth and merit. We can be certain that "outstanding birth" does not signify patrician status. Although it is unclear whether or not the priesthood was originally reserved for members of the patriciate, we have secure evidence that plebeians were serving as *curiones* by the end of the third century BC at the latest. C. Mamilius Atellus (pr. 207 BC), the first plebeian *curio maximus*, was elected to that post in 209 BC and must have been a *curio* for several years before that date.[127] It does appear, however, that the *curiones* were typically members of the elite.[128] Livy includes the *curio maximus* Ser. Sulpicius (cos. 500 BC) among the "illustrious men" (*clari viri*, 3.7.7) who perished in a plague in 463 BC. Mamilius' predecessor, M. Aemilius Papus (d. 210 BC), was a member of the prominent Aemilian *gens* and the brother of a consul, while both Mamilius and his successor, C. Scribonius Curio (pr. 193 BC), were elected to the aedileship and the praetorship.[129] The curionate may have offered a viable alternative to successful elites who wished to obtain a religious office but had failed to gain entrance to any of the major priestly colleges. Since elite marriage patterns indicate that the wives of the *curiones* were likely drawn from the same social circles as their husbands, the provision offers some insight into the status of curial wives as well.

---

[126] For a similar criterion for the Vestal order, see chapter 4.

[127] Livy 27.8.1–3, with Rüpke 2008: 782, No. 2334, though see also Palmer 1970: 146, n. 2; Feig Vishnia 1996: 229, n. 182.

[128] During the imperial period, members of the curial priesthood appear to have been drawn exclusively from among the senatorial and equestrian elite and included several former consuls (Scheid and Granino Cecere 1999: 83–84).

[129] For M. Aemilius Papus, see Rüpke 2008: 517, No. 520. For C. Scribonius Curio, see Rüpke 2008: 880, No. 2995.

Dionysius also specifies that the *curiones* had to be over fifty years of age. The existence of a minimum age for entrance to the curionate is rather surprising.[130] The Vestal order had strict age requirements, but religious offices reserved for adults did not typically specify age as a prerequisite.[131] The practical effects of this provision can be more readily deduced than the reasons for its institution. By age fifty, most men had reached the pinnacle of their magisterial or military careers and were settling into a new role in society defined by experience and wisdom.[132] The curial priesthood, therefore, may have been regarded as the capstone of a relatively successful elite career and a venue for continued public activity beyond the office-holding years. At the same time, since the risk of dying increased dramatically after age fifty, the minimum age requirement may often have resulted in a relatively brief tenure in office.[133]

Since Roman brides tended to be ten or more years younger than their husbands, we may estimate that the wives of the *curiones* would typically have been in their late thirties or early forties when they entered office.[134] Many of these women were reaching the end of their childbearing years.[135] Even so, it is possible that some had a child young enough to serve as a *camillus* or *camilla* when they entered the curionate.[136] According to Dionysius, the *camilli* served until manhood (by which he likely means the assumption of the *toga virilis* at age sixteen) and the *camillae* until they married.[137] As their children matured, however, many couples would have been forced to employ another provision described by Dionysius:

> τοῖς δὲ ἄπαισιν ἐκ τῶν ἄλλων οἴκων τοὺς χαριεστάτους καταλεγέντας ἐξ ἑκάστης φράτρας, κόρον καὶ κόρην, τὸν μὲν ἕως ἥβης ὑπηρετεῖν ἐπὶ τοῖς ἱεροῖς, τὴν δὲ κόρην ὅσον ἄν ᾖ χρόνον ἀγνὴ γάμων. (*Ant. Rom.* 2.22.1)

[130] In fact, Rüpke (2008: 782, No. 2334, n. 5) recently expressed doubt about the authenticity of this requirement and suggests that it may have come into effect only during the Augustan period, if ever.

[131] See chapter 4.

[132] Studies suggest that during the period of the Republic, the age of office holding was the thirties and forties (see especially Harlow and Laurence 2002: 104–116).

[133] For a discussion of ancient mortality rates, see Parkin 1992: 92–110; Saller 1994: 12–25.

[134] It is notoriously difficult to determine age at first marriage in the Roman world. Written sources suggest that the median age was nineteen for men and fourteen for women (see Hopkins 1965: 309–327; Lelis, Percy and Verstraete 2003: 15–20, 29–72, 91–101, 103–24). Using the evidence of funerary inscriptions, Saller (1987; 1994) and Shaw (1987) estimate that men and women typically married in their late twenties and late teens, respectively. Most recently, Scheidel (2007) has argued that men probably married in their late twenties or early thirties, but that it is impossible to conclude with any degree of certainty whether women married in their early, mid, or late teens. Remarriage would obviously affect the age difference between spouses (see, for example, Bradley 1991a: 156–176, 1991b).

[135] The age of menopause varies widely, typically beginning around the age of forty (Parkin 1992: 123).

[136] Although Palmer (1970: 80) suggested that a man in his fifties would not have qualifying children, the age of his wife, who would probably have been in her mid to late thirties or early forties, is more relevant to the question at hand. Most women married in their teens but did not achieve full fecundity until their early twenties (Parkin 1992: 124). The model life tables simulated by Saller (1994: 68–69) and census data from Roman Egypt (Bagnall and Frier 1994: 136–137) show that the average age at maternity in the ancient world was in the mid twenties. Historians estimate that Roman women bore an average of five children over the course of their childbearing years, though only two or three typically survived infancy (Parkin 1992: 111–119; Bagnall and Frier 1994: 138–144; Saller 1994: 42, n. 71). All of this suggests that some curial priestesses may have had children young enough to serve as priestly assistants, at least when they first entered office.

[137] Dion. Hal. *Ant. Rom.* 2.22.1.

[Romulus ordered that] for those who had no children, the most beautiful boy and girl out of the other households of each *curia* should be chosen, the boy to assist in the religious rites until the age of manhood, and the girl for as long as she remained unmarried.

Curial priests who found themselves in this situation presumably included not only childless couples, but also those whose children no longer qualified for service as *camilli* or *camillae*. The experience of religious service must have varied from couple to couple and even changed over the course of an individual career.

Dionysius does not describe the ritual obligations of the *curiones* or their wives in any detail. He does, however, report that the curial priestesses performed "whichever rites could not lawfully be celebrated by a man according to the native custom" (εἴ τι μὴ θέμις ἦν ὑπ' ἀνδρῶν ὀργιάζεσθαι κατὰ νόμον τὸν ἐπιχώριον, *Ant. Rom.* 2.22.1). Just as the *flaminica Dialis* and the *regina sacrorum* presided over sacrifices that their husbands could not perform, so too did the wives of the *curiones*. Unfortunately, however, the function and composition of their ritual program is very uncertain. The verb ὀργιάζω can signify the celebration of mystery rites, but it can also be used in a more general sense to describe a variety of rites assigned to priests and priestesses alike.[138] Dionysius probably had the latter sense in mind when he chose the word for this passage. In the absence of specific evidence, we must turn to the category of rites designated as "belonging to a *curio*" (*curionia sacra*, Festus (Paulus) 54L), for it is among these rituals that we may imagine a role for the wife of the *curio*.

Each *curia* maintained a curial building, also known as a *curia*, where "*curiales* offered the sacrifices appointed for them together with their priests and feasted together on festival days" (συνέθυόν τε τοῖς ἱερεῦσιν οἱ φρατριεῖς τὰς ἀπομερισθείσας αὐτοῖς θυσίας καὶ συνειστιῶντο κατὰ τὰς ἑορτὰς, Dion. Hal. *Ant. Rom.* 2.23.2).[139] Like the Temple of Vesta, the *regia*, and the houses of the *flamines*, the *curiae* were part of a network of archaic cult sites that received fresh laurel garlands on March 1, the first day of the ritual calendar.[140] According to Dionysius, the hearth in each curial building was sacred to Vesta, perhaps indicating a close connection between the *curiae* and Vesta in her role as protectress of the community.[141] Since the task of tending the domestic and communal hearth generally fell to women, it seems very likely that the wives of the *curiones* were responsible for the hearths in the curial buildings.

The *curiones* offered sacrifices to Juno Curitis on *curiales mensae* (curial tables) that stood in the curial buildings.[142] Additionally, each *curia* sacrificed

---

[138] *LSJ* s.v. ὄργια.

[139] For the curial buildings, see also Varro *Ling.* 5.155; Festus 180–182L; Dion. Hal. *Ant. Rom.* 2.65.4–2.66.1.

[140] Ov. *Fast.* 3.135–3.140; Macrob. *Sat.* 1.12.6. See chapter 1.

[141] Dion. Hal. *Ant. Rom.* 2.65.4–66.1. For the public cult of Vesta, see especially chapters 4 and 6.

[142] Dion. Hal. *Ant. Rom.* 2.23.5, 2.50.3; Festus 56L. Festus derives the name of Juno Curitis from the belief that she carried a spear (*curitim Iunonem appellabant, quia eandem ferre hastam putabant*, 43L).

to its own *genius* (life-force) and patron deity.[143] The *genius* was a generative and protective deity worshipped in a variety of social contexts.[144] There was a cult of the *genius* of the Roman people (*genius publicus populi Romani*) near the Forum and a cult of the *genius* of the city of Rome (*genius urbis Romae*) on the Capitol.[145] In the household, each family worshipped the *genius* of their *paterfamilias* and the *iuno* (female *genius*) of their *materfamilias* (female head of household).[146] Professional guilds (*collegia*), private clubs (*sodalitates*), army units, and cities throughout Italy also had their own particular *genii*, whose worship reinforced a sense of corporate identity. The *genii* and patron deities of the *curiae* presumably served a similar function. As in the household, worship of the curial *genius* was almost certainly communal and gender-inclusive, requiring the participation of male and female *curiales* as well as curial priests and priestesses.

The ritual calendar included two public festivals common to all thirty *curiae*. The first was the Fordicidia on April 15.[147] Ovid describes this festival in some detail in the fourth book of the *Fasti*:

> tertia post Veneris cum lux surrexerit Idus,
>   pontifices, forda sacra litate bove.
> forda ferens bos est fecundaque, dicta ferendo:
>   hinc etiam fetus nomen habere putant.
> nunc gravidum pecus est, gravidae quoquo semine terrae:
>   Telluri plenae victima plena datur.
> pars cadit arce Iovis, ter denas curia vaccas
>   accipit et largo sparsa cruore madet.
> ast ubi visceribus vitulos rapuere ministri
>   sectaque fumosis exta dedere focis,
> igne cremat vitulos quae natu maxima virgo est,
>   luce Palis populos purget ut ille cinis. (629–640)

When the third day has dawned after the Ides of Venus, offer a sacrifice, *pontifices*, with a *forda* cow. A *forda* cow is a cow that is carrying, and is called fertile from her carrying; they think that the fetus also has its name from this fact. Now the cattle are pregnant, and the earth also is pregnant with seed. A full victim is given to full earth. Some fall on the cita-

---

[143] Dion. Hal. *Ant. Rom.* 2.23.1–2. We are almost entirely ignorant about the gods worshipped by individual *curiae*, though Varro implies that the *curia Acculeia* had a special relationship with the mysterious goddess Angerona (*Ling.* 6.23, with Palmer 1970: 106–109; Estienne 2005b: 110).

[144] Gradel 2002: 36–44; Liu 2009: 259–262.

[145] Palombi 1995b.

[146] For the *genius* of the *paterfamilias*, see Orr 1978: 1560–1575; Fröhlich 1991: 22–23; Foss 1997: 199. For the *iuno*, see Fröhlich 1991: 23; Rives 1992; Boëls-Janssen 1993: 268–271; Schultz 2006b: 124–125.

[147] The ancient sources for the Fordicidia are Varro *Ling.* 6.15; Ov. *Fast.* 4.629–672; Festus 74 and 91L.

del of Jove; the *curiae* receive thirty cows and are soaked, sprinkled with plentiful blood. But when the attendants have seized the calves from the wombs of their mothers and placed the divided entrails on the smoking hearths, the eldest virgin [i.e., the *virgo maxima*] burns the calves in the fire, so that the ashes may purify the people on the day of Pales.

Ovid here describes a complex, interrelated festival requiring coordination among various priestly figures at various sacred sites throughout the city. The *pontifices* sacrificed a pregnant cow (*forda*) on the Capitol. At the same time (or perhaps later on the same day), the members of the thirty *curiae* offered identical victims in their curial buildings.[148] Once the ritual slaughterers (*victimarii*) had butchered the animal, the *curiones* burned the entrails of the mother cows on the curial hearths. The calves, however, were carried to the Temple of Vesta, where the *virgo maxima* (the chief Vestal Virgin) burned their remains in the flame of Vesta. As the temple was off-limits to men, the task of delivering the victims to the *virgo maxima* may have fallen to the curial priestesses.

Ovid's lengthy etiology reveals that he understood the Fordicidia as a ritual to ensure the fertility of the flocks, herds, and fields.[149] Because the earth and the cattle were both "pregnant" at this time of year, a pregnant cow (*forda*) was sacrificed. The calf embryo symbolized the buried grain (*semen*), and its sacrifice was exchanged for the successful germination of the crop.[150] At the same time, the ritual facilitated the celebration of the Parilia on April 21, an agricultural festival and celebration of the foundation of the city.[151] The Vestals combined the ashes of the calves with beanstalks and blood from the tail of the October Horse to produce the *februa*, or "cleansing agents," which they distributed to the people for the purification of the flocks.[152] The Fordicidia thus underscores the association between the *curiae* and the hearth of Vesta, where offerings from each *curia* were gathered together and transformed into a new ritual substance for the benefit of the entire community.

The second major curial festival, the Fornacalia, fell in the middle of February and was celebrated in honor of the oven-goddess Fornax.[153] According to Ovid, the *curio maximus* announced the date of this moveable feast with "proscribed words" (*legitimis verbis*, *Fast.* 2.527), while each *curia* displayed in the Forum a tablet marked with its own particular symbol (*multa circum pendente tabella*, / *signatur certa curia quaeque nota*, 529–530). These tablets presumably

---

[148] See also Varro *Ling.* 6.15. For the role of the *curiones* at this festival, see Scheid and Granino Cecere 1999: 91–92.

[149] Ov. *Fast.* 4.641–672.

[150] The sacrifice conforms to the ordinary symbolic rule that a divinity is provided with victims that are homologous to it (i.e., male or female, depending on its sex). It also provides the divinity, although in a different form, with what it is expected to produce in return for the sacrifice (Dumézil 1970: 371–372).

[151] For the Parilia, see chapter 6.

[152] Ov. *Fast.* 4.731–734. For the role of the Vestals at the Fordicidia, see chapter 6.

[153] For the Fornacalia, see Festus 73, 82, 298L; Ov. *Fast.* 2.519–532, 6.313–314; Plin. *H.N.* 18.8; Plut. *Quaest. Rom.* 89 = *Mor.* 285d; Varro *Ling.* 6.13; Robinson 2003.

provided instructions for the *curiales* about when, where, and how they were to celebrate the festival. Romans who did not know their curial affiliation or who were prevented from celebrating the Fornacalia with their *curiae* were obliged to observe the rites on February 17 at the so-called Feast of Fools (*stultorum feriae*, Ov. *Fast*. 2.531–532).[154] The coincidence of the *stultorum feriae* with the feast of Quirinus, the god of the *Quirites* and perhaps of the *curiae* as well, may have been intentional.

The written sources suggest that the Fornacalia involved the roasting of *far* (emmer wheat), a staple of the ancient diet and a ubiquitous element of the sacrificial system.[155] The Romans employed *far* as a grain offering at public and private ceremonies and the Vestal Virgins used it to make *mola salsa*, the salted grain that priests and magistrates sprinkled on the heads of sacrificial victims at all public sacrifices. According to Pliny the Elder, however, only roasted *far* could be offered to the gods.[156] The Fornacalia thus celebrated Fornax, the goddess who taught the Romans how to transform raw grain into a product fit for consumption or sacrifice. The *curiones* and their wives presumably had an official role at the festival, although the ancient sources are silent on the matter.

Our sources for the religious life of the *curiae* are fragmentary and impressionistic. Even so, the evidence confirms that there were priestly couples in the *curiae*, married priests and priestesses with a significant (if poorly understood) ritual role. As in the household, civic cult required women's presence and active participation. It is clear, moreover, that the *curiae* and their priestly couples belong to an early phase of Roman religion. This is evident not only from the festivals they celebrated, but also from the fact that the curial buildings were adorned with laurel to mark the new year in a ritual that included the *regia*, the Temple of Vesta, and the houses of the *flamines* as well. All of these spaces were associated with demonstrably ancient cults and priesthoods involving women. Early Rome was populated by an impressive number of priestesses who have left only faint traces in the historical record.

Priestly Couples on the Seven Hills?

A late republican inscription suggests that there may have been priestly couples affiliated with the hills (*montes*) of Rome as well:

> [magistri] et flamin(es) montan(orum) montis Oppii de pequnia mont(anorum) montis Oppii sacellum claudend(um) et coaequand(um) et arbores serundas coeraverunt. (*CIL* 6.32455)

---

[154] See also Varro *Ling*. 6.13; Plut. *Quaest. Rom.* 89 = *Mor.* 285d; Festus 304, 418L.
[155] Plin. *H.N.* 18.8; Festus 73, 82L. For the ritual significance of *far*, see also chapter 6.
[156] Plin. *H.N.* 18.8.

The *magistri* (officials) and *flamines montanorum* of the Mons Oppius have overseen the enclosing and leveling of a shrine and the planting of trees with the funds of the residents of the Mons Oppius.

The text of this inscription reveals that the residents of the Mons Oppius formed a distinct religious community with priests, a treasury, and a shrine. The *magistri* and *flamines* were evidently empowered to undertake initiatives funded by their fellow *montani* (residents of a hill), including the refurbishment of the shrine and the planting of trees, perhaps as part of a sacred grove.[157] The shrine may have belonged to the *genius* of the Mons Oppius or to another god with a longstanding connection to this hill.[158] In either case, the inscription suggests that the *flamines* and *magistri* of the Oppian Hill supervised the maintenance of at least some sacred spaces belonging to their religious communities.

We know little else about the *montes* and their religious activities, though we hear of *sacra publica* performed on their behalf (*pro montibus*, Festus 284L). Varro confirms that the communities of the hills celebrated at least one common festival, the Septimontium (Seven Hills), on December 11:

> dies Septimontium nominatus ab his septem montibus, in quis sita urbs est; feriae non populi, sed montanorum modo. (*Ling.* 6.24)

> Septimontium Day was named from these seven hills on which the city is situated; it is a festival not of the people (*populus*), but only of those who live on the hills (*montani*).

According to the Augustan antiquarian Antistius Labeo, the Septimontium involved the Palatine, Velia, Fagutal, Subura, Cermalus, Caelius, Oppius, and Cispius.[159] This list of eight toponyms, however, is inconsistent with the traditional etymology of Septimontium from *septem montes* (seven hills).[160] It is also at odds with sources that include the Capitoline, Aventine, and Quirinal hills among the canonical seven. Modern efforts to explain these discrepancies have yielded less than satisfactory results.[161] The form and function of the rites are also poorly understood, though a festival celebrated on behalf of the *montani* presumably required the participation of the *flamines montanorum*. There were sacrifices on the Palatine and the Velia, and John Lydus, a sixth-century AD Byzantine author, mentions a procession around the city.[162] Domitian celebrated the Septimontium by distributing bread to the senators and equestrians

---

[157] Palmer (1970: 122–132) argues for an equation between the hills and the *curiae*. As Smith (2006: 360) points out, however, we do not know whether all of the hills were represented in the *curiae*, as the Mons Velia was in the Curia Veliensis, or even whether the *curiae* were geographic entities.

[158] Palmer (1970: 127) speculates that the *sacellum* was one of the Argei shrines.

[159] Festus 476L.

[160] For a different etymology, see Holland 1953.

[161] Fulminante (2014: 75–77) reviews the relevant evidence.

[162] Festus 476L; Lyd. *Mens.* 4.155.

and baskets of food to the people, but Suetonius implies that this was his own innovation.[163]

The late republican inscription from the Mons Oppius raises the possibility that priestly couples were a feature of religious life on the hills of Rome. The title *flamen* certainly implies that the priesthood was structured along the lines of the *flamonia* of Jupiter and Mars. Once again, however, we must be content with what is plausible, rather than what is known as fact.

Conclusion

Joint priesthoods filled by married couples were a central, perhaps even defining, feature of civic cult in early Rome. In fact, evidence suggests that the total number of priestly couples far exceeded the number of *pontifices*, augurs, and *quindecemviri* combined. A focus on gender thus exposes serious flaws in traditional approaches to Roman priesthood, which tend to look for a common priestly function or uniform hierarchy. The Roman constitution distributed ritual authority and sacrificial capacity widely, to women as well as to men. Religious officials could be individual men or women, members of a board of peers, or part of a priestly couple. In light of this variety, any single definition of the Roman "priest" dissolves. In its place, we must develop a more nuanced and flexible description of priestly service, one that accounts fully for individual priestesses and priestly couples. In light of the fact that the husband and wife who constituted a priestly couple entered office together and served only until one or the other died, the mutual dependence of married priests must occupy a central position in any new model proposed. Indeed, public cult required male and female priests to cooperate with one another as men and women, not just as religious officials. Far from challenging or confusing traditional gender roles and ideologies, priestly service reinforced them. The remaining chapters expand upon this observation, looking first at individual priestesses and then at the college of Vestal Virgins.

[163] Suet. *Dom.* 4.5, with Scullard 1981: 203.

CHAPTER THREE

Salian Virgins, *Sacerdotes*, and *Ministrae*

This chapter focuses primarily on *sacerdotes* (priestesses) associated with the public cults of Mars, Fortuna Muliebris, Bona Dea, Liber, Magna Mater, and Ceres.[1] Even though the *sacerdotes* of Bacchus were not entrusted with any *sacra publica* (public rites), they are included as well, since the senate took an active role in regulating their status during the notorious Bacchanalian affair in 186 BC. Finally, a discussion of female support personnel supplements the priestly material. Without these women, many of whom were *libertae* (freedwomen) and *servae publicae* (public slaves), the ritual system would have ground to a halt. Though often fragmentary and problematic, the evidence under consideration in this chapter allows us to explore important questions about the nature of women's religious activities and the position of priestesses within civic cult at Rome. As a group, these priestesses and cultic assistants further complicate traditional accounts of Roman "priesthood" and confirm that women were involved in official religious service at nearly every level.

The Salian Virgins

Of all the priestesses under consideration in this chapter, the enigmatic *saliae virgines* (Salian Virgins) may be the most intriguing.[2] Festus provides our only evidence for these priestesses in an entry that challenges deeply held views about Roman religion and the role of women in public cult:

> salias virgines Cincius ait esse conducticias, quae ad salios adhibeantur cum apicibus paludatas; quas Aelius Stilo scribsit sacrificum facere in regia cum pontifice paludatas cum apicibus in modum saliorum. (Festus 439L)

> Cincius says that the *saliae* are virgins who are assembled (*conducticias*), wearing the *apex* and armed and equipped (*paludatas*), to assist the *salii*,

---

[1] Priestesses associated with the cult of Magna Mater and the Greek rites of Ceres are considered in this chapter because their activities belonged to the *sacra publica* during the republican period. Female cult personnel affiliated with nonpublic cults, such as the cult of Isis, which began to receive public support only under Claudius (r. AD 41–54), are not. For women's roles in the Roman cult of Isis, see Heyob 1975; Takács 1995.

[2] For the *saliae virgines*, see especially Glinister 2011, with further bibliography.

and Aelius Stilo has written that they perform a sacrifice in the *regia* with the *pontifex*, armed and equipped and wearing the *apex* in the manner of the *salii*.[3]

The interpretation of this passage is contested. According to the translation I have adopted here, the passage tells us how these priestesses dressed (like the *salii*), where they sacrificed (in the *regia*), and with whom they were associated in the ritual sphere (the *salii* and a *pontifex*). I shall discuss each of these observations in turn before considering the problematic adjective *conducticius*, a term that has long shaped modern analyses of the *saliae*.

According to Festus, the antiquarians Cincius Alimentus (first century BC) and Aelius Stilo (ca. 154–74 BC) agreed that the *saliae* dressed *paludatas cum apicibus*.[4] Some modern scholars have understood *paludatas* to mean that the women wore the *paludamentum*, a military cloak used by generals and other high-ranking officials.[5] If this is true, then we must conclude that Stilo is mistaken when he claims that they dressed *in modum Saliorum*, since the ancient sources describe the *salii*, Roman priests named from their dancing (*ab salitando*, Varro *Ling.* 5.85), as wearing an embroidered tunic (*tunica picta*), a bronze breastplate, and the *trabea*, a robe associated with the kings of Rome.[6] The late Republican antiquarian Veranius, however, tells us that in the augural books, *paludatae* means, "armed" or "equipped."[7] In a ritual context, therefore, *paludatas* and *in modum Saliorum* suggest that the *saliae* dressed exactly like the *salii* and like them bore arms.[8] These arms included a bronze helmet adorned with an *apex* (an olive-wood spike), a sword, a spear, and an *ancile* (shield). We will return to the significance of this transvestism, which has attracted considerable scholarly attention.[9]

Aelius Stilo tells us that the *saliae* performed a sacrifice (*sacrificium facere*) in the *regia* with a *pontifex*. Although we lack a precise ritual context, this evidence points to an official priestly status for the *saliae* and indicates that their sacrifice was a public rite. Modern scholars, however, have generally held that the girls were hired and thus of low social status.[10] By employing the adjective *conducticius*, Thomas Habinek writes, "Cincius makes it seem as though the Salian maidens were geishas or *hetairai*."[11] In her detailed analysis of the word

[3] Translated by Glinister 2011: 117. For alternative translations of certain key terms, including "*paludatas cum apicibus*" and "*conducticias*," see the notes below.
[4] For the identity of the sources cited in this passage, see Glinister 2001: 108.
[5] See, for example, Liou-Gille 2006: 62; Feeney and Katz 2006: 241.
[6] For the costume of the *salii*, see Livy 1.20.4; Dion. Hal. *Ant. Rom.* 2.70.2–3. Schäfer 1980 discusses the visual evidence.
[7] Festus 298L, with Glinister 2011: 109.
[8] Glinister 2011: 109.
[9] See, for example, Torelli 1984: 76, 107–108, 111–112; Versnel 1993: 158, n. 104; Habinek 2005: 17, 255–256; Glinister 2011: 255–256; Glinister 2011: 122–123.
[10] See, for example, Rose 1949: 164; Scholz 1970: 30, n. 51; Torelli 1984: 111; Beard 1990: 21; Beard, North, and Price 1998: 24; Habinek 2005: 255–256; Feeney and Katz 2006: 241.
[11] Habinek 2005: 256.

and its root verb, *conducere*, however, Fay Glinister concludes that *conducticius* could mean "assembled" or "brought together," rather than "hired."[12] Although most known examples of the adjective are related to hiring or leasing someone or something, Glinister cites a passage in Cicero's *De inventione* where *conductio* means "a bringing together:" *quare in longis argumentationibus ex conductionibus aut ex contrario complecti oportet* (therefore in long arguments one ought to state the conclusion by bringing major and minor together, or by a contrary statement, 1.74).[13] This suggests that the adjective may simply indicate that the *saliae* were brought together to assist the *salii*.

Even if *conducticius* does mean "hired," however, the term may be compared to the *captio* (capture) of a new Vestal, who was led away by the *pontifex maximus* "as if she had been taken in war" (*veluti bello capta*, Gell. *N.A.* 1.12.13–14). Our sources apply the same terminology to the appointment of new *flamines*, *pontifices*, and augurs.[14] No one, however, would argue that these priests were actually seized as captives. As Glinister observes, this parallel suggests that *conducticius* may be the technical term for the selection of new *saliae* and *salii*, who were "hired" or "conscripted" into a "Salian army."[15]

It is unnecessary, therefore, to assume that the *saliae* were lowborn women hired on a temporary basis. In fact, their sacrifice in the *regia* suggests the opposite, that the *saliae* were public religious officials, perhaps female counterparts of the *salii*.[16] It seems very likely, moreover, that they were the daughters of elite Roman families, just as the male *salii* were required to be patricians well into the imperial period.[17] At the time of their selection, *salii* also had to be *patrimi et matrimi*, that is, with both parents living.[18] The same requirement applied to the Vestal Virgins and perhaps to the *saliae* as well.

During the Republican period, there were two groups (*sodalitates*) of twelve *salii* each: the *salii Palatini* and the *salii Collini*.[19] According to the Roman etiological tradition, Numa established the first group to serve the god Mars after a shield (*ancile*) fell from heaven during a severe plague.[20] This shield, the nymph

---

[12] Glinister 2011: 115–116.

[13] The *Oxford Latin Dictionary* (s.v. *conductio* 2) defines this use as "a bringing together (of the premises of an argument)."

[14] Gell. *N.A.* 1.12.15–17.

[15] Glinister 2011: 117–118.

[16] Glinister 2011: 110–111.

[17] Cic. *Dom.* 38; Dion. Hal. *Ant. Rom.* 2.70.1; Lucan 9.478.

[18] Dion. Hal. *Ant. Rom.* 2.71.4. For the significance of this requirement, see chapter 4.

[19] For the *salii*, see Wissowa 1912: 555–559; Cirilli 1913; Schäfer 1980; Rüpke 1990: 23–27; Estienne 2005c.

[20] Livy 1.20.2; Dion. Hal. *Ant. Rom.* 2.70.1; Ov. *Fast.* 3.365–392; Plut. *Num.* 13.1–7. Ennius (*Ann.* 114) merely says that Egeria gave the shield to Numa. The *salii Palatini* maintained a cult place (*curia*) on the Palatine where they kept the *lituus* of Romulus (Cic. *Div.* 1.17). The *salii Collini* (sometimes called *Agonenses*), on the other hand, traced their origins to Tullus Hostilius and were devoted to Quirinus, the deified Romulus (Livy 1.27.14; Dion. Hal. *Ant. Rom.* 2.70.1, 3.32.4). They had a cult place (*curia*) on the Quirinal. In reality, of course, the *salii* were not unique to Rome and are attested in a number of other cities in Latium and Etruria, though not always in association with the same gods. The Romans themselves were aware of the existence of non-Roman *salii*. See Serv. Auct. ad *Aen.* 8.285 for the claim

Egeria explained, came "for the salvation of the city" (ἐπὶ σωτηρίᾳ τῆς πόλεως, Plut. *Num.* 13.2), and Numa accordingly had eleven copies made in order to protect the original from theft. Dionysius adds that he instituted sacrifices in honor of the shield, which was stored along with the copies in the *sacrarium Martis* (shrine of Mars) in the *regia*.[21] It seems very likely, therefore, that the *saliae* sacrificed to the *ancile* when they entered the *regia* in the company of a *pontifex*.[22]

According to Cincius, the *saliae* were also summoned to join the *salii* (*ad salios adhibeantur*) at an unspecified time and place.[23] Their martial costume suggests that the girls may have participated in the ritual dance that was the main function of the Roman *salii*.[24] On March 1, 9, 14, 19 and 23 and on October 19, the *salii* leapt and danced through the city in full dress singing the ancient Salian Hymn.[25] They were directed by a lead singer (*vates*) and a lead dancer (*praesul*), who set the steps for the other priests to follow.[26] In his account of the reign of Numa, Livy describes the scene as follows:

> Salios item duodecim Marti Gradivo legit, tunicaeque pictae insigne dedit et super tunicam aeneum pectori tegumen; caelestiaque arma, quae ancilia appellantur, ferre ac per urbem ire canentes carmina cum tripudiis sollemnique saltatu iussit. (1.20.4)

> He [i.e., Numa] likewise chose twelve *salii* for Mars Gradivus, and gave them the honor of the *tunica picta* and over the tunic a bronze breastplate, and ordered them to bear the heavenly shields, which are called *ancilia*, and to process through the city, chanting their hymns to the triple beat of their solemn dance.

---

that Veii and Tusculum had *salii* before Rome. For a discussion of the evidence for non-Roman *salii*, see Glinister 2011: 111–4, with further bibliography. The existence of a *praesula* from Tusculum (see further below) suggests that these non-Roman *salii* had female counterparts as well.

[21] For the spears of Mars, see Gell. *N.A.* 4.6.1–2; Cass. Dio 44.17.2; Serv. ad *Aen.* 7.603, 8.3.

[22] Glinister 2011: 126. Other suggestions for the identity of the recipient(s) of the sacrifice include the goddesses mentioned in the Salian Hymn (Cirilli 1913: 111), Ops (Liou-Gille 2006), and Nerio, a quality of Mars sometimes identified as his wife (Porte 1989: 104).

[23] Livy uses *adhibere* to describe the children who had been summoned to participate in expiatory rites in 190 BC (*ad id sacrificium adhibiti*, 37.3.6).

[24] Glinister 2011: 124. Varro (*Ling.* 5.85) and Festus (438L) derive the name of the priesthood from their leaping (*ab saliendo*) and dancing (*a saltando*). See also Dion. Hal. *Ant. Rom.* 2.70.4; Ov. *Fast.* 3.387. The *salii* also had a role at the Regifugium on February 24 (Festus 346L), but the text of Festus is too fragmentary to say anything more definitive.

[25] For the dates, see Estienne 2005c. Varro (*Ling.* 7.26–27) quotes the beginning of the hymn as evidence for archaic spelling and Quintilian (*Inst.* 1.6.40) notes that in his day, even the *salii* did not understand the words they sang. The hymn's content is not well understood. Varro (*Ling.* 7.26–27) implies that it mentioned the Camenae, while Festus (3L) records that there were verses in honor of Juno, Minerva, and Janus. Vergil (*Aen.* 8.285–304) suggests that the *salii* sang a hymn in honor of Hercules at the Ara Maxima. Ovid (*Fast.* 3.384) says that the song contained verses in praise of Mamurius Veturius, whom the ancients identified as the craftsman who produced eleven copies of the *ancile* that had fallen from heaven (see also Dion. Hal. *Ant. Rom.* 2.71.2; Plut. *Num.* 13.7). Modern scholars, however, suspect that this is a late addition to the tradition (Bremmer 1993; Estienne 2005c: 86). During the imperial period, the names of the emperors were added, beginning with that of Augustus (Aug. *R.G.* 10; Tac. *Ann.* 2.83).

[26] Festus 334L; *Vir.* 3.3.1. The title *magister* is also attested (Val. Max. 1.1.9).

Dionysius of Halicarnassus adds that the *salii* processed through the city to the Forum, the Capitol, and "many other places, both public and private" (πολλοὺς ἄλλους ἰδίους τε καὶ δημοσίους τόπους, *Ant. Rom.* 2.70.2). The dances were almost certainly associated with the beginning of the campaigning season (marked by the Tubilustrium on March 23) and with its end (celebrated by the Armilustrium on October 19).[27]

What role the *saliae* played in the ritual dances of the *salii* is uncertain. Their martial costume and the existence of a *praesula* from Tusculum suggest that the girls may have danced as well, following the example of their own lead dancer:

D(is) M(anibus) / Flaviae Ver(a)e praesul(a)e / sacerdot(um) Tus-culanor(um) / vix(it) ann(is) VI, me(n)s(ibus) XI, die(bus).. / fecit Fl[avi........]. (*CIL* 6.2177)

To the spirits of Flavia Vera, *praesula*, priestess of the Tusculans. She lived six years, eleven months, [. . .] days. Flavia/us set this up.

The fact that Flavia Vera was only six years old when she died may indicate that the office of *praesula* was primarily honorific during the early imperial period. In fact, the *saliae virgines* may have disappeared from Rome by the age of Augustus—neither Livy nor Dionysius of Halicarnassus mention the priest-esses in their discussions of the *salii*. Flavia Vera's epitaph nonetheless suggests that the priesthood was remembered in parts of Latium.

Even if the *saliae* did not participate in the dance itself, they may have attended the elaborate banquets that followed the processions. In fact, *adhibere* can also mean, "to invite (as a guest), summon (to a feast)."[28] The ancient sources imply that the *salii* feasted in one of the temples of Mars, perhaps the Temple of Mars Gradivus in the Campus Martius, and that the statue of the god was provided with a couch (*pulvinar*) and table as at a *lectisternium*.[29] There is some precedent for mixed gender priestly banquets—the Vestals attended a pontifical banquet in honor of the inauguration of a new *flamen* and *flaminica Martialis* in 69 BC—so it is not impossible to believe that the *saliae* were in-cluded in the festivities celebrated by the *salii*.

Uncomfortable with the traditional interpretation of the Salian dance as a martial ritual, some modern scholars have argued that the activities of the *salii* and *saliae* were initiation rites marking the transition from childhood into adulthood.[30] But it is difficult to understand how a ritual involving such a small

[27] Wissowa 1912: 144, 557; Estienne 2005c: 86. For a different interpretation of the Tubilustrium, see Rüpke 1995: 214–221. For an interesting (if not entirely persuasive) analysis of the meaning of the rite, see also Glinister (2011: 128–132), who suggests that the *salii* were concerned with the fertility of the community (among other things).

[28] *OLD* s.v. *adhibeo* 4.

[29] Hor. *Carm.* 1.37.1–4; Suet. *Claud.* 33.1; Estienne 2005c: 86.

[30] Torelli 1984: 106–115; Versnel 1993: 158, n. 104; Habinek 2005: 17. For a criticism of this view, see Rüpke 1990: 25; Feeney and Katz 2006: 241; Glinister 2011: 119–121.

group of Romans could have functioned as an initiation rite (in contrast to the donning of the *toga virilis* at the Liberalia, for instance). Furthermore, the lengthy tenures of several known *salii* argue against associating their activities with traditional rites of passage. Although it was apparently common for a *salius* to resign his office when he took up another major priesthood or a curule magistracy, Ap. Claudius Pulcher (cos. 143 BC) held the augurate and the Salian priesthood simultaneously.[31] L. Furius Bibaculus "bore the *ancilia*, preceded by his six lictors" (*sex lictoribus praecedentibus arma ancilia tulit*, Val. Max. 1.1.9) during his praetorship in about 219 BC.[32] Valerius Maximus tells us that that he did so at the direction of his father, who was then head of the group (*a patre suo collegii Saliorum magistro iussus*, 1.1.9).[33] Finally, Polybius reveals that P. Cornelius Scipio Africanus (cos. 205, 194 BC) was still a *salius* at age forty-six during the war against Antiochus III in 190 BC, when he was unable to move his camp for thirty days during the celebration of the sacrifices.[34]

The *saliae*, on the other hand, could only have remained in office as long as they were *virgines*. It is possible that they committed to a lengthy period of service; the Vestal Virgins, for instance, served for a minimum of thirty years. It seems more likely, however, that a *salia* resigned her position when she married, as did *camillae*, the young assistants of the curial couples.[35] If membership was fluid, this could explain why we hear so little about them. This variability also means, as Glinister writes, "that at any given moment no *Salia* was likely to have been older than, say, a teenager (unless we assume the office was long-term, like that of the Vestals). Her male counterparts, meanwhile, could range in age from young boys right through to middle-aged or even geriatric men, and, even more tellingly, could include a father and son as colleagues."[36] Such drastic variation in the ages of Salian priests and the possibility of a prolonged tenure in office make it difficult to interpret the priesthood and its rituals as a rite of passage.

The martial character of the Salian rites must be retained and scholarly opinions about the role of women in Roman religion revised accordingly. The *saliae* sacrificed (*sacrificium facere*) on behalf of the Roman people in the *regia*, the site of numerous sacrifices by public priestesses.[37] Their costume and as-

---

[31] Hahm (1963: 81, n. 27), for instance, claims, "it was not permissible to hold the saliate together with a major priesthood." For the priestly career of Claudius, see Plut. *Ti. Gracch.* 4.1; Macrob. *Sat.* 3.14.14; Rüpke 2008: 619–620, No. 1225; Glinister 2011: 120–121. This is the same Claudius who triumphed illegally with the assistance of his Vestal daughter in 143 BC (see chapter 4), an indication that there was some flexibility regarding the regulation that the daughter of a *salius* be exempt from the Vestal order (see chapter 4).

[32] See also Lactant. *Div. inst.* 1.21.47; Brennan 2001; Rüpke 2008: 701, No. 1782; Glinister 2011:121.

[33] Rüpke 2008: 701, No. 1781.

[34] Pol. 21.13.10. See also Livy 37.33.6–7; Rüpke 2008: 642, No. 1372.

[35] Dion. Hal. *Ant. Rom.* 2.22.1, with chapter 2.

[36] Glinister 2011: 121.

[37] For the sacrifice of the Vestals and a *sacerdos publicus* in the shrine of Ops Consiva, see chapter 6. For the *flaminica*'s sacrifice to Jupiter on the *nundinae*, see chapter 1. For the *regina*'s sacrifice to Juno, see chapter 2.

sociation with the *salii* suggests a martial ritual connected to the success of Rome's military operations. The success of the campaigning season was just as important to women as it was to men, and rituals surrounding this important activity consequently involved priestesses as well as priests.

The *saliae* should probably be understood as the female counterparts of the patrician *salii*. As such, they modeled the same pattern of ritual service that we have observed in the archaic priesthoods described in the previous two chapters. There are clear differences, most significantly the fact that the *salii* and the *saliae* were never married to one another. The *saliae* were virgins and may often have been much younger than the *salii*. In fact, like Vestal virginity, discussed more fully in chapter 4, Salian virginity may have performed an ideological function. As intact virgins, the *saliae* symbolized the object of their sacrifices: the inviolability of the city and the strength of its military. Marriage would have interfered with this important goal. Despite their departure from the model set by the priestly couples, however, the *saliae* add to the perception that Roman religion frequently relied upon cooperation between the male and female halves of the same priesthood.

The Priestesses of Fortuna Muliebris

Like the Salian priesthood, the cult of Fortuna Muliebris (Feminine Fortune) associated women with civic life and the security of the city.[38] Our sources for this cult and its priesthood are comparatively rich; Livy, Dionysius of Halicarnassus, and Plutarch provide relatively expansive etiologies.[39] These narratives offer a fascinating window into the construction and interpretation of women's priestly service during the republican period.

According to Roman tradition, the cult of Fortuna Muliebris was founded in 488 BC. The disgraced general Cn. Marcius Coriolanus, who had gone into exile after opposing a distribution of grain to the plebs, was encamped outside the walls of Rome at the head of a Volscian army. When the senate failed to negotiate a peace, Rome's *matronae* persuaded Coriolanus' wife and mother to join them in an embassy (*ingens mulierum agmen*, Livy 2.40.3) to the enemy camp. They were determined, Livy writes, "that since the arms of men could not defend the city, the women should defend it with their prayers and tears" (*quoniam armis viri defendere urbem non possent, mulieres precibus lacrimisque defenderent*, 2.40.2). After some debate, the senate officially sanctioned

[38] Fortuna, the personified goddess of fate and chance, was worshipped under a variety of cult titles as the protector of a range of activities and social groups. For a discussion of the individual cults, see especially Champeaux 1982.

[39] Livy 2.40.1–13; Dion. Hal. *Ant. Rom.* 8.39.1–8.56.4; Plut. *Cor.* 33.1–37.3. For a discussion of the foundation legend and the cult of Fortuna Muliebris at Rome, see Mommsen 1870; Gagé 1963: 48–63; Bonjour 1975; Champeaux 1982: 335–373; Mustakallio 1990; Boëls-Janssen 1993: 376–377; Fantham 2002: 44; Schultz 2006b: 37–44, 143–144.

their mission. The impassioned speech of his mother Veturia, the embraces of his wife Volumnia, and the tears of the entire company of women finally persuaded Coriolanus to withdraw his army from Roman territory.[40] Like the Sabine women before them, the *matronae* protected the city from destructive male violence by reminding Coriolanus of his duty to his family and to the state. The Romans greeted their return, Dionysius tells us, with great joy and "songs of triumph" (παιᾶνας, *Ant. Rom.* 8.55.1).

Following their remarkable "victory," the *matronae* asked for permission to found, with their own money, a temple to Fortuna Muliebris at the fourth milestone on the Via Latina at the place where they had interceded for their country. This request is quite extraordinary. In general, the only Romans permitted to dedicate new temples were magistrates who had been granted permission by the appropriate authority.[41] As Celia Schultz has noted, however, the women may have felt entitled to ask for permission to dedicate a temple because the senate had ratified their embassy to Coriolanus and thereby granted them a quasiofficial status.[42] Having vowed to grant the *matronae* whatever they requested, the senate agreed to establish a temple, but employed public funds for the purpose and delegated the task of the actual foundation to the consul, Proculus Verginius Tricostus Rutilus (cos. 486 BC). The episode thus highlights the opportunities for female participation in public religion alongside some of its limitations.[43] The senate permitted the women to establish a new public cult in honor of their role in resolving a military crisis, but refused to allow them to fund and found the temple themselves.

The senate did allow the women to choose one of their number to serve as the cult's first priestess (ἱέρεια, Dion. Hal. *Ant. Rom.* 8.55.4). They selected Valeria, who had orchestrated the embassy to Coriolanus and the Volscians.[44] Her role as mediator between the *matronae* on the one hand and Veturia and Volumnia on the other translated quite naturally into her role as priestess of Fortuna Muliebris.[45] On December 1, she commemorated the first anniversary of the embassy with a sacrifice on behalf of the people (ὑπὲρ τοῦ δήμου, Dion. Hal. *Ant. Rom.* 8.55.4). The fact that the *matronae* were permitted to elect their own priestess highlights the extent to which women's ritual activities replicated other forms of civic participation. Valeria's election was not unique. In 214 BC, the *matronae* chose Sulpicia, the wife of Q. Fulvius Flaccus (cos. 237, 224, 212, 209 BC), as the most virtuous (*pudicissima*) woman in Rome and granted her the

---

[40] For Veturia's influence over her son, see Champeaux 1982: 344; Hallett 1984: 247–252; Mustakallio 1990: 129–130.

[41] Orlin 1997: 162–167. In the early Republic, the power to authorize temple dedications resided with the senate or the tribunes of the plebs. The plebs later took over this responsibility.

[42] Schultz 2006b: 43–44, 167, n. 74.

[43] For this point, see especially Schultz 2006b: 37–44.

[44] Dion. Hal. *Ant. Rom.* 8.55.4.

[45] As noted by Champeaux 1982: 348.

honor of dedicating the cult statue of Venus Verticordia (Heart-Turner).[46] Admittedly, some would argue that the standard by which the women judged one another—chastity (*castitas*)—undercuts their autonomy.[47]

As we have seen, the senate had insisted upon covering the expenses of the newly founded cult with funds from the public treasury, a move that emphasized its official status. The *matronae*, however, dedicated a second cult statue with money that they themselves had collected.[48] This image reportedly twice told the women that they had made their dedication in accordance with divine will (*rite me, matronae, dedistis riteque dedicastis*, Val. Max. 1.8.4).[49] Although the senators had not initially approved the use of private funds, the double prodigy confirmed the women's right to commemorate their victory with their own money and in accordance with their own wishes. The senate accordingly ordered new annual sacrifices, presumably in honor of the second statue.[50]

Valeria, in her capacity as priestess of Fortuna Muliebris, introduced her own initiative regulating access to the miraculous image:

αἱ δὲ γυναῖκες ἐν ἔθει κατεστήσαντο τῇ τῆς ἱερείας χρησάμεναι γνώμῃ, τῷ ξοάνῳ τούτῳ μήτε στεφάνους ἐπιτιθέναι μήτε χεῖρας προσφέρειν γυναῖκας, ὅσαι δευτέρων ἐπειράθησαν γάμων, τὴν δὲ τιμὴν καὶ θεραπείαν αὐτοῦ πᾶσαν ἀποδεδόσθαι ταῖς νεογάμοις. (Dion. Hal. *Ant. Rom.* 8.56.4)

And the women, having sought the advice of their priestess, established it as a custom that no women who had been married a second time should place fillets (*stephanoi*) on this statue or stretch out their hands to it, but that all the honor and worship paid to it should be entrusted to the newly-married women.

Valeria and the *matronae* restricted certain forms of ritual participation to newly married women (νεογάμοις), more specifically, to newly married *univirae* (one-man women).[51] The ancient sources do not address the issue directly, but it seems reasonable to assume that the priestess of Fortuna Muliebris was required to be a *univira* as well.[52] Valeria's insistence on univirate status reveals that, like the priesthood of the *flaminica Dialis*, the cult of Fortuna Muliebris reinscribed an ideology of gender that privileged women who remained in a

---

[46] Pliny H.N. 7.120–1. Valerius Maximus describes her as the most holy of women (*sanctissima*), and stresses that she surpassed all in chastity (*cunctis castitate praelata est*, 8.15.12).

[47] As stressed by Richlin 2014: 221. For a discussion of women's agency, see the introduction.

[48] In reality, the existence of two cult statues within the temple may indicate that Fortuna Muliebris possessed a dual nature, though modern scholars disagree about the details (see, for example, Gagé 1963: 48–63; Champeaux 1982: 335–373; Boëls-Janssen 1993: 376–377; Mustakallio 1990).

[49] See also Dion. Hal. *Ant. Rom.* 8.56.2–3; Plut. *Cor.* 37.3.

[50] Dion. Hal. *Ant. Rom.* 8.56.4.

[51] For a fuller discussion of *univirae*, see chapter 1.

[52] Champeaux 1982: 348–349; Boëls-Janssen 1993: 376–377; Schultz 2006b: 75. Gagé (1963: 48–63) argues instead that the priestess of Fortuna Muliebris was a virgin.

single marriage throughout their lives.[53] At the same time, the political and military focus of the cult's foundation legend contributes significantly to our understanding of this concept: good *univirae* were expected to act on behalf of their city.

As Schultz has stressed, Fortuna Muliebris was not simply "another deity concerned with feminine matters," at least not as they have been defined in modern scholarship.[54] As wives, mothers, and citizens, *matronae* had an interest in the security and success of Rome and her empire. The ritual sphere provided them with an arena in which to express their civic-mindedness. When the senate failed to reach an agreement with Coriolanus, Rome's *matronae* gathered at the public temples in order to perform supplications and sacrifices.[55] They subsequently formed a procession from the Temple of Jupiter to the house of Veturia, where Valeria emphasized the bonds forged by ritual practice, begging the mother of Coriolanus to "have mercy on women who once shared with you the same sacrifices and rites" (ἐλέησον . . . γυναῖκας κοινωνησάσας ἱερῶν ποτε καὶ ὁσίων, Dion. Hal. *Ant. Rom.* 8.40.3).[56] The extraordinary embassy to Coriolanus was possible because Valeria and her fellow *matronae* routinely cooperated on behalf of the community.[57]

Although the historical veracity of the legend has been called into question, there are reasons to believe that it is not a complete fabrication.[58] At the very least, we should assume that the details of the story made sense to the early imperial audience for whom our sources were writing. Perhaps the women in our written sources are empowered to select Valeria as the first priestess of Fortuna Muliebris because the priesthood was an elected office during the historical period. The dedication of a second cult statue and the privileged role granted to newly married *univirae* presumably reflect historical realities as well. The valorization of the embassy to Coriolanus, moreover, suggests that the cult addressed women as citizens with an interest in the welfare of the city. Each year, the priestess of Fortuna Muliebris commemorated the peaceful victory of the "great army of women" (*ingens mulierum agmen*, Livy 2.40.3) with a public sacrifice. This sacrifice and its etiology furnished a model for all Roman *matronae*; women were not equal to men in the public sphere, but they were capable of ritually and politically significant action.

[53] The cults of Mater Matuta and Pudicitia were also restricted to *univirae*. For a discussion of the evidence, see Champeaux (1982: 352–360), who compares such provisions to the patrician monopoly over certain priesthoods prior to the *lex Ogulnia* of 300 BC.

[54] Schultz 2006b: 38–39.

[55] Dion. Hal. *Ant. Rom.* 8.39.1–2.

[56] As stressed by Mustakallio 1990.

[57] See also Culham 1982 for the suggestion that women utilized contacts developed in the ritual sphere to coordinate their opposition to the *lex Oppia* in 195 BC.

[58] For arguments against the historical validity of the story, see Mommsen 1870: 24; Gagé 1963: 48–63; Champeaux 1982: 342–360; Scheid 1992c: 388–390. For a different view, see Schultz 2006b: 40–41.

Piatrices

Women also routinely participated in the public expiation of prodigies, including especially *supplicationes*, rituals in which men and women visited temples throughout the city to offer prayers and sacrifices on behalf of the civic community.[59] There is even tantalizing evidence for priestesses with expertise in expiatory sacrifices. According to Paul the Deacon, the *piatrix* was a *sacerdos* "accustomed to performing expiations" (*expiare erat solita*, 233L) who was also known by the title *saga* (wise woman).[60] Given that *piatrices* are absent from ancient discussions of public cult, Celia Schultz has suggested that they catered to private individuals, rather than the state.[61] The importance of female worshippers in supplications and other public expiatory activities, however, suggests an official role. A Sibylline oracle preserved by Phlegon of Tralles, for instance, calls for rites to be performed by "sacrificially knowledgeable old women" (ἐπισταμένως θυσίαν γραῖαι, *Mir.* 10.22–3 Diels). As Rebecca Flemming has pointed out, this text may refer to the *piatrices*, who were "experienced in sacred matters" (*perita sacrorum*, Festus (Paulus) 427L).[62] If this interpretation is correct, it suggests that priestesses could participate in public rituals designed to palliate divine anger and to restore order to the civic community.

The *Sacerdotes* and *Antistites* of Bona Dea

In early December 62 BC, P. Clodius Pulcher (tr. pl. 58 BC) disguised himself as a female musician and crept into the house of C. Julius Caesar (cos. 59 BC), where Rome's elite *matronae* had gathered to celebrate the secret rites of Bona Dea (Good Goddess).[63] His presence in the house—the ancient sources allege that he had come for a rendezvous with Caesar's wife Pompeia—vitiated a public sacrifice and ignited a political firestorm. Given the notoriety of the scandal and the elite context of the ritual itself, the December rites of Bona Dea have long obscured other aspects of her cult, including the fact that it supported an impressive range of priestly officials and ancillary staff. Although the evidence for these women is quite fragmentary, it is possible to recover some of their activities and even to identify several priestesses by name.

---

[59] See especially Schultz 2006b: 28–37.
[60] The fragmentary entry in Festus (232–234L) includes two additional alternate titles for the *piatrix*: *simulatrix* and *expiatrix*.
[61] Schultz 2006b: 28.
[62] Flemming 2007: 106–107. For the oracle, see also MacBain 1982: 127–135.
[63] For the scandal, see chapter 6. For Bona Dea and her cult, see especially Piccaluga 1964; Brouwer 1989; Mastrocinque 2014. For a more gendered approach, see also Versnel 1992; Boëls-Janssen 1993: 429–468, 2008: 273–295.

The Romans regarded the title Bona Dea as a descriptive epithet designed to protect the identity of a goddess "whose name it is not right for men to know" (*cuius ne nomen quidem viros scire fas est*, Cic. *Har. resp.* 37).[64] Citing Varro as his source, the late third-century AD Christian writer Lactantius suggests that this prohibition was a sign of respect for the deity's extraordinary *pudicitia* (sexual virtue):[65]

> eandem Varro scribit tantae pudicitiae fuisse, ut nemo illam quoad vixerit praeter suum virum mas viderit nec nomen eius audierit, idcirco illi mulieres in operto sacrificant et Bonam Deam nominant. (*Div. inst.* 1.22.10)

> Varro writes that this same goddess demonstrated such great *pudicitia* that no man except her own husband ever saw her or heard her name while she was living. For this reason, women sacrifice to her in secret and call her Bona Dea.

The name of the Good Goddess and the content of her rites were the property of Rome's women. Despite the taboo against revealing her name, however, Roman antiquarians speculated freely about Bona Dea's true identity. She was sometimes associated with Fauna, who is variously reported as the wife, sister, or daughter of the nature god Faunus.[66] On the authority of the late republican grammarian Gavius Bassus, Lactantius reports that Fauna's name was Fatua and that she foretold women's fates, as her husband Faunus did men's.[67] Sextus Clodius, another of Lactantius' late republican sources, claims that Faunus beat his wife to death with myrtle twigs because she had drunk a jar of wine. Macrobius, on the other hand, tells us that Faunus fell in love with his daughter Fauna and first beat her with a myrtle branch and then plied her with wine when she resisted his sexual advances.[68] The god achieved his aim only after he had turned himself into a snake.

These less than flattering (and seemingly paradoxical) myths presumably grew out of an impulse to explain certain cultic realities, including the prohibition against bringing myrtle into the temple of Bona Dea and the curious practice by which the women called the wine for libations "milk" (*lac*) and its container a "honeypot" (*mellarium*).[69] As Nicole Boëls-Janssen has noted, moreover, one point of correspondence between the otherwise contradictory myths is the fact that Faunus punishes Fauna for her disobedience in both ver-

---

[64] See also Serv. Auct. ad *Aen.* 8.314.

[65] See also Macrob. *Sat.* 1.12.27.

[66] Varro *Ling.* 6.55, 7.36; Plut. *Quaest. Rom.* 20 = *Mor.* 268d–e; Arn. *Adv. Nat.* 1.36; Serv. ad *Aen.* 7.47; Serv. Auct. ad *Aen.* 8.314; Lactant. *Div. inst.* 1.22.9–1.22.11; Justin *Apol.* 43.1.8. For a discussion and evaluation of the Fauna myths, see especially Boëls-Janssen 2008.

[67] Lactant. *Div. inst.* 1.22.9–1.22.11.

[68] Macrob. *Sat.* 1.12.24.

[69] For modern attempts to explain the meaning of the "milk" and "honeypot" within the cult of Bona Dea, see especially Versnel 1992.

sions, which may indicate that the cult of Bona Dea addressed the maintenance of traditional gender hierarchies.[70] According to this interpretation, the myths served an ideological as well as an etiological function.

Other sources suggest that the Romans regarded Bona Dea as a fertility goddess. Visual representations typically show her seated on a throne holding a cornucopia, with a serpent wrapped around her right arm.[71] Citing Cornelius Labeo, the author of several works on Roman religion in the third century AD, Macrobius claims that some equated her with the earth goddess Terra, who was also known as Maia or Mater Magna (Great Mother):

> adfirmant quidam, quibus Cornelius Labeo consentit, hanc Maiam cui mense Maio res divina celebratur terram esse, hoc adeptam nomen a magnitudine, sicut et Mater Magna in sacris vocatur, adsertionemque aestimationis suae etiam hinc colligunt quod sus praegnans ei mactatur, quae hostia propria est terrae . . . auctor est Cornelius Labeo huic Maiae, id est terrae, aedem Kalendis Maiis dedicatam sub nomine Bonae Deae et eandem esse Bonam Deam et terram ex ipso ritu occultiore sacrorum doceri posse confirmat: hanc eandem Bonam Faunamque, Opem et Fatuam pontificum libris indigitari. (Macr. *Sat.* 1.12.20–21)

> Some assert, and Cornelius Labeo is in agreement with them, that this Maia, who is honored with sacrifices in May, is Terra, and that she obtained this name from her magnitude, just as she is also called "Great Mother" (Mater Magna) in her rites. They also adduce as evidence for this claim the fact that a pregnant sow is sacrificed to her, which is a victim appropriate to the earth . . . Cornelius Labeo agrees that a temple was dedicated to this Maia (that is, Terra) under the name of Bona Dea on the Kalends of May, and he maintains that an exceptionally secretive rite of her cult demonstrates that she is the same as Bona Dea and Terra. This same goddess is invoked as Bona Dea, Fauna, Ops, and Fatua in the books of the *pontifices*.

The equation of Bona Dea with Terra and Maia presumably represents an antiquarian attempt at systemization.[72] The fact that the *dies natalis* (foundation day) of Bona Dea's Aventine temple coincided with a feast day sacred to Maia may have provided the initial impetus for their identification. It is unlikely, however, that the three deities were ever fully equated with one another, at least on the level of ritual practice.[73] Maia received a sacrifice from the *flamen Vulcanalis* on the Kalends of May, which may indicate that she was regarded as the

[70] Boëls-Janssen 2008: 287–290.
[71] Brouwer 1989: xxi.
[72] Brouwer (1989: 354) suggests that the identification of Terra and Maia with Bona Dea may have originated with Varro.
[73] In book 5 of the *Fasti*, for example, Ovid mentions both Maia and Bona Dea without positing a close relationship between them.

wife of Vulcan.[74] The rites of Bona Dea celebrated on the same day, on the other hand, were strictly off limits to men and under the control of a female *sacerdos publica* (public priest).

Perhaps the most intriguing proper name proposed by our antiquarian sources is preserved in Paul's epitome of the lexicon of Festus, where we learn that she was called Damia and her priestess the *damiatrix*:

> damium sacrificium quod fiebat in operto in honore Deae Bonae; dictum a contrarietate quod minime esset δαμόσιον, id est publicum. Dea quoque ipsa Damia et sacerdos eius damiatrix appellabatur. (60L)

> The *damium* was a sacrifice that took place in secrecy in honor of Bona Dea; it was thus named because of its opposite meaning, as it was least of all public. Also the goddess herself was called Damia and her priestess the *damiatrix*.

The proper name Damia belonged to a Greek goddess worshipped throughout southern Italy, including at Tarentum, where there was a festival in her honor called the Dameia. Indeed, some scholars have hypothesized that the cult of Damia was imported to Rome following the capture of Tarentum in 272 BC and merged with the cult of Bona Dea.[75] We can only be certain that the *damiatrix* offered a sacrifice known as the *damium* in secret (*in operto*) and in the company of Roman women (*mulieres*).[76] Whether these women believed that they were honoring Bona Dea or Damia, or some combination of the two, is an open question.

The principal sanctuary of Bona Dea was located on the Aventine below the rock (*saxum*) where Remus was supposed to have established his augural station during the infamous contest with Romulus.[77] At least one modern scholar has argued that a temple was standing there by the fifth century BC, but most push its foundation into the late second century BC on the authority of Ovid's *Fasti*.[78] The poet's evidence on this point, however, is even more problematic than usual:

> templa patres illic oculos exosa viriles
>   leniter acclini constituere iugo.
> dedicat haec veteris Crassorum nominis heres,
>   virgineo nullum corpore passa virum:

---

[74] Macrob. *Sat.* 1.12.18.

[75] Wissowa 1912: 216–217; Fowler 1899: 105. Against this view, see Latte 1960: 228–231; Brouwer 1989: 238–239.

[76] Festus (Paulus) 60L; Plac. *Gloss.* 59 (Pirie and Lindsay).

[77] For the *aedes Bonae Deae Subsaxanae* (*Not. Cur.* Reg. 12), see Platner and Ashby 1929: 85; Brouwer 1989: 400–402; Richardson 1992: 59–60; Ziolkowski 1992: 19–21; Chioffi 1993.

[78] For a date in the fifth century BC, see Merlin 1906: 171–177. For a date in the late second century BC, see Latte 1960: 229, n. 13; Ziolkowski 1992: 19–21; Herbert-Brown 1994: 131–145. Richardson (1992: 60) suggests that the *aedes* was very ancient but does not offer a date.

Livia restituit, ne non imitata maritum
    esset et ex omni parte secuta suum. (5.152–158)[79]

There, on the gently sloping hillside, the fathers established the temple
that hates the eyes of men. A descendant of the ancient name of the
Crassi dedicated it, who with her virgin body had submitted to no man.
Livia restored it so that she might imitate her husband and follow him in
every way.

According to Ovid, the senate called for the establishment of a temple to Bona
Dea but delegated responsibility for the actual dedication to a "virgin" (*virgo*),
since, he notes, the sanctuary "hates the eyes of males" (*oculos exosa viriles*).
The virgin in question can be none other than the Vestal Licinia, the daughter
of C. Licinius Crassus (tr. pl. 145 BC), who dedicated an altar (*ara*), a shrine
(*aedicula*), and a ritual couch (*pulvinar*) beneath the rock (*sub saxo*) in 123
BC.[80] Ovid equates this dedication with the original foundation of the temple
and would thus have us believe that there was no temple of Bona Dea on the
Aventine until the late second century BC.

There are several obstacles to accepting Ovid's claim. First, Cicero describes the site where Licinia erected her shrine as a public place (*locus publicus, Dom.* 136) and a sacred space (*loco augusto, Dom.* 137), implying that
there was a temple standing on the Aventine prior to her dedication. Second,
he reveals that Licinia acted on her own initiative. In fact, on the advice of
the pontifical college, the senate ultimately declared the dedication invalid because Licinia had not obtained the permission of the Roman people.[81] Cicero's
De domo sua, therefore, directly contradicts the view that Bona Dea had no
temple on the Aventine prior to 123 BC. It likewise calls into question the hypothesis that the temple was never an *aedes publica* (public temple), but rather
an embellishment of Licinia's original shrine and, therefore, a *sacrum priva-
tum* (private dedication).[82] The interest taken by the senate and the *pontifices*
suggests that we are dealing with a sanctuary belonging to the official public
religion.[83]

---

[79] Some editors read *Clausorum* in place of *Crassorum* in line 155 and thus argue that the dedicator
was a Claudia. This reading is a late interpolation in the manuscript tradition, however, and it seems
better to retain *Crassorum* (see Alton, et al. 1973: 150).

[80] Cic. *Dom.* 136. For a fuller discussion of Licinia's dedication, see chapter 7.

[81] Cic. *Dom.* 127. Licinia had evidently violated the *lex Papiria*, which required prior authorization by
the plebs for the dedication of any shrine (Cic. *Dom.* 127; Ziolkowski 1992: 220–234; Orlin 1997: 166–
171). Herbert-Brown (1994: 138–145, followed by Johnson 1997: 409) suggests that Licinia's dedication
was declared invalid following her conviction on a charge of *incestum* and subsequent execution in 113
BC. Cicero (*Dom.* 136), however, clearly indicates that the shrine was removed because Licinia had not
received the proper authority to make the dedication.

[82] As suggested by Latte 1960: 229, n. 3; Ziolkowski 1992: 19–21; Herbert-Brown 1994: 131–145. In
support of this position, Ziolkowski (1992: 20) claims that, "worship of Bona Dea was exclusively feminine." As we have seen, however, gender exclusivity in no way disqualifies a rite, let alone an entire cult,
from public status.

[83] See Brouwer 1989: 400.

If there was a public temple of Bona Dea standing on the Aventine in 123 BC, then Ovid has either confused or deliberately conflated the original foundation with Licinia's failed dedication. The latter possibility is more likely in light of the poet's disingenuous comments about the Vestal's chastity: "*virgineo nullum corpore passa virum*" (who with her virgin body had submitted to no man, *Fast*. 5.156). In 114 BC, Licinia was accused of having multiple lovers and convicted at one of the most notorious *incestum* (unchastity) trials in the order's history.[84] The decision to focus on Licinia cast Livia, Bona Dea's most recent patron, in a less flattering light. As Patricia Johnson has argued, this "historical revisionism" allowed Ovid to undercut the effect of Livia's patronage of a goddess known for her extraordinary *pudicitia*.[85] Ovid had an ulterior motive for suggesting that Licinia dedicated the original temple, and his testimony for the date of its foundation cannot be accepted.

In fact, the Romans themselves believed that the Aventine temple of Bona Dea was very ancient. In a poem explaining the origins of the Ara Maxima, Propertius describes how Hercules happened upon the enclosed sanctuary (*loca clausa*) following his victory over the monster Cacus.[86] Within the sacred grove young girls could be heard celebrating a festival in the company of a priestess.[87] Hercules, Propertius continues, knocked on the door (*foris*) of the sanctuary and asked to be allowed to drink from the stream within. The elderly priestess, however, cautioned him not to defile the sanctuary or its secret rites:[88]

> at talibus alma sacerdos
> puniceo canas stamine vincta comas:
> "parce oculis, hospes, lucoque abscede verendo;
> cede agedum et tuta limina linque fuga.
> interdicta viris metuenda lege piatur
> quae se summota vindicat ara casa" (Prop. 4.9.51–56).

But the kindly priestess (*sacerdos*) her white hair bound with a purple band, replied, "Spare your eyes, stranger, and leave this revered grove. Come now, depart, leave this threshold in safe flight. The altar that protects itself in this hidden shrine is forbidden to men, and avenges its pollution by a dreadful law."

Enraged at her refusal to admit him and undeterred by her stern warning, Hercules broke down the door and drained the spring dry. The hero pledged to ban all women from worshipping at the Ara Maxima in retaliation for their refusal

---

[84] Livy *Per*. 63; Plut. *Quaest. Rom*. 83 = *Mor*. 283f–284c; Cass. Dio 26, fr. 87.3; Oros. 5.15.22; Macrob. *Sat*. 1.10.5–6 (= Fenestella fr. 11 Peter); Ascon. 45–46C; Obseq. 37; Zon. 7.8.

[85] Johnson 1997: 409.

[86] Prop. 4.9.21–30.

[87] Piccaluga (1964) suggests that the *puellae* were celebrating an initiation rite, but Propertius may not have had a specific festival in mind (Boëls-Janssen 2008: 275–276).

[88] For the exclusion of men from Bona Dea's sanctuary, see also Tib. 1.6.21–4; Prop. 4.9.53–60; Ov. *Ars. am*. 3.637–638, *Fast*. 5.153; Festus 348–350L; Lactant. *Div. inst*. 3.20.3–4; Macrob. *Sat*. 1.12.26.

to admit him to the sanctuary of Bona Dea. The proximity of the Ara Maxima to the sanctuary of Bona Dea evidently gave rise to an interrelated etiology.[89] It is striking, however, that the Romans regarded Bona Dea and her shrine as the older cult.[90] The all-male rites at the Ara Maxima were conceptualized as a reaction to the women-only rites of Bona Dea at her nearby altar, rather than as a natural state of affairs.

In addition to the antiquity and gender exclusivity of the temple, another important detail to emerge from this poem is the fact that the sanctuary was surrounded by an enclosure wall. Archaeological evidence from outside Rome, including from the sanctuary of Bona Dea at Ostia, confirms that this arrangement was customary.[91] The wall presumably protected the secret rites from exposure. Its existence suggests, moreover, that the priestess and her female staff exercised absolute control over a sanctuary from which the *pontifex maximus* himself was excluded.

According to Macrobius, the *dies natalis* (foundation day) of the Aventine temple was celebrated on May 1.[92] The festival included the sacrifice of a pregnant sow (*sus pregnans*), perhaps by the *sacerdos*, to encourage the earth to bear good fruit.[93] The surviving *fasti* (ritual calendars) do not record the festival, though this does not prove that it was not a public rite.[94] As we have seen, Cicero describes the temple as a public place (*locus publicus, Dom.* 136), which implies a public cult as well.

In addition to the literary evidence, epigraphic sources record the existence of priestesses of Bona Dea. As is often the case, much of this evidence comes from the imperial period, and it is uncertain to what extent it reflects the operation of the cult under the Republic. A funerary inscription from the third or fourth century AD mentions a *sacerdos Bonae Deae* and her protégée or foster child (*alumna*):

> D(is) M(anibus) Aelia Nice / sacerdos Bon(a)e Deae / se biva conparavit sibi et / alumn(a)e suae Cl(audiae) Nice et / Ael(iae) Thalasse et Ael(iae) Serapiae et / Cl(audiae) F(r)tunat(a)e et Lucciae Felicitati et / Valerio Menandro et . . . (*CIL* 6.2236)

---

[89] As Beard, North, and Price (1998: 174) write, "when the antiquarians, historians and poets of the late Republic and early empire speculated on the myth and ritual of this particular cult site at the Ara Maxima, more was involved than the simple physical *location* of the cult. In this case, ideas of *place* lead straight to ideas of demarcation of *gender*, that is, to rival claims about the religious *place* of women. Stories of Rome *situated* the Roman system of cultural norms and practices." (Emphasis in original.) For full discussion (and varying interpretations) of this poem as a commentary on Roman constructions of gender, see Cyrino 1998; Janan 1998; Lindheim 1998; Staples 1998: 13–36; Welch 2005: 112–132.

[90] Propertius did not invent this myth; a quotation in Macrobius (*Sat.* 1.12.27–28) shows that Varro provided essentially the same story.

[91] For the evidence, see Brouwer 1989: 407–412.

[92] Macrob. *Sat.* 1.12.20.

[93] Macrob. *Sat.* 1.12.20.

[94] As Scheid (2003: 55) emphasizes, other important public festivals, including the October Horse, are absent from the extant calendars as well. For a more pessimistic view, see Brouwer 1989: 371–372.

> To the souls of the departed. Aelia Nice, priestess of Bona Dea, has built this (tomb?) when still alive, for herself, for her pupil Claudia Nice, for Aelia Thalasse and Aelia Serapia, for Claudia Fortunata, Luccia Felicitas, Valerius Menander, and . . . [95]

The names of the dedicatees, which combine Latin *nomina* with mostly Greek *cognomina,* are indicative of freed status.[96] Even so, the title *sacerdos Bonae Deae* suggests that Aelia Nice served at an official sanctuary, either on the Aventine or elsewhere in the city.[97] Religious officials affiliated with private voluntary associations (*collegia*) did not bear the title *sacerdos,* but were known instead as *magistrae* (officials).[98] The term *alumna* is more problematic, but may indicate that Claudia Nice was Aelia Nice's apprentice.[99]

Perhaps a role for Aelia Nice and Philematio, a freedwoman of Livia who also bore the title *sacerdos Bonae Deae,* can be found in the goddess's healing cult.[100] Although this aspect of her identity is not much discussed in the literary sources, Bona Dea is associated with Hygieia, the Greek healing goddess, in an inscription from a now lost statuette from Rome.[101] She is addressed as Bona Dea Oclata (= Oculata) in an inscription from the republican period, perhaps on account of her role as a healer of eye diseases.[102] In a votive from the late first century BC a public slave by the name of Felix Asinianus thanks the goddess for restoring his vision. Given up by professional physicians, this grateful patient recovered his sight through the aid of the goddess and a ten-month course of treatment:

> Felix publicus / Asinianus pontific(um) / Bonae deae agresti Felicu(la) / votum solvit iunicem alba(m) / libens animo ob luminibus / restitutes derelictus a medicis post / menses decem bineficio dominaes medicinis sanatus per / eam restituta omnia ministerio Canniae Fortunatae. (*CIL* 6.68 = *ILS* 3513)

> Felix Asinianus, public slave of the *pontifices,* fulfilled his vow to Bona Dea Agrestis Felicula, willingly and with good cause, (sacrificing) a white heifer on account of his eyesight having been restored. Abandoned by doctors, he recovered after ten months by taking medicines, by the aid of

---

[95] Translated by Brouwer 1989: 37.
[96] Brouwer 1989: 377.
[97] Brouwer 1989: 371.
[98] Brouwer 1989: 371.
[99] Brouwer 1989: 377; Takács 2008: 106–107.
[100] *CIL* 6.2240.
[101] *CIL* 6.72 = *ILS* 3514, with Latte 1960: 228–231.
[102] *CIL* 6.75 = *ILS* 3508, with Brouwer 1989: 27. This inscription, along with another slightly later dedication (*CIL* 6.36.766), was found in the garden of S. Maria dell'Orto in Trastevere, perhaps indicating that there was a small shrine to Bona Dea Oclata in this area during the late republican period (as suggested by Brouwer 1989: 304).

the Mistress. Through her, all things were restored during Cannia Fortunata's term in office.[103]

While credit belongs to Bona Dea above all, Felix also commemorates the service (*ministerio*) of Cannia Fortunata, who presumably supplied the medicines that restored his sight. The votive fails to record a title for Cannia Fortunata, but the term *ministerium*, which can refer to the activities of a wide variety of religious officials, suggests that she held an official position within the healing cult.[104] In fact, we may be able to associate her with the *antistites* who managed a pharmacy within the Temple of Bona Dea:

> quidam Medeam putant, quod in aede eius omne genus herbarum sit ex quibus antistites dant plerumque medicinas, et quod templum eius virum introire non liceat propter iniuriam quam ab ingrato viro Iasone perpessa est. (Macrob. *Sat.* 1.12.26)

> Some think that she [i.e., Bona Dea] is Medea, because all kinds of herbs are found in her temple, and the *antistites* regularly dispense medicines that they have produced from these herbs, and because men are not permitted to enter her temple on account of the injury she suffered from her ungrateful husband Jason.

It is unclear whether Macrobius means the *aedes* on the Aventine or a separate shrine located elsewhere in the city. Clusters of inscribed dedications to Bona Dea suggest that there may have been secondary sanctuaries on the Caelian, in the Regio Transtiberina (modern Trastevere), and near the third milestone on the Via Ostiensis.[105] It is possible that these shrines were accessible to male worshippers like Felix Asinianus, who would have been excluded from the Aventine temple. In fact, of the thirty-one inscribed dedications to Bona Dea from the city of Rome, thirteen were made by men and six were made by men and women together.[106] These dedications reveal that the cult did not exclude men entirely, even though it forbade their participation at particular times and in particular places. In her capacity as a healing deity, Bona Dea and her priestesses welcomed worshippers of either sex.

The meaning of the title *antistes* is also uncertain.[107] It appears occasionally as a synonym for *sacerdos* in the written sources.[108] Other evidence suggests that

---

[103] I have modified Brouwer's (1989: 53) translation only slightly. For a discussion of the difficulties involved in dating the inscription, see Brouwer 1989: 53–54.

[104] See, for example, the citations in *TLL* s.v. *ministerium*.

[105] For the cult center on the Caelian Hill, see Brouwer 1989: 302. For the two shrines in the Transtiberina, see Brouwer 1989: 303–304.

[106] Brouwer 1989: 258; Takács 2008: 102–109.

[107] For a discussion of the evidence, see Wissowa 1912: 370, n. 3, 483; Gaspar 2012: 48–49; *TLL* s.v. *antistes*.

[108] See, for example, Plaut. *Rud.* 624 (*antistita* for *sacerdos Veneris*); Livy 1.20.3 (*antistites* for *virgines Vestales*); Val. Max. 1.1.1 (*antistes* for *sacerdos Cereris*).

the term usually referred to officials who performed nonsacrificial functions, such as the overseer of a temple or—in the case of the healing cult of Bona Dea—a priestess skilled in the art of pharmacology and medical botany.[109] Cannia Fortunata may have been an *antistes* herself, or she may have served as an assistant (*ministra*) to the *antistites* who supervised the temple pharmacy. Epigraphic evidence suggests that the temple staff provided essential services, interacting with male and female worshippers on a regular basis. A detailed picture of their training and methods is impossible, of course, but one feature to emerge from this discussion is simply the fact that they existed.

The Roman cult of Bona Dea incorporated a heterogeneous collection of rites, worshippers, and priestly officials. At her secretive December rites, the Vestal Virgins sacrificed a sow (*porca*) on behalf of the Roman people (*pro populo*) in the company of elite *matronae*.[110] The *damiatrix* also performed a secret sacrifice. The *sacerdos* mentioned by Propertius presumably had a ritual program as well, perhaps including the sacrifices on the *dies natalis* of the Aventine temple. These rites addressed the welfare (*salus*) of the city and the fertility of the flocks and fields. Other priestesses affiliated with the cult of Bona Dea, some with freed status, performed an unspecified ritual program. At least some of these women saw to the health (*salus*) of individual citizens, extending the reach of Rome's priestesses into yet another sphere of ritual activity.

The *Sacerdotes* of Liber and Bacchus

Our written sources mention the existence of priestesses of Liber, an Italic god of wine and a member of the Aventine triad of Ceres, Liber, and Libera.[111] According to Varro, elderly women sacrificed to Liber for a fee during the Liberalia on March 17, when young men put aside the *toga praetexta* (purple-bordered toga), and took up the *toga virilis* of the adult man:

> Liberalia dicta, quod per totum oppidum eo die sedent <ut> sacerdotes Liberi anus hedera coronatae cum libis et foculo pro emptore sacrificantes. (Varro *Ling.* 6.14)

> It is called the Liberalia because on that day old women wearing ivy wreaths on their heads sit in all parts of the town as priestesses of Liber, with cakes and a small portable stove, on which they offer the cakes on behalf of any purchaser.

---

[109] Cicero (*Verr.* 2.4.99), for instance, distinguishes between *sacerdotes* and "*antistites* of the temple" (*fani antistitae*) at the Temple of Ceres in Catina (modern Catania) in Sicily.

[110] Cic. *Har. resp.* 12, *Att.* 1.13.3, with chapter 6.

[111] For Liber and his cult, see especially Bruhl 1953. See also Holland 2011 for an interesting discussion of the probable relationship between Ceres, Liber, and Libera.

It is unclear whether or not these sacrifices were connected to the donning of the *toga virilis*. Perhaps fathers and sons purchased a *libum* (sacrificial cake) on their way to the Forum. The phrase *pro emptore* (on behalf of a purchaser) certainly suggests that the ritual was private in nature. Even so, it seems unnecessary to assume that the women were only "claiming to be priestesses."[112] A first-century BC inscription from Aquinum records a *sacerdos Liberi publica* (public priestess of Liber), at the very least confirming that women in Latium could serve Liber in an official capacity.[113]

Ovid, our only other source for priestesses of Liber, connects their sacrifices to Liber's discovery of honey and to the offering of *liba*, the sacrificial cakes that bore his name: "Father Liber enjoys honey, and rightly do we give to its discoverer the shining honey, poured over a warm cake" (*melle pater fruitur, liboque infusa calenti / iure repertori splendida mella damus*, *Fast.* 3.761–762).[114] What is most striking about Ovid's interpretation of the festival, however, is his attempt to account for the gender of the *sacerdotes Liberi*. Building upon Liber's assimilation with Bacchus, the Latin Dionysus, Ovid highlights that god's well-known association with women:

> femina cur praesit, non est rationis operatae:
>   femineos thyrso concitat ille choros.
> cur anus hoc faciat, quaeris? vinosior aetas
>   haec erat et gravidae munera vitis amat.
> cur hedera cincta est? hedera est gratissima Baccho . . . (*Fast.* 3.763–768)

> The reason why a woman presides is not a secret: he [i.e., Bacchus] stirs bands of female worshippers with his *thyrsus*. Why does an old woman offer this sacrifice, you ask? That age is fonder of wine and loves the gifts of the heavy vine. Why is she wreathed with ivy? Ivy is dearest to Bacchus . . .

Ovid's explanation for the gender of the priestesses resorts to common stereotypes regarding women, especially older women, and the consumption of wine. Ironically, however, none of the ancient sources claim that the *sacerdotes* poured libations of wine at the Liberalia. Instead, they offered sacrificial cakes (*liba*) on portable hearths (*foculi*), objects associated with the positive, nurturing role of women within the household.

Ovid is surely correct, however, to stress the close association between female worshippers and Liber/Bacchus. Greco-Roman myth and ritual practice

---

[112] Prescendi 2005: 486. Edlund-Berry (1994: 29–30) and Schultz (2006b: 7, 79) hold out the possibility that the *sacerdotes* were public officials.

[113] *CIL* 10.5322 = *ILS* 3353, with Gaspar 2012: 86.

[114] The etymological link between Liber and *libum* was popular, even if false (Bruhl 1953: 15–16). Ovid also alludes to the more popular association between Liber and *liber* (free) when he calls the *toga virilis* the "free toga" (*toga libera*, *Fast.* 3.771).

assigned a prominent role to women in the wine god's cult. From the frenzied maenads of Euripides' *Bacchae* to the enigmatic priestesses at the Liberalia, the presence of women dominates the Bacchic tradition. In fact, female *sacerdotes* were at the center of one of the most infamous episodes in Roman history: the violent suppression of the Bacchanalian cult by the senate and consuls in 186 BC.[115] The scandal and its aftermath provide a fascinating case study of Roman efforts to define priestly roles according to gender.[116] For this reason, the episode deserves our attention, even though the cult in question was not publicly funded.

Livy, our primary narrative source for the Bacchanalian affair, suggests that the senate was particularly outraged by reports that members of the cult were forcing new initiates to engage in *stuprum* (illicit sexual intercourse).[117] He traces this shocking development to Paculla Annia, a Campanian *sacerdos* who first initiated men into the cult of Bacchus.[118] Previously, Livy tells us, the initiation rites had been restricted to women, who selected *matronae* to act as priestesses in turn (*sacerdotes in vicem matronas creari solitas*, Livy 39.13.8). Accusations of corruption, debauchery, and even murder soon followed Paculla Annia's innovations. The senate acted swiftly to restrict the celebration of the cult and imprisoned or executed about seven thousand people.[119]

Our only other source for this episode, an inscription found at Tiriolo in Calabria (ancient Bruttium), confirms that the senate imposed severe and wide-ranging limitations on Bacchic worship, though it casts doubt on certain aspects of Livy's sensationalized narrative.[120] The so-called *senatus consultum de Bacchanalibus* preserves a letter drawn up at a meeting of the senate on the Nones of October 186 BC in the Temple of Bellona with both consuls presiding. Addressed to the allies (*foideratei*), it outlines various decisions made by the senate about the Bacchic initiation cult, including specific instructions about how the text was to be publicized and enforced. Most significantly, the letter shows that the senate sought to regulate certain forms of Bacchic worship in Rome and Italy, rather than to eradicate the initiation cult entirely. While some

---

[115] The bibliography on this subject is enormous. For a detailed treatment of the episode with extensive bibliography, see Pailler 1988.

[116] For the importance of gender in the Bacchic scandal, see especially Cancik-Lindemaier 1996a; Flower 2002a; Schultz 2006b: 82–92.

[117] Livy devotes twelves chapters to the scandal (39.8.1–19.7). For accusations of debauchery and *stuprum*, see especially 39.8.7–8, 39.10.6–9, 39.13.10–14, 39.15.9–14.

[118] Livy 39.13.9.

[119] Livy 39.14.3–10, 39.17.1–7. Although Livy claims that Postumius "discovered" the Bacchic cult in 186 BC, worship of Dionysus was widespread in Italy, particularly in southern Italy and Campania, from an early period (see, for example, Jeanmaire 1951; Bruhl 1953; Nilsson 1957; North 1979). Furthermore, as Livy himself points out, the consuls were assigned the task of suppressing the "domestic conspiracy" (*intestinae coniurationis*, 39.8.1) at the beginning of the year while other business was put on hold, which suggests that the senate had decided to take the situation seriously even before the new consuls took office (Flower 2002a: 82).

[120] *CIL* 1².581 = *ILS* 18 = *ILLRP* 511. For a text and translation of this inscription, see Flower 2002a: 93–96.

practices were subject to an absolute ban, including the performance of rituals in secret (*in [o]quoltod*, 14), exceptions were possible in most cases. When considered as a group, the rulings target two main areas of concern: the structure of the cult groups and the role of men within them.

According to the senate's letter, no man, whether citizen (*ceivis Romanus*), Latin (*nominus Latini*), or ally (*socium*), was permitted to enter a meeting of Bacchic women (*Bacae*) without the authorization of the urban praetor and the senate (7–9).[121] An additional ruling, moreover, emphasizes that mixed cult groups of men and women could include no more than two men and three women. Larger mixed-gender groups were required to obtain permission to meet from the urban praetor and the senate (19–22). Despite Livy's preoccupation with allegations of *stuprum*, the *senatus consultum de Bacchanalibus* reveals that mixed-gender groups were allowed under certain conditions. Even so, the senate evidently assumed that most cult groups would be composed entirely of women. The letter places no restriction on the size of women-only cult groups, allowing them to meet in public (*in poplicod*) or in private (*in preivatod*), provided that they obtain the consent of the urban praetor and the senate (15–16).

The letter also regulates the assignment of priesthoods and other leadership positions within the Bacchic initiation cult:

> sacerdos nequis vir eset; magister neque vir neque mulier quisquam eset; / neve pecuniam quisquam eorum comoine[m h]abuise ve[l]et; neve magistratum, / neve pro magistratu[d], neque virum [neque mul]ierem quiquam fecise velet. (10–12)

> Let no man be a *sacerdos*, let no man or woman be an official (*magister*), let none of them be willing to have money in a common fund, let no one be willing to appoint either a man or a woman as an official (*magister*) or an acting official (*promagister*).

The senate banned men from any leadership role within the cult of Bacchus, whether as *sacerdos*, *magister* or *promagister*, without the possibility of an exception. It also prohibited members of the cult from appointing women as *magistrae* or *promagistrae*. The absolute ban on *magistri/magistrae* and *promagistri/promagistrae* was almost certainly motivated by a fear that the cult groups were organizing themselves along the lines of *collegia* (voluntary associations). This ruling should be taken together with the provisions banning oaths, contracts, and the maintenance of common funds.[122] Fearful of potentially seditious activity, the senate prohibited all organizational structures that endowed the initiation cult with the formality of a *collegium*.

While the senate's letter prohibits men from serving as *sacerdotes*, it presumes that women will continue to serve in this capacity, presiding over cult groups

---

[121] For the various civic statuses outlined in the letter, see Sherwin-White 1973.
[122] For a discussion of this point, see especially, Gruen 1990: 76; Takács 2000; Flower 2002a: 89.

composed entirely of women as well as those including men and women together. Gender appears as an important factor in determining access to religious office, though in this case it is used to deny men official positions in cults where female priests were the norm. Indeed, the *senatus consultum de Bacchanalibus* appears to support Livy's assertion that prior to the reforms of Paculla Annia, members of the Bacchic initiation cult elected *matronae* to serve as *sacerdotes*. The interpretation offered here challenges the notion that the senate suppressed the Bacchanalian cult in order to limit the growing influence of women in Roman society.[123] Far from providing an example of the systematic marginalization of women in the ritual sphere, the Bacchanalian affair reveals that that the senate affirmed priestly roles for women, even granting them authority over male initiates.

The *Sacerdotes* of Magna Mater

The senate's efforts to regulate the Bacchanalian cult in Italy notwithstanding, the Romans were known, even in the ancient world, for their habit of importing foreign cults and, on occasion, foreign priests to go along with them.[124] Among the antiquarians, foreign practices that had found a home in the city were known collectively as *sacra peregrina* ("foreign rites").[125] As Eric Orlin has shown, however, the incorporation of cults from alien communities was more complex than this straightforward categorization allows.[126] Some foreign deities were thoroughly naturalized. The cult of Venus Erycina, for instance, a goddess from Mt. Eryx in Sicily who received a temple on the Capitoline Hill in 215 BC, was stripped of its Punic elements and reshaped to conform to traditional Roman practice.[127] Other cults remained ideologically "foreign" even after they had been formally consecrated as public rites. The cult of the Magna Mater, which employed foreign priests and priestesses to oversee her traditional rites as well as aediles to organize the quintessentially Roman *ludi Megalenses* (Megalesian Games), offers a case in point. Decisions about when and how to incorporate foreign cults allowed the Romans to craft an ideology

---

[123] According to Scheid (1992c: 393), for example, "The (real or alleged) role of women in the scandal of 186 BCE and the reaffirmation of the authority of fathers, husbands, and guardians point to a larger problem that Rome had to face since the end of the third century: matrons." For a summary of earlier views, see Paillier 1988: 523–596.

[124] For a recent discussion of this topic, see Orlin 2010.

[125] Festus 268L: *peregrina sacra appellantur, quae aut evocatis dis in oppugnandis urbibus Romam sunt coacta aut quae ob quasdam religiones per pacem sunt petita, ut ex Phrygia Matris Magnae, ex Graecia Cereris, Epidauro Aesculapi, quae coluntur eorum more, a quibus sunt accepta* (Those rites are called foreign that have been led to Rome after the gods were "evoked" at a time when their cities were under siege, or which were sought on account of various religious motivations during peacetime, such as those of the Magna Mater from Phrygia, of Ceres from Greece, and of Aesculapius from Epidaurus, which are conducted according to the custom of those from whom they were received). For this translation and a discussion of the passage, see Orlin 2002: 3–4.

[126] Orlin 2002: 3–4.

[127] Orlin 2010: 71–76.

of "Romanness" even as they continued to practice the openness that defined the Roman approach to expansion.[128] This self-conscious manipulation of ritual practice also allows us to analyze how the Romans viewed priestly service, and the extent to which they were willing to accept new female religious practitioners into the existing ritual system.

In 204 BC, following a consultation of the Sibylline Books, the Romans brought Magna Mater (Cybele) to Rome from Asia Minor with the help of King Attalus of Pergamum.[129] There is some debate regarding the precise origins of the cult, with the majority of the written sources reporting that the Romans obtained the goddess from Pessinus in Anatolia.[130] Material evidence from her sanctuary in Rome and her official cult title, "Mater Deum Magna Idaea" (Great Idaean Mother of the Gods), on the other hand, suggests the Pergamene sanctuary at Mount Ida as a more likely source for the Roman cult.[131] The Romans received the goddess (in the shape of an aniconic black stone) with great fanfare. According to Livy, the leading matrons of the city (*matronae primores civitatis*, 29.14.10) took turns carrying the goddess from the port to the Palatine, where her image was installed in the Temple of Victoria until a new sanctuary could be built nearby.[132]

The cult of Magna Mater was formally adopted as an official public cult under the auspices of the Sibylline Books and the appropriate civic authorities. Within the first decade of her arrival, the Romans established a specifically Roman festival in her honor, the *ludi Megalenses*, which were inaugurated in 194 BC with a performance of Plautus' *Pseudolus*.[133] In spite of her enthusiastic welcome, however, certain aspects of Magna Mater's worship were clearly defined as non-Roman and entrusted to the foreign priests and priestesses imported along with the cult.[134] These officials were permitted to leave

[128] See especially Beard 1994; Scheid 1995; Orlin 2010.

[129] For this episode, see especially Livy 29.10.4–11.8, 29.14.5–9, 29.37.2, 36.36.3–5. The bibliography on the Magna Mater and her priests is extensive. I have relied primarily upon Vermaseren 1977; Thomas 1984; Beard 1994; Summers 1996; Roller 1999; Orlin 2010; Latham 2012.

[130] See, for example, Cic. *Har. resp.* 28; Livy 29.10.6; Diod. Sic. 34.33.1–3; Strabo 12.5.3; Cass. Dio 17.61; App. *Hann.* 7.9.56; Arn. *Ad. nat.* 7.49; Amm. 22.9.5–7; Vir. 3.46. Pessinus was home to the most important Magna Mater cult in Asia Minor during the first century BC and later, a fact that very likely influenced the narrative we find in the ancient sources (Roller 1999: 269; Orlin 2010: 79). Historically, however, there is evidence that Pergamum did not control the interior of Phrygia as early as 204 BC, when King Attalus facilitated Rome's adoption of Magna Mater (Gruen 1990: 16; Roller 1999: 268–269; Orlin 2010: 80).

[131] Only Ovid (*Fast.* 4.249) explicitly cites Mount Ida as Magna Mater's original home, but Livy (29.10, 14) and Cicero (*Har. Resp.* 27–28, *Sen.* 45) also refer to the goddess as the Idaean mother. Furthermore, numerous Attis figurines found in the sanctuary on the Palatine demonstrate that her worship was more Hellenized than Phrygian from an early date (Roller 1999: 274–278). For arguments in favor of Mount Ida, see also Gruen 1990: 16–20; Orlin 2010: 79–81. For the cult title, see Ziegler 1969.

[132] For a discussion of the role of the Roman *matronae* in receiving the goddess, see Roller 1999: 264–271. The Temple of Magna Mater was dedicated in 191 BC (Livy 36.36.3–5).

[133] For the first *ludi Megalenses*, see Livy 34.54.3; Roller 1999: 278–279; Orlin 2010: 156–159. The games were organized by the *curule aedile* (Livy 34.54.3; Cic. *Har. resp.* 27; Cass. Dio 37.8.1) until 23 BC, when they were turned over to the praetor (Cass. Dio 54.2.3).

[134] This seeming hostility toward the more exotic elements of the cult was once interpreted as evidence that the Romans did not fully realize what they were getting when they imported Magna Mater (see, for example, Vermaseren 1977: 96; Scullard 1981: 98–99). Numerous recent discussions, however,

the sanctuary only for the procession on the *dies natalis* (foundation day) of the Palatine temple and for the *ludi Megalenses*.[135] Furthermore, as Dionysius of Halicarnassus stresses, these offices were off limits to Roman citizens, who were not allowed to participate in the procession or to worship the goddess according to her "Phrygian" rites.[136]

The *galli*, who reportedly castrated themselves in a ritual frenzy, fascinated (and often repelled) Roman authors.[137] As Mary Beard has written, "they stalk the pages of Roman literature as mad, frenzied, foreign eunuchs."[138] At the same time, these sources are largely silent on the matter of female officials within the cult. Indeed, the absence of specific commentary on Metroac priestesses suggests that the Romans found official roles for women unremarkable. The *galli* raised the hackles of Roman authors because their dress, behaviors, and sexual proclivities violated traditional gender categories. The priestesses of Magna Mater, on the other hand, were merely foreign. As we shall see, it was the exotic cacophony of their ritual practices, rather than their gender, that marked their alterity.

There is abundant epigraphic evidence for priestesses and female attendants of Magna Mater both in Rome and elsewhere in Roman Italy. The beautifully carved sarcophagus of Metilia Acte and her husband, Junius Euhodus, records her service as *sacerdos Magnae Deum Matris* at Ostia in the late second century AD.[139] Funerary inscriptions from Rome record seven female *sacerdotes* of Magna Mater, all from the imperial period and all with Greek names suggesting foreign or servile origins.[140] Livia Briseis and Claudia Acropolis, for instance, were freedwomen of the imperial family.[141] The existence of freed priestesses confirms that the old restriction on citizen participation in the cult of Magna Mater had been set aside as early as the principate of Tiberius.[142] At least some of these

---

have shown that the Romans were far from ignorant about the cult when they brought it to Rome. As we shall see, the careful delineation of "traditional" and "foreign" ritual practices within the cult served an important ideological function.

[135] Graillot 1912: 76. This restriction raises a number of important questions, including where the *galli* lived. Wiseman (1982) has suggested that they maintained a "clubhouse" near the temple of Magna Mater on the Palatine.

[136] Dion. Hal. *Ant. Rom.* 2.19.5.

[137] See, for example, Lucr. 2.610–628; Catull. 63; Ov. *Fast.* 4.193–244; Juv. 6.511–516; Mart. 3.81; Beard 1994; Roller 1999: 300–308; Orlin 2010: 100–104. Latham (2012) has recently argued that we should be more sensitive to the possibility that Roman attitudes toward the *galli* evolved over time. "In the late republic," he writes, "the *galli* were depicted as charming curiosities, in the Augustan era they were threateningly foreign and effeminate, while in the high empire they became sexually aberrant fanatics" (2012: 109).

[138] Beard 1994: 174.

[139] *CIL* 14.371, with Wood 1978.

[140] *CIL* 6.496 (*CCCA* 3.10; Rüpke 2008: 772, No. 2266); *CIL* 6.508 (*CCCA* 3.235; Rüpke 2008: 886, No. 3038); *CIL* 6.502 (*CCCA* 3.251; Rüpke 2008: 504, No. 413); *CIL* 6.2261 (*CCCA* 3.276; Rüpke 2008: 704, No. 1801); *CIL* 6.2260 (*CCCA* 3.291; Rüpke 2008: 609, No. 1154); *CIL* 6.2259 (*CCCA* 3.360; Rüpke 2008: 508, No. 450); *AE* 1997.157 (Rüpke 2008: 590, No. 1037).

[141] Livia Briseis: *CIL* 6.496 (*CCCA* 3.10; Rüpke 2008: 772, No. 2266). Claudia Acropolis: *CIL* 6.2260 (*CCCA* 3.291; Rüpke 2008: 609, No. 1154).

[142] Wissowa 1912: 320. The fact that Livia Briseis describes herself as *liberta Augustae* dates her epitaph to the principate of Tiberius (AD 14–37), when Livia was formally known as Livia Augusta (as noted by Rüpke 2008: 772, No. 2266).

women may have been affiliated with the temple on the Palatine and Magna Mater's public cult.[143] The imperial evidence must be interpreted with great care, however, particularly since we know that the cult underwent momentous changes during the principate of Claudius, when Attis received his own festival in March.[144]

In contrast to the abundance of epigraphic evidence from the imperial period, our republican sources focus almost exclusively on the colorful *galli*. There is secure evidence, however, that the goddess employed priestesses during the republican period as well.[145] Dionysius of Halicarnassus, whose *Antiquitates Romanae* were complete by about 7 BC, provides important evidence for the organization of the Metroac priesthood prior to the reforms of Claudius:

θυσίας μὲν γὰρ αὐτῇ καὶ ἀγῶνας ἄγουσιν ἀνὰ πᾶν ἔτος οἱ στρατηγοὶ κατὰ τοὺς Ῥωμαίων νόμους, ἱερᾶται δὲ αὐτῆς ἀνὴρ Φρὺξ καὶ γυνὴ Φρυγία καὶ περιάγουσιν ἀνὰ τὴν πόλιν οὗτοι μητραγυρτοῦντες, ὥσπερ αὐτοῖς ἔθος, τύπους τε περικείμενοι τοῖς στήθεσι καὶ καταυλούμενοι πρὸς τῶν ἑπομένων τὰ μητρῷα μέλη καὶ τύμπανα κροτοῦντες. (*Ant. Rom.* 2.19.4)

For the praetors celebrate sacrifices and games in her honor every year according to the Roman custom, but a Phrygian man and a Phrygian woman serve as priests of this goddess and lead her procession through the city, playing the part of begging priests (*metragyrtai*), as is their custom, wearing carved images upon their breasts and striking their drums (*tympana*) while their attendants accompany them, playing music in honor of the goddess on the flute.

According to Dionysius, a priestly hierarchy existed within the cult of Magna Mater in which the priest and priestess, a Phrygian man and a Phrygian woman, were situated above the *galli*. Like the famous *gallus* in a second-century AD funerary portrait from Rome, the priest and priestess wore icons of the goddess on their chests, an accessory without parallel in native Roman cult.[146] Dionysius also reports that they played the drum (*tympanum*) and begged for alms, a practice that stood in stark contrast to the traditional notion that priests should offer sacrifices for the benefit of the people, but never ask for anything in return.[147] The priestess of Magna Mater, in other words, looked, sounded, and worshipped like an exotic foreigner.

---

[143] As suggested by Beard 1994: 173.

[144] Further innovations were introduced under the Antonines, including certain mystical elements that came to dominate the cult in the late antique period. For a discussion of the development of the cult of Magna Mater during the imperial period, see Fishwick 1966; Vermaseren 1977: 122–123; Roller 1999: 315–316.

[145] As stressed by Wissowa 1912: 320.

[146] For a photograph and discussion of this image, see Beard, North and Price 1998: 2.211. The female figure on the altar of the Vicus Sandaliarius, whom Rose (1997: 105–106) has identified as a priestess of Magna Mater, wears a diadem and a torque, but not a medallion bearing an image of the goddess.

[147] Beard 1994: 176. For the collection of alms, see also Cic. *Leg.* 2.22, 40.

The procession described by Dionysius is very likely the one that opened the *ludi Megalenses* on April 4.[148] Lucretius, who presumably witnessed the procession on numerous occasions, also emphasizes its raucous sights and sounds in a famous digression in book two of the *De rerum natura*.[149] His account confirms much of what Dionysius tells us about the ritual, including the clanging music provided by the *galli*:

> tympana tenta tonant palmis et cymbala circum
> concava, raucisonoque minantur cornua cantu,
> et Phrygio stimulat numero cava tibia mentis. (2.618–620)

> They make the tightly stretched drums thunder with their palms, and the hollow cymbals crash all around. The horns blare out a raucous warning, and the hollow flute rouses their minds to frenzy with a Phrygian beat.

The priests, he continues, carry a statue (*imago*, 609) of the goddess wearing a mural crown (*murali corona*, 606) enthroned on a chariot drawn by yoked lions (*sedibus in curru biiugos agitare leones*, 601).[150] Overjoyed by the spectacle, the crowds lining the streets strew her path with coins and shower her statue and her priests with rose petals.[151] Once again, the *galli* overshadow the priestess of Magna Mater, but we should probably assume her presence nonetheless.

The ethnicity of the priest and priestess, whom Dionysius describes as Phrygian, requires further comment, particularly in light of the evidence that the Roman cult of Magna Mater had its origins in the Pergamene shrine at Mount Ida, rather than the Phrygian sanctuary at Pessinus.[152] Although it is possible that the Romans imported priests from Pessinus during the late first century BC, the label "Phrygian" was more likely a kind of shorthand that could be applied to any non-Roman element of the cult, regardless of its true source.[153] In fact, the term tends to confirm that the Romans associated the cult of Magna Mater with Mount Ida and thus with their Trojan heritage. Greek writers had been equating the Trojans with the Phrygians since Aeschylus.[154] Roman authors continued the practice, in spite of its frequently pejorative connotations in Greek literature. In the *Aeneid*, for instance, Numanus taunts Aeneas and his Trojan warriors as "Phrygian women" (*Phrygiae*, 9.617) who are better suited

---

[148] The *lavatio* in March, during which the statue of the goddess was washed in the river Almo, is also a candidate, but this ritual is not securely attested before the middle of the first century AD and may not have formed an important part of the cult during the republican period. For a discussion of the evidence, see Summers 1996: 343.

[149] Although a number of scholars have doubted the authenticity of this description, Summers (1996) and Roller (1999: 297–299) argue persuasively that the description reflects actual Roman practice.

[150] A bronze group in the Metropolitan Museum of Art in New York depicts a similar scene (Inv. No. 97.22.24). For the iconography of the Roman Magna Mater, see also Summers 1996: 344–345, 363–364.

[151] Lucr. 2.626–628. As Summers (1996: 362) points out, other authors associate the worship of Magna Mater with showers of rose petals as well (see, for example, Hor. *Carm.* 3.19.18; Ov. *Fast.* 4.346).

[152] See above.

[153] Roller 1999: 293–296.

[154] Hall 1988, 1989: 38–39.

to the ecstatic worship of the Idaean mother than to the battlefield. Dionysius' text thus tells us nothing more than that the priest and priestess were foreigners, perhaps from Asia Minor, but not necessarily from the Phrygian heartland.

The clear boundaries erected around the *galli* and the Phrygian priest and priestess reveal deep-seated anxieties about the style of worship demanded by the Magna Mater.[155] The ecstatic dancing, the clanging of symbols, the begging for alms, and the voluntary castration of the *galli* were inconsistent with traditional modes of ritual practice. Even so, this tendency to highlight the exotic "otherness" of the Magna Mater and her priests does not imply that the cult was unwelcome at Rome. In fact, Magna Mater was closely associated with military victory during the republican period, beginning with Rome's defeat of Carthage in the Second Punic War. Rather, the importation of foreign priests and priestesses allowed the Romans to integrate Magna Mater into the framework of public cult without compromising either the essence of the foreign cult or their own ideas about appropriate style of worship. While many aspects of the Magna Mater cult attracted comment from Roman authors, the gender of Metroac priestesses did not. As we have seen, there was nothing extraordinary about female priestly officials in a Roman context, and it should come as no surprise that the Romans did not remark upon the goddesses' priestess, choosing instead to dwell on the gender-bending *galli*.

The *Sacerdos Cereris*

The Romans articulated the worship of Magna Mater as an exotic foil to traditional Roman practice. They did not, however, emphasize the alterity of "foreign" rituals and priests in precisely the same way on every occasion. As Eric Orlin has written, "the line between Roman and non-Roman might be drawn differently in different contexts."[156] The importation of a Greek priestess of Ceres from at least the third century BC exemplifies the flexibility of the Roman approach to foreign ritual practices. Like the priestess of Magna Mater, the *sacerdos Cereris* relied upon her ethnicity to legitimize her position within the public cult of Ceres. She was, however, more thoroughly "Romanized" than her Phrygian counterpart. Whereas the priestess of Magna Mater celebrated rituals from which Roman citizens were excluded, the *sacerdos Cereris* presided over rites involving Rome's *matronae*. She even received a special grant of Roman citizenship. Both a citizen and a stranger, the *sacerdos Cereris* retained "just the right amount of priestly foreignness."[157]

[155] On this point, see especially Orlin 2010: 100–104.
[156] Orlin 2010: 104.
[157] The quote is taken from the title of Isayev's 2011 article, "Just the Right Amount of Priestly Foreignness: Roman Citizenship for the Greek Priestess of Ceres."

The cult of the Italic grain goddess Ceres was very ancient. Her primary festival, the Cerialia (April 19), very likely dates to the regal period.[158] Other agricultural rites associated with Ceres, including the sacrifice of the first fruits of the harvest, the Ambarvalia in May, the Feriae Sementivae (Festival of Sowing) in January, and the joint festival of Ceres and the earth goddess Tellus in December, almost certainly belong to this early period as well.[159] Her sanctuary on the Aventine Hill dates at least to the early fifth century BC when, according to the written sources, Sp. Cassius (cos. 493 BC) dedicated a temple to Ceres, Liber, and Libera.[160] While Greek influence is evident and was undoubtedly present from an early date, the triad established in 493 BC was essentially an Italic one.[161] During the historical period, Ceres had a *flamen Cerialis* and perhaps a *flaminica* as well, suggesting that her worship was not only very old, but also very Roman.[162]

At an unknown later date, perhaps in the middle of the second century BC, the Romans introduced new Greek rites, the so-called *Graeca sacra Cereris*, probably from Magna Graecia, along with a Greek priestess, the *sacerdos Cereris*.[163] The Greek rites are first attested at Rome during the Hannibalic War (218–201 BC). Following Rome's catastrophic defeat at Cannae in 216 BC, a festival associated with the Greek rites had to be suspended (*intermissum*) because "there was not a single *matrona* untouched by mourning at that time" (*nec ulla in illa tempestate matrona expers luctus fuerat*, Livy 22.56.4).[164] The rites may have been relatively new in this period. Given the widespread popularity of the cult of Demeter throughout Magna Graecia as early as the eighth century BC, however, it is possible that the Romans adopted her rites at an early date, perhaps not long after foundation of the Aventine temple.[165] Regardless of the precise historical context for this innovation, it is important to emphasize that the Greek rites supplemented, rather than displaced, the Roman cult of Ceres and its native cultic personnel.[166] The result was a self-consciously hybridized public cult in which "native" and "foreign" elements coexisted for the good of the community.

The fullest evidence for the status of the *sacerdos Cereris* appears in Cicero's speech in defense of L. Cornelius Balbus (cos. 40 BC), who stood accused of falsely claiming Roman citizenship. Near the end of a lengthy discourse on the enfranchisement of foreigners, Cicero touches upon the Greek priestess of Ceres:

---

[158] Spaeth 1996: 4.
[159] Spaeth 1996: 5.
[160] Dion. Hal. *Ant. Rom.* 6.17.94.
[161] For a discussion of Greek influence on the Ceres cult, see Spaeth 1996: 103–113. For the Italic character of the cult, see especially Le Bonniec 1958: 292–305; Orlin 1997: 100, 2010: 104.
[162] See chapter 2.
[163] For the date, see Le Bonniec 1958: 390–395; Scheid 1995: 23–24; Spaeth 1996: 11–13; Bendlin 2002: 60–61; Orlin 2010: 104–105, 107–109); Isayev 2011: 378.
[164] See also Val. Max. 1.1.15.
[165] As suggested by Flower 2002a: 87, n. 29.
[166] For this point, see Scheid 1995: 23.

sacra Cereris, iudices, summa maiores nostri religione confici caerimo-
niaque voluerunt; quae cum essent adsumpta de Graecia, et per Grae-
cas curata sunt semper sacerdotes et Graeca omnino nominata. sed cum
illam quae Graecum illud sacrum monstraret et faceret ex Graecia delig-
erent, tamen sacra pro civibus civem facere voluerunt, ut deos immorta-
lis scientia peregrina et externa, mente domestica et civili precaretur. Has
sacerdotes video fere aut Neapolitanas aut Veliensis fuisse, foederatarum
sine dubio civitatum. (*Balb.* 55)

Our ancestors, judges, desired that the sacred rites of Ceres be performed
with the strictest religious observance and reverence. And since these
rites were acquired from Greece and always performed by Greek priestesses, they were generally called Greek rites. But, although they chose a
woman from Greece to perform and teach the Greek rite, they nevertheless desired that a citizen perform rites on behalf of citizens, so that she
might pray to the immortal gods with a foreign and external knowledge,
but with the mind of a citizen and native. I see that, as a rule, these priestesses were either from Naples or Velia, federated cities without question.

Several important pieces of evidence emerge from this discussion, including
the fact that the *sacerdos Cereris* was a public priestess (*sacerdos publica*).[167] An
undated inscription from Rome gives her title as "public priestess of Ceres for
the Roman people, the *Quirites*" (*sacerdos Cereris publica populo Romano Quiritibus, CIL* 6.2182).[168] This title confirms that her ritual program was conducted
at public expense on behalf of the Roman people, or as Cicero writes, "for the
citizens" (*pro civibus*), a variation on the traditional formula "for the people"
(*pro populo*) and better suited to the case at hand.

Cicero also addresses the paradox at the heart of her position within the
Roman cult of Ceres. On the one hand, her authority over the *Graeca sacra
Cereris* was rooted in her ethnicity and in her familiarity with the cult of Demeter, the Greek counterpart of Ceres. Demeter was especially dominant in the
most fertile areas of Magna Graecia. Her priestesses are attested epigraphically
in towns throughout the region, though Cicero singles out Neapolis and Velia
as cities that regularly contributed *sacerdotes Cereris* to Rome.[169] He stresses
that both were "federated communities" (*civitates foederatae*), cities bound to
Rome by a treaty (*foedus*), but lacking the privileges associated with citizenship

---

[167] As noted by Pomeroy 1975: 214; Spaeth 1996: 105; Böhm 2003: 85; Schultz 2006b: 75–81; Isayev
2011; Gaspar 2012: 98; Šterbenc Erker 2013: 158–162. Scheid (1993: 57) also classifies the *sacerdos
Cereris* as a public priestess but argues that her status had no broader implications for the role of women
in Roman religion since the cult was a naturalized one and did not represent "an evolution in Roman
religious convictions." Although I disagree with his conclusions, Scheid is correct that Roman religious
convictions did not "evolve" following the introduction of the *sacerdos Cereris*; prior to her arrival in
Rome, numerous women were already serving public cult in an official capacity.

[168] See further below.

[169] For the Italian priestesses of Demeter/Ceres, see Peruzzi 1995; Zimmermann and Frei-Stolba 1998;
Gaspar 2012: 100–110.

until the end the Social War (91–89/82 BC), when Rome enfranchised all Italian communities south of the Po River. The Romans may have imported priestesses from Sicily as well. On a funerary inscription dated to the late republican period, Casponia Maxima is named as the "public priestess of Ceres" (*sacerdos Cereri* (sic) *publica populi Romani, CIL* 6.2181).[170] She is also explicitly described as "Sicilian" (*sicula*). The *sacerdos Cereris* did not simply live in southern Italy or Sicily; she was an authentically Greek woman in possession of invaluable "foreign knowledge" (*peregrina scientia*).[171]

In order to facilitate her service as a public priestess, however, the *sacerdos Cereris* was made a Roman citizen. Cicero cites the case of Calliphana, a priestess from Velia, who received a grant of citizenship from the Roman people on a motion of the praetor C. Valerius Flaccus (cos. 93 BC).[172] Citizen status was a requirement for most priesthoods in the ancient world; like magistrates, priests conducted public business on behalf of the Roman people (*pro populo*) and were expected to be members of the people themselves.[173] The *sacerdos Cereris* was no exception. As Rebecca Flemming has stressed, she "addressed the gods on exactly the same basis as any other public religious official, her authority came from her own, properly arrived at, position in the Roman constitution."[174] At the same time, of course, implicit in the grant of citizenship is an understanding that the priestess was not exchanging one identity for another, but rather adding to the identity that she already possessed.[175]

The evidence for the marital status of the *sacerdos Cereris* is less secure than the evidence for her Greek origins and Roman citizenship. At Athens, the priestess who presided at the Thesmophoria was a married woman, as was the priestess of Demeter and Kore at Eleusis.[176] Modern scholars, however, have generally followed Tertullian in arguing that priestesses of Ceres in the Roman world remained celibate throughout their period of service.[177] In a catalogue of pagan religious officials and cults especially devoted to chastity, the early Christian theologian claims that the *sacerdotes* of Ceres dissolved their marriages with the consent of their husbands and lived as celibate widows (*Cereris sacerdotes viventibus etiam viris et consentientibus amica separatione viduantur, De monog.*

---

[170] Rüpke 2008: 599, No. 1096.
[171] Valerius Maximus also comments on the fact that the Romans employed a "skilled ministrant" (*perita antistes*, 1.1.1) to administer the Greek rites of Ceres.
[172] Cic. *Balb.* 55. See also Val. Max. 1.1.1b, with Rüpke 2008: 591, No. 1042. Orlin (2010: 107) cautions against accepting Cicero's testimony "at face value," and we should consider the possibility that the orator is extrapolating from an exceptional grant made at a time of great political conflict regarding the enfranchisement of the Italian allies.
[173] At Rome, only the priests of Magna Mater present an exception to this general rule. The Etruscan *haruspices* were primarily "consultants" whose status is not strictly analogous to that of priests who sacrificed or prayed on behalf of the Roman people (Isayev 2011: 383–384).
[174] Flemming 2007: 104.
[175] As stressed by Isayev 2011: 375.
[176] For the ancient evidence, see Connelly 2007: 41–42.
[177] See, for example, Wissowa 1912: 301; Le Bonniec 1958: 411–412; Peruzzi 1995: 10; Spaeth 1996: 115.

17.4).[178] Tertullian, however, was a native of Carthage, and his knowledge of specific cultic regulations was likely shaped by his North African context. Indeed, he specifies in a separate treatise on chastity that the practice of amicable divorce was observed by the ministrants of African Ceres.[179] The cult of Ceres in Africa differed from her Hellenized cult in Italy in several respects.[180] It would be foolhardy to assume that Tertullian's testimony applies with equal force to the sexual status of *sacerdotes Cereris* serving in Rome and Italy during the republican period.

Even so, the epigraphic evidence appears to confirm that Italian *sacerdotes Cereris* were generally unmarried. Nearly all of the inscriptions from the republican period are epitaphs that mention only the name of the *sacerdos* and her title, thus providing no explicit information about her marital status.[181] The only exception is the funerary inscription of Caesia, daughter of Novius Caesius, who was commemorated by her *nepos*, Quintus Caesius, son of Quintus.[182] While *nepos* can mean both "nephew" and "grandson," the similarity of Quintus' name to Caesia's suggests that he is her brother's son.[183] Since Roman testamentary practices typically held the heir responsible for the expense of erecting a funerary monument, the epitaph suggests that Caesia had no direct descendants of her own and thus left her estate to her nephew.[184] While the sample of republican inscriptions is admittedly small, the complete absence of commemorations made by husbands or children is highly unusual, and tends to indicate that Italian *sacerdotes Cereris* were generally unmarried.[185]

The Greek *sacerdos Cereris* did not participate in an official capacity in any of the Roman rites of Ceres. Instead, she presided over a Greek festival known at Rome as the *sacrum anniversarium Cereris* (the annual rites of Ceres).[186] This festival was observed exclusively by women. According to Paul's epitome of Festus, it commemorated "the finding of Proserpina" (*inventionem Proserpinae*, 86L), the daughter of Ceres, who had been abducted by the god of the

---

[178] In the Greek world, priesthoods that required perpetual celibacy were typically held by postmenopausal widows, rather than by young virgins (Bremmer 1987b; Connelly 2007: 43–44). While Tertullian may be mistaken that African *sacerdotes Cereris* divorced their husbands in order to take up their posts, the notion that some priesthoods required the service of a celibate widow is certainly correct.

[179] Tert. *Cast.* 13.2.

[180] As stressed by Rives 1995: 49; Schultz 2006b: 76; Gaspar 2011. For the cult of Ceres in Roman North Africa, see also Drine 1994; Hinz 1998.

[181] Schultz (2006b: 76) is particularly pessimistic about the value of the epigraphic evidence.

[182] *CIL* 1².3110 = 10.6103 (now at Gaeta).

[183] As concluded by Schultz 2006b: 76.

[184] For the responsibilities of heirs regarding funerary monuments, see Champlin 1991: 169–180.

[185] Inscriptions of imperial or uncertain date from Roman Italy do record married *sacerdotes Cereris* (see, for example, *CIL* 9.4200 (Amiternum?), 10.1036 = *ILS* 6365 (Pompeii), 10.6109 (Formiae), with Schultz 2006b: 77–78). Although Isayev (2011: 385) may be correct that the *sacerdos Cereris* at Rome could have been a *matrona* in the imperial period as well, her interpretation of Plut. *Mul. virt.* 26 is unconvincing.

[186] For the *sacrum anniversarium Cereris*, see Spaeth 1996: 107–113; Šterbenc Erker 2013: 84–112. The Roman sources consistently refer to this rite as "Greek." See, for example, Cic. *Balb.* 55 (*Graecum sacrum*); *Leg.* 2.21 (*Cereri Graeco sacro*); Festus (Paulus) 86L (*Graeca sacra festa*).

underworld. This mythological etiology suggests that the *sacrum anniversarium Cereris* was related to the Greek Thesmophoria, the primary festival of the cult of Demeter Thesmophoros and her daughter, Persephone.[187] One of the most widely attested festivals in the ancient Mediterranean, the Thesmophoria was characterized by secrecy, gender exclusivity, and the sacrifice of a pig.[188] The ancient sources indicate that on its second day, the Nesteia, or "Fasting," the women sat on the ground and fasted in a ritual reenactment of Demeter's grief for the loss of her daughter.[189] As Barbette Spaeth has noted, the rites of the Nesteia correspond closely to a Roman ritual recorded by Servius:[190]

> Proserpinam raptam a Dite patre Ceres cum incensis faculis per orbem terrarum requireret, per trivia eam vel quadrivia vocabat clamoribus. unde permansit in eius sacris, ut certis diebus per compita a matronis exerceatur ululatus. (ad *Aen.* 4.609)

> When Ceres with blazing torches was searching over the whole earth for Proserpina, who had been seized by Dis Pater, she called her with shouts where three or four roads meet. For this reason it remains a custom in her rites that on certain days a lamentation is raised at the crossroads by the *matronae*.

Following this ritual mourning at the crossroads, the Roman *matronae* celebrated the "finding" (*inventio*) of Proserpina with sacrifices and a procession, just as worshippers at the Thesmophoria commemorated the return of Persephone on the final day of the festival, the Kalligeneia, or "Fair Birth."[191] This and other similarities between the two festivals, including the imposition of a period of ritual chastity, tend to confirm that the Roman *sacrum anniversarium Cereris* was a close adaptation of the Greek Thesmophoria.[192]

The Thesmophoria, and by extension the *sacrum anniversarium Cereris*, is generally understood as a fertility festival in which citizen women helped to guarantee the continued wellbeing of the city through the production of crops and legitimate children. More recent scholarship on the festival has also emphasized how it reinforced traditional gender roles in Greek society by isolating

---

[187] Ovid likewise relates "the yearly time of the rite of Ceres" (*annua Cerealis tempora sacri, Am.* 3.10.1), to the rape of Persephone, Demeter's terrible grief, and the eventual reunion of the two goddesses. For a discussion of the myth and its relationship to the *sacrum anniversarium*, see Šterbenc Erker 2013: 113–43.

[188] For the Thesmophoria, see Parke 1977: 82–88; Brumfield 1981: 70–103; Simon 1983: 18–22; Burkert 1985: 242–246; Detienne 1989; Winkler 1990; Dillon 2001: 110–120.

[189] Plut. *Demetr.* 30.5, *De Is. et Os.* 69 = *Mor.* 378d–e.

[190] Spaeth 1996: 107–108.

[191] For the Kalligeneia, see Isaeus 3.80; *IG* II² 1184. For the sacrifices and procession at the *sacrum anniversarium Cereris*, see Plut. *Fab. Max.* 18.1–2; Spaeth 1996: 108; Šterbenc Erker 2013: 102–109.

[192] Le Bonniec 1958: 422. For a discussion of the evidence for sexual abstinence before and during the Thesmophoria, see Dillon 2001: 113, 325 n. 24, with further references. For the importance of abstinence at the *sacrum anniversarium Cereris*, see Ov. *Am.* 3.10, with Spaeth 1996: 110–111; Šterbenc Erker 2013: 96–102.

the ritual practice of women and emphasizing their responsibility for fertility.[193] The *sacrum anniversarium Cereris* almost certainly performed this important ideological function at Rome as well. In fact, Spaeth has argued that the cult of Ceres emphasized the link between matronal *castitas* (chastity) and the flourishing of human and agricultural fertility. [194] The festival thus confirmed the centrality of women to the success of the Roman state, even as it defined their role in terms that conformed to the prevailing patriarchal ideology.

While the primary model for the *sacrum anniversarium Cereris* was undoubtedly the Thesmophoria, Cicero and Varro describe the rites as *initia* (initiations), suggesting that they incorporated aspects of the Eleusinian cult of Demeter as well.[195] The Eleusinian Mysteries and the Thesmophoria are typically analyzed and interpreted separately, but the two cults shared a common etiological myth, addressed the same deities, and were both connected with fertility.[196] In fact, the Homeric *Hymn* to Demeter links the myth of the abduction and recovery of Persephone to the foundation of the mysteries at Eleusis. It is not surprising, therefore, that the Romans fused two separate Demeter festivals into one composite rite known as the *sacrum anniversarium Cereris*. One crucial difference between the Eleusinian Mysteries and the *initia* performed at Rome, however, is the gender of their respective participants: the Eleusinian Mysteries were open to men and women of all social statuses, including slaves, while the rites of the *sacrum anniversarium Cereris* were restricted to *matronae*, married citizen women.

It seems very likely that the *sacerdos Cereris* also presided over the mysterious *mundus patet* ritual, which took place on August 24, October 5, and November 8 at a subterranean pit known as the *mundus Cereris*.[197] The location of the *mundus Cereris* remains a mystery.[198] It reportedly contained an entrance to the underworld through which, when open, the *di manes* (spirits of the dead) returned to the upper world.[199] The three *mundus patet* days were consequently classified as *religiosi* and considered unsuitable for weddings, military campaigns, and *comitia* (assemblies). The significance of the ritual and the dates on which it was observed are unclear, though the opening on August 24 may have coincided with the *sacrum anniversarium* and the return of Proserpina.[200] It is also possible that the *mundus* fulfilled the function of the *megaron* (underground

[193] See especially Zeitlin 1982; Winkler 1990; Versnel 1993.
[194] See especially Spaeth 1996: 108–119. For a critique of this interpretation, see Šterbenc Erker 2013: 89–96.
[195] Cic. *Leg.* 2.21; Varro *Rust.* 3.1.5. For the identification of the *initia Cereris* with the *sacrum anniversarium*, see Le Bonniec 1958: 423–437; Spaeth 1996: 59–62; Šterbenc Erker 2013: 85. For a different interpretation, see Wagenvoort 1980.
[196] For this point, see Nixon 1995.
[197] Bendlin 2002: 59–61.
[198] Bendlin (2002: 54–59) convincingly refutes earlier attempts to identify the *mundus Cereris* with either the *umbilicus urbis* (naval of the city) or the foundation pit described by Plutarch in his *Life* of Romulus (11.2).
[199] Festus 124–126, 144–146L; Festus (Paulus) 125–127, 145–147L; Macrob. *Sat.* 1.16.17–18.
[200] Bendlin 2002: 67–19.

pit) into which women celebrating the Thesmophoria descended to retrieve the rotten remains of piglets deposited there at an earlier date.[201] In any case, evidence from Magna Graecia, including the epitaph of a *sacerdos Cerialis mundalis* from Capua, suggests that the *mundus* arrived in Rome from southern Italy, perhaps in the middle of the second century BC.[202]

The Greek rites of Ceres were thoroughly integrated within the traditional framework of the Roman cult of Ceres. At the same time, however, an insistence on the external origins of the rites and of the *sacerdos Cereris* allowed the Romans to articulate an ideology of openness that legitimated their imperial project. Roman attitudes toward the Greek priestess of Ceres thus allow us to examine how concerns about the "otherness" of foreign rites intersected with ideas about the gender of priestly figures. While the ancient sources emphasize the ethnicity of the *sacerdos Cereris*, they treat her gender as a perfectly natural aspect of her priestly identity. Given the well-attested presence of numerous public priestesses within the Roman system, this is hardly surprising. Despite modern claims to the contrary, the alterity of the Greek priestess was articulated through her cultural origins and foreign expertise, not through her gender.[203]

Support Personnel

Thus far, the focus has been on women whom I have described as public "priestesses." But no Roman religious official ever worked in isolation. Ancillary staff maintained the temples of the gods and saw to the daily management of the sanctuaries in which they served. Animal sacrifice in particular required a large cast of support personnel, many of whom were *servi publici* (public slaves) or *liberti* (freedmen).[204] While their subordinate status tends to render them less visible in the written sources, sculpted reliefs on Roman temples and altars include an impressive range of *victimarii* (ritual slaughterers), musicians, and assistants of various kinds carrying jugs filled with wine, boxes of incense, and baskets containing fruit or sacrificial cakes.[205] The figures depicted in these scenes are generally male. Epigraphic and written evidence, however, confirms that the republican altar was occasionally crowded with women as well.

As we have seen, some Roman priestesses possessed the authority to offer blood sacrifices. It should come as no surprise, therefore, that women participated in animal sacrifices in other capacities as well. In fact, the only *popa*

---

[201] Bendlin 2002: 63.
[202] *CIL* 10.3926 = *ILS* 3348, with Zimmermann and Frei-Stolba 1998: 114–115. For the date, see Bendlin 2002.
[203] See, for example, Scheid 1993: 57; Isayev 2011: 386.
[204] Purcell 1983; Horster 2007: 332–334.
[205] For examples, see Ryberg 1955; Fless 1995.

(ritual slaughterer) known by name is a *liberta* (freedwoman), Critonia Philema, whose funerary inscription describes her as *"popa de insula"* (ritual slaughterer of the island, *CIL* 6.9824).[206] As Emily Hemelrijk has noted, the existence of a female *victimarius* is "highly surprising," at least if our expectations are governed by the visual evidence alone.[207] In Roman art, *popae* are invariably muscular young men wearing nothing but a *limus* (apron) and carrying a *dolabra* (ax) or *malleus* (mallet) with which they will fell the sacrificial victim.[208] Even so, female *popae* must have existed. We may assume, for instance, that the *victimarius* who slaughtered and butchered the victim at the December rites of Bona Dea was a woman—even the *imagines* (ancestor masks) of male ancestors were removed from the house during the celebration of this festival.[209]

Other women-only rituals such as the *sacrum anniversarium Cereris*, the Matronalia, the Carmentalia, and the annual festivals of Mater Matuta, Fortuna Muliebris, and Venus Verticordia undoubtedly required female assistants as well. Female *victimarii* may even have belonged to the *collegium victimariorum*, a professional organization composed of "those who serve the priests, the magistrates, and the senate" (*qui ipsi et sacerdotibus et magistr(atibus) et senatui apparent, CIL* 6.971 = *ILS* 4963), though none are specifically attested. In fact, it is possible, perhaps even probable, that women-only sacrifices included female *haruspices*, who examined the *exta* (entrails) of the sacrificial victim and announced whether or not it had been accepted by the gods.[210]

Other support personnel have left traces in the antiquarian tradition. Paul the Deacon describes a group of otherwise unknown specialists who bore the title *simpulatrix*:

> simpulum vas parvulum non dissimile cyatho, quo vinum in sacrificiis libabatur; unde et mulieres rebus divinis deditae simpulatrices. (Festus (Paulus) 455L)

> A *simpulum* is a small vessel, not dissimilar to a *cyathus*, from which wine used to be poured out as an offering in sacrifices; from which, also, women devoted to divine matters are called *simpulatrices*.

---

[206] The significance of the phrase *"de insula,"* which could mean "of the island," or "of the apartment block" is uncertain. Lanciani (cited in Besnier 1902: 75) suggested that she plied her trade on the Tiber Island (*insula*), while Hemelrijk (2009: 263–264) has proposed that she sold sacrificial victims from a stall in an apartment block (*insula*). Foxhall (2013: 139) suggests that Critonia Philema ran a butcher's shop, but the word *popa* generally refers to ritual slaughterers, rather than to commercial butchers (see, for example, Cic. *Mil.* 24.65; Prop. 4.3.62; Suet. *Calig.* 32.3; Serv. ad *Aen.* 12.120). See also Rüpke 2008: 649, No. 1419.

[207] Hemelrijk 2009: 263.

[208] For examples, see Fless 1995, especially Plates 36.1, 36.2, 37.2, 40.2, 41.2.

[209] See chapter 6.

[210] Despite bearing the same title as the group who advised the senate on the expiation of prodigies, it seems likely that the *haruspices* who read the *exta* at sacrifices belonged to a different group of religious officials, perhaps of a lower social status (North 1990a: 53). Plautus (*Mil.* 692, with Dickie 2001: 157) mentions *haruspicae* (female *haruspices*) who were evidently available for private consultations.

As the *simpulum* was a ladle used to dip wine and pour libations at sacrificial rites, it is natural to assume that a *simpulatrix* used the *simpulum* to handle wine on regular ritual occasions.[211] This is confirmed by an anonymous scholiast on Juvenal, who describes the *simpuvium* (an alternative for *simpulum*) as a vessel "suited for sacrifice, from which the *pontifices* used to offer libations," and explains that from the *simpuvium*, "the woman who offers the cup is called the *simpuviatrix*" (*illa dicitur simpuviatrix quae porrigit poculum ipsud*, 6.343).[212] That a group of women "devoted to divine matters" and bearing the name of a sacrificial vessel could assist the male *pontifices* highlights the extent to which women were involved in public sacrifice at Rome.

Roman sacrifices and processions typically included a parade of assistants carrying ritual implements, boxes of incense, trays of horticultural offerings, and jugs of wine. On certain occasions, this task inevitably fell to women. Festus, for instance, reports that the *canifera* was a woman (*mulier*) who carried a wicker basket known as the *canua*.[213] Other public rituals employed *camilli* and *camillae*, freeborn children with both parents living.[214] The *flaminia sacerdotula* was one such assistant devoted to assisting the *flaminica Dialis*.[215] According to Dionysius of Halicarnassus, the *tutulatae*, freeborn girls who assisted at curial sacrifices, performed the same duties assigned to Greek basket bearers known as *kanephoroi* and *arrhephoroi*.[216] Athenian *kanephoroi*, including the maidens on the Parthenon frieze, wore richly embroidered festival mantles that marked their special ritual status, and we may perhaps imagine that Roman *camillae* and *tutulatae* had a special costume as well.[217]

Other women served as ritual musicians. Aelia Recepta was a *tympanistria* (drummer) of Magna Mater, presumably playing her instrument during the public procession at the *ludi Megalenses* on April 4.[218] An epitaph from Rome of unknown date records the service of Fulvia, a freedwoman who died at age fifteen, as a *tibicen*.[219] Attendants serving in this capacity played the double flute at public sacrifices in order to drown out inauspicious sounds.[220] Like the *victimarii* and other religious professionals, *tibicines* were organized into a *collegium*.[221]

Epigraphic evidence from Rome reveals the existence of female *aedituae* (temple custodians) as well. Lollia Urbana, a freedwoman, is commemorated

---

[211] Schultz 2006b: 133; Flemming 2007: 96. For the *simpulum* (or *simpuvium*), see Siebert 1999: 47–51, 236–239.

[212] The commentary dates to the fifth century AD, though the present tense verbs in the second half of the note clearly indicate an earlier source (Cameron 2010: 576).

[213] Festus 57L.

[214] For the role of children in public cult at Rome, see especially Mantle 2002; Vuolanto 2010.

[215] Festus (Paulus) 82L.

[216] Dion. Hal. *Ant. Rom.* 2.22.2.

[217] For the *kanephoroi* and their costume, see Roccos 1995.

[218] *CIL* 6.2264 = *ILS* 4165, with Rüpke 2008: 508, No. 455.

[219] *CIL* 6.33970 = *ILS* 5240, with Gaspar 2012: 147.

[220] Pliny *H.N.* 28.3; Fless 1995: 80–84.

[221] *CIL* 6.240.

as *aeditua* and *ministra* of an unknown deity.[222] Another inscription records Doris, slave of Asinius Gallus, as *aeditua* of a temple of Diana.[223] Lora Holland has suggested that she may have worked at the temple on the Vicus Patricius, which was open only to women.[224] Other temples that forbade access to men presumably employed female *aeduae* as well, even if they have left no trace in the historical record. Temple custodians lived near the temple and performed a variety of important functions, from regulating access, managing offerings, and keeping the sanctuary neat and clean.[225]

Conclusion

The religious landscape of republican Rome was inhabited by an impressive variety of female religious officials. The Vestal Virgins, the *flaminica Dialis*, and the *regina sacrorum* may have been the most prominent priestesses in the city, but they were not alone. As we have seen in this chapter, some of their colleagues speak to us, albeit indirectly, from fragmentary written sources and the handful of inscriptions that have survived the vicissitudes of time. Others presumably existed, even if they have left no mark on the historical record. Evidence from outside the city is suggestive. Inscriptions from Italy memorialize *sacerdotes* of Juno Populona, Minerva, Venus, and Venus and Ceres together.[226] An epitaph from Beneventum records a female *sacerdos* of Juno Regina, and it stands to reason that her Roman cult, which had been imported from Veii in 396 BC, supported a priestess as well.[227] Tellus, Diana, Fortuna, Mater Matuta, Juno Lucina, Pudicitia, Venus Verticordia, and Feronia, to name just a few of the myriad female deities with cults at Rome, may also have had priestesses of their own.[228] Priestesses attested at Rome during imperial period, such as the

---

[222] *CIL* 6.2213, with Rüpke 2008: 774, No. 3.

[223] *CIL* 6.2209, with Rüpke 2008: 662, No. 1497.

[224] Holland 2012a: 115. For the Temple of Diana on the Vicus Patricius, see Plut. *Quaest. Rom.* 3 = *Mor.* 264c.

[225] Varro *Ling.* 5.50; Graf 2002; Rüpke 2008: 13; Holland 2012a: 114–115; Gaspar 2012: 142–143.

[226] For the *sacerdotes Iunonis Populonae*, see *CIL* 10.4789 = *ILS* 3112 and *CIL* 10.4790. For the *sacerdos Minervae*, see *CIL* 9.307 = *AE* 1990.202. For the *sacerdotes Veneris*, see *CIL* 9.2569 = *ILLRP* 273; *CIL* 9.3166; *CIL* 9.3167; *CIL* 9.3429 (*sacerdos Veneris Felicis*); 10.1207 (*sacerdos Ioviae Veneriae Abellanorum*). For the *sacerdotes Cereris et Veneris*, see *CIL* 9.3087 = *ILLRP* 65; *CIL* 9.3090 = *ILS* 3351 = *ILLRP* 66; *CIL* 10.5191 = *ILLRP* 63. Green (2007: 235, 251, 278, 282, 285) mentions priestesses of Diana at Aricia; though not attested in epigraphic or written sources, they presumably existed. For a discussion of the epigraphic evidence from Italy, see Zimmermann and Frei-Stolba 1998; Schultz 2006b: 69–74; Gaspar 2012; Richlin 2014.

[227] *CIL* 9.2111. For the *evocatio* of Juno Regina, see Livy 5.21.3–7. There may have been other priestesses of Juno in Rome and Latium, where her cult was particularly strong (Gaspar 2012: 71). In Vergil's *Aeneid* (7.415–20), the Fury Allecto disguises herself as Calybe, an elderly *sacerdos Iunonis* from Ardea. Ovid (*Am.* 3.13.2) mentions Falscian *sacerdotes Iunonis* without specifying gender.

[228] There may even be some visual evidence for a priestess of Diana at Rome in the second century AD. An altar from the city now in the Ny Carlsberg Glyptotek (Inv. No. 858, with Hemelrijk 2009: 261, n. 27; Gaspar 2012: 75) depicts a veiled woman sprinkling incense on an altar. She is assisted by two attendants, one carrying a box and the other holding a knife and leading an ox. A deer on the other side

sacerdos of Dis Pater, may have existed under the Republic as well.[229] Among other things, this chapter should prompt us to consider how much we have lost.

Though incomplete, the evidence discussed here allows us to draw some preliminary conclusions about the nature of female priesthood. The first is its eclecticism; no single model of service predominates. Some priestesses had colleagues, including the *saliae*, who may have formed a religious sorority (*sodalitas*) on the model of the *salii*. The *sacerdotes Liberi* and the priestesses affiliated with the healing cult of Bona Dea also served alongside colleagues, though it is unlikely that they were organized into an official priestly college (*collegium*). Support personnel, on the other hand, were very likely members of professional organizations (*collegia*). Other priestesses operated more or less independently, assisted only by ancillary staff and laywomen. Some presumably served for life, while others, such as the *saliae*, may have held their priesthood only for a season. They were active in native and "foreign" cults and served both male and female deities, challenging the view that Roman religion followed a strict gender order, according to which the sex of the deity determined the sex of his or her priest.[230]

The second feature to emerge from this material confirms a conclusion reached in the previous chapters, namely that gender was not the sole criterion for selection to the priesthood. Ethnicity, age, social standing, and marital status were important factors in determining an individual's opportunities for priestly service. Some offices may even have required prior training or a specialized skill set. The *sacerdos Cereris*, for instance, was chosen for her familiarity with the Greek rites of Demeter and Persephone, while the *antistites* of Bona Dea may have been expected to demonstrate expertise in medical botany before taking up a position in the temple pharmacy.

The religious rites performed by the priestesses in this chapter defy generalization. Some addressed agricultural fertility and the perpetuation of the city through the production of a stable food supply. Others were connected to warfare, the welfare of the city, and the expiation of prodigies. The *sacerdotes Liberi* may have presided over semiprivate sacrifices on the Liberalia, a day of great significance within the life course of the Roman male. The priestesses and support personnel associated with the healing cult of Bona Dea treated ailing Romans from both ends of the social spectrum. Some of these rites enacted beliefs about female chastity (*castitas*) and fidelity in marriage. At the same time, however, they reveal that femininity had many facets; ritual did not confine women to the margins of society, but rather positioned them right at the heart of the civic community.

---

of the altar suggests a link with the cult of Diana, and may indicate that the woman shown on the front is a priestess of the goddess.

[229] *CIL* 6.2243, with Rüpke 2008: 712, No. 1865. An inscription from 259 BC records a *sacerdos Caelestis* (*CIL* 6.37170 = *ILS* 4438 = *AE* 1893.79), though Rives (1995: 68–69) and Gaspar (2012: 74) suggest that she may have served in a private association of freedwomen, presumably of African descent, since Caelestis was an important African deity.

[230] See, for example, Latte 1960: 171. For a critique of the idea of a "gender rule" in Roman religion, see also Schultz 2000, 2006b: 50–57, 61–69; Gaspar 2012: 85–91.

CHAPTER FOUR

The Vestal Virgins

The six Vestal Virgins belonged to the pontifical college (*collegium pontificum*), the largest and one of Rome's most prestigious religious orders. Chosen for their role between the ages of six and ten, they were committed to serve the cult of Vesta for a minimum of thirty years. Most remained Vestals for life.[1] They must often have been the longest serving priests in their generation. The Vestals lived together in the sanctuary of Vesta in the heart of the Roman Forum, Rome's civic and religious center. They were synonymous with the continued welfare of the city and inseparable from the Romans' view of themselves. Rome, the poet Horace emphasizes, will stand "as long as the *pontifex* climbs the Capitol beside the silent virgin" (*dum Capitolium / scandet cum tacita virgine pontifex, Carm.* 3.30.7–9). In addition to guaranteeing Rome's future, the Vestal priesthood was cherished as one of the most ancient religious institutions in the city. While the written sources attribute the foundation of the Roman cult to Numa, they also tell us that Rhea Silvia, the mother of Romulus and Remus, was a Vestal at the Latin city of Alba Longa.[2] Vestals had been worshipping Vesta even before the foundation of the city.

Written and visual evidence for the Vestals abounds, allowing us to write a more comprehensive account of the order than is possible for almost any other Roman priesthood.[3] In fact, given their prominence in the ancient literature, the Vestals tend to eclipse other priestesses in modern scholarship as well. Many have concluded that they were the only female priests at Rome and some have even supposed that they were regarded as "honorary men."[4] The previous chapters, however, have shown that the Vestals were not the only women at

---

[1] The Vestal Occia, for example, served for fifty-seven years (Tac. *Ann.* 2.86). In fact, there is no secure evidence that a Vestal ever chose to the leave the order after thirty years. Bätz (2012: 141–162) provides a detailed discussion of this question.

[2] For Rhea Silvia's status as a Vestal, see Livy 1.4.2; Dion. Hal. *Ant. Rom.* 1.75.1–77.4; Ov. *Fast.* 2.383–386, 3.11. For the institution of the Vestal order by Numa, see Cic., *Rep.* 2.64.14; Dion. Hal. *Ant. Rom.* 2.64.5–67.1; Ov. *Fast.* 6.257–260; Plut. *Num.* 9.5. Epigraphic evidence from Alba Longa and from other towns nearby confirms that the Vestals were central to the religious structures of early Latium (Beard, North, and Price 1998: 51). The fullest discussion is Granino Cecere 2003, with further bibliography.

[3] The bibliography on the Vestals is consequently quite sizeable. Some of the most important contributions include Giannelli 1913; Rose 1926; Worsfold 1934; Koch 1958; Hommel 1972; Guizzi 1968; Beard 1980; Cancik-Lindemaier 1990; Beard 1995; Cancik-Lindemaier 1996b; Martini 1997a, 1997b; Staples 1998; Saquete 2000; Martini 2004; Parker 2004; Thompson 2005; Mekacher 2006; Wildfang 2006; Mustakallio 2007; Thompson 2010; Bätz 2012; Schultz 2012.

[4] Hopkins 1983, with the introduction.

the republican altar. The order stood as one among several models of priestly service available to women and must, therefore, be examined in light of the gender-inclusive nature of Roman civic cult.

The first of four focusing on the Vestals, this chapter considers the social profile of prospective priestesses and explains how they were chosen for their extraordinary role in Roman society. It also outlines their legal status, which set them apart from ordinary Romans, and the privileges they were granted in exchange for their service to the state. Finally, the chapter considers the ritual function of Vestal virginity and its symbolic role in the Roman political imagination. While the first two sections in particular are largely descriptive, they provide essential background for further discussion of the Vestal order. The arguments presented here are informed in turn by the reconsideration in chapter 5 of the Vestal costume, the analysis of the order's ritual obligations in chapter 6, and in chapter 7 the investigation of the relationship between individual Vestals and their families. Together, these chapters emphasize the Vestals' role as guardians of the communal hearth in the Temple of Vesta. The eternal flame on the hearth symbolized the permanence of the city and its empire, and the Romans accordingly feared its extinction "above all misfortunes" (ὑπὲρ ἅπαντα τὰ δεινὰ), looking upon it as "an omen portending the destruction of the city" (ἀφανισμοῦ τῆς πόλεως σημεῖον, Dion. Hal. *Ant. Rom.* 2.67.5). In the tangled web of questions surrounding the Vestal order, each thread leads back to this central occupation and its power to direct the fate of Rome.

Becoming a Vestal Virgin

Principles of Selection

A set of strict selection criteria governed access to the Vestal order. Before choosing a new priestess, the *pontifex maximus* scrutinized her age, legal status, and physical condition, as well as the legal and social standing of her parents. Once again, just as we have seen in other chapters, it is clear that sacral law treated gender as just one of many factors determining access to priestly office. Absolute physical virginity was the most important qualification. Other conditions are more puzzling and seemingly unconnected at first glance, but together reveal a concern for the candidate's ritual and social purity. As the ritually pure, virginal daughters of "ideal" Roman families, Vestals were ideal representatives of the family writ large at the public hearth of Vesta.

The only extant discussion of the selection criteria for the Vestal order appears in the *Noctes Atticae* (*Attic Nights*) of Aulus Gellius (*ca.* AD 125–after 170), a compendium of miscellaneous information compiled from earlier sources.[5] Gellius generally cites his sources and occasionally quotes from their

---

[5] For Gellius' relationship to his antiquarian sources, see the introduction.

works, allowing us to peel back at least one layer separating us from the republican period. In his discussion of the Vestal priesthood, Gellius cites two jurists active during the reign of Augustus—M. Antistius Labeo (d. before AD 22) and C. Capito Ateius (cos. suff. AD 5)—who are known to have written on the Twelve Tables and the pontifical law respectively. The provisions assembled in the following passage presumably reflect the relevant portions of these texts and ultimately the legal decisions of the *pontifices* regarding the selection of Vestal Virgins:

> qui de virgine capienda scripserunt, quorum diligentissime scripsit Labeo Antistius, minorem quam annos sex, maiorem quam annos decem natam negaverunt capi fas esse; item quae non sit patrima et matrima; item quae lingua debili sensuve aurium deminuta aliave qua corporis labe insignita sit; item quae ipsa aut cuius pater emancipatus sit, etiamsi vivo patre in avi potestate sit; item cuius parentes alter ambove servitutem servierunt aut in negotiis sordidis versantur. sed et eam, cuius soror ad id sacerdotium lecta est, excusationem mereri aiunt; item cuius pater flamen aut augur aut quindecimvirum sacris faciundis aut septemvirum epulonum aut salius est. sponsae quoque pontificis et tubicinis sacrorum filiae vacatio a sacerdotio isto tribui solet. praeterea Capito Ateius scriptum reliquit neque eius legendam filiam qui domicilium in Italia non haberet, et excusandam eius qui liberos tres haberet. (*N.A.* 1.12.1–8)

> Those who have written about the taking of a virgin (of whom Labeo Antistius has written most carefully) maintain that it is not permitted to take a girl of less than six and more than ten years of age; or one whose father and mother are not alive; or one who has exhibited a speech impediment, an impaired sense of hearing, or some other bodily defect; or one who has been emancipated herself or whose father has been emancipated, even if she is in the power (*potestas*) of her grandfather and her father is alive; or one whose parents, either one or both, were slaves or engaged in low occupations. But they also say that one whose sister was selected for this priesthood obtains an exemption; or one whose father is a *flamen*, an *augur*, one of the *quindecimviri sacris faciundis* (the fifteen men for performing sacred rites), one of the *septemviri epulones* (the seven men for sacrificial banquets), or a *salius* (dancing priest of Mars). It is also customary for an exemption from that priesthood to be given to the betrothed of a *pontifex* and the daughter of a *tubicen sacrorum* (a priest officiating at the Tubilustrium). Moreover, Capito Ateius has left a record that the daughter of a man who does not have a residence in Italy must not be chosen, and the daughter of one who has three children must be excused.

It is clear that the selection criteria recorded here were not developed at one time as part of a coherent program for choosing a new Vestal. Instead, they represent a gradual accretion of provisions over time, perhaps on an ad hoc basis. The exemption offered to the daughter of a man with three children, for instance, almost certainly postdates the introduction of the *ius liberorum* (right of children) under the marriage laws of Augustus, which granted special privileges to couples with large families.[6] Other requirements are more difficult to date. In general, the profile of the "ideal" candidate developed in this chapter is valid only for the late republican and the early imperial periods; it cannot be applied with confidence to early Rome, though some of the provisions, particularly those related to the candidate's legal status, were undoubtedly very ancient.

Gellius begins with the age of candidacy: only girls between the ages of six and ten could be chosen as Vestals. The minimum age limit may reflect a belief that a child under age six was too young to be removed from her family or properly fulfill a Vestal's cultic responsibilities.[7] At age six, however, a prospective Vestal had nearly reached her seventh year, the age at which children normally began to participate in public and private religious rituals.[8] A girl who lived to age six had also survived the most dangerous years of her childhood. Nearly fifty percent of Roman girls died before their sixth birthday, while those who reached this milestone were more likely to survive into adulthood and could be expected to fulfill the required thirty-year period of service.[9]

In her recent study of the Vestal order, Robin Wildfang suggests that the lower age limit was also designed to ensure that no physical imperfection would manifest itself in a newly selected Vestal.[10] Vestals had to be physically sound in order to perform their ritual obligations, such as harvesting *far* (emmer wheat) or drawing water to cleanse the temple.[11] Wildfang's observation, however, is particularly relevant to the prohibition against choosing a girl with a speech impediment.[12] Roman legal texts regularly refer to children under the age of seven as *infans*, literally "not speaking," while Pliny the Elder believed that they overcome childish speech patterns only at age six.[13]

The lower age limit thus allowed the *pontifex maximus* to determine that a candidate could speak clearly. The prohibition against choosing a girl "lacking in speech or hearing," as Gellius writes, was itself related to her ability to perform her ritual program. The Romans believed that prayers had to replicate traditional formulae exactly in order to be effective.[14] Any omission or mispro-

---

[6] For the Augustan marriage legislation, see Treggiari 1991: 60–80.

[7] As suggested by Wildfang 2006: 44.

[8] For the role of children in Roman ritual, both public and private, see Néraudau 1984: 226–31; Harlow and Laurence 2002: 37; Mantle 2002; Prescendi 2010; Vuolanto 2012.

[9] Saller 1994: 22–25, with Table 2.1.

[10] Wildfang 2006: 44.

[11] See also Bätz 2012: 73.

[12] For this provision, see also Fronto *Epist.* 149N. The fact that Pliny the Elder (*H.N.* 11.174) is reluctant to believe that the *pontifex* Metellus had a stutter may indicate that he knew of a rule that *pontifices* should be free of speech impediments as well.

[13] Plin. *H.N.* 11.174, with Néraudau 1984: 53–55; Harlow and Laurence 2002: 37.

[14] See, for example, Cic. *Dom.* 139–140; Livy 41.16.1; Plin. *H.N.* 28.10–11. For a general discussion of Roman prayer, see Appel 1909; Hickson 1993: 1–15.

nunciation automatically forced a repetition (*instauratio*) of the entire rite.[15] A girl who could not hear or speak properly would not be able to pray effectively and could not be entrusted with the responsibilities of the Vestal priesthood.[16]

The requirement that new Vestals be free from physical defects also reflects a general demand for physical perfection in the ritual sphere. Blemishes of any kind disqualified an animal for use as a sacrificial victim.[17] Even internal imperfections discovered during the inspection of a victim's entrails could invalidate the offering and necessitate a repetition of the sacrifice.[18] Vestals were likewise expected to be perfect physical specimens, at least when they entered the order.[19] In reality, the conditions of service may have been more flexible than Gellius suggests. In 14 BC, for instance, the *virgo maxima*, the chief of the Vestal order, was unable to assist her colleagues in rescuing the *sacra* (sacred objects) from a fire threatening the Temple of Vesta because she was blind.[20] It seems that Vestals who developed physical impairments later in life were permitted to continue serving, presumably because their training and years of experience made them valued members of the order.

The age of candidacy requirements also prohibited the selection of a girl older than ten, ensuring that a new Vestal entered the order well before she reached puberty.[21] This rule very likely alleviated concerns about whether or not the candidate was still a virgin.[22] A Vestal's virginity was central to her priestly identity. The harsh punishment that awaited Vestals who violated their oath of chastity was a strong deterrent to those in office, and the upper age limit minimized the risk that a candidate had lost her virginity before entering the order.[23] Furthermore, the very young age at which a new Vestal was chosen may have ensured that she was not simply unmarried, but also not betrothed or spoken for in any way. Although betrothals could take place at any age, the majority of marriages were contracted not long before consummation.[24] Since Roman girls tended to marry in their middle to late teens, it seems very likely that few would have been betrothed before age ten.[25]

Other selection criteria addressed a prospective Vestal's family situation. Gellius reports, for instance, that a girl chosen as a Vestal had to be *patrima et*

[15] See, for example, Livy 41.16.1.
[16] Wildfang 2006: 43–44. For the prayers of the Vestals on behalf of the Roman people, see chapter 6.
[17] According to Pliny the Elder (*H.N.* 8.183), for instance, the gods would not accept a lame animal.
[18] See, for example, Cic. *Div.* 2.37.
[19] The Romans were clearly uneasy about employing priests with physical defects (see, for example, Dion. Hal. *Ant. Rom.* 2.21.3; Pliny *H.N.* 7.105; Sen. *Controv.* 4.2; Plut. *Quaest. Rom.* 73 = *Mor.* 281c-d). Whether or not this translated into an official ban (as argued by Wissowa 1912: 491; Szemler 1972: 31) is less clear (doubts expressed by Morgan 1974).
[20] Cass. Dio 54.24.2.
[21] On the average age of menarche for Roman girls, see Harlow and Laurence 2002: 13–15, 56.
[22] As noted by Wildfang 2006: 42.
[23] Vestals convicted of losing their virginity—the official term was *incestum*—were buried alive outside the Colline Gate (Plut. *Num.* 10.4). See further below.
[24] Corbett 1930: 1–23; Treggiari 1984; Gardner 1986: 45–47; Treggiari 1991: 138–160; Harlow 2010.
[25] For age at first marriage, see chapter 2.

matrima at the time of her initiation, a requirement she shared with the *salii* and with children who served as priestly attendants (*camilli* and *camillae*).[26] Festus says that *patrimes et matrimes* (elsewhere, *patrimi et matrimi*) were children whose parents were both living (*matrimes ac patrimes dicuntur, quibus matres et patres adhuc vivunt*, 113L).[27] This definition is corroborated by Dionysius of Halicarnassus and Cassius Dio, who translate *patrimi et matrimi* with the Greek term ἀμφιθαλεῖς, literally "blooming on both sides," that is, on both the father's and the mother's side.[28] Such children performed a variety of ritual tasks in the Greek world as well.[29]

Some have argued that this regulation ensured that candidates would be fairly young when selected, since the high mortality rate at Rome meant that relatively few children could expect to reach adulthood with both parents living.[30] But age at death is not an exact science, and the stipulation that a candidate be *patrima et matrima* would not have been a foolproof method for regulating age. The traditional explanation, moreover, amounts to no more than a reworking of the upper age limit discussed above. It seems more likely that the two requirements served different purposes. Death was a bad omen that could attach itself to close relations. Apuleius claims that a widow is "a woman of evil omen and unlucky" (*scaevi ominis mulier et infausti, Apol.* 92). The death of a parent at a young age may have indicated that a child was unlucky or out of favor with the gods.[31] Only children who exemplified perfection and completeness were eligible to serve in the ritual sphere; the death of a parent, like a speech impediment or a missing appendage, disqualified a candidate for the Vestal order.

Gellius does not say that the parents of a prospective Vestal had to be married in order to submit their daughter for consideration. Tacitus, however, reports that in AD 19, Tiberius (r. AD 14–37) chose the daughter of Domitius Pollio

---

[26] For the *sallii*, see Dion. Hal. *Ant. Rom.* 2.71.4. For priestly attendants (*camilli* and *camillae*), see Dion. Hal. *Ant. Rom.* 2.22.1; Macrob. *Sat.* 1.6.14; Festus (Paulus) 38, 82L. The requirement may have applied to children participating in public supplications (*supplicationes*) as well (Livy 37.3.6).

[27] Festus (266L) adds elsewhere that the adjective *patrimus* was used to designate a person whose father was still living in nonreligious contexts as well (see also Festus (Paulus) 267L). Servius (ad *Georg.* 1.31) claims that *patrimi et matrimi* were children born to a couple married by *confarreatio*, but modern scholars generally discount his testimony (see especially Richard 1978: 241–244). For a discussion of the term, see also Koch 1949; Fless 1995: 45–48; Prescendi 2010: 88–89; Bätz 2012: 71–73.

[28] Dion. Hal. *Ant. Rom.* 2.21.1, 71.4; Cass. Dio 59.7.1. For the translation of this term, see *LSJ*, s.v. ἀμφιθαλεύς.

[29] Garland 1990: 145.

[30] See most recently Wildfang 2006: 44, with further bibliography.

[31] As suggested by Koch 1949; Néraudau 1984: 229; Mustakallio 2007: 189. Seneca the Elder's *sacerdos prostituta* (prostitute priestess), who had been kidnapped by pirates, sold into a brothel, but managed (she claimed) to preserve her virginity throughout, may shed further light on this provision. In addition to the dispute over her chastity, the candidate's bad luck (*infelicitas*) surfaces as an impediment to her selection. One of the declaimers argues, for instance, that chastity, innocence, and good fortune (*pudicitiam, innocentiam, felicitatem*, 1.2.19) must be prized above all in a woman seeking a religious office. If the insistence on *felicitas* can be extended beyond the particulars of this *controversia*, it would lend support to the interpretation offered here that a girl who had lost one (or both) of her parents was too unlucky to serve as a Vestal.

instead of the daughter of Fonteius Agrippa, "because her mother remained in the same marriage: for Agrippa had diminished his house by divorce" (*quod mater eius in eodem coniugio manebat; nam Agrippa discidio domum imminuerat, Ann.* 2.86). It is impossible to determine whether this episode reflects the conventional approach to selecting a Vestal. The Romans disapproved of divorce, especially divorce of a virtuous wife who had borne legitimate children, but the practice was never explicitly prohibited, except in the case of the *flamen Dialis* and perhaps the remaining *flamines maiores* and the *rex sacrorum* as well.[32] In light of other extant provisions about the composition of a prospective Vestal's family, however, it seems likely that the daughters of divorced couples were not often competitive candidates for the priesthood.

Vestals were chosen from complete and "ideal" families in which both parents were living and very likely still married. This expectation of perfection extended to a candidate's legal status as well, though in this context, "ideal" refers to the legal construct known as the Roman *familia*, rather than to the lived reality of familial relations at Rome.[33] According to Gellius, neither a prospective Vestal nor her father could ever have been emancipated from the *patria potestas* (paternal power) of their *paterfamilias* (male head of household). An ancient concept predating the codification of the Twelve Tables in the middle fifth century BC, *patria potestas* articulated the legal relationship between the *paterfamilias* and the members of his household.[34] The *paterfamilias* was the sole legal owner of his family's property. He could expose infants, exercise the right of life and death over his children, sell them into slavery, or emancipate them from his power. Under normal circumstances, *patria potestas* was a lifelong power, and even an adult man, his children, and his property technically remained in the control of his father as long as he was living. Emancipation, on the other hand, legally severed the bond of *potestas*, making the emancipated son or daughter legally independent (*sui iuris*).[35]

Jane Gardner has suggested that the Romans prohibited an emancipated child from entering the Vestal order because she was an orphan in the eyes of the law and thus no longer *patrima et matrima*.[36] This compelling proposal does not explain, however, why the daughters of emancipated fathers were also ineligible. The reason for this provision may be related to the original purpose of emancipation itself. Some argue that in archaic Rome, emancipation and the associated loss of inheritance rights allowed a *paterfamilias* to punish

[32] Treggiari 1991: 471–473. Although actual statistics are irrecoverable, Treggiari (1991: 473–482, 1996a: 31–46) has argued that divorce was not nearly as prevalent in the late Republic as scholars once believed.

[33] For this distinction, see Gardner 1998: 1–5; Saller 1994: 71–101.

[34] Family members in the *potestas* of the *paterfamilias* included his wife (if she had married with *manus*), their children, the children of their sons, their daughters-in-law (if they had married with *manus*), and all household slaves. For a full discussion of *patria potestas* see, for example, Crook 1967; Lacey 1986; Saller 1994: 102–132.

[35] For the procedure and legal effects of emancipation, see Gardner 1998: 10–15. Unlike a son, an emancipated daughter remained in her father's guardianship (Gardner 1986: 14–15; 1998: 12, 85–93).

[36] Gardner 1986: 22, followed by Bätz 2012: 74.

a wayward son by casting him out of the family.[37] Although this position is not universally accepted, it highlights the disruption caused by emancipation. Whatever its initial intent, the practice fragmented the family and undermined the proper succession of *potestas* through the male agnatic line. Such meddling with the order of things was evidently serious enough to disqualify a family from presenting their daughter as a candidate for the Vestal priesthood.[38]

The ban on emancipation provides indirect evidence for other aspects of a prospective Vestal's family situation. A Roman citizen had *potestas* only over children born to him by his *matrona*, the woman with whom he had *conubium* (legal ability to marry).[39] Children born to a man by a concubine or a slave did not enter his *potestas* but derived their legal status from their mother instead.[40] A Vestal candidate, in other words, had to be the product of a *iustum matrimonium*, a legal marriage contracted by two citizens with *conubium* for the sake of producing legitimate children.[41] In early Rome, only full Roman citizens (*cives*) and communities with the Latin right (*ius Latii*) had the *conubium* to marry one another.[42] Citizens of Italian municipalities with a diminished form of citizenship (*civitas sine suffragio*) did not possess *conubium* with Roman citizens. The tradition is uncertain, but it appears that patricians and plebeians did not possess *conubium* with one another until after the introduction of the *lex Canuleia* in 445 BC.[43] The evidence thus suggests that Vestals were drawn only from "ideal" families constituted in accordance with legal and social norms. The nature of this ideal changed over time—the *lex Canuleia*, for instance, radically redefined legal marriage in fifth-century BC Rome, as did the marriage laws of Augustus in the first century BC—but the civil status of a Vestal and her family remained a concern well into the imperial period.

Other provisions underscore the elite social status of Vestal Virgins and their families. Gellius reports, for instance, that the daughters of freedmen as well as the daughters of parents who had been engaged in a base or degrading occupation (*sordidum negotium*) were prohibited from joining the Vestal order. Elite Romans generally held a very dim view of craftsmen and wage-laborers.[44] Certain trades and professions were officially considered base (*sordidi*) and disqualified a citizen from political activity and membership in the equestrian or senatorial orders (*ordines*).[45] Cicero's well-known catalogue of occupations in the *De officiis (On Duties)* provides some indication of how the Romans cate-

---

[37]Girard 1911: 190; Nicholas 1962: 80; Thomas 1982: 554–555; Borkowski 1994: 107. Against this interpretation, see Gardner 1998: 6–10, 67–68, 104–110, 112.

[38]For similar comments, see Staples 1998: 139; Bätz 2012: 74–75.

[39]Treggiari 1991: 43.

[40]Treggiari 1991: 49–54.

[41]For this definition of legal marriage, see Treggiari 1991: 11–12.

[42]Ulp. 5.3–5, with Treggiari 1991: 43–54.

[43]Livy 4.1.1–3.

[44]On Roman attitudes toward work, see De Robertis 1963: 21–97; Treggiari 1980; D'Arms 1981: 20–47, 149–171; Joshel 1992b: 62–91.

[45]Nicolet 1980: 80–81; Grieve 1985: 425–426, n. 49; Dyck 1996: 335.

gorized work, and may clarify the occupational profile of a prospective Vestal's family.[46] Not surprisingly, Cicero extols agriculture as the only truly honorable (*liberalis*) pursuit for a freeborn man. Professions like medicine, architecture and teaching are acknowledged as respectable (*honestae*), while all others are classified as base (*sordidi*) for one reason or another, especially those catering to pleasure and self-indulgence (fishmongers, poulterers, butchers, cooks, perfumers, dancers and stage artists are singled out for particular censure).[47]

While some base professions were simply regarded as unworthy of freeborn citizens, others were held as unclean and polluting. Undertakers (*libitinarii*), for example, were ritually polluted on account of their constant contact with the dead.[48] The children of men and women who engaged in such occupations were likewise polluted and may have been disqualified from serving as ritual agents in the public sphere.[49] The exclusion from the Vestal order of any girl whose father or mother had performed a "base occupation" may reasonably be ascribed to this ritual rationale, and goes hand in hand with the requirement that she be physically unblemished. We cannot be certain about which professions disqualified a family from offering their daughter as a candidate for the Vestal order, or even whether sacral law approached the question with any consistency over time. Even so, the general picture is one in which certain members of Roman society were prohibited from participating in public religion in a priestly capacity because they or their parents had engaged in a stigmatized occupation.

The exclusion of the daughters of freedmen and freedwomen can likewise be attributed to a desire to maintain social distinctions. In all periods, the Roman elite exhibited a hearty disdain for former slaves and their children, particularly those whose wealth and success threatened to efface time-honored social distinctions. Former slaves were prohibited from holding magistracies or positions in the major and minor colleges.[50] Although their freeborn sons were legally permitted to do so, the stigma of a freed parent was often an impediment to advancement.[51]

Despite this deeply ingrained prejudice against freedmen and their children, the historian Cassius Dio reports that Augustus enacted an extraordinary measure in AD 5 in response to a shortage of candidates for the Vestal order:

ἐπειδή τε οὐ ῥᾳδίως οἱ πάνυ εὐγενεῖς τὰς θυγατέρας ἐς τὴν τῆς Ἑστίας ἱερατείαν ἐπεδίδοσαν, ἐνομοθετήθη καὶ ἐξ ἀπελευθέρων γεγεννημένας

---

[46] Cic. *Off.* 1.150–151, with De Robertis 1963: 52–63; Finley 1973: 41–61; D'Arms 1981: 23–24; Treggiari 1980; Joshel 1992b: 66–69; Dyck 1996: 331–338.

[47] Cic. *Off.* 1.150.

[48] Bodel 2000: 135–144; Lindsay 2000: 157–160. A late first century BC or early first century AD inscription from Puteoli (*AE* 1971 88) prohibits *libitinarii* from entering the town except to collect or dispose of a corpse or to inflict a punishment.

[49] See, for example, Cass. Dio 46.4.2–5.3, 7.4.

[50] This is not to say that freedmen were excluded from participating in public religion on every occasion (Beard, North and Price 1998: 260–261).

[51] See, for example, Hor. *Sat.* 1.6.

ἱερᾶσθαι. καὶ ὁ μὲν κλῆρος αὐτῶν, ἐπεὶ πλείους ἠμφεσβήτησαν, ἐν τῷ συνεδρίῳ παρόντων τῶν πατέρων σφῶν, ὅσοι γε ἵππευον, ἐγένετο, οὐ μέντοι καὶ τοιαύτη τις ἀπεδείχθη. (55.22.5)

Since the highborn were reluctant to contribute their daughters for the order of Vesta, it was enacted that the daughters of freedmen also be Vestals. The casting of lots in their case [i.e., in the case of the daughters of freedmen], seeing that there were still other candidates [i.e., the daughters of freeborn fathers], took place in the senate with the fathers in attendance—at least insofar as these were *equites*; however, it was not a freedman's daughter who was elected.[52]

An anecdote related by Suetonius reveals that Augustus had faced similar opposition several years earlier. On this occasion, the *princeps* attempted to shame the recalcitrant nobles into offering their daughters by swearing that if one of his own granddaughters were eligible, he would have proposed her name.[53] When faced with renewed intransigence in AD 5, Augustus adopted this astonishing solution.[54] Marie-Thérèse Raepsaet-Charlier has suggested that the law was actually more cunning than it appears at first glance.[55] On the one hand, the measure allowed Augustus to flatter the freed population by extending to them a considerable honor. At the same time, however, he was undoubtedly counting on the fact that the proposal would motivate the elite to participate in the sortition. Despite their initial reluctance to submit their daughters to the order, the prospect of a freedman's daughter in the Vestal order reignited the interest of freeborn fathers. A freedman's daughter was not selected in AD 5.

Scholars have rightly questioned the impact of this episode on the order's subsequent history.[56] Did the principate of Augustus represent a major turning point in the way access to the Vestal order was defined? A survey of Vestals from the imperial period provides no definitive answers. Of thirty-eight known Vestals, eight belonged to senatorial families, fifteen were probably of senatorial birth, one was a member of an equestrian family, and fourteen are of unknown origin.[57] Ultimately, however, Gellius' assertion that the daughters of freedmen

---

[52] I have adopted Swan's (2004: 157) translation of this text.

[53] Suet. *Aug.* 31.3. Suetonius does not provide a date for this episode, but it must have occurred between July 4, 13 BC, when Julia was old enough to be chosen as a Vestal (and Augustus had returned to Rome from Gaul), and late March of 12 BC, when her father Agrippa died (as argued by Scheid 1999: 15; Mekacher and Van Haeperen 2003: 72–74).

[54] It is interesting that despite the evident importance of the Vestal order to Rome's continued existence, fathers could not be forced to relinquish their daughters to the order, otherwise Augustus could simply have chosen a new Vestal without resorting to such a radical measure.

[55] Raepsaet-Charlier 1984: 257–260.

[56] Most believe (rightly, I think) that the measure had no lasting impact on the Vestal order (see, for example, Münzer 1937: 48; Koch 1958: 1744; Raepsaet-Charlier 1984: 257; Mekacher and Van Haeperen 2003: 75). For a different view, see Giannelli 1913: 51; Gardner 1986: 22; Takács 2008: 81.

[57] Raepsaet-Charlier 1984: 259.

were excluded is a reliable indication that Augustus did not permanently expand access to the Vestal order in AD 5.[58]

Though he appears to have relied upon Labeo's commentary for the restrictions discussed thus far, the plural verb "they say" (*aiunt*, 1.12.6) suggests that Gellius changed sources for his discussion of "exemptions" from the order. The wording in this section, in any case, clearly indicates that we are dealing with provisions of a different character from those that precede them. Whereas Gellius tells us that it would not be "right" (*fas*, 1.12.1) to select a girl with a speech impediment, he writes in the following section that certain girls were entitled to an exemption (*excusatio*, 1.12.6; *vacatio*, 1.12.7). Prosopographical evidence confirms that the exemptions mentioned by Gellius did not categorically exclude a girl from joining the order. Although the sister of a Vestal could be excused, the Oculata sisters served together during the reign of Domitian (r. AD 81–96) and were convicted of *incestum* (unchastity) at the same trial.[59] Despite their nonbinding nature, the exemptions merit brief discussion.

According to Gellius, the sisters of Vestals, the daughters of *flamines*, augurs, *quindecimviri*, *septemviri*, and *salii*, and the fiancées of *pontifices* and *tubicines* were excused from serving in the Vestal order.[60] Given the nature of this list, it seems probable that the exemptions had a religious basis.[61] As I argue in chapter 1, the daughter of a *flamen* may have assisted her parents as the *flaminia sacerdotula*.[62] Perhaps the daughters of other priests on the list also participated in rituals celebrated by their fathers. If these girls were already serving in an official capacity, then it would have been inappropriate to remove them from this role. Exemption was not granted to the sisters, daughters, and fiancées of all priests, however, and the absence from the list of several prominent figures is curious. Why was the daughter of an *augur* excused but not the daughter of a *pontifex* or the *rex sacrorum*? Did Gellius (or his source) omit these priesthoods unintentionally? Or does the extant list represent only those priesthoods whose members had filed for exemption at the time when the source was compiled? Much remains uncertain.

It is also possible that the exemptions were motivated by more material considerations. The exemption granted to the sister of a Vestal, for instance, could reasonably be understood in the context of elite competition for priestly offices. It is true that daughters were important assets for cementing political alliances through marriage.[63] Even so, some fathers may have appreciated the utility of having a Vestal daughter, and the Roman elite, who preferred to distribute

---

[58] Mekacher and Van Haeperen 2003: 75.

[59] Suet. *Dom.* 8.4, with Mekacher and Van Haeperen 2003: 68; Bätz 2012: 80. For the opposing view, see Porte 1989: 67; Koch 1958: 1744.

[60] The daughter of a *flamen Dialis* would have been ineligible anyway, since the *flamen Dialis* was released from the *potestas* of his *paterfamilias* when he took office (Gai. *Inst.* 1.130, 3.114; Ulp. 10.5).

[61] Wildfang (2006: 45) suggests as much, though she does not offer a specific solution.

[62] See chapter 1.

[63] For a discussion of the evidence, see especially Dixon 1985.

power and prestige widely, may have considered it unfair for a single family to monopolize new spots.[64] With only six Vestals serving at any given time, each fulfilling a term of at least thirty years, vacancies in the order were probably few and far between. Unable to find a reason why it would be *nefas* (prohibited) for a Vestal's sister to be elected to the order as well, the Romans decided that such a girl should be exempt, a condition that likely exerted social if not religious pressure on a father to withhold his second daughter from consideration.[65] Such an explanation assumes that the office was desirable at the time these exemptions became customary, which rules out the reign of Augustus, when candidates for the order were relatively scarce.[66]

Before concluding his discussion, Gellius cites Capito Ateius for two further provisions. The father of a candidate, he reports, could not have his *domus* (house) outside Italy. This provision very likely dates to the late Republic or early principate, when Roman citizens first began to settle in the provinces in large numbers.[67] Capito also reported that the daughter of a man with three children must be excused from joining the order.[68] This exemption presumably postdates the introduction of the *ius liberorum* under the marriage laws of Augustus, which granted freeborn mothers of three children exemption from *tutela* and allowed fathers of the same number to ascend the *cursus honorum* more quickly.[69] Perhaps Augustus sought to increase the rewards of a large family by exempting parents with three children from submitting one of their daughters to the order at a time when the elite were generally disinclined to do so.

The Selection Process

After describing the conditions of service and provisions for exemption, Gellius turns to the mode of selection:

> De more autem rituque capiundae virginis litterae quidem antiquiores non exstant, nisi quae capta prima est a Numa rege esse captam. Sed Papiam legem invenimus, qua cavetur ut pontificis maximi arbitratu virgines e populo viginti legantur sortitioque in contione ex eo numero fiat

---

[64] See also Bätz 2012: 79. There was rule, perhaps introduced by the *lex Domitia* of 104 BC, that only one member of a family could serve in one of the major priestly colleges at any given time (see Cass. Dio 39.17.1, with North 1990b). This condition ensured that positions in the major colleges were shared among the most important elite families.

[65] It is probably not coincidental that the only pair of Vestal sisters known to us served during the reign of Domitian, when competition for the office was not particularly fierce.

[66] North (1990b) makes a similar argument with respect to male priesthoods. Others have interpreted the exemptions differently, stressing that families reluctant to surrender their daughters to the Vestal order may have been eager to find exemptions (see, for example, Bätz 2012: 80–83).

[67] For a discussion of settlement abroad, see Sherwin-White 1973: 225.

[68] Wildfang (2006: 42–43) argues that the daughter of a man with three children was excluded from the order. The wording is admittedly ambiguous, but it seems very unlikely that men with three children were prohibited from offering their daughters as Vestals.

[69] For the *ius liberorum*, see Gardner 1986: 202–1, 194–198.

et cuius sors virginis ducta erit, ut eam pontifex maximus capiat eaque Vestae fiat. (*N.A.* 1.12.10–11)

With regard to the custom and ritual for taking a virgin, indeed, no ancient accounts are extant, except that the first one taken was taken by Numa. But we have found the *lex Papia*, in which it is prescribed that the *pontifex maximus* select twenty virgins from among the people, and that a choice from that number be made by lot in a *contio* (a nonvoting assembly), and that the *pontifex maximus* take the one whose lot is drawn, and she becomes Vesta's.

Though Gellius alludes to some uncertainty in the sources, most ancient authors report that the king nominated new Vestals directly.[70] Modern scholars speculate that in the early Republic, the *pontifex maximus* exercised this prerogative by virtue of his position as president of the pontifical college.[71] Direct nomination allowed the *pontifex maximus* to exert unilateral control over access to the order. Presumably, personal interest and political affiliation often influenced his decision. Later, however, the *lex Papia* established a new procedure for the selection of Vestals, stipulating that they be chosen in a *contio* (a nonvoting assembly) by lot from a group of twenty virgins nominated in advance by the *pontifex maximus*. This reduced the role of the *pontifex maximus* in the selection of new Vestals and subjected the process to greater public scrutiny.

According to Gellius, the *pontifex maximus* selected candidates for the lot "from the people" (*e populo*), that is, from among the entire citizen body. For this reason, historians tend to argue that the *lex Papia* granted plebeian candidates access to the order for the first time, and this has ignited a lively debate regarding the date of the law, as scholars attempt to place it within an appropriate sociopolitical context.[72] It seems more likely, however, that plebeians had always been eligible for the Vestal order.[73] There was at least one plebeian Vestal as early as the fourth century BC, Minucia, who was executed for *incestum* (unchastity) in 337 BC.[74] Unfortunately, we know too little about the order's early history to be certain.[75] Whether or not the *lex Papia* altered the constituency of the Vestal order by admitting plebeians, the larger pool of candidates mandated

---

[70] See, for instance, Cic. *Rep.* 2.26; Livy 1.20.3; Dion. Hal. *Ant. Rom.* 2.64, 3.2.67; Plut. *Num.* 10.1. Roman historians claim that Rhea Silvia was also directly nominated by the Alban king Amulius (Livy 1.3.11; Dion. Hal. *Ant. Rom.* 1.76; Plut. *Rom.* 3).

[71] See, for example, Mommsen 1887–1888: 25–26; Wissowa 1912: 487, 510; Giannelli 1913: 49.

[72] The date of the *lex Papia* will probably never be known with certainty. Some scholars, including most recently Rüpke (1996b: 277–279, with further bibliography), have proposed that it should be dated to 65 BC, a year in which one of the tribunes was named C. Papius. Those arguing for a date in the third or second century BC include Niccolini 1934: 382–383; Guizzi 1968: 73–77; Rawson 1974: 210–211; Van Haeperen 2002: 96–102; Mekacher and Van Haeperen 2003: 70–72; Bätz 2012: 117–123.

[73] As argued by Mommsen 1887–1888: 3, 567, n.2; Klose 1910: 33.

[74] Livy 8.15.7–8; *POx.* 12.3.33–36, with Klose 1910: 35–36, No. 4; Rüpke 2008: 802–803, No. 2463.

[75] We know the names of only twenty Vestals from the Republican period and only four from the period before the *lex Ogulnia* of 300 BC opened the major priestly colleges to plebeian candidates.

by the law resulted in a more transparent and seemingly equitable process of selection.

Although the *lex Papia* curtailed the power of the *pontifex maximus*, it did not go as far as the *lex Domitia* of 104 BC, which empowered the people directly. In accordance with the provisions of this law, members of the priestly colleges were elected in a special session of the *comitia tributa* (tribal assembly) from a list of three nominees, prepared in advance by members of the relevant college. Vestals, by contrast, were chosen by lot.[76] Though election may have seemed inappropriate when the candidate was a young girl, the religious implications of the lot were undoubtedly a factor as well.[77] Given that ancient Greeks and Romans viewed sortition as an expression of divine will, the *lex Papia* introduced a process of selection that seemed to leave the final decision to Vesta.[78]

However we interpret the law's original intent, the provisions of the *lex Papia* suggest that the Vestal order was a highly coveted priesthood: the increased number of candidates and the use of sortition would have reduced the potential for aristocratic strife concerning the selection process.[79] As I argue in chapter 7, the prestige and influence of individual Vestals was not insignificant; some parents may have been eager to see their daughters selected to the order, even if this meant sacrificing a potentially advantageous alliance through marriage. It is more difficult to tell, however, whether or not the law was intended to make the order more accessible to plebeian candidates and, if so, whether or not it succeeded.

Gellius relates that the procedure outlined by the *lex Papia* was rarely used in his day.[80] Instead, the senate typically granted an exception to the law if a man of respectable birth offered his daughter to the *pontifex maximus*, provided that she met all requirements for admission. Although the *lex Papia* had not been formally repealed, it had evidently outlived its usefulness. As we have already seen, the selection process was in a state of flux during the early principate. Raepsaet-Charlier suggests that the incident narrated by Suetonius, which has been dated to about 12 BC, precipitated this transformation.[81] But the details of the selection process in AD 5, when a shortage of candidates prompted Augustus to open the order to the daughters of freedmen, suggest otherwise. The radical nature of the solution indicates that Augustus was attempting to fill the requisite slate of twenty candidates in accordance with the *lex Papia*, as opposed to finding one or two fathers willing to offer their daughters as Vestals.

---

[76] The Romans also used the lot in a more limited way to select the seventeen tribes (out of a total of thirty two) that would elect a new *pontifex maximus* and, following the *lex Domitia* of 104 BC, any member of one of the major priestly colleges (Rosenstein 1995: 50, n. 26).

[77] See, for example, Wildfang 2006: 47; Bätz 2012: 125.

[78] Rosenstein 1995: 50. In fact, the Greeks often chose their priests by lot (for the ancient evidence, see Headlam 1933: 5–6).

[79] Guizzi 1968: 69–70.

[80] Gell. *N.A.* 1.12.12.

[81] Raepsaet-Charlier 1984: 256.

At the same time, the unusual circumstances surrounding the sortition of that year, which took place in the senate rather than in a *contio*, seem to suggest that the *lex Papia* was not strictly observed.

The first securely attested implementation of the new procedure dates to AD 19, when the death of the Vestal Occia created a vacancy in the order. According to Tacitus, Fonteius Agrippa and Domitius Pollio offered their daughters to the *pontifex maximus* Tiberius, who chose the daughter of Pollio.[82] The fact that only two senators offered their daughters, coupled with the provision of a dowry for the runner-up, suggests that there was once again a shortage of candidates. The new method of selection overcame this problem not by altering the requirements for eligibility, but by dispensing with the necessity of finding twenty girls for the lot. The transition also placed control of the selection of new Vestals more securely in the hands of the emperor, by virtue of his position as *pontifex maximus*, and the senate, who sanctioned his decision by granting an exemption from the *lex Papia*.[83] The process outlined by the *lex Papia* was the product of a characteristically republican struggle for religious authority and access to public religious offices. As social and political circumstances changed under Augustus and his successors, the practice of selecting a new Vestal was renegotiated to account for the *princeps* and his new position within the Roman religious system.

Initiation: The Rite of *Captio*

Once the *pontifex maximus* had selected a candidate, he "seized" her in a rite known as the *captio*, the same procedure used during the inauguration of a new *flamen Dialis* or *rex sacrorum*.[84] Once again, Gellius provides the most detailed account of this ritual, including the formula spoken by the *pontifex maximus*:

> "capi" autem virgo propterea dici videtur, quia pontificis maximi manu prensa ab eo parente in cuius potestate est, veluti bello capta, abducitur. in libro primo Fabii Pictoris, quae verba pontificem maximum dicere oporteat, cum virginem capiat, scriptum est. ea verba haec sunt: "sacerdotem Vestalem, quae sacra faciat quae ius siet sacerdotem Vestalem facere pro populo Romano Quiritibus, uti quae optima lege fuit, ita te, Amata, capio." (*N.A.* 1.12.13–14)

Therefore, it seems that the virgin is said to be "taken" because she is grasped by the hand of the *pontifex maximus* and led away from the parent in whose *potestas* she is, as if she had been taken in war. In the

---

[82] Tac. *Ann.* 2.86.1–3.
[83] Mekacher and Van Haeperen (2003: 76, 79) argue that the selection of a new Vestal was actually made by the senate, not the *pontifex maximus*, but neither Tacitus (*Ann.* 2.86) nor Gellius (*N.A.* 1.12.12) support this claim.
[84] Livy 27.8.4; Gai. *Inst.* 3.114, with Guizzi 1968: 34–45. See also chapter 1.

first book of Fabius Pictor are recorded the proper words for the *pontifex maximus* to say when he takes a virgin. The words are, "I take you, Amata, just as she who was [taken] in perfect formality, to be a Vestal priestess, to perform the rites that are lawful for a Vestal priestess to perform on behalf of the Roman people, the *Quirites*."

This passage has been the subject of intense scrutiny, particularly because of what it reveals (or seems to reveal) about the nature of the relationship between the Vestals and the *pontifex maximus*. Many scholars have identified similarities between the *captio* and the Roman wedding.[85] The *pontifex maximus* took the initiate from her *paterfamilias* and led her away "as if she had been taken in war" (*veluti bello capta*, Gell. *N.A.* 1.12.13), just the bride was removed from the lap of her mother in a simulated abduction (*rapi simulatur virgo ex gremio matris*, Festus 354L). He addressed the new Vestal as "Amata," perhaps meaning "Beloved."[86] Finally, the Vestal hairstyle, the *seni crines* (six-tressed hairstyle), was otherwise worn only by brides on their wedding day.[87] Taken together, these details suggest to some that the *captio* was a symbolic wedding between the Vestal and the *pontifex maximus*. This position is generally held in tandem with a belief that the Vestals represented the wife of the archaic king and the flame of Vesta his domestic hearth.[88]

There are, however, compelling differences between the *captio* and the Roman wedding.[89] As we shall see in chapter 5, it is far from certain that the Vestals adopted the *seni crines* from the bride, or that their obligation to wear this coiffure on a daily basis symbolized their perpetually "liminal" (i.e., bridal) status. At the wedding, moreover, the bridegroom pretended to seize the bride from the lap of her mother or closest female relative in a ritual that recalled the rape of the Sabine women. She was then led in procession to the home of her new husband (*domum deductio*) and, even more importantly, to the bridal bed (*lectus genialis*), where the marriage would be consummated. The *pontifex maximus*, on the other hand, took the initiate from her *paterfamilias* and delivered her into the care of her colleagues at the House of the Vestals. There is no indication that he offered her fire and water or that she performed any of the rituals associated with a traditional wedding ceremony. Furthermore, the Romans apparently did not understand the title "Amata" as a term of endearment, regardless of its relationship to the verb "to love" (*amare*). Gellius, for instance,

---

[85] See, for example, Dragendorff 1896: 299; Santinelli 1904: 63, with the discussion in Beard 1980: 13–14.

[86] Many scholars argue that the title Amata is the perfect passive participle of the verb *amare* (to love), and should thus be translated as "beloved" (see, for example, Guizzi 1968: 130–131, with earlier bibliography).

[87] See, for example, Jordan 1886: 43–56; Guizzi 1968: 110–112; Beard 1980: 16; La Follette and Wallace 1993; La Follette 1994; Mustakallio 1997: 74, 2007: 187.

[88] See, for example, Jordan 1886: 47; Dragendorff 1896: 281–302; Santinelli 1904; Wissowa 1912: 509–10.

[89] For the Roman wedding, see especially Hersch 2010.

records a tradition that the *pontifex maximus* addressed the initiate in this way because the first Vestal was named Amata.[90]

The ancient sources do not support interpreting the *captio* ritual as a symbolic marriage between the *pontifex maximus* and the Vestal initiate, nor do they permit us to identify the priestesses of Vesta as the republican counterparts of the archaic queen. As Beard has written, "it is unacceptable special pleading" to maintain that the absolute physical virginity expected of Vestals was merely a generalized form of chastity, like the *pudicitia* (sexual virtue) required of Roman *matronae* (married women).[91] But Beard's suggestion that the priestesses were interstitial figures in a perpetual state of transition is equally unsatisfactory.[92] The *captio* ritual must be understood on its own terms. It effected a change in social status by legally and physically removing the candidate from her household and making her a Vestal priestess (*sacerdos Vestalis*, Gell. *N.A.* 1.12.14).[93] This transformation, discussed more fully below, was immediate and complete; a Vestal could never return to her former position in the social hierarchy. Though she remained an unmarried *virgo* (virgin), she exchanged her place in her natal household for a life of priestly service on behalf of the Roman people (*pro populo Romano Quiritibus*, Gell. *N.A.* 1.12.14). The ritual formula quoted by Gellius confirms that she acquired an official position in civic cult.[94] The phrase "in perfect formality" (*optima lege*, *N.A.* 1.12.14), the same formula used for the creation of magistrates, indicated not only that the *pontifex maximus* was taking the Vestal in a perfectly legal way, but also that she would enjoy complete possession of all the rights and privileges of her office.[95] No longer a private individual, the initiate had become a public priestess.

The Legal Status of the Vestal Virgins

When a young girl began her new life as a Vestal, she assumed an extraordinary position for a person of her age and gender. The legal status of an ordinary elite woman was defined at all times by her relationship to the men in her life.[96] A daughter was subject to the authority (*potestas*) of her *paterfamilias*. A

---

[90] Gell. *N.A.* 1.12.19.

[91] Beard 1980: 15.

[92] Beard 1980: 21. See also Takács (2008: 80–86), who has recently written that the Vestals "remained in a perpetual 'rite of passage' loop, between status (unmarried and married) and a gendered (female and male) sphere."

[93] Wildfang 2006: 38–39. Gellius does not describe a separate inauguration ceremony, which suggests that the *captio* ritual fully integrated the candidate into the Vestal priesthood.

[94] For the source of the quotation, see the introduction.

[95] See, for example, Cic. *Phil.* 11.12.30; Festus 204, 216L, with Botsford 1909: 186–187; Brouwers 1933; Radke 1972: 431; Kroppenberg 2010: 427.

[96] For a discussion of the legal status of Roman women, see especially Gardner 1986.

wife might be under the control (*manus*) of her husband.[97] During the republican period, a woman who had become legally independent (*sui iuris*) upon the death of her father or husband passed into the guardianship (*tutela*) of her nearest male relative. A Vestal, however, was bound by none of these conditions. In a state that continually emphasized the importance of the family, the Vestals must have stood out as the only Romans without one.[98] Having been freed from *patria potestas*, she was no longer a daughter.[99] As a Vestal she was the wife of no man and as a virgin she could not be a mother. While other women were subject to the *tutela* of a male relative, a Vestal never had a guardian. Unlike a man who became *sui iuris*, however, a Vestal did not become the head of her own *familia* with her own *potestas*. As Holt Parker has commented, "she did not cease to be a woman, but she ceased to be like any other woman."[100] Together with her virginity, considered more fully below, a Vestal's unique legal status isolated her from traditional kinship structures and defined her position in relation to the community as a whole.[101] Her unique ability to represent and even symbolize the collective was vitally important to the fulfillment of her ritual obligations at the communal hearth of Vesta.[102]

According to Gellius, a Vestal's legal relationship to her birth family was severed at the moment she entered the order:

> virgo autem Vestalis, simul est capta atque in atrium Vestae deducta et pontificibus tradita est, eo statim tempore sine emancipatione ac sine capitis minutione e patris potestate exit et ius testamenti faciundi adipiscitur. (*N.A.* 1.12.9)

---

[97] For *manus* marriage, see chapter 1.

[98] As observed by Culham 2004: 142.

[99] Some scholars have argued that the Vestals were in the *potestas* of the *pontifex maximus* (see, for example, Fowler 1899: 147; Wissowa 1912: 158, n. 7; Giannelli 1913: 60; Lacey 1986: 126), but this is not strictly accurate (Gardner 1986: 23; Staples 1998: 183, n. 39; Parker 2004: 573; Mekacher 2006: 32). The *pontifex maximus* did have the authority to inflict corporal punishment (see below), but this alone is not enough to prove that he had *potestas* over the Vestals. In fact, he exercised some disciplinary control over all members of the pontifical college, male as well as female.

[100] Parker 2004: 572. Although Beard (1980: 17) suggested that a Vestal's legal status was "defined in male terms," her position was not entirely analogous with that of other Roman women or men. For a critique of Beard's analysis of the legal status of the Vestals, see also Gardner 1986: 24–25; Staples 1998: 141; Parker 2004: 572–574.

[101] As stressed by Cancik-Lindemaier 1990: 14–15; Staples 1998: 143–145; Parker 2004: 571–573; Wildfang 2006: 73–74; Kroppenberg 2010: 422–424. Gallia (2015: 77) has recently argued that release from *potestas* was simply "the means by which their [i.e., the Vestals'] status was assimilated to that of the other priests under the purview of the pontifical college," a suggestion that effaces important distinctions within the extended pontifical college. The *flamen Dialis* was released from *potestas* (see below), but it is not at all clear that *pontifices* underwent a similar change in status (though it is admittedly unlikely that many had living fathers when they entered the college). The status of the *flaminicae maiores* and the *regina sacrorum*, moreover, who were very likely full members (see chapter 1), differed from that of the Vestals, suggesting an alternative model for assimilating priestesses within the structure of the college. More generally, while I agree that the "lived experience" of many Vestals differed from the "symbolic" ideal presented in this chapter (see Gallia 2015: 77–89), this tension is to be expected (see chapter 7). For the isolation of the Vestals from their families, see also Cornell 1981: 28; Fraschetti 1984: 101; Gardner 1986: 25; Mustakallio 1992: 56, 2007: 190–191; Bätz 2012: 92–94, 287–299.

[102] See chapter 6.

As soon as the Vestal Virgin is taken, led to the House of the Vestals, and handed over to the *pontifices*, she immediately at this time leaves the power (*potestas*) of her father without undergoing emancipation and without the diminution of her rights, and obtains the right to make a will.

In this passage, Gellius clearly indicates that the *captio* ritual itself released a Vestal from *patria potestas*, rather than any of the standard legal procedures used to achieve this change in status.[103] The procedure had to be unique, since *coemptio*, a form of ritual sale that could be invoked to emancipate children in *potestas*, would have placed the initiate into another man's power, thereby defeating the purpose of the ritual.[104] The *captio* severed a Vestal's legal ties to any individual family and established her as a public priestess of Vesta, fully committed to the welfare of the entire community. Roman sacral law took a similar approach to the *flamen Dialis* (and perhaps to the remaining *flamines* and the *rex sacrorum* as well) by stipulating his release from *patria potestas*.[105] Although the implications were not as dramatic, it is significant that his status was defined by his relationship to his wife the *flaminica* and by their obligation to the Roman people. Certain priests at Rome, including the Vestal Virgins, were uniquely identified with the community, rather than with individual Roman families.

Release from *patria potestas* had other important consequences that tended to reinforce the significance of a Vestal's relationship to the community. Upon entrance to the Vestal order, an initiate lost her rights of intestate succession.[106] Gellius quotes the relevant passage from Labeo's commentary on the Twelve Tables, Rome's earliest written law code:

> praeterea in commentariis Labeonis, quae ad duodecim tabulas composuit, ita scriptum est: "virgo Vestalis neque heres est cuiquam intestato, neque intestatae quisquam, sed bona eius in publicum redigi aiunt."
> (*N.A.* 1.12.18)

Moreover, in the commentaries of Labeo, which he composed on the Twelve Tables, the following is recorded: "A Vestal Virgin is not heir to

---

[103] Aside from the death of the *paterfamilias*, *patria potestas* could be extinguished through emancipation, adoption, the loss of citizenship through *capitis deminutio* (literally, "decrease of head"), or, in the case of a daughter, marriage with *manus*. The fact that a Vestal was not removed from *patria potestas* by any formal legal procedure has led some scholars to speculate that her father's *potestas* was merely suspended, like that of the father of a child captured in war (see Guizzi 1968: 66, 196, with further bibliography). Gardner (1986: 25) rightly rejects this hypothesis, pointing out that a captive had no rights, while the Vestals enjoyed many legal privileges.

[104] As observed by Parker 2004: 572–573.

[105] Gai. *Inst.* 1.130, 3.114; Ulp. 10.5.

[106] The ancient sources do not specify whether the *flamen Dialis* lost his rights of intestate succession as well, though Gardner (1986: 24) is inclined to think that he did not. Under Justinian, sons who reached the consulship or became bishops were released from their father's *potestas* without any corresponding loss of inheritance rights (*Nov.* 81.pr.3), a provision that may have been based on a privilege traditionally granted to *flamines Diales*.

any intestate person, nor is anyone her heir if she should die intestate, but they say that her property is transferred to the state."

Roman law observed strict rules concerning the designation of an heir in the case of intestacy.[107] The *sui heredes*, who were first in the line of succession, were all those who had been in the *potestas* of the deceased man, that is, his sons and daughters (including any adopted children), the children of his sons, and his wife if she had married with *manus*.[108] The *sui heredes* inherited equal portions of the estate irrespective of gender. If there were no *sui heredes*, agnatic relatives could be named as heirs, and finally, if all other options had been exhausted, members of the deceased man's *gens* (clan).[109]

Vestals, however, were explicitly excluded from the line of intestate succession. Having been released from her father's *potestas*, a Vestal was no longer one of his *sui heredes* and had no right of intestate succession. She also lost the right to inherit from her agnates, whose relationship to her had been determined by her position as a child in the *potestas* of her *paterfamilias*. The loss of automatic inheritance rights was reciprocal. If a Vestal died without a will, her property automatically passed to the state (*in publicum*), which stood in the place of her agnates. This provision reaffirms the notion that a Vestal belonged to the community as a whole, rather than to an individual family. Her property may have financed public rituals performed on behalf of the Roman people, perhaps those connected with the cult of Vesta, though Gellius does not say that this was the case.[110]

Even though Vestals were excluded from intestate succession, they could receive specific bequests and were free to make their own wills by virtue of exemption from guardianship (*tutela*).[111] The latter privilege in particular set them apart from other Roman women, who received testamentary powers only gradually.[112] In Roman law, a will was valid only if made by someone possessing testamentary capacity (*testamenti factio*). Although many of the conditions necessary to attain this capacity were equally valid for men and women, others affected them differently. Testators were required to be legally independent (*sui iuris*), which meant that men and women with a living *paterfamilias* as well as women married with *manus* could not make their own will unless they were

---

[107] On intestate succession, see Crook 1973; Gardner 1986: 190–200, 1998: 24–46.

[108] Women could not have *sui heredes*, but they could be *sui heredes* as daughters, granddaughters, or wives *in manu* (Gardner 1986: 190).

[109] Agnates were all persons who were descended from the same male ancestor and who would be in that ancestor's *patria potestas* if he were still living. Both male and female agnates could inherit through intestate succession, but succession between generations could pass through the male line only, since a woman's children would be in the *potestas* of their father, rather than that of their maternal grandfather. A woman could thus inherit from her father's brother, while a man could not inherit from his mother's brother (Gardner 1986: 191).

[110] Moyle 1912: 183. Against this interpretation, see Guizzi 1968: 166–167; Gardner 1986: 23–24.

[111] Gell. *N.A.* 1.12.9; Plut. *Num.* 10.3.

[112] For the testamentary powers of Roman women, see Watson 1971: 22–23; Buckland 1963: 288; Gardner 1986: 165–169.

emancipated. Until the reign of Hadrian (r. AD 117–138), the testamentary powers of a freeborn woman without a living *paterfamilias* were restricted as well, even if she was married without *manus*. If she wished to make a will, she was required to sever all legal ties to her agnates, typically by undergoing a *coemptio*, that is, a change in status.[113] Once the *coemptio* was complete, she obtained a guardian (*tutor*), whose consent was necessary in order for her will to be valid.

Guardianship over adult women (*tutela mulierum*) was of great importance in Roman law and society.[114] Ordinarily, any adult woman who was not under the *potestas* of her father or in the *manus* of her husband was subject to *tutela*. Most men designated a *tutor* for their wives and daughters in their wills. In cases where no provision had been made, the office fell to a woman's male agnates, either collectively or to the one most closely related. The *tutor* was responsible for safeguarding the interests of the family with respect to the property of the woman under his supervision. His consent was required for any action that might diminish the estate and transfer property out of the family, including marriage with *manus* or the creation of a dowry.[115] Under the *lex Iulia* of 18 BC and the *lex Papia Poppaea* of AD 9, freeborn women were exempt from *tutela* if they had borne three children. During the republican period, however, only the Vestal Virgins enjoyed this privilege.

According to the mid-imperial jurist Gaius (fl. *ca.* AD 140–180), the Vestals received exemption from *tutela* under a provision enshrined by the Twelve Tables.[116] Freedom from guardianship provided the Vestals with an unusual degree of legal and financial independence. Unlike most women during the republican period, Vestals were free to manage and to dispose of their own estates, which may often have been quite substantial. According to Livy, the Vestals received a yearly *stipendium* (pay) at public expense.[117] The primary source of their fortunes, however, must have been bequests from family members and wealthy patrons. Literary and epigraphic evidence indicates that individual Vestals owned slaves and property. In 337 BC, for instance, Minucia was ordered to "keep her slaves in her power" (*familiamque in potestate habere*, Livy 8.15.7–8) prior to her trial on a charge of *incestum* (unchastity). In the first century BC,

---

[113] Gai. *Inst.* 1.113–115.

[114] For *tutela mulierum*, see Gai. *Inst.* 1.142–196; Watson 1967: 102–154; Gardner 1986: 14–22.

[115] Actions that might diminish the estate included the alienation of property (e.g., through the manumission of slaves), undertaking contractual obligations, creating a dowry, marrying with *manus*, accepting an inheritance, and making a will (Gardner 1986: 18). Women were granted complete control over certain types of property, including jewelry, clothes, furniture, and houses and land outside of Italy. They were also free to purchase property without tutorial consent and could even lend money. Unlike the *tutor* of a minor, the *tutor* of an adult woman did not administer her property. Instead, his power was essentially negative, enabling him to prevent an action (Gardner 1986: 21).

[116] Gai. *Inst.* 1.144–145. See also Plut. *Num.* 10.3, with Guizzi 1968: 3–30.

[117] Livy 1.20.3. Mommsen (1887–1888: 2, 64) suggested that the *stipendium* should be regarded as a kind of dowry. Gardner (1986: 24), on the other hand, equates it with the *peculium*, that is, the property held by a person in another's *potestas*. But the dowry was a one-time gift and the Vestals were not subject to anyone's *potestas*. As Wildfang (2006: 71) has suggested, the *stipendium* of a Vestal should probably be compared to the *stipendium* paid to a soldier at the end of each annual campaign.

Licinia was accused of *incestum* with her cousin, M. Licinius Crassus (cos. 70 BC), because they had met together in private to discuss the purchase of a piece of her property.[118] Evidence from the imperial period suggests that these episodes were not aberrations.[119] Vestals were not dependent upon their fathers or husbands for financial support. They owned property and were free to dispose of it as they saw fit, without the intervention of a male guardian.[120]

Gaius reports that the ancients (*veteres*) had exempted the Vestals from *tutela* "on account of the honor of their priesthood" (*in honorem sacerdotii, Inst.* 1.145). A Vestal's legal autonomy was undoubtedly a source of status and prestige within the community. On its own, however, such an explanation is inadequate. Exemption from legal guardianship was very likely a "side effect" of the process of freeing a Vestal from male control.[121] Having ensured that a candidate for the order belonged to an "ideal" Roman family, the *pontifex maximus* subsequently oversaw her removal from this family through the ritual of *captio*. Her new position outside of traditional kinship structures had both ritual and symbolic functions. A Vestal's legal situation established her priestly competence, isolating her from her natal family and enabling her to serve and represent all Roman families. While other women tended the hearths of their fathers or husbands, a Vestal cared for the eternal flame of Vesta on the common hearth of the Roman people, which stood in the heart of the city and served to unite the individual families of Rome into a single community.

Vestal Privileges

Alongside their exceptional legal status, the Vestals enjoyed a variety of unusual privileges. Some of these were closely related to their ritual obligations. Like the *flamines*, the *rex sacrorum*, and *matronae* (married women), they were permitted to ride in *carpenta* (covered carriages) within the city on festival days.[122] They also enjoyed the privilege of *sacrosanctitas* (sacrosanctity), the same personal inviolability that protected tribunes from physical harm.[123] Like tribunician inviolability, Vestal *sacrosanctitas* was a function of public office. It was undoubtedly perceived as an honor, but even more importantly as a practical means of ensuring that the priestesses did not become ritually impure: a Vestal was consecrated to Vesta (*sacer*) and it was contrary to ritual law (*nefas*) to touch her. The provision of personal inviolability guaranteed that the Vestals could continue to perform their ritual obligations on behalf of the community.

---

[118] Plut. *Crass.* 1.2.
[119] See, for example, *CIL* 6.2146, 6.2147, 6.2148, 15.7126, 15.7127.
[120] Mekacher (2006: 32) has suggested that the *pontifex maximus* or an older member of the Vestal order advised young priestesses on legal and financial matters.
[121] Gardner 1986: 24; Parker 2004: 572–574.
[122] *CIL* 1.206. See also Livy 1.21.4; Tac. *Ann.* 12.42.
[123] Plut. *Ti. Gracch.* 15.6. For tribuncian *sacrosanctitas*, see Lintott 1999: 122–128.

Vestals were also permitted to employ a *lictor*.[124] Dio reports that the Romans first granted this privilege in 42 BC after one of the priestesses was insulted on her way home from a dinner party.[125] It seems more likely, however, that the Vestals had been attended by *lictores* on festival days already and were granted the additional privilege of a fulltime *lictor* after the incident in 42 BC. Generally speaking, Roman *lictores* accompanied high-ranking magistrates, representing their authority (*imperium*) and, when necessary, enforcing it through physical force.[126] The Vestals, on the other hand, were accompanied by *lictores curiatii*, a special class of *lictores* attached to the pontifical college.[127] Unlike their civil counterparts, *lictores curiatii* carried only two *fasces*.[128] Their presence thus clearly communicated a Vestal's status as a public priestess and member of the pontifical college. Presumably they also provided some degree of physical protection, alerting passersby that they should not touch (or insult) the Vestal in their midst.

The Vestals received additional public honors under Augustus and Tiberius, including the right to sit in prominent seats at the theater.[129] This privilege may have been instituted by the *lex Iulia Theatralis* (after AD 5), which imposed new restrictions on seating at theatrical performances and other spectacles as part of a multifaceted effort to restore distinctions between the various social orders (*discrimina ordinum*).[130] According to Suetonius, Augustus relegated women to the upper tiers of the theater during gladiatorial spectacles, granting special seating only to the Vestals, who sat in the lower level opposite the praetor's tribunal.[131] Cicero indicates that the Vestals had reserved seats during the republican period as well, but the location of their box must have been even more prominent following the *lex Iulia Theatralis*, when men and women no longer sat together at the games.[132] It does not necessarily follow, however, that this arrangement invested the Vestals with an aura of masculinity, as argued by Beard and those who have followed her.[133] The Vestals sat in special seats at the theater because they were public priestesses.[134] In fact, the fourth century AD author Arnobius claims that all the major priestly colleges had reserved seats

---

[124] For the Vestals' right to a *lictor*, see Plut. *Num.* 10.3; Cass. Dio. 47.19.4; Sen. *Controv.* 1.2.3, 7; Saquete 2000: 112. The Vestals on the altar frieze of the Ara Pacis Augustae (fig. 5.5) and on the Cancelleria Reliefs (fig. 5.7) are accompanied by *lictores*.

[125] Cass. Dio. 47.19.4.

[126] For the *lictores* see, for example, Gladigow 1972; Purcell 1983; Gizewski 2005.

[127] The *lictores curiatii* summoned the *comitia curiata* (Gell. *N.A.* 15.27), assisted at sacrifices *pro populo Romano* (*CIL* 6.1846–1847, 1852, 1885–1892, 14.296), and accompanied various priests (Ov. *Fast.* 2.21–24; Plut. *Quaest. Rom.* 113 = *Mor.* 291b; Festus (Paulus) 82L; *CIL* 12.6038).

[128] See Figs. 5.5 and 5.7, with Ryberg 1955: 41.

[129] Suet. *Aug.* 31.3, 44.3.

[130] For the *lex Iulia Theatralis*, see Rawson 1987.

[131] Suet. *Aug.* 44.3.

[132] Cic. *Mur.* 73, with Rawson 1987: 97. See also chapter 7.

[133] Beard 1980.

[134] Rawson 1987: 91, 109. Greek priestesses regularly sat in the *prohedria* (front seats) of Greek theaters as well (for the evidence, see Connelly 2007: 205–215).

at public spectacles, and an inscription from the Colosseum identifying those reserved for the Arval Brethren confirms his assertion.[135] The Vestals' prominent position in the theater reaffirmed their priestly status and official position within the community.

Augustus also enhanced the legal status of the Vestals as part of his marriage legislation. The *lex Papia Poppaea* of AD 9, which amended and supplemented certain provisions in the *lex Iulia* of 18 BC, guaranteed the Vestals the same privileges as freeborn mothers of three children.[136] Even though they already enjoyed freedom from *tutela*, the grant of the *ius trium liberorum* (right of three children) was necessary in order to exempt the Vestals from a provision in the *lex Papia Poppaea* that prevented the unmarried and childless from inheriting testamentary bequests.[137] Interestingly, the prohibition applied only to those whose estates were valued at more than one hundred thousand sesterces. The grant of the *ius trium liberorum* thus suggests that some Vestals controlled considerable property by this period.

According to Tacitus, Tiberius and the senate continued to provide incentives for service in the Vestal order. When Cornelia was "taken" (*capiebatur, Ann.* 4.16.5) in place of the Vestal Scantia in AD 23, she received two million sesterces. To put this number in perspective, we need only consider that Augustus imposed a property qualification of one million sesterces for entrance to the senatorial order.[138] Four years earlier, in AD 19, Tiberius had awarded one million sesterces to the runner-up in the selection process. The memory of the difficulties faced by Augustus undoubtedly influenced his decision to offer such large financial inducements.[139]

Augustus and Tiberius apparently hoped that these incentives would encourage more members of the Roman elite to offer their daughters as priestesses of Vesta. The privileges, however, must also be considered alongside their efforts to align the imperial household and domestic hearth with the public cult of Vesta.[140] Augustus established a shrine to Vesta in his house on the Palatine and assigned new ritual obligations to her priestesses. He also honored his female relatives with privileges that were analogous to those enjoyed by the Vestals.[141] His wife Livia and sister Octavia had been associated with the order even during the triumviral period, when they were granted personal inviolability (*sacrosanctitas*), immunity from guardianship (*tutela*), and honorific portrait statues.[142] Tiberius allowed Livia to employ a *lictor* when she sacrificed to the divinized Augustus and, perhaps on account of her status as *flaminica*

---

[135] Arnob. *Adv. Nat.* 4.35.4; *ILS* 5049.
[136] Cass. Dio 56.10.2.
[137] Gardner 1986: 24.
[138] Cass. Dio 54.17.3.
[139] See above.
[140] As discussed more fully in chapter 6.
[141] See especially Willrich 1911; Bauman 1981; Bartman 1999: 94–95; Barrett 2002: 142–144.
[142] Cass. Dio 49.38.1.

Divi Augusti, to sit with the Vestals in the theater.[143] These privileges associated the Vestal order more closely with the imperial household and undoubtedly benefitted both sides.

Vestal Virginity

A Vestal's legal and ritual status was predicated upon her virginity, the *sine qua non* of the Vestal priesthood. Virginity set the Vestals apart from other Romans. Chastity (*castitas*) before marriage and sexual virtue (*pudicitia*) thereafter were valued in the ancient world, but lifelong virginity generally was not. Women were expected to marry and to provide heirs for their husbands and citizens for the state. Vestals, on the other hand, served the community by preserving their virginity. Cicero opines that chastity allowed the Vestals to be more vigilant in caring for the flame of Vesta (*advigiletur facilius ad custodiam ignis, Leg.* 2.29), presumably because they had no familial obligations to divert their attention from the communal hearth.[144] Indeed, as I argue above, ensuring a Vestal's independence from male authority was a chief desideratum of pontifical law. As an overall solution to the question of perpetual *castitas*, however, this explanation represents just one piece of the puzzle. Perpetual virginity was almost certainly connected to concerns about ritual purity. It had important symbolic functions as well. In the same passage from the *De legibus*, Cicero suggests that Vestal virginity was useful for demonstrating "that the nature of women permits complete chastity" (*naturam feminarum omnem castitatem pati*, 2.29). In fact, as we shall see, in the person of the Vestal, we may read the working out of ideas about ritual purity, proper womanly conduct, and the ideological functions of the female body.

Until fairly recently, modern explanations for Vestal virginity have assumed that the priesthood originated in the household of the early kings of Rome.[145] Those who hold that the Vestals were the republican counterparts of the king's daughters argue that their virginity was simply an institutionalized form of the *castitas* expected of young girls before marriage. Those who interpret the Vestals as surrogates for the wife of the king, on the other hand, compare their virginity to the *pudicitia* required of Roman *matronae*. The latter position is deeply problematic given the number of priestesses in the order and the central importance of their virginity. In general, the Vestals seem better suited to the role of daughters. Ultimately, however, scholarly preoccupation with the origins of the Vestal order is misguided.[146] Even if we could trace the public cult

---

[143] Tac. *Ann.* 1.14.2, 4.16.5; Cass. Dio 56.46.2; Barrett 2002: 160–161.

[144] As suggested by Parker 2004: 90–93; Wildfang 2006: 52.

[145] For a discussion of the arguments for and against this position with earlier bibliography, see Beard 1980.

[146] For a fuller discussion of this point, see Parker 2004: 565.

of Vesta to the royal household, determining whether the Vestals represented the wife or the daughters of the king would not sufficiently account for their complex and varied ritual role during the historical period.

In her seminal article "The Sexual Status of Vestal Virgins," Mary Beard attempted to move beyond the confines of the "wives or daughters" debate by refusing to choose between the two alternatives. Beard argued that neither the virginal nor the matronal aspects of Vestal identity, considered more fully in chapter 6, should be ignored. More tentatively, she suggested that they possessed masculine qualities as well, primarily, she argued, because their unique legal status was "defined in male terms" and because they were permitted certain "male" privileges such as the services of a lictor.[147] The Vestals were interstitial figures whose sexual status crossed all boundaries and included virginal, matronal, and even masculine dimensions. Drawing upon structural anthropology, particularly the work of Mary Douglas, Beard maintained that this "sexual ambiguity" was the very thing that made the Vestals sacred figures. The "ambiguity model" reframed the terms of the debate by advancing an explanation that emphasized liminality over a unified gender identity.

Although Beard's description has been extremely influential, the thesis is untenable, at least in its extreme form.[148] As Beard herself has stressed, classifying aspects of the Vestal experience as masculine fails to interrogate how the priesthood itself contributed to the production and maintenance of gender categories and ideologies and obscures how and why the Romans distributed priestly authority between the sexes.[149] Important work by Ariadne Staples and Holt Parker has shifted the focus from Vestal ambiguity back to Vestal virginity and its symbolic functions.[150] Both scholars begin from the premise that in the ancient world, female chastity was thought to underpin the stability of the family and the city.[151] For the Romans, women constituted a kind of cognitive map by physically representing the boundaries of the social group.[152] Their sexual status was figured as a sign that the body politic was internally unified and impervious to assault. The failure of female chastity, on the other hand, placed the entire community at risk. Beginning with Tarpeia, who fell in love with the Sabine king Titus Tatius and betrayed the city to the enemy, Roman myths

[147] Beard 1980: 17.

[148] For an assessment of Beard 1980's impact on later scholarship, see especially Beard 1995; Staples 1998; Parker 2004: 563–564.

[149] Beard 1995, with the introduction.

[150] Staples 1998; Parker 2004. My own analysis of Vestal virginity owes much to these studies, though we are not in agreement on every point.

[151] See especially Ortner 1978. For a specifically Roman focus, see Joshel 1992a; Hänninen 1999a; Henry and James 2012. Giovannini's (1981: 412) analysis of the symbolic status of women in rural Sicily demonstrates the persistence of this cultural trope: "for the Garrese, a young woman's virginity constitutes an important personal attribute. But her physical intactness is also viewed as a sign that her family possesses the unity and strength necessary to protect its patrimony from encroachment. . . . As a family member, *la Vergine* can synecdochically (part for whole) convey the message that her family is a viable entity with its boundaries intact."

[152] For the body as a "cognitive map," see especially the work of Mary Douglas (1966, 1970).

about women reveal a deep fear of invasion and even annihilation as a result of female unchastity.[153] The violation of chastity through rape was also deployed as an image of destabilization within the state. The rapes of Rhea Silvia and Lucretia and the threatened rape of Verginia led, respectively, to the overthrow of the wicked usurper Amulius, the foundation of the Republic, and Rome's liberation from the tyranny of the *decemviri*.[154] Women's bodies—either chaste and inviolate or penetrated and despoiled—served as metaphors for the welfare of the civic community and catalysts for political action.

The legendary rape of Lucretia began as a violation of a private household. Her story (and her body) was politicized only after her death, when Brutus displayed her corpse to the citizens of Collatia in order to arouse their fury against the Tarquins.[155] Tarpeia, on the other hand, was a Vestal who had consecrated her *castitas* to the community. Unlike an individual citizen woman, a Vestal who faltered in her commitment to absolute virginity rendered the entire city vulnerable to attack. The Sabine occupation of the Capitol mythologized the link between Vestal virginity and the integrity of the city walls. Other ancient sources likewise draw an implicit connection between the Vestals and the *pomerium*, the sacred boundary of the city. Priestesses of Vesta were credited with the ability to root fugitives to the spot, provided they had not yet crossed the *pomerium*.[156] Vestals also enjoyed the right of burial within this boundary, even if they had been convicted of *incestum*, the official term for loss of *castitas*.[157] Vestal bodies served to objectify the boundaries of the city and projected an image of strength and inviolability.

The *virgo maxima* Cornelia, who was convicted of *incestum* and buried alive under the emperor Domitian, articulated the association between Vestal chastity and the welfare of the city in even more explicit terms. Maintaining her innocence until the very end, Cornelia asked repeatedly, "does Caesar think that I have been unchaste, when he has conquered and triumphed while I have been performing the rites?" (*me Caesar incestam putat, qua sacra faciente vicit triumphavit*, Pliny *Ep.* 4.11.7).[158] Cornelia's plea hinges on the relationship between her virginity and the efficacy of the *sacra* (religious rites) in her care. If she had performed the *sacra* unchastely, Domitian's campaigns would have been doomed to failure. The fact that he succeeded, so her argument goes, is proof of her chastity.

---

[153] Varro *Ling.* 5.41; Prop. 4.4; Livy 1.11.5–9; Dion. Hal. *Ant. Rom.* 2.38.1–40.3; Ov. *Met.* 14.776; Ov. *Fast.* 1.261–262; Val. Max. 9.6.1.

[154] For the rape of Rhea Silvia by Mars, see Livy 1.4.2; Dion. Hal. *Ant. Rom.* 1.75.1–77.4; Ov., *Fast.* 2.383–386, 3.11. For the rape of Lucretia by Sextus Tarquinius, see Livy 1.57–60; Dion. Hal. *Ant. Rom.* 4.64–85. For the attempted rape of Verginia by the *decemvir* Appius Claudius, see Livy 3.44–58. For a discussion of these legends, see especially Joshel 1992a.

[155] Livy 1.59.1–5.

[156] Pliny *H.N.* 28.13.

[157] Serv. ad *Aen.* 11.206. Bätz 2012: 165–195 provides a detailed discussion of burial within the *pomerium*.

[158] For an interesting discussion of this episode, see Gallia 2012: 86–127.

Cornelia's defense suggests that a Vestal's sexual status was more than a symbol of Rome's inviolability. It also guaranteed her ritual purity and her ability to perform her ritual program.[159] Both Cicero and Gellius stress that the gods had to be approached "chastely" (*caste*).[160] Officiants were required to wash their hands before offering a sacrifice of any kind, large or small.[161] More elaborate rituals, including purification rites such as the Argei festival, often required a period of sexual abstinence.[162] For the Vestals, who were in constant contact with the divine as they ministered at the hearth of Vesta, sexual activity was simply impossible.[163] Roman authors extend this line of reasoning one step further, emphasizing the virginal status of the goddess Vesta. "What wonder if a virgin delights in a virgin servant," Ovid writes, "and admits only chaste hands to her rituals?" (*quid mirum, virgo si virgine laeta ministra / admittit castas ad sua sacra manus, Fast.* 6.289–290).[164] As simplistic as this explanation may seem, it suggests that Vestal virginity operated on more than one level.[165] In addition to its symbolic significance, virginity was grounded in the reality of cultic duties, explored more fully in chapter 6.

The sacral significance of Vestal virginity comes to the fore most clearly in accounts of its absence. By transgressing divinely sanctioned rules against ritual purity, an unchaste Vestal disrupted the fragile relationship between Rome and her gods, the *pax deorum* (literally, "the peace of the gods"). In the Roman imagination, the principal sign that an unchaste Vestal was polluting the rites was the spontaneous extinction of the sacred flame in the Temple of Vesta. The gods might also express their displeasure through other prodigies, pestilences, or even military defeats.[166] In 114 BC, Helvia, the virgin daughter of L. Helvius, was struck by lightning and killed instantly while traveling from Rome to Apulia.[167] The explosive force of the lightning bolt shredded her clothing and left her body fully exposed. The *haruspices* interpreted this horrific event as a sign that there was trouble in the house of Vesta; three Vestals were

[159] For a discussion of ritual purity in the Greek world, see Parker 1996. For the Roman world, see the various essays in Bradley and Stow 2012, especially Lennon 2012: 49–52.

[160] Cic. *Leg.* 2.19 (*caste*); Gell. *N.A.* 4.9.9 (*castitate*).

[161] Plaut. *Aul.* 612.

[162] The *flaminica Dialis*, for example, was required to abstain from sexual activity during the period from June 7 to June 15 (Ov. *Fast.* 6.226–232).

[163] For this explanation, see especially Rose 1926: 442–443; Guizzi 1968: 102–108; Mustakallio 1992: 62. Compare also Plutarch's (*Cat. Mai.* 20.5) observation that indecent speech was to be avoided in the presence of the Vestals.

[164] See also Plut. *Num.* 9.5.

[165] Compare the story of Sulpicia, who was chosen as the most pure (*sanctissima*) of women on account of her outstanding *castitas* (Val. Max. 8.15.12). Given that the competition had been established to select a woman to consecrate the statue of Venus Verticordia, *castitas* must here refer to both her sexual virtue and her ritual purity.

[166] Dion. Hal. *Ant. Rom.* 2.67.5. Staples (1998: 150–151) places special emphasis on the connection between Vestals and the flame: "The intimate relationship between a Vestal's virginity and the sacred fire is underscored by the fact that the loss of virginity was signified by the loss of the fire . . . the spontaneous extinguishing of the fire and a Vestal's unchastity were equivalent occurrences, both omens of disaster."

[167] Plut. *Quaest. Rom.* 83 = *Mor.* 283f–284c; Oros. 5.15; Obseq. 97.

convicted of *incestum* and put to death during the ensuing scandal.[168] Similarly, on at least two occasions, Vestals were found guilty of *incestum* in the wake of serious plagues that attacked pregnant women and livestock with particular vehemence.[169] The loss of Vestal chastity placed the entire community in danger of divine retribution.

As soon as an allegation of *incestum* was made, the accused Vestal was ordered to refrain from her duties (*sacris abstinere*, Livy 8.15.7) in order to prevent further contamination of the rites.[170] She was then tried before the pontifical college.[171] The priestess was permitted to speak in her own defense.[172] If the *pontifices* voted to condemn her, she was ordered to remove her ritual headdress, signifying the termination of her status as a Vestal in good standing.[173] The *pontifices* placed her in a litter and carried her through the city in a solemn procession resembling a funeral (ζῶσαι γὰρ ἔτι πομπεύουσιν ἐπὶ κλίνης φερόμεναι τὴν ἀποδεδειγμένην τοῖς νεκροῖς ἐκφοράν, Dion. Hal. *Ant. Rom.* 2.67.4). "No other spectacle is more appalling," Plutarch adds, "nor does any other day bring more gloom to the city than this" (οὐδὲ ἐστὶν ἕτερον θέαμα φρικτότερον, οὐδ᾽ ἡμέραν ἡ πόλις ἄλλην ἄγει στυγνοτέραν ἐκείνης, *Num.* 10.6). When the procession reached the Campus Sceleratus just inside the Colline Gate, the *pontifex maximus* and the other priests averted their gaze as the Vestal descended into an underground chamber that had been dug below or perhaps within the walls of the city.[174] The chamber contained a bed, a burning lamp, and small portions of "the necessities of life" (τῶν πρὸς τὸ ζῆν ἀναγκαίων,

---

[168] For a discussion of the Roman approach to prodigies and expiation, see especially MacBain 1982.

[169] Dion. Hal. *Ant. Rom.* 9.40.3; Oros. 4.5.6–9, with Mustakallio 1992. See also Livy 2.42.14–18 for the execution of a Vestal in the midst of the Volscian War (ca. 483 BC).

[170] See also Dion. Hal. *Ant. Rom.* 2.68.3–5; Plut. *Num.* 10.4.

[171] Cic. *Har. resp.* 13; Livy 4.44.11–12, 8.15.7–8; Dion. Hal. *Ant. Rom.* 2.67.3, 8.89.4–5, 9.40.3; Pliny *Ep.* 4.11. For a discussion of the unique procedure for handling accusations of Vestal *incestum*, see especially Cornell 1981; Lovisi 1998. Despite Richardson's (2011) claims to the contrary, there is no compelling evidence that the *pontifices* failed to keep records of *incestum* trials in the pontifical archives. Annalists presumably consulted these archives for notices concerning the trial and interment of unchaste Vestals (as suggested by Ogilvie 1965: 349, 602; Oakley 1998: 577).

[172] Macrobius (*Sat.* 1.10.5), for instance, tells us that Licinia "was ordered to plead her case" (*Liciniam virginem ut causam diceret iussam*) in 114 BC. Vestals were not subjected to a physical examination during the trial, presumably because the (erroneous) concept of the hymen and hymeneal blood as a sign of virginity was not as pervasive in the Roman world as it is today (Sissa 1990: 105–123). In fact, ancient medical and gynecological treatises explicitly deny that virgins are "sealed" with a "virginal membrane" (*membrana virginalis*, Serv. ad *Aen.* 1.651) or "hymen" (ὑμήν, Sor. *Gyn.* 1.16–17). Greek and Roman chastity tests were far more likely to involve the supernatural (Sissa 1990: 105–106). Propertius (4.8.1–16), for instance, describes the famous snake ritual at the sanctuary of Juno Sospita in Lanuvium, during which unmarried girls descended into a cave bearing offerings to a snake that accepted the gifts only if the girls were chaste (*castae*, 13). In fact, the execution of a Vestal may reasonably be understood as a trial by ordeal: if she were pure, Vesta would presumably rescue her from her underground tomb (Pomeroy 1975: 211; Staples 1993: 133; Parker 2004: 586; Kroppenberg 2010: 430–431).

[173] Dion. Hal. *Ant. Rom.* 8.89.4–5.

[174] The following description synthesizes accounts found in Dion. Hal. *Ant. Rom.* 2.67.4; Plut. *Num.* 10.4–7, *Quaest. Rom.* 96 = *Mor.* 286f–287a; Serv. ad *Aen.* 11.206. For the location of the chamber, see Richardson 2011, who notes that the *agger*, which Plutarch describes as "inside the city" (ἐντὸς τῆς πόλεως ὀφρὺς γεώδης παρατείνουσα πόρρω· καλεῖται δὲ χῶμα διαλέκτῳ τῇ Λατίνων, *Num.* 10.4), was actually part of the wall.

Plut. *Num.* 10.5), such as bread, water, milk, and oil. These provisions absolved the priests of the Vestal's death by placing her fate in the hands of Vesta.[175] Once she had disappeared from view, the ladder was pulled up and the entrance sealed with earth. Despite the funereal character of the ceremony, the Vestal received no monument and none of the customary funerary rites.[176]

Following errors in the execution of a prayer or sacrifice, it was possible to secure the goodwill of the gods through a repetition of the ritual (*instauratio*), perhaps accompanied by further expiatory rites (*piacula*).[177] The offence of an unchaste Vestal, on the other hand, could not be handled according to standard piacular practice. Once penetrated, a Vestal could never become inviolate again. Her continued existence perpetuated the original offense and exacerbated the anger of the gods.[178] Vestals convicted of *incestum* were buried alive. If an unchaste Vestal embodied invasion and vulnerability, her live interment restored order and reaffirmed the boundaries of the city. Entombed beneath (or perhaps within) the defensive walls, she was permanently incorporated into the physical boundary of Rome.[179]

Although Dionysius and Plutarch describe the live interment of an unchaste Vestal as a punishment (κόλασις), the form of her trial, the details of her conveyance to the Colline Gate, and the location of her burial all suggest that it was not an ordinary execution.[180] Nor, strictly speaking, was it a sacrifice.[181] An unchaste Vestal was impure and polluted; the charge against her, the *crimen incesti*, was of not being *castus*, that is, of being sexually and ritually impure.[182] An unchaste Vestal would not have been an acceptable offering to the gods. The fact that she removed her ritual headgear, the *infula* and *vittae*, which symbolized ritual purity and adorned sacrificial victims as well as priests, tends to confirm that the Romans did not regard her as a sacrifice.[183]

[175] Staples (1998: 133, 150–152) and Martini (2004: 247–248) suggest that the provisions allowed the Romans to maintain the "ritual fiction" that the priestess was not really put to death, but this view is contradicted by the written sources, which insist upon her execution.

[176] Plutarch (*Quaest. Rom.* 96 = *Mor.* 287a), however, tells us that the priests made annual offerings at the site, perhaps as part of the Parentalia (see chapter 6).

[177] Livy 2.36.1–7.

[178] As noted by Cornell 1981: 35; Fraschetti 1984: 121, 125; Lovisi 1998: 705; Richardson 2011: 102.

[179] There is an interesting correspondence with Joshel's (1992a: 122) observation that in Livy's history of early Rome, "women's bodies literally become building material—the stuff of physical and political topography. Women who are supposed to have lived are transformed into places and spaces." Tarpeia, for instance, is buried beneath the shields of the Sabines and becomes the Tarpeian Rock, the place from which traitors were hurled to their deaths.

[180] Dion. Hal. *Ant. Rom.* 2.67.3; Plut. *Num.* 10.4, with Koch 1958: 1748–1750. More recently, Gradel (2002: 237) has argued that the live interment of a Vestal was "simply a form of human execution." Against this interpretation, see Cornell 1981: 32–33; Lovisi 1998: 702–703; Wildfang 2006: 56–57; Richardson 2011: 94–95; Schultz 2012: 124.

[181] For the unchaste Vestal as a human sacrifice, see Parker 2004: 575–588; Wildfang 2006: 58; Baschirotto 2012. Against this view, see Prescendi 2007: 235–241; Schultz 2010: 530–534; Richardson 2011: 98–100; Schultz 2012.

[182] *OLD* s.v. *incestum*. Although Koch (1958: 1749) held that an unchaste Vestal was guilty of *Blutschande* (incest), because, in his view, all Romans were the brothers of the Vestals, his arguments are based on a narrow application of the Latin term.

[183] For the *infula* and *vittae*, see chapter 5.

Celia Schultz has shown, moreover, that the ancient sources do not use sacrificial vocabulary to describe the unchaste priestess as a victim (*hostia* or *victima*) or her death as a sacrifice (*immolare* or *sacrificare*).[184] When the Romans discuss the live interment of pairs of Gauls and Greeks in the Forum Boarium, by contrast, they explicitly identify the ritual as a sacrifice (*sacrificium*) and the couples as human victims (*hostiae*). The distinction is particularly clear in Livy's account of the events following the Roman losses at Cannae and Canusium in 216 BC, a year in which two Vestals, Opimia and Floronia, had been convicted of *incestum*. One had been buried alive at the Colline Gate and the other had killed herself. The *pontifex maximus* scourged L. Cantilius, a *scriba pontificus* (pontifical scribe) and the man who had corrupted Floronia, so severely that he died under the blows. Convinced that this misfortune was a terrible portent (*prodigium*), the Romans sent an embassy to Delphi and consulted the Sibylline Books, which recommended the live interment of a pair of Gauls and a pair of Greeks in the Forum Boarium.[185] Unlike the entombment of the unchaste Vestal, which is described in relatively neutral terms (*necata fuerat*, 22.57.2), the burial of the Gauls and Greeks is identified as one of a number of unusual "sacrifices" (*sacrificia extraordinaria*, 22.57.6). The ancient evidence suggests, Schultz writes, "that the ancients had more than one intellectual category for rites that required a human death."[186]

In place of human sacrifice, Schultz employs the more nuanced concept of ritual murder, "the killing of a human being for religious purposes, repeated in specific circumstances in a prescribed fashion that marks it off from profane killing."[187] There are crucial differences between ritual murder as a category of religious activity and human sacrifice, a specific example of the broader phenomenon. Ritual murder is not typically part of a regular cycle of festivals, for instance, nor is the victim intended as an offering to the gods.[188] In Rome, the most common form of a ritual murder, aside from the burial of a Vestal, was the disposal of a polluted individual, especially the disposal of hermaphrodites.[189] The Romans treated androgynous infants as prodigies (*prodigia*). On the advice of the *haruspices*, they typically placed them in a box and set them adrift in the sea. Following the removal of the hermaphrodite, they performed a fairly regularized set of expiatory rites, including offerings to Ceres and Proserpina by the *matronae*, a procession of twenty-seven virgins, and the sacrifice of two cows to Juno. The Roman treatment of a hermaphroditic birth thus included a ritual murder and a program of expiatory rites to restore the *pax deorum*.

[184] Schultz 2012.
[185] See also Livy *Per.* 22; Plut. *Fab.* 18.3.
[186] Schultz 2012: 125.
[187] Schultz 2010: 518.
[188] Schultz 2010: 518.
[189] There are fourteen androgyne births reported in the prodigy lists between 209 and 92 BC. For a discussion of the evidence, see especially MacBain 1982: 127–135; Schultz 2010: 529–530.

In the same way, the Roman procedure for dealing with an unchaste Vestal involved ritual murder and rites of expiation. Dionysius of Halicarnassus tells us that after the burial of the convicted priestess, the Romans rekindled the flame in the temple with many expiatory rites (πολλαῖς αὐτὸ θεραπείαις ἐξιλασκόμενοι κατάγουσι πάλιν εἰς τὸ ἱερόν, *Ant. Rom.* 2.67.5). Even the accidental extinguishment of the eternal flame, punished by scourging, rather than interment, might be followed by piacular sacrifices.[190] In fact, Livy suggests that the live burial of Gauls and Greeks in 216 BC was meant to expiate the pollution of Floronia and Opimia's unchastity.[191] The interment of Gauls and Greeks in 114/113 BC also coincided with the only other conviction of a Vestal for *incestum* in the period between the Hannibalic War and the reign of Domitian.[192] The coincidence of these ritual murders, along with Livy's commentary on the events of 216 BC, indicate that the discovery of an unchaste Vestal required exceptional expiatory rites above and beyond the live burial of the priestess herself.

Does this mean that, like a hermaphroditic child, an unchaste Vestal was regarded as a *prodigium*?[193] It is certainly true that both hermaphrodites and unchaste Vestals violated sexual categories: one combined two sexes in the same body, the other combined unchastity with membership in the Vestal order.[194] Unlike an androgynous infant, however, an unchaste Vestal had (in theory) contaminated these categories willingly. She was not a prodigy, but rather the author of a serious ritual error that had prompted the gods to send prodigies as an expression of their anger.[195] The location of the chamber in which the unchaste Vestal was buried also suggests that the Romans drew an important distinction between the hermaphrodite and the compromised priestess. Livy tells us that an androgynous child was placed in a box and drowned in the sea in order to remove its polluting presence from Roman territory (*ager Romanus*).[196] The unchaste Vestal, on the other hand, was interred within the *pomerium*, the sacred boundary of the city.[197] As Schultz has suggested, this practice may

---

[190] Livy 28.11.6–8.

[191] See also Plut. *Quaest. Rom.* 83 = *Mor.* 283f–284a.

[192] Livy *Per.* 63; Plut. *Quaest. Rom.* 83 = *Mor.* 283f–284a; Cass. Dio 26, fr. 87.3; Oros. 5.15.22; Macrob. *Sat.* 1.10.5–6 (= Fenestella fr. 11 Peter); Ascon. 45–46C; Obseq. 37; Zon. 7.8. On the basis of Livy *Per.* 20, Cichorius (1922: 7–16) argued that the first known burial of Gauls and Greeks in 228 BC may have coincided with the ritual murder of an unchaste Vestal as well. This association is not secure, however, particularly because the other ancient sources for the trial of Tuccia record her acquittal (see above and below). Even so, a connection between Vestal unchastity and the burial of Gauls and Greeks in 216 and 114/113 BC seems secure and has been widely accepted (see, for example, Schultz 2012). Against this interpretation, see Eckstein 1982.

[193] Wissowa (1923–1924) was the first to argue that the unchaste Vestal was a prodigy. See also Fraschetti 1984: 99–100, 113–114; Parker 2004: 575–578.

[194] Schultz 2012: 130.

[195] Wildfang 2006: 56. See also Cornell 1981: 30–32; Staples 1998: 133–134; Richardson 2011: 95, 98–100; Schultz 2012: 130.

[196] Livy 27.37.6. See also Cic. *Rosc. Am.* 70–72 (for the similar treatment of parricides); Livy 39.22.5.

[197] See above.

be related to the Roman practice of burying damaged or obsolete cult objects within the boundaries of the sanctuary. "Like a broken statuette or bones left over from a burned sacrifice," she writes, "an unchaste Vestal might be seen, in a sense, as a decommissioned sacred entity, as something polluted but still sacred: not profane, but not ritually perfect (and therefore not ritually usable) either."[198] Given her close association with the boundaries of the city, a Vestal could not be removed from the *pomerium*. She was buried alive and a new flame was kindled on the hearth.

This discussion has attempted to make sense of the ritual murder of Vestals within the framework of the ritual system, which was governed by the contractual nature of the *pax deorum*. It goes without saying, however, that Vestals convicted of *incestum* were not necessarily guilty of this crime.[199] Livy even casts doubt on the justice of the execution of Oppia in 483 BC. Foreign wars, conflict between the patricians and the plebeians, and especially the religious terror excited by daily prodigies, rather than evidence of her guilt, Livy tells us, resulted in her condemnation and punishment (*qui terrores tamen eo evasere ut Oppia virgo Vestalis damnata incesti poenas dederit*, 2.42.18).[200] The Vestals served as a convenient mechanism for restoring stability in times of panic and crisis. When circumstances demanded a spectacular public expiation, a Vestal was deemed to have lost her virginity. Male codefendants appear only occasionally in the historical record, suggesting that a Vestal could be convicted of *incestum* even in the absence of a male paramour. [201] The Roman elite knew what they were up to, even if they maintained the fiction that they were punishing a Vestal guilty of *incestum*, rather than offering up a scapegoat to relieve the religious hysteria of the masses.

The vulnerability of Vestals facing charges of *incestum* is illustrated clearly in the myths of Tuccia and Aemilia. Both Vestals were falsely accused of this crime and were absolved only when Vesta granted their prayers to perform miraculous deeds proving their innocence. In 178 BC, the fire of Vesta went out through the negligence of the *virgo maxima* Aemilia, who had left the hearth in the care of a novice. When the *pontifices* began their investigation, Aemilia prayed to Vesta and threw a strip of linen upon the hearth, and "from the ashes, which had long been cold and retained no spark, fire blazed up through the linen" (ἐκ τῆς κατεψυγμένης πρὸ πολλοῦ καὶ οὐδένα φυλαττούσης σπινθῆρα τέφρας ἀναλάμψαι φλόγα πολλὴν διὰ τῆς καρπάσου, Dion. Hal. *Ant. Rom.* 2.68.5). Tuccia, on the other hand, was falsely accused of *incestum* even though her informer was unable to point to the extinction of the flame as

---

[198] Schultz 2012: 133. For the prohibition against removing objects that had been dedicated to the gods from their sanctuaries, see Gai. *Inst.* 2.2–5.

[199] Parker 2004: 585.

[200] As noted by Levene 1993: 158.

[201] For the details, see Parker 2004: 581–582.

evidence.[202] When the *pontifices* asked her to present a defense, she first prayed to Vesta and then carried a sieve full of water from the Tiber to the Forum. Tuccia was acquitted and her accuser, Dionysius tells us, was never seen or heard from again. Suspected of *incestum* and put on trial before the *pontifices*, Aemilia and Tuccia proved their innocence only by completing impossible, miraculous tasks. The connection between Vestal virginity and the welfare of the state meant that the Vestals were under the constant threat of wrongful execution.[203]

Conclusion

A girl embarking upon a career as a Vestal priestess had to be a virgin between the ages of six and ten, in full possession of her limbs and faculties, and the legitimate daughter of two living, freeborn citizens who had never engaged in any base occupation. Only a perfect candidate from an "ideal" family could be consecrated to Vesta. The *captio* ritual, however, formally severed the candidate's ties to her family and established her as a public priestess with an obligation to set aside personal loyalties in the service of the community of Rome. Sacral law promoted the fiction that Vestals belonged to the entire community, even though reality occasionally belied this ideal.[204]

Virginity was the single most important aspect of a Vestal's priestly identity. For the Romans, the safeguarding of the eternal flame and the inviolability of the city depended upon the Vestals preserving their virginity, such that the integrity of Vestal bodies was bound inextricably to that of the community. What is more, the very high profile of the Vestals in Roman society allowed the priestesses to model the virtue of chastity for married and unmarried women alike. Cicero alludes to this exemplary function of Vestal virginity in the *De legibus*, where he suggests that other women (*mulieres*) may learn from the Vestals "that the nature of woman permits complete purity" (*naturam feminarum omnem castitatem pati*, 2.29). The Vestals presumably understood the ideological force of their virginity, though other aspects of their identity, such as their sacrificial capacity or their membership in the pontifical college, may have been just as important to their sense of self, if not more. Exemption from *patria potestas* and *tutela* allowed the Vestals to manage and distribute their wealth without the interference of a guardian, granting them an unusual degree of indepen-

---

[202] Dion. Hal. *Ant. Rom.* 2.69.1; Val. Max. 8.5.1.

[203] Admittedly, we hear of only thirteen Vestals who were buried alive in the more than one thousand year history of the Vestal order. Another six were convicted of *incestum* but committed suicide before their sentences could be carried out (for the details, see Parker 2004). The chronological distribution is far from even, with the majority of cases clustering in the first few centuries of the Republic and again under the notoriously tyrannical emperors Domitian and Caracalla. Even so, the fact remains that the Romans sanctioned the murder of Vestals accused of exercising their sexuality.

[204] See chapter 7.

dence. Their right to be attended by a lictor enhanced their visibility within the city and ensured that they would be noticed wherever they went. In the chapters that follow, I will trace how the Vestals expressed their identity through their ritual costume, how they carried out their ritual obligations, and how they leveraged their status for political gain.

CHAPTER FIVE

The Costume of the Vestal Virgins

In 420 BC, the Vestal Postumia was accused of *incestum* (unchastity). Though innocent of the charge, Livy tells us, she was suspected "on account of a style more charming and a manner more open than is fitting for a virgin" (*propter cultum amoeniorem ingeniumque liberius quam virginem decet*, 4.44.11). The *pontifices* acquitted Postumia, but the *pontifex maximus* nonetheless ordered her "to dress with greater regard for sanctity than for sophistication" (*coli . . . sancte potius quam scite*, 4.44.12). Nearly a century later, Minucia's style of dress, likewise deemed more elegant than her situation as a Vestal required (*mundiorem iusto cultum*, Livy 8.15.7), raised questions about her *castitas* (chastity) and led to her conviction for *incestum* on the testimony of her slaves. The *pontifices* buried her alive near the Colline Gate. For a Vestal Virgin, decisions about what to wear could be a matter of life and death.

These episodes, regardless of their historicity, illustrate the timeless truth that costume is a powerful visual language.[1] Clothing and other physical adornment construct and communicate identity and position the wearer within the larger social group. At Rome, the *toga praetexta* (purple-bordered toga) distinguished priests and magistrates from ordinary citizens, while a gold ring indicated membership in the equestrian order. The accusations leveled against Postumia and Minucia reveal that clothes also conveyed information about the character and morality of the man or woman who wore them.[2] The long and concealing *stola* (a slip-like dress worn over the tunic), for instance, symbolized and preserved the modesty and *pudicitia* (sexual virtue) of the Roman *matrona* (married woman), for whom this dress was specially reserved. Elegists and antiquarians alike insist upon an association between this garment and the virtues it signified.[3] Augustus may have mandated the *stola* on public occasions and at least one moralist during

---

[1] Important studies of Roman clothing include Bonfante-Warren 1973; Sebesta and Bonfante 1994; Croom 2002; Cleland, Harlow, and Llewellyn-Jones 2005; Edmondson and Keith 2008; Olson 2008; Harlow 2012; Harlow and Nosch 2014. For the Vestal costume and hairstyle, see especially Dragendorff 1896; Beard 1980: 15–16; La Follette and Wallace 1992; La Follette 1994: 57–60; Mekacher 2006: 44–49; Wildfang 2006: 12–16; Olson 2008: 27; La Follette 2011; Stephens 2013, January 4; Gallia 2014; Lindner 2015: 99–125, 164–186.

[2] For the ways in which clothing interacted with the Roman moral system, see especially Bonfante 1994; Heskel 1994; Sebesta 1997; Olson 2002, 2008; La Follette 2011. As Olson (2002, 2008: 40–41, passim) has recently stressed, however, there was a vast difference between the "normative" sartorial ideals expressed by the literary and visual evidence and the "normal" appearance of the average Roman man or woman.

[3] See further below and chapter 1.

his reign argued that any *matrona* who refused to wear it should be prosecuted for adultery (*pro stupro*).[4] A married woman who appeared in public without her *stola*, so it was argued, was virtually indistinguishable from a prostitute.[5] As Seneca the Elder observes, "For a woman the only glory is *pudicitia*, and so she must take care both to be and to be seen to be chaste" (*feminae quidem unum pudicitia decus est; itaque ei curandum est esse ac videri pudicam, Controv.* 2.7.9).

Like the dress of a respectable *matrona*, the costume of a Vestal rendered visible her social status and moral probity. The full Vestal regalia included the *seni crines* (six-tressed) hairstyle, a headdress composed of the *infula* and *vittae* (woolen bands), a veil known as the *suffibulum*, a *palla* (mantle), the soft shoes of a priestess, and, as I argue here, a long *tunica* (tunic), rather than a *stola*, as others have argued. Through a detailed analysis of the Vestal costume, this chapter analyzes how its constituent parts worked together to define and represent a Vestal's position as a public priestess and ideal virgin. As I argue in the previous chapter, these two facets of her identity were inextricably linked and absolutely central to her role in Roman society. A Vestal's virginity guaranteed her ritual purity and her ability to secure the inviolability of the city. In addition to these vital ritual and symbolic functions, her absolute *castitas* provided a template of feminine virtue after which other women could model their behavior. The Vestal costume performed important work with respect to this exemplarity; it was a crucial means by which the identity of a Vestal Virgin was constructed, perceived, and even emulated.[6] A nuanced reading of the Vestal dress is, therefore, absolutely essential to our ability to understand and interpret the role of these priestesses in Roman society.

Hairstyle and Headdress

The *Seni Crines*

One of the most important elements of the Vestal costume was its distinctive hairstyle, the *seni crines*. A fragmentary entry in the lexicon of Festus provides the most detailed literary evidence for the *seni crines*:

> senis crinibus nubentes ornantur, quod [h]is ornatus vetustissimus fuit. quidam quod eo Vestales virgines ornentur, quarum castitatem viris suis †sponoe *** a ceteris . . . (454L)

---

[4] For Augustus' efforts to legislate Roman dress, see Suet. *Aug.* 40.5, with Sebesta 1997. For the suggestion that women who did not wear the *stola* be tried for adultery, see Tert. *Pall.* 4.9.2, with McGinn 1998: 161–162. All of this implies, of course, that some women rebelled against expectations of their dress and behavior.

[5] Olson 2002: 400–401. Consider also the stories of C. Sulpicius Galus (cos. 166 BC), who divorced his wife because he learned that she had gone out in public with her head uncovered (Val. Max. 6.3.10), and of Claudia Quinta, whose reputation for virtue was called into question on account of her manner of dress (*cultus*) and propensity to appear in public with her hair arranged in various ways (*ornatis varie prodisse capillis*, Ov. *Fast.* 4.309).

[6] Compare Levine's (1995: 104) brief comments on this point.

Brides are adorned with the *seni crines*, because this was the most ancient style. Certain people [think that brides wear the *seni crines*] because the Vestal Virgins are adorned with it, whose chastity for their own husbands †brides *** by others . . .

According to Festus, the *seni crines* was a very ancient hairstyle worn by brides and Vestals. Mary Beard has argued, therefore, that the hairstyle showed the liminal status of the Vestals between virgin and *matrona*.[7] Festus, however, suggests a different interpretation. Although the second sentence is lacunose, it is clear that certain authors held not that the Vestals wore the *seni crines* because they were like brides, but rather that brides wore the *seni crines* because it was used by the Vestals and, moreover, because the hairstyle symbolized their *castitas* (chastity). When a bride dressed her hair in the *seni crines* style, she declared to the community and to her new husband that she had lived up to the ideal set by the Vestal Virgins, just as the *flammeum*, the veil of the *flaminica Dialis*, represented her promise to model the marital fidelity embodied by this priestess.[8] According to the reading offered here, the *seni crines* symbolized a virtue shared by brides and Vestals, without necessarily implying a confusion of social categories.[9] As Karen Hersch has recently stressed, moreover, most scholars understand *seni* as an adjective derived from the cardinal number *sex* (six), and consequently view the *seni crines* as a coiffure in which the hair was divided into six sections.[10] The number of tresses in a Vestal's *seni crines* hairstyle corresponded to the number of women active in the Vestal order and served as "a symbolic representation of the totality of her group."[11] Taken together, the testimony of Festus and the number of sections in the hairstyle suggest that it was associated primarily with the Vestals.

While Festus stresses the moral implications of the *seni crines*, he does not describe how the hairstyle was achieved. Visual evidence has likewise failed to reveal precisely what the Vestal hairstyle looked like. In part, this may be a function of the fact that brides and Vestal Virgins were extremely modest. In Roman art, brides are generally shown wearing the voluminous *flammeum*, which tends to obscure the details of the hair beneath. Visual depictions of the Vestals likewise tend to depict the priestesses heavily veiled. The interpretation of these images has proved exceedingly problematic.[12]

---

[7] Beard 1980: 16, 21.

[8] See chapter 1.

[9] As Gallia 2014: 235 has recently suggested.

[10] Hersch 2010: 765–766. For the etymology and translation of *seni*, see Ernout and Meillet 1959: 151, 621; La Follette and Wallace 1993; La Follette 1994: 56–60. Giannecchini (1980) has rejected the numerical interpretation and proposed two alternative etymologies, maintaining that *seni crines* should be translated either as "bound hair" or "cut hair." His arguments are refuted convincingly by La Follette and Wallace 1993. More recently, Stephens (2013, January 4) has argued that the Vestal *seni crines* was constructed of seven braids on the basis of a detailed reconstruction of the hairstyle of a Vestal portrait now in the Galleria degli Uffizi in Florence (fig. 5.10). I consider her suggestion in more detail below.

[11] Hersch 2010: 75–76. For an illuminating discussion of the social and symbolic functions of female hairstyles, see Bartman 2001.

[12] For a discussion of the limitations of art as a source for ancient dress and adornment, see Van Deman 1908; Lindner 1995: 98–129; Bartman 2001: 7–8; Connelly 2007: 86–87; Olson 2008: 3–4.

FIGURE 5.1. Relief fragments from Rome showing the heads of two Vestal Virgins. Second century AD. Inv. Nos. 12491/1–2, Antiquario Palatino, Rome. Photo: Scala / Art Resource, NY, ART181977.

The Vestals appear on nine sculpted reliefs dating from the late first century BC through the late second century AD. These reliefs originated on public monuments in Rome, the Campanian city of Surrentum (modern Sorrento), and Caleacte (modern Marina di Caronia) in Sicily. On many of these reliefs, the Vestals appear in the company of the emperor and other members of the priestly hierarchy, which further underscores the prominence of their position at the center of civic cult and reminds us that the Vestals (and their costumes) were on public display at major religious festivals throughout the year. Nearly all of the relief sculptures depict the Vestals with their hair parted at the center and waved back beneath the *infula* and *suffibulum*, which disguise the hair beneath and complicate efforts to elucidate the appearance of the *seni crines*.[13] This arrangement is clearly visible, for example, on two Vestal heads from the Antonine period that may have originated in the House of the Vestals (fig. 5.1).[14] The Vestal on a relief fragment now in the British Museum (fig. 5.2) and the figures on the heavily restored Villa Albani Relief are shown wearing the same style.[15] Though not as readily discernible, the central part with loosely waved hair can be seen on a relief from the principate of Augustus now in Palermo (fig. 5.3), as well as on the so-called Banqueting Vestals

[13] Mekacher 2006: 46.

[14] For a discussion of the heads, now on display in the Antiquario Palatino (Inv. Nos. 12491/1, 12491/2), see Thompson 2005: 155; Mekacher 2006: 164, 252–253.

[15] For the relief in the British Museum (Inv. No. 1805,0703.263), see Bonanno 1979; Thompson 2005: 139–143; Mekacher 2006: 164, 249. For the Villa Albani Relief (Inv. No. 1010), see Thompson 2005: 99–102; Mekacher 2006: 250–251.

FIGURE 5.2. Relief fragment, perhaps from Rome, showing a Vestal Virgin and a flamen. Late first century AD. Inv. No. 1805,0703.263, British Museum, London. Photo © Trustees of the British Museum.

Relief, which dates to the principate of Claudius (fig. 5.4).[16] Unfortunately, the heads of the Vestals on the altar frieze of the Ara Pacis Augustae (fig. 5.5) and the roughly contemporaneous Sorrento Base (fig. 5.6) are badly damaged, making it is impossible to assess how the hair of these figures was depicted.[17]

---

[16] For the Palermo Relief, now in the Museo Archeologico Regionale in Palermo (Inv. No. 1539), see Rizzo 1932; Degrassi 1955: 152–154; Ryberg 1955: 51–53; Guarducci 1964; Degrassi 1966–1967: 111–115; Guarducci 1971: 95–96; Cappelli 1990; Thompson 2005: 89–95; Mekacher 2006: 156–162, 251. For a discussion of the relief's iconography, see also chapter 6. For the Banqueting Vestals Relief, now on display in the Museo dell'Ara Pacis Augustae (Inv. No. 2391), see La Rocca 1992; La Rocca 1994; Thompson 2005: 174–178; Mekacher 2006: 156, 249.

[17] The bibliography on the Ara Pacis is enormous. For the altar relief I have consulted Moretti 1948: 76–79, 182–186, 279–282; Ryberg 1949: 89–90, 1955: 41–48; Simon 1968: 14–15; Torelli 1982: 36; Conlin 1997: 101, figs. 237–239, 246–247; Thompson 2005: 42–52. For the Sorrento Base, now in the Museo

FIGURE 5.3. Relief showing Vesta, Augustus, and four Vestal Virgins, late first century BC. Inv. No. 1539, Museo Archeologico Regionale, Palermo. Photo: K. Anger, Neg. D-DAI-Rom 96.989.

In contrast to the generally uniform style visible on the reliefs discussed thus far, the only fully intact Vestal on the so-called Cancelleria Reliefs is depicted wearing a closely cropped coiffure beneath her *infula* (fig. 5.7).[18] Short locks of hair appear combed across her forehead and behind her ear, with no evidence of longer hair coiled at the top or back of her head. On the basis of this sculpture, some have speculated that the Vestals actually wore their hair in a short "bowl" cut and arranged their woolen *infulae* in imitation of the *seni crines*.[19] These scholars point to the "hair tree" (*capillata*), so named "because the hair of the Vestal Virgins is brought to it" (*quoniam Vestalium virginum capillus ad*

Correale di Terranova in Sorrento (Inv. No. 3657), see Rizzo 1932; Ryberg 1955: 49–53, 74; Guarducci 1964; Kolbe 1966–1967; Guarducci 1971; Cappelli 1990; Cecamore 1994–1995; Thompson 2005: 74–99; Mekacher 2006: 154–155, 250.

[18] The Cancelleria Reliefs, excavated from beneath the Palazzo della Cancelleria in Rome in the late 1930s, are now in the Museo Gregoriano Profano in the Vatican (Frieze A: Inv. Nos. 13389–13391; Frieze B: Inv. Nos. 13392–13395). It seems very likely that all six Vestals appeared as a processional group on Frieze B, though only one has been fully preserved. For a discussion of this frieze, see especially Thompson 2005: 114–144; Mekacher 2006: 46–47, 162–164, 251–252, with further bibliography. For a summary discussion of the issues surrounding the date of the Cancelleria Reliefs, see Oppermann 1985: 44–52; Kleiner 1992: 191–192.

[19] Jordan (1886: 47–48) made a similar argument prior to the discovery of the Cancelleria Reliefs. Sensi 1980–1981: 68; La Follette and Wallace 1993; La Follette 1994: 57–59; Martini 1997b: 477–479.

FIGURE 5.4. Relief fragment from Rome showing six Vestal Virgins at a ritual banquet. Early first century AD. Inv. No. 2391, Museo dell'Ara Pacis Augustae, Rome. Photo: K. Anger, Neg. D-DAI-Rom 2000.0106.

eam defertur, Pliny *H.N.* 16.235).[20] But Pliny the Elder does not say that the Vestals cut off *all* of their hair and brought it to the tree; he may simply mean that they deposited the clippings there when they had their hair trimmed.[21] The *flamen* and *flaminica Dialis* were required to bury their hair and nail clippings beneath a "fruitful tree" (*felix arbor*), and the Vestals may have observed a similar ritual at the "hair tree."[22] As Molly Lindner has stressed, moreover, not every Vestal portrait depicts the *infula* wound around the subject's head the same number of times, which makes it difficult to interpret their headdress as a representation of the *seni crines*, at least if we adhere to the standard translation of "six-tressed."[23] The short hairstyle of the Vestal on the Cancelleria Reliefs may reflect the order's tumultuous history under Domitian, who pursued three

[20] See also Festus 50L.
[21] Stephens (January 4, 2013), for instance, suggests that a Vestal would have needed to trim the hair around her face in order to achieve the prominent roll visible on so many of the portrait statues.
[22] Gell. *N.A.* 10.15.15, 26.
[23] Lindner 2015: 115.

FIGURE 5.5. Relief from the Ara Pacis Augustae in Rome showing six Vestal Virgins. Museo dell'Ara Pacis Augustae, Rome. Photo by author.

FIGURE 5.6. Side A of the Sorrento Base showing Vesta, Livia, and six Vestal Virgins. Late first century AD. Inv. No. 3657, Museo Corrreale di Terranova, Sorrento. Photo: Hutzel, Neg. D-DAI-Rom 57.1470.

FIGURE 5.7. Detail of Frieze B of the Cancelleria Reliefs showing Roma and five Vestal Virgins. Late first century AD. Inv. Nos. 13392–13393, Musei Vaticani (Gregoriano Profano), Rome. Photo: Behrens, Neg. D-DAI-Rom 2007.0011.

accusations of *incestum* during his brief reign.[24] Unfortunately, however, we are no longer in a position to fully understand the message that the relief was intended to convey about the status of the Vestals in this period.

With the exception of the Cancelleria Reliefs, the relief sculptures depict the Vestals with their hair dressed in a relatively uniform style. The ten Vestal portrait statues and nine portrait heads, on the other hand, exhibit considerable iconographic variation with respect to their hairstyles.[25] These portraits, recovered from the House of the Vestals and the surrounding area, date to the second and early third centuries AD. While the hair on many of the statues is obscured by the Vestal headdress, they provide compelling evidence that the Vestal *seni crines* involved braids. On a portrait head from the Hadrianic period now in the British Museum, a single braid is visible between the roll of hair on the Vestal's forehead and the first turn of her *infula* (fig. 5.8).[26] A similar gap is visible on a

[24] Suet. *Dom.* 8.4; Pliny *Ep.* 4.11.9. Thompson (2005: 122) argues that the hairstyle was a sign of asceticism. Although her suggestion lacks Roman comparanda, it has the virtue of relating the Vestal's unusual appearance to the historical circumstances of Domitian's reign.

[25] The fullest discussion of the portraits is Lindner 2015. See also Lindner 1995; Mekacher 2006: 215–230.

[26] The provenance of this head is unknown. It was acquired by a private collector in 1922 and purchased by the British Museum in 1979 (Inv. No. 1979, 1108.1). The head has been dated to the Hadrianic period on the basis of a similarity to portraits of the empress Sabina, making it one of the earliest surviving Vestal portraits (Lindner 1995: 281–282). For a full discussion, see Lindner 2015: 130–132.

FIGURE 5.8. Head of a Vestal Virgin. Early second century AD. Inv. No. 1979, 1108.1, British Museum, London. Photo © Trustees of the British Museum.

FIGURE 5.9. Portrait of a Vestal Virgin. Early second century AD. Inv. No. 639, Museo Nazionale Romano (Terme), Rome. Photo: Alinari / Art Resource, NY, ART424634.

late Hadrianic portrait of a Vestal now in the collection of the Museo Nazionale Romano; no incised hatch marks are visible, but the braid was presumably rendered in paint (fig. 5.9).[27] While these veiled portraits conceal the rest of the coiffure, it appears that their sculptors sought to present a complete picture of Vestal insignia, including the headdress, veil, and *seni crines* hairstyle beneath it.

At least three Vestal portraits depict enough of the hair on the back of their subjects' heads to allow for a tentative reconstruction of the *seni crines*.[28] All three show a series of braids beneath the *infula* and *vittae*. Janet Stephens, a practicing hairdresser and "hair archaeologist," has recently applied her unique expertise to the question.[29] Her detailed analysis of the Uffizi Vestal, a bust from the early Antonine period (fig. 5.10), reveals how to section, braid, and tie the hair into an elegant turban-like coiffure with six main braids. This reconstruction appears to account for the hairstyles worn by the subjects of two other Vestal portraits in the Antiquario Forense and may also explain the low bun concealed beneath the veil of the late Hadrianic portrait in the Museo Nazionale Romano. Stephens also suggests that the figure in the Uffizi portrait wears a seventh braid constructed from the ends of the hair used to create a prominent roll over the Vestal's forehead. This hair roll, however, which is visible in every extant Vestal portrait, likely served as a support for the Vestal headdress by preventing the woolen bands of the *infula* from slipping down over the forehead of the priestess.[30] The seventh braid identified by Stephens is not part of the *seni crines* proper, but rather an element of the Vestal headdress. The portraits thus appear to confirm the traditional interpretation of the *seni crines* as a hairstyle composed of six braids.

The *Infula* and *Vittae*

On top of the *seni crines* hairstyle, Vestals wore a distinctive ritual headdress composed of the *infula*, a woolen band made from white and scarlet threads that was wrapped around the head up to six times, and *vittae*, which were attached to the *infula* and hung down on either side of the head.[31] A version of this headdress appears on every extant Vestal portrait as well as on those sculpted reliefs that preserve enough detail for analysis.[32] Symmachus describes

---

[27] For a discussion of this portrait, now in the collection of the Museo Nazionale Romano (Inv. No. 639), see Lindner 2015: 132–133.

[28] These are the Vestal portrait in the Galleria degli Uffizi in Florence (fig. 5.10), a portrait in the Antiquario Forense, which may represent the same woman as the Uffizi Vestal (Inv. No. 424492), and the portrait of a young Vestal in the Antiquario Forense (Inv. No. 424934).

[29] Stephens 2013, January 4.

[30] For a discussion of the Vestals' hair roll, see Lindner 2015: 113–114.

[31] Ancient descriptions of the *infula* include Lucr. 1.87–88; Verg. *Georg.* 3.487, *Aen.* 2.430, 10.538; Serv. ad *Aen.* 10.538; Prud. *Contra Symm.* 2.1085, 1094; Isid. *Orig.* 19.30.4; Festus (Paulus) 100L. The fullest modern discussion of the Vestal headdress is Lindner 2015: 110–118.

[32] For the importance of the *infula* in identifying a portrait as a Vestal, see Lindner 2015: 146, 159–162, 208–210.

FIGURE 5.10. Portrait bust of a Vestal Virgin. Early second century AD. Inv. No. 1914/150, Galleria degli Uffizi, Florence. Photo: Alinari / Art Resource, NY, ART313434.

the woolen *vittae* as the glory (*decus*) of the Vestal order, suggesting that the headdress was indeed a universally recognized symbol of a Vestal's priestly status.[33] The connection between the Vestal headdress and Vestal identity was so strong, in fact, that the bands were removed from the head of a priestess convicted of being unchaste.[34]

Our antiquarian sources confirm the priestly and sacral significance of the *infula*. In his epitome of Festus, for instance, Paul notes that *infulae* "are woolen

[33] Symmachus *Relat.* 3.11.
[34] Dion. Hal. *Ant. Rom.* 8.89.4–5. Dionysius notes elsewhere that a Vestal who chose to retire from service was expected to lay aside the insignia of her office (*Ant. Rom.* 2.67.2). Consider also the fact that Roman Catholic priests who are deprived of the right to exercise their priestly functions are said to be "defrocked," a term that highlights the very close association between clerical garments and priestly status.

threads with which priests, sacrificial victims, and temples are veiled" (*infulae sunt filamenta lanea, quibus sacerdotes et hostiae templaque velantur*, 100L). Isidore of Seville, a Christian bishop who produced a compendium of earlier antiquarian works in the early seventh century AD, adds that priests wore the *infula* wrapped around their heads like a diadem (*in modum diadematis*, *Orig.* 19.30.4). Based on these passages, we may conclude that the bands of the *infula* communicated a Vestal's priestly status. They presumably served an apotropaic function as well.[35] Like human hair, wool was believed to embody strength because of its ability to grow without the assistance of any external force. It retained this strength even after it had been sheared from the sheep and turned into yarn, making it an ideal fabric for priestly costumes and sacrificial victims.[36]

While the *infula* appears on every Vestal portrait, not every Vestal wears the band wound around her head the same number of times. The two Vestals in the Antiquario Palatino each wear four turns (fig. 5.1), as does the only fully preserved Vestal on the Cancelleria Reliefs (fig. 5.7). The figure on the fragmentary relief in the British Museum (fig. 5.2), however, is shown with just two rows beneath her veil. The portrait statues likewise reveal considerable variation, with the number of turns ranging from one to six. The reason for this variety is not immediately clear. Lindner has proposed that the Vestals used the turns of the *infula* to differentiate status within the order, which was governed by an internal hierarchy based on the age of the priestesses.[37] She suggests that the eldest Vestal, the *virgo maxima*, wore six turns of the *infula*, the next in order five, and so on down to the youngest, who wore only one turn. The fact that both priestesses on the Antiquario Palatino relief are shown wearing four turns of the *infula* argues against this solution, though it is possible that the Vestals were ranked in pairs, with the youngest priestesses wearing two turns of the *infula*, the middle two four, and the eldest two six turns each. This interpretation finds support in the fact that the two senior Vestals performed certain rituals in tandem.[38] If this hypothesis is correct, it would provide further insight into the inner dynamics of the Vestal order and reveal how the status of each member was represented visually to the outside world.

The *infula* communicated a Vestal's priestly status. The *vittae*, on the other hand, were more closely associated with her *castitas* and *pudicitia*. Ovid and Tibullus mention *vittae* in connection with chaste *matronae* and indicate that they were worn as a sign of modesty (*insigne pudoris*, Ov. *Ars am.* 1.31), while Servius claims that prostitutes and slaves were not permitted to wear the headbands.[39] Many scholars consequently list the *vittae* as part of the traditional

---

[35] Sebesta 1994: 47.
[36] Oswald and Haase 2010.
[37] Lindner 2015: 159–162. For the internal hierarchy of the Vestal priesthood, see also chapter 6.
[38] See chapter 6.
[39] Ov. *Ars am.* 3.483, *Rem.* 386, *Pont.* 3.3.51–52; Tib. 1.6.67. See also Plaut. *Mil.* 790–793; Verg. *Aen.* 7.403; Sebesta 1994: 49; Fantham 2008; Olson 2008: 36–38.

FIGURE 5.11. Torso of a Vestal Virgin. Late second century AD. Atrium Vestae, Rome. Photo by author.

attire of the Roman *matrona*, and it has even been argued that the Vestals' right to wear them is a sign that they were regarded as married women.[40] The matronal *vittae*, however, were used to bind up the *tutulus*, the distinctive hairstyle of a *materfamilias* (mother of the family) and the *flaminica Dialis*.[41] On the Vestal portraits, on the other hand, the *vittae* appear as cloth loops originating at the back of the *infula* and hanging down over the shoulders (fig. 5.11).[42] To my knowledge, no portrait of a non-Vestal woman shows the *vittae* as cloth loops, which indicates that this arrangement was unique to the Vestal order.[43] The *vittae* of a Vestal, therefore, simultaneously symbolized her *pudicitia* and distinguished her from *matronae* who shared this virtue, but arranged their headbands differently in order to mark their distinct status in the social order.[44] Together with the *seni crines*, the *vittae* communicated a Vestal's special status

[40] Serv. ad *Aen.* 7.403. For the *vittae* as an element of the costume of the *matrona*, see Sebesta 1994: 48–50; Olson 2008: 36–39. For the *vittae* as a sign of the matronal status of the Vestals, see Beard 1980: 14–15.

[41] Varro *Ling.* 7.44, with Sebesta 1994: 49–50. See also chapter 1.

[42] Lindner (2015: 157) notes that the width and appearance of these *vittae* clearly indicate that they were made from a different piece of cloth than the *infula*. While the *vittae* are not visible on every Vestal portrait, a statue lacking *vittae* may, nonetheless, be securely identified as a Vestal if both the *infula* and *suffibulum* are present. For the relationship between the *infula* and *vittae* on extant Vestal portraits, see also Stephens 2013, January 4.

[43] See also Lindner 1995: 74; Fantham 2008: 167–168; Olson 2008: 38–39.

[44] Unmarried girls may have worn *vittae* as well; at least that is what Propertius implies when he refers to marriage as a time when "a different headband" (*altera vitta*, 4.11.34) was placed upon the bride's head. The *vittae* would thus mark something unmarried girls, *matronae*, and Vestals held in common (*pudicitia*), rather than a particular social status (Gallia 2014: 225).

FIGURE 5.12. Denarius of M. Aemilius Lepidus showing a veiled and laureate female head on the obverse (left) and the Basilica Aemilia on the reverse (right), 61 BC. (*RRC* 419/3a). Inv. No. 1867,0101.1119, British Museum, London. Photo © Trustees of the British Museum.

as a chaste virgin and, with the *infula*, signified her membership in the Vestal order.

The only extant Vestal portraits from the republican period are also the tiniest. Even so, they tend to confirm what I have argued thus far about the Vestal hairstyle and headdress. The earliest image dates to 88 BC, when L. Titurius Sabinus placed an image of his ancestor Titus Tatius on the obverse of a *denarius* that showed a representation of the punishment of Tarpeia on the reverse.[45] Her hair, however, is unbound as a sign of her distress. In 58 BC, M. Aemilius Lepidus, the future *triumvir*, minted a *denarius* showing a bust portrait of a woman traditionally identified as the Vestal Aemilia on the obverse and a representation of the Basilica Aemilia on the reverse (Figure 5.12).[46] She wears a veil, a bun at the back of her head, and a lumpy band on her forehead that presumably represents either the *infula* or the roll of hair required to secure this headdress.[47] Her laurel wreath is without parallel on portraits in other media and suggests that this is the Vestal recorded as the mother of Romulus and Remus in an alternative version of the tradition, rather than the Vestal who rekindled the flame on the hearth of Vesta with nothing but a strip of white linen.[48] She holds a scepter and a *simpulum* on one of the triumviral gold

[45] *RRC* 344/2b, with Flower 2002b: 166.

[46] *RRC* 419/3a–b, with Zehnacker 1973: 510; Flower 2002b. For the revised date, see Hersh and Walker 1984. The absence of clearly rendered *vittae* is surprising, though perhaps not reason enough to challenge the traditional identification.

[47] On some examples, including fig. 5.11, what may be wisps of hair appear beneath the roll, suggesting that it is the *infula*.

[48] For the tradition recording Aemilia as the mother of Romulus and Remus, see Plut. *Rom.* 2. We know that the Basilica Aemilia had a frieze showing scenes from the life of Romulus; it is possible that the Vestal Aemilia appeared in one of these scenes (Flower 2002b: 169).

FIGURE 5.13. Aureus of L. Livineius Regulus showing the head of M. Aemilius Lepidus the *triumvir* on the obverse (left) and the Vestal Aemilia on the reverse (right), 42 BC. (*RRC* 494/1). Inv. No. 1864,1128.11, British Museum, London. Photo © Trustees of the British Museum.

coins minted in Rome in 42 BC, though the condition of the extant examples makes it difficult to say anything definitive about her hair or headdress (fig. 5.13).[49] The third Vestal portrait appeared in 41 BC, when C. Clodius Vestalis designed an issue featuring his ancestor Claudia seated on a chair holding a *simpulum*, her hair bound by the characteristic *infula* and *vittae* (fig. 7.1).[50] Claudia had earned her reputation for *pietas* (piety), and her status as a worthy ancestor, when she protected her father from a violent tribune during his illegal triumph in 146 BC.[51]

Coins depicting the goddess Vesta seem to imitate the hairstyle and headdress of her priestesses and thus provide additional evidence for their appearance during the republican period. A veiled head of Vesta wearing the *infula*, a bun at the back of her head, and a prominent hair roll graces the obverse of a *denarius* issued by Q. Cassius Longinus in 55 BC (fig. 6.1).[52] An almost identical image appears on coins minted by P. Sulpicius Galba in 69 BC and L. Cassius Longinus in 63 BC.[53] Though diminutive, these republican coins suggest that the Vestal hairstyle and headdress survived the transition from Republic

[49] *RRC* 494/1, with Zehnacker 1973: 611–613; Flower 2002b: 169.
[50] *RRC* 512/1–2, with Zehnacker 1973: 522; Flower 2002b: 169. Sydenham (1952: 185, Nos. 1134–1135) and Seaby (1967: 32, Claudia 13) identify the figure as Claudia Quinta, who famously proved her virtue when she received the ship of the Magna Mater in 204 BC (Cic. *Cael.* 14.34; Prop. 4.10.51–52; Livy 29.14; Ov. *Fast.* 4.305–345). As Leach (2007: 5) points out, however, the "Vestalization" of Claudia Quinta, who is characterized as a *matrona* in the Republican sources, appears first in Statius (*Silv.* 1.2.245–246) and is likely "a product of later sources that may well have confused her with two other Claudian woman [*sic.*] of the Roman Republic."
[51] See chapter 7.
[52] *RRC* 428/1.
[53] *RRC* 406/1, 413/1.

to principate largely unscathed. In light of this evidence, we can be more confident about describing the nature of the Vestal costume on the basis of the imperial portraits and reliefs.

The *Suffibulum*

When they presided over or participated in a public sacrifice, the Vestals also wore a short veil known as the *suffibulum*. To pray or sacrifice with one's head veiled (*capite velato*) was a quintessentially Roman practice.[54] A man would cover his head by pulling up a fold of his *toga*, while a woman generally veiled herself with her *palla*. In practical terms, the veiled head communicated that a sacrifice was underway. It also suppressed unfavorable sights and sounds and allowed the officiant to focus on the ritual, in the same way that the music played by the *tibicines* (players of the double flute) or other musicians prevented inauspicious noise. In place of the ordinary veil, some priests wore special head coverings, including the *flamines*, who put on a *pilleus*, a close fitting cap with an olivewood spike (*virgula oleagina*, Festus 9L) attached to its top, before sacrificing.[55] The *suffibulum* worn by the Vestals was likewise unique to their office.[56] It expressed their priestly status and distinguished them from other women who might be present at a public sacrifice.

The *suffibulum* was a short white veil that had a purple border and was fastened under the chin with a *fibula* (clasp).[57] The veil is clearly visible on a late Hadrianic portrait now in the collection of the Museo Nazionale Romano (fig. 5.9). This is the only Vestal statue that depicts the veil pinned at the sternum as it is shown on the relief sculptures. It falls over the Vestal's shoulders, but has been arranged rather artificially to reveal the *vittae* as well. Although the figure is damaged, it appears that she was originally shown sprinkling grain or incense on a small altar with her right arm and holding a *patera* or a small box in her extended left hand. The Vestals on the Sorrento Base (fig. 5.6) also wear *suffibula* secured with rosette brooches, while the figures on the Palermo Relief (fig. 5.3) are shown wearing veils fastened with small round *fibulae*. The *suffibula* of the priestesses on the Banqueting Vestals Relief are particularly well articulated (fig. 5.4). On this image, the short veil is fastened at the sternum with a simple round brooch and the cloth, which is clearly distinguished from the fabric of the *tunica*, falls just over the shoulders of the Vestals. Although the heads of five of the six Vestals on the altar relief of the Ara Pacis Augustae are badly damaged, the smallest figure at the front of the procession does appear

---

[54] For the Roman habit of sacrificing *capite velato*, see Freier 1963; Scheid 1995; Fantham 2008; Huet 2012.

[55] For the *pilleus*, see Festus 9L; Serv. Auct. ad *Aen.* 7.688; Isid. *Orig.* 7.12.18–19, 19.30.5. The *flamen Dialis* wore a special version of this cap, the *albogalerus*, which was made from the hide of a white victim that had been offered to Jupiter (Gell. *N.A.* 10.15.32 (= Varro *Div.* 2.51); Festus 9L).

[56] With one exception, for which see chapter 6.

[57] Varro *Ling.* 6.21; Festus (Paulus) 475L.

to be wearing a short veil fastened at her sternum (fig. 5.5). The praetextate border on the *suffibulum* is no longer visible on any of these sculptures, though it was almost certainly painted on along with other details that have been lost over time.[58]

Dress

Tunica and *Palla*

The hairstyle and headdress of the Vestals is described in some detail by our ancient authors and its various elements are confirmed by the visual evidence. The nature of their dress, however, is less certain. Generally speaking, ancient references to the clothing worn by Vestals are vague and uninformative. Propertius, Valerius Maximus, Dionysius of Halicarnassus, and Ambrose mention fabrics and colors but are silent regarding cut or style.[59] In the absence of more explicit information, some modern scholars have argued that the Vestals wore the toga on the basis of a brief notice in Paul's epitome of the lexicon of Festus: "a virgin sacrificing with the fold of her toga thrown back over her shoulder was called an *armita*" (*armita dicebatur virgo sacrificans, cui lacinia togae in humerum erat reiecta*, 4L).[60] This evidence, however, is hardly conclusive. No other ancient source suggests that the Vestals wore the toga, and none of the extant visual representations depict them dressed in this garment. Furthermore, the term *virgo* itself is not sufficient proof that Paul is referring to the Vestals, who are normally called *Vestales virgines* in the lexicon.[61] It is more plausible that the toga-wearing *armitae* were citizen girls who had a specific and otherwise unknown sacrificial role that involved throwing the fold of their *togae praetextae* over their shoulders.[62]

The absence of any systematic discussion of the Vestal dress in the ancient sources tends to support my earlier claim that their hairstyle and headdress

---

[58] For a discussion of praetextate garments and their ritual significance, see chapter 1.

[59] Propertius (4.11.54–55), Valerius Maximus (1.1.7), and Dionysius of Halicarnassus (*Ant. Rom.* 2.68.5) report that a Vestal named Aemelia miraculously reignited the flame on the hearth of Vesta with a garment made of white linen (*carbasus*), but provide no further details about its cut or color. Mekacher (2006: 47) points out that the linen cloth must have been closely linked to Aemilia's story, as it appears in all three versions of the *exemplum* but is not associated with the Vestals in any other ancient source. Ambrose implies that the Vestals wore purple robes (*purpuratarum vestium murices*, *Ep.* 18.11). The text in which this claim is found, however, is highly polemical and perhaps more than a little tendentious. The *suffibulum* had a purple edge, but it is unlikely that the Vestals wore entire garments died with this color, particularly during the imperial period, when purple was generally reserved for members of the imperial family.

[60] Giannelli 1913: 90; Guizzi 1968: 112, n. 49; Boëls-Janssen 1993: 102.

[61] See, for example, Festus 454L; Festus (Paulus) 14, 475L. See also Martini 1997b: 483, n. 115.

[62] Roman girls wore the *toga praetexta* until marriage (see, for example, Cic. *Verr.* 2.1.113; Prop. 4.11.33–34; Festus 282–284L; Macrob. *Sat.* 1.6.7; Arnob. *Ad. Nat.* 2.67). It seems likely, however, that most girls wore a *tunica* on a daily basis and the *toga praetexta* only on certain ritual occasions (see Sebesta 1994: 46–47, 2005; Olson 2008: 15–20).

were more significant markers of Vestal status.[63] Nonetheless, the question of what kind of dress the Vestals wore is a vital one. Nearly all recent studies of the Vestals have begun from the premise that they wore the *stola*, the traditional over-dress of a married woman.[64] The *stola* was a long, slip-like garment with over-the-shoulder straps and a deep V-shaped neckline (fig. 5.14). It was worn over the *tunica* and belted under the breast with a plain cord.[65] The *stola* was a mark of honor that distinguished the wearer as a member of a specific social group, the *ordo matronarum*, composed of citizen wives living in a *iustum matrimonium* (legal marriage).[66] In fact, the *stola* was virtually synonymous with matronly status in the Roman mind. According to Paul the Deacon, the Romans "generally used to call *matronae* those women who had the right to wear the *stola*" (*matronas appellabant eas fere, quibus stolas habendi ius erat*, 112L). Many recent studies of the Vestals have thus assumed that the Vestal costume and hair-style created a special, deeply ambiguous status between the virgin, the bride, and the married woman. By borrowing from both the married woman and the bride, so it has been argued, the Vestal appeared as a perpetually liminal figure caught in the moment of transition between two normal phases in a woman's life.[67] Close analysis reveals, however, that the costume of the Vestals was unique to their priestly order and did not borrow from the dress of other women. As I have suggested above, it was the bride who imitated the characteristic Vestal hairstyle, the *seni crines*, rather than the Vestals who imitated the bride. In what follows, I argue that the Vestals wore a long *tunica*, rather than the *stola*, in keeping with their status as absolute physical virgins. The *tunica* underscored their exemplary virginity and worked alongside the *seni crines* and the Vestal headdress to convey the moral and ritual purity of the priestesses. ·

Scholars who have argued that the Vestals wore the *stola* point to a letter of Pliny the Younger, where the author notes that Cornelia, who was buried alive in AD 91, wore a *stola* to her tomb:[68]

---

[63] This may have been fairly typical of Roman priestesses. Compare, for example, Vergil's description of Allecto disguising herself as Calybe, the priestess of Juno: "*Allecto torvam faciem et furialia membra / exuit, in vultus sese transformat anilis / et frontem obscenam rugis arat, induit albos / cum uitta crinis, tum ramum innectit olivae; / fit Calybe Iunonis anus templique sacerdos*" (Allecto lays aside her dreadful features and avenging limbs, transforming herself into the appearance of an old woman. She furrows her loathsome forehead with wrinkles, puts on white hair and a *vitta*, and fastens them with a branch of olive; she becomes Calybe, the elderly priestess of Juno and her temple, *Aen.* 7.415–419). While Allecto's *vitta* and an olive branch are carefully described, Vergil makes no mention of any special dress.

[64] See, for example, Beard 1980: 16; Scheid 1992c: 381–384; Mustakallio 1997: 74; Beard, North and Price 1998: 52; Scheid 2003: 132; Mekacher 2006: 46; Wildfang 2006: 13; Mustakallio 2007: 187; Gallia 2012: 118–119, 2014: 223, 228–229. Martini (1997b: 486–487), Staples (1998: 146), Olson (2008: 27), and Lindner (2015: 12, 255) express doubt, but do not fully challenge the prevailing consensus. Bartman (1999: 95) describes their dress as a "girded tunic."

[65] On the *stola*, see, for example, Sebesta 1994; Croom 2002: 75–78; Olson 2008: 27–33.

[66] Sebesta 1997: 531; Olson 2008: 27.

[67] See especially Beard 1980, followed by Scheid 1992c, 1993; Wildfang 2006: 13; Takács 2008: 85–86, 110. See also chapter 4.

[68] For the circumstances surrounding Cornelia's trial and execution, see Gallia 2012: 86–127.

FIGURE 5.14. Portrait of a woman wearing a *stola* from the Isola Tiberina in Rome. Early first century AD. Museo Nazionale Romano (Terme), Rome. Drawing by Amy Welch.

cum in illud subterraneum demitteretur, haesissetque descendenti stola, vertit se ac recollegit, cumque ei manum carnifex daret, aversata est et resiluit foedumque contactum quasi plane a casto puroque corpore novissima sanctitate reiecit. (4.11.9)

When she was taken down into that underground chamber, her *stola* caught on something as she was descending. She turned to free it, and when the executioner offered his hand to her, she pulled back and recoiled in disgust, and thrust his polluting touch from her chaste and pure body as if by a final act of piety.

While at first glance this passage appears to confirm an association between the Vestals and the *stola*, its testimony is open to criticism on several fronts. First, it is very unlikely that Cornelia wore her usual Vestal costume to her tomb. According to Dionysius of Halicarnassus, the *pontifices* removed the *infula* and *vittae* (στέμματα, *Ant. Rom.* 8.89.5) from the head of a Vestal convicted of *incestum*. While Dionysius does not say that the condemned Vestal removed her dress as well, it seems very likely that she was required to lay aside all garments explicitly associated with her former status as a priestess of Vesta. An important aspect of the public spectacle surrounding the execution of an unchaste Vestal was surely the fact that she no longer looked like a priestess.

If a disgraced Vestal did not wear her traditional costume to her death, then Pliny's letter appears to confirm that the Vestals did not normally wear the *stola*. I would like to suggest, however, that such a literal reading of the letter is unnecessary. In fact, it is very unlikely that Cornelia actually wore a *stola* to her tomb. As we have seen, the *stola* simultaneously identified the wearer as a *matrona* and reinforced an expectation of moral conduct. Prostitutes and adulteresses were forbidden to wear the dress because they failed to exhibit chaste or modest behavior. One ancient author even claims that adulteresses were required to remove the *stola* and to put on the *toga* as a sign of their dishonor.[69] These women were denied the dignity of the *stola* because they had broken the moral code associated with the garment. It is difficult to imagine that a disgraced Vestal, whose unchastity threatened not only the integrity of her family, but also the wellbeing of the entire Roman community, was allowed an honor withheld from disreputable wives.

Why, then, does Pliny use this inaccurate and misleading term? First, it is important to remember that he was not writing a technical treatise about the costume of the Vestals, but rather describing Cornelia's final, dramatic act of piety. The entire passage offers a subtle critique of Domitian, who had now presided over the execution of four Vestals, by casting doubt on Cornelia's guilt.[70] "I

[69] Acr. ad Hor. *Sat.* 1.2.63, with Sebesta 1994: 50–51; McGinn 1998: 156–171; Olson 2002: 393–397; Dixon 2014.

[70] For the trial and deaths of the Oculata sisters and Varonilla in AD 83, see Suet. *Dom.* 8.3–4; Cass. Dio 67.3.3–4; Juv. 4.9–10.

do not know whether she was innocent," Pliny writes, "but she certainly appeared to be so" (*nescio an innocens, certe tamquam innocens ducta est*, 4.11.9). Domitian, we are left to assume, sent an innocent Vestal to her death. Within this explicitly polemical context, Pliny employs the word *stola* in a general sense to describe the length of Cornelia's garment. This use is not without precedent. Cicero, for example, chose the term to describe the robe worn by the cult statue of Artemis at the Greek city of Segesta in Sicily:

> erat admodum amplum et excelsum signum cum stola; verum tamen inerat in illa magnitudine aetas atque habitus virginalis; sagittae pendebant ab umero, sinistra manu retinebat arcum, dextra ardentem facem praeferebat. (*Verr.* 2.4.74)

> It was a statue with a *stola*, quite large and tall; despite its great size, it had the age and appearance of a maiden. Arrows hung from her shoulder; she grasped a bow in her left hand and, in her right, held forth a burning torch.

While it is nearly impossible to imagine that the cult state of Artemis from Segesta actually wore a Roman *stola*, she may have been dressed in a long *chiton*. In fact, it has been argued that the archaistic Pompeii Artemis is a copy of the statue from Segesta, which had been taken to Rome in the late first century BC.[71] Cicero, who had knowledge of the original, likely chose the word *stola* in order to indicate that Artemis wore a long, flowing dress, rather than her more typical double-girded *chiton*. We may presume, therefore, that Pliny likewise uses *stola* to indicate that Cornelia wore a long dress as she descended the steps of her tomb.

Pliny's letter, therefore, does not provide incontrovertible evidence that the Vestals wore the *stola*. While it is sometimes claimed that the *stola* is "clearly represented" on sculptures depicting the Vestals, the visual evidence also fails to substantiate the traditional association between the Vestals and the matronly garment.[72] The Vestal portraits are shown wearing *tunicae*, the basic garment of every Roman woman.[73] Several statues wear their *tunicae* belted beneath

---

[71] Giuliano 1953. Even if, as Fullerton has argued (1990: 22–29), the Pompeii Artemis is a copy of an original Roman statue of the Augustan period, this original is likely to have been influenced by archaic Greek models, including, perhaps, the Artemis of Segesta.

[72] Beard 1980: 16, n. 36. See also Wildfang (2006: 13), who writes, "[t]he various sculptures of senior Vestal Virgins found within the *atrium Vestae* . . . are all portrayed dressed in a *stola*." Although Thompson (2005: 191) reports that the Vestal on the Cancelleria Reliefs is shown wearing a stola, I was unable to discern any evidence to support this claim. Mekacher (2006: 47–48) identifies a *stola* strap that has slipped off the shoulder of the sixth Vestal from the left on the Banqueting Vestals Relief. Close examination of the monument, however, reveals that the fold of fabric in question does not continue over the front of the arm and cannot be part of a *stola* strap. In my opinion, this garment is her *palla*.

[73] Lindner 2015: 133, 258. Among known Vestal portraits, only a lost portrait formerly in the collection of the Palazzo Giustiniani may have shown a Vestal wearing a *stola*. As Lindner (2015: 141–143) emphasizes, however, the head, which clearly identifies the portrait as a Vestal, and the torso, which wears *stola*, do not belong together. The statue appears in the first catalog published by the owner of

the breast with a Hercules knot, perhaps in order to signify their virginity (fig. 5.11).[74] Over their *tunicae*, the portraits wear *pallae,* large rectangular mantles that could be wrapped around the body and used to veil the head (fig. 5.15).[75] Together with the long *tunica*, the *palla* conveyed the modest chastity of the Vestals. Even though most of the portraits are not actually veiled, the mantle serves an important symbolic purpose, reminding the viewer that the subject of the portrait was an honorable woman who took care to preserve her modesty when she was in public.

The *palla* on a Vestal statue also expressed the subject's priestly status by imitating the iconographic conventions of Hellenistic portraiture. The precise configuration of the *palla*, which is worn wrapped around the right arm of the Vestal and arranged in a horizontal roll at her abdomen, mimics the drapery patterns found on portraits of Greek priestesses (fig. 5.16).[76] The young Vestal depicted in figure 17, which dates to the late second century AD, even wears a Greek *peplos* beneath her *palla*. The use of classicizing drapery patterns and formulaic poses is fairly typical of female portraiture at Rome.[77] Honorific statues of women tend to replicate standard types, such as the so-called Large Herculaneum Woman, which convey information about the subject's social identity by means of a visual "cliché."[78] Only the portrait heads attached to these stock bodies were carved with individualized facial features and hairstyles. The clothed bodies of the Vestal statues, therefore, communicate information about virtue and priestly status in a general sense, but are of little value as evidence for specific Vestal attire in any period.

While the classically idealizing portrait statues fail to solve the question of the Vestal dress, the official public reliefs in which the priestesses appear may provide more concrete evidence for their costume and appearance. The majority of the relief sculptures show the Vestals wearing *pallae* and *suffibula* over long dresses, which obscure the details of the garment beneath and make it impossible to determine whether the distinctive shoulder straps of the *stola* are present. The fully preserved Vestal on the Cancelleria Reliefs, however, does not wear a *suffibulum,* nor does she have her *palla* drawn up over her head. Instead, she wears it wrapped under her right arm and draped over her left shoulder (fig. 5.18). This arrangement clearly reveals her right shoulder, upon which no sign of the strap of the *stola* is visible. The Cancelleria Reliefs, therefore, which are

---

the Giustiniani collection in 1631, which indicates that the restoration had taken place even before this date. For the *tunica*, see Croom 2002: 78–79; Olson 2008: 25–26.

[74] Festus (55L) associates the *nodus Herculaneus* with brides. As Mekacher (2006: 157–158) has emphasized, the knot is absent from written descriptions of the Vestal costume.

[75] For the *palla*, see Croom 2002: 89–91; Sebesta 1994: 48–49; Olson 2008: 33–36.

[76] Lindner 2015: 236–237; Mekacher 2006: 47. For a discussion of the costume of Greek priestesses, see Connelly 2007: 85–115.

[77] For a discussion of the practice, see especially Trimble 2011.

[78] For this terminology, see Trimble 2011: 127.

FIGURE 5.15. Portrait statue of a Vestal Virgin, middle of the second century AD. Antiquario Forense, Rome. Photo: Eisner, Neg. D-DAI-Rom 68.3911.

FIGURE 5.16. (opposite page) Portrait statue of a Vestal Virgin, early third century AD. Inv. No. 4384, Antiquario Forense, Rome. Photo: Behrens, Neg. D-DAI-Rom 2006.0422.

FIGURE 5.17. Portrait statue of a Vestal Virgin, late second century AD. Inv. No. 4385, Antiquario Forense, Rome. Photo: Eisner, Neg. D-DAI-Rom 68.3921.

FIGURE 5.18. Detail of Frieze B of the Cancelleria Reliefs showing a Vestal Virgin, late first century AD. Inv. No. 13392, Musei Vaticani (Gregoriano Profano), Rome. Photo: HIP / Art Resource, NY, AR931818.

roughly contemporaneous with Pliny's letter, suggest that the Vestals wore long *tunicae*.

The priestesses of Vesta were career virgins who were required to maintain their virginity throughout their period of service. They were not married women, and there is no evidence that the Romans saw them as such. One of the reasons that modern scholars have been willing to do so is their conviction that the Vestals wore the *stola*, a view that is not well supported by the ancient evidence. Instead, the literary and visual material considered here suggests that the Vestals wore the *tunica*, which must originally have been standard dress for all Roman women. When they appeared in public, they also veiled themselves with a *palla* in order to preserve their modesty. It was dangerous for Vestals like Postumia and Minucia to wear excessively elegant clothing precisely because such garments might draw attention to their bodies and turn them into objects of desire. A long *tunica* and voluminous *palla*, on the other hand, carefully concealed a Vestal's body from the public gaze and helped to ensure that her virginity, which guaranteed the inviolability of the Roman state, remained intact. A modest costume was particularly important since, as Laetitia La Follette observes, the Vestals were continually exposed to the public eye as they carried out their ritual obligations.[79] While the headdress and accessories of the Vestals emphasized their priestly status, the *tunica* and *palla* communicated their virginity and extreme modesty.

Shoes and Accessories

"Soft" Shoes

The final element of the Vestal costume for which we have secure visual evidence is its special shoes, known to modern scholars as "soft" shoes.[80] These closed-toe shoes were likely made of very soft leather or felt and are clearly visible on the feet of the Vestals on the Ara Pacis (fig. 5.5), the Sorrento Base (fig. 5.6) and the Cancelleria Reliefs (fig. 5.7). They also appear on all of the portrait statues whose feet have been preserved. Although female members of the imperial family are sometimes depicted wearing footwear of this type, soft shoes were generally reserved for priests and priestesses.[81] Soft shoes are thus an important, if generally overlooked, element of the Vestal costume. At Rome, footwear was another means of differentiating social status.[82] Senators, *equites*, soldiers, *sacerdotes*, actors, citizens and noncitizens all wore distinctive shoes that reflected their position in Roman society. The soft shoes worn by the Vestals

---

[79] La Follette 2011: 155.
[80] For a discussion of the Vestals' footwear, see Mekacher 2006: 48.
[81] Lindner 1995: 245.
[82] For a discussion of Roman footwear, see Goldman 1994.

marked their priestly status and, for this reason, were carefully depicted on relief sculptures and portrait statues.

The Medallion of the *Virgo Maxima*

Generally speaking, the Vestal Virgins are not represented wearing jewelry, which might have attracted attention to their physical appearance or been misunderstood as a sign of *luxuria* (luxury).[83] As we have seen, priestesses whose dress and comportment was judged to be excessively elegant could face accusations of *incestum*. Most Vestals, therefore, appear to have refrained from wearing ornaments of any kind, aside from the *fibula* with which they fastened their *suffibula*. There are, however, two exceptions to this general rule. A large pendant hangs from a scarf around the neck of a portrait of the *virgo maxima* Coelia Concordia, who served in the late fourth century AD.[84] The pendant is carved as a three-part circle with a row of alternating rectangular, oval, and circular depressions on the widest band. These depressions almost certainly held gems or paste imitations. Given Coelia Concordia's status, we might speculate that her medallion was a special ornament reserved for the chief Vestal Virgin.[85]

A portrait from the Severan period also wore a medallion that is now lost (fig. 5.16). Seven holes drilled across the chest of the portrait form the outline of a necklace that once supported a large metal pendant, traces of which are visible between the breasts of the figure.[86] While the inscription associated with this portrait is no longer extant, it may also depict a *virgo maxima*. Unfortunately, however, these statues are late and any conclusions formed on the basis of their testimony are highly speculative. While the chief Vestal may have been distinguished by a special ornament during the later empire, it is uncertain whether she wore a similar medallion during the republican period as well.

Conclusion

The Vestal costume was unique to the Vestal order. While its individual elements appeared in the costumes of other women or other priests, no other Roman wore the same configuration of dress, headdress, and hairstyle assigned to the Vestal Virgins. Each component of the costume should be understood as one part in a system of visual signs. The *seni crines* symbolized a Vestal's virginity, the central and defining characteristic of the Vestal order.

---

[83] As stressed by La Follette 2011: 155–156.

[84] For a discussion of this portrait statue, now on display in the Galleria Colonna (Inv. No. 87), see Picozzi 1990: 157–162; Lindner 1995: 262–269. The inscription on the statue base identifying the subject as the *virgo maxima* Coelia Concordia is *CIL* 6.2145 = *ILS* 1261.

[85] Lindner 1995: 263–264.

[86] A reddish stain and a small amount of metal are visible on the original statue, though not on the copy in the *atrium*. For a discussion of this portrait, see Lindner 1995: 377–383.

The *infula* and *vittae*, on the other hand, represented her priestly status and may have signified her rank within the order. The *suffibulum* likewise expressed a Vestal's position as a priestess and emphasized her right to preside over public sacrifices. The *tunica* and *palla* shielded her from the public gaze and advertised her moral character. Like modest *matronae*, the Vestals were expected to communicate their chastity and modesty through their clothing. Those who did not were subject to scrutiny and even, on occasion, to accusations of *incestum*. Finally, her special soft shoes completed the ensemble and indicated that she was permitted to walk on sacred ground. The Vestal costume rendered visible a Vestal's unique position in Roman society. It made her instantly recognizable in public and, in a society that emphasized rank and status by means of distinctive sartorial markers, must have granted the wearer a high degree of prestige.

CHAPTER SIX

The Ritual Activities of the Vestal Virgins

According to an obscure cult formula (*verba sacrorum*) recorded by Servius in his commentary on Vergil's *Aeneid*, the Vestal Virgins approached the *rex* (perhaps the *rex sacrorum*) on a certain day (*certe die*) and asked, "Are you on the alert, king? Be alert!" (*vigilasne rex? vigila*,10.228). This unusual address has been much discussed in modern scholarship as evidence for a special relationship between the Vestals and either the archaic king or the republican *rex sacrorum*.[1] Of far greater significance, however, is the light it sheds on their role as guardians of the city of Rome.[2] The Vestals protected the Roman community by maintaining their absolute physical virginity, by praying for the welfare (*salus*) of the Roman people, by tending the eternal flame of Vesta, and by guarding the *pignora imperii*, the "pledges of empire" that resided within the *aedes Vestae* (Temple of Vesta). Fixed in the heart of the Forum at the very center of Roman civic life, the Vestals were the ritual defenders of the city and its inhabitants.

The extensive ritual program assigned to the Vestal order further emphasizes the connection between these priestesses and the wellbeing of the community. They participated in various rites designed to cleanse the city of ritual impurity. At the Fordicidia, the October Horse, and the December rites of Bona Dea, they played a role in guaranteeing the fertility of the fields and flocks. They were also involved in rites concerned with the preservation of the food supply, on which the security of the city depended, and with the transformation of raw grain into a substance suitable for consumption. Perhaps most significantly, the Vestals prepared *mola salsa*, the salted grain used to consecrate sacrificial victims and thereby to maintain Rome's relationship with the gods.

---

[1] See, for example, Latte 1960; Guizzi 1968: 109; Dumézil 1970: 586.
[2] As noted by Beard, North, and Price 1998: 58, n. 182; Bätz 2012: 296–298, with the reservations expressed by Cameron 2011: 604–605. Mueller (2002: 203, n. 21) has also suggested that the formula contextualizes the Vestals' subordination to the *pontifex maximus* by revealing that the priestesses "recognized their own part in making sure other priests lived up to their responsibilities."

Membership in the *Collegium Pontificum*

The Vestals were members of the extended pontifical college, a body that included the *pontifices*, the *rex sacrorum*, and the *flamines maiores*.[3] The wives of the *flamines*, the *flaminicae*, and the *regina sacrorum* were likely full members as well. The chief of the college, the *pontifex maximus* exercised a certain degree of authority over the other members of the college. His official residence, the *domus publica* (public house), adjoined the *atrium Vestae*, and he was responsible for the selection and *captio* (capture) of new Vestals. The *pontifex maximus* also presided over special meetings of the pontifical college convened to try a Vestal suspected of *incestum* (unchastity).[4] Though he could scourge the priestesses for minor offenses, the pontifex maximus did not exercise *patria potestas* (paternal power) or *tutela* (guardianship) over them.[5]

Other implications of the Vestals' membership in the pontifical college have not been as fully explored. As we shall see, they cooperated with other members of the college on a number of ritual occasions. Pontifical *cenae* (banquets) also provided opportunities for priests to create and solidify social bonds.[6] According to one pontifical source cited by the early fifth-century AD author Macrobius, four Vestals were present at a banquet celebrated in 69 BC in honor of the inauguration of L. Cornelius Lentulus Niger (pr. ca. 61 BC) as *flamen Martialis*.[7] The guest list included the distinguished consulars Q. Caecilius Metellus Pius (cos. 80 BC), Q. Lutatius Catulus (cos. 78 BC) and Mam. Aemilius Lepidus (cos. 77 BC). The Vestals shared a dining couch with Publicia, the new *flaminica Martialis*, and her mother, Sempronia. It is possible, perhaps even probable, that the wives of other male priests were present as well.[8] By virtue of their position in the pontifical college, the Vestals were connected to many of the most powerful men and women in Rome.

A similar pontifical *cena* may be the subject of a fragmentary relief from a state monument of the Claudian period (fig. 5.4).[9] The Banqueting Vestals relief depicts the six priestesses seated behind a low table. They are clearly identifiable by their *suffibula* (sacrificial veils), suggesting that the occasion was a religious one. The first five Vestals from left to right are shown frontally while the sixth, whose head is now lost, is partially reclining with her back to the viewer.

---

[3] For the composition of the *collegium pontificum*, see Wissowa 1912: 501; Van Haeperen 2002: 80–84.
[4] For a detailed discussion of the evidence for pontifical oversight of *incestum* trials, see Johnson 2007.
[5] Dion. Hal. *Ant. Rom.* 2.67.3; Plut. *Num.* 10.3. For the legal status of the Vestals, see chapter 4.
[6] As Rüpke (2012: 45) observes regarding *cenae sacerdotalis* (priestly meals), "an event that is marked out as religious can also offer an occasion for intensified social interaction, however much communicative practice on such occasions was constrained by formal and informal rules specific to the event." See also Rüpke 1998; Scheid 2005c; Martens 2015.
[7] Macrob. *Sat.* 3.13.10–11. For the date of the banquet, see Taylor 1942; Tansey 2000.
[8] The first two *triclinia* held a total of eighteen *pontifices* (Tansey 2000: 247, n. 40), which suggests that the third could have accommodated up to three additional female guests if the women were reclining; more if they were seated (for women's dining posture, see Roller 2006: 96–156).
[9] For further discussion and bibliography, see chapter 5.

Several female figures, presumably priestly attendants, are visible in the background.[10] A seventh seated female figure depicted in profile on the far right of the relief holds her hand beneath her chin in a gesture reminiscent of the so-called *pudicitia* pose.[11] She may represent a *flaminica*.[12] The scene bears a striking resemblance to Macrobius' account of the pontifical banquet in 69 BC. Indeed, it has been suggested that the relief represents a banquet celebrating the inauguration of Claudius (r. AD 41–54) as *flamen Augustalis*.[13] Although uncertainty regarding the original context of the relief precludes precise identification, it nonetheless illustrates an important and generally underappreciated facet of the Vestals' participation in social and religious life at Rome, one that is corroborated by the literary sources.

Although the ritual obligations of the Vestals were less obviously political than those of the male *pontifices*, their role within the pontifical college did allow them to exert influence over matters with significant political consequences. Evidence from the late Republic suggests that the Vestals could advise the senate on questions related to their sphere of responsibility, a category of religious activity from which they are almost always excluded by modern scholars.[14] In 61 BC, the Vestals were embroiled in the trial of P. Clodius Pulcher (tr. pl. 58 BC), who stood accused of violating the secret rites of Bona Dea two years earlier, when he entered the house of Julius Caesar (where the *matronae* had gathered) disguised as a flute girl.[15] The Vestals had repeated the sacrifice immediately (*instaurassent*, Cic. *Att.* 1.13.3), but the prank was a serious ritual offense.[16] Clodius had violated the sanctity of a public rite and placed the entire community in danger of retribution from the gods. When pressed to take action, the senate referred the matter to the Vestals and *pontifices*, who pronounced the matter a violation of divine law (*postea rem ex senatus consulto ad virgines atque ad pontifices relatam idque ab iis nefas esse decretum*, Cic. *Att.* 1.13.3).[17] Although Clodius was ultimately acquitted, the so-called Bona Dea scandal suggests that the Vestals had a more significant role

---

[10] Fless 1995: 40–41.

[11] The *pudicitia* pose, which takes its name from Roman coins bearing an allegory of Pudicitia, was a popular format in Greek and Roman portraiture (Masséglia 2015: 124–5). Figures in this pose are typically shown with one hand beside or beneath their chin, often grasping a fold of the *palla* (cloak).

[12] Thompson 2005: 177.

[13] Ryberg 1955: 72–73. Felletti Maj (1977: 291) suggests that the scene depicts a *lectisternium*, but there is no concrete iconographical evidence in the relief to support this interpretation (as stressed by Dunbabin 2003: 223, n. 6).

[14] See, for example, Beard 1990; Scheid 1993; Gaspar 2012: 152–153.

[15] For a detailed account of the Bona Dea scandal, see Tatum 1999: 62–86, with further bibliography.

[16] The religious implications of the Bona Dea scandal do not receive adequate consideration from Bauman (1992: 62–63) or Wildfang (2006: 98–99).

[17] Tyrell and Purser (1904: 199) bracketed "*ad virgines atque*" as "doubtful," arguing, "we are not aware that the Vestal Virgins had any jurisdiction as regards matters of ritual, and we know that they were subject to the Pontifices." As Shackleton Bailey (1965: 304) has stressed, however, "it is idle to question the text," particularly on the basis of a belief that the Vestals could not have exercised such an important role in Roman society.

within the pontifical college than is often assumed.[18] They could evidently make the decision to perform an *instauratio* (repetition of a rite) without consulting the *pontifex maximus* and, even more tellingly, pronounce judgment on the behavior of a member of the political elite.

Ritual Activities within the Precinct of Vesta

The Temple of Vesta and the House of the Vestals

The Vestals performed many of their most important ritual obligations within the precinct of Vesta, which sat at the southeast end of the Forum near the *regia* and the *domus publica*, the headquarters and official residence of the *pontifex maximus*. The archaeological evidence indicates that the area emerged as a cult site over the course of the sixth century BC.[19] An altar stood in the precinct by the end of this period at the latest, a sure indication that Vesta's cult involved sacrifice from an early date.[20]

The earliest remains of a temple date to the end of the third century BC, though a shrine of some kind presumably existed prior to this date.[21] The written sources claim, in this instance with some validity, that the first *aedes Vestae* was a round building constructed of wattle and daub with a thatched roof in the manner of a primitive Italic hut.[22] The Romans retained the round form and diminutive size of the temple throughout its history, perhaps in an effort to emphasize the antiquity and permanence of Vesta's cult.[23] The late republican temple appears as a round building with six columns on a *denarius* issued by Q. Cassius Longinus in 55 BC (fig. 6.1).[24] A figure holding a scepter and perhaps a *patera* stands on the peak of the roof and large gryphon-head antefixes adorn the eaves. This temple was destroyed in the great fire of AD 64, and the remains visible today date to the restoration carried out by the Severan empress Julia Domna (AD 185–217) following a fire in AD 191.

From an early date, the precinct of Vesta included a residence for the Vestal Virgins. The earliest remains, situated behind the temple, date to the end of the third century BC.[25] During the republican period, the house of the Vestals was

[18] Johnson (2007: 159, 162–163) has even suggested that they may have been able to vote on issues of this kind.

[19] Scott 2009: 8–18. For a discussion of the archaeological evidence, see also Mekacher 2006: 81–102; Caprioli 2007.

[20] Scott 2009: 15.

[21] Scott 2009: 18–21. The Temple of Vesta reportedly burned in 241 BC (Livy *Per.* 19). It was damaged again in 210 BC during the war with Hannibal (Livy 26.27.1–4, 14), setting the stage for the significant rebuilding that took place at the end of the third century BC

[22] Ov. *Fast.* 6.261–266.

[23] As suggested by Scott 2009: 24, 77.

[24] *RRC* 428/1, including a discussion of the significance of the voting urn, tablet, and curule chair on the reverse.

[25] Scott 2009: 18.

FIGURE 6.1. Denarius of Q. Cassius Longinus showing Vesta on the obverse (left) and the *aedes Vestae* on the reverse (right), 55 BC. (*RRC* 428/1). Inv. No. 1901,0407.169, British Museum. Photo © Trustees of the British Museum.

a rectangular building with a series of six rooms of a equal size, presumably the bedrooms of the six priestesses, and a slightly larger common room opening onto an enclosed courtyard.[26] In the late Republic, perhaps not long after Caesar was elected *pontifex maximus* in 63 BC, several rooms were added to the residence, including one that appears to have served a ritual purpose.[27] A coarseware pot buried in the floor of this room held the remains of an animal sacrifice and a ritual banquet, confirming that ritual activity was not restricted to the temple, but extended into the house of the Vestals as well.[28] The residence of the Vestals remained relatively modest in size, even after Augustus donated the adjacent *domus publica* in 12 BC, until the reign of Trajan (r. AD 98–117), when the building was enlarged and embellished significantly.[29] It was refurbished under Julia Domna and remained the home of the Vestal order until the end of the fourth century AD.

Tending the Eternal Flame

The central focus of the *aedes Vestae* was not a cult statue of the goddess Vesta, but rather her presence in the living flame (*vivam . . . flammam*, Ov. *Fast.* 6.291) on the hearth.[30] This hearth was the physical and symbolic heart of the city,

---

[26] Scott 2009: 18, 28, figs. D1, D24.
[27] Scott 2009: 35–52.
[28] Scott 2009: 38, 42–43.
[29] For the development of the residence of the Vestals during the imperial period, see Scott 2009: 66–77.
[30] For the goddess Vesta, see Hommel 1972. In addition to the flame, there was a deep shaft in the interior of the temple, known as the "*favissa*" since its discovery in the nineteenth century, which ran

just as the family hearth was the focal point of the Roman home.[31] Its eternal flame (*ignis inextinctus*, Ov. *Fast.* 6.297) was thought to guarantee the eternity and inviolability of the city of Rome. Indeed, Livy's Camillus invokes the fires of Vesta (*Vestae ignes*, 5.54.7) as an argument against moving the community to Veii after the Gallic sack in the early fourth century BC. It is not difficult to imagine how this sympathetic connection between the flame and the city developed. Fire was a vital resource without which the community could not hope to survive: it provided light and heat and allowed early Romans to cook food, to fire ceramics, and to burn offerings to their gods. A communal hearth would have ensured that the city was never without a source of fire. Located in the center of the city, the hearth of Vesta bound individual families together into a stable and secure community.

As caretakers of the flame the Vestals took an active role in safeguarding the community. They were also subject to intense scrutiny when the flame burned out. The extinction of Vesta's fire portended the destruction of the city and was generally regarded as a sign that one of the Vestals had violated her vow of chastity.[32] Even its accidental extinguishment was taken very seriously. Following a list of frightful prodigies reported to the senate in 206 BC, Livy notes that the Romans were even more terrified by the news that the flame in the *aedes Vestae* had gone out.[33] An investigation established that the Vestal in charge of the fire on the night in question had simply been careless. The senate ordered a sacrifice and a *supplicatio*, an expiatory rite in which all Romans, male and female alike, were encouraged to visit public temples throughout the city to offer prayers and sacrifices. The offending Vestal was flogged by the *pontifex maximus* according to the usual custom.[34]

Given the importance of the eternal flame, it stands to reason that the Vestals were expected to maintain constant vigilance over the hearth. No ancient literary source addresses this question directly, but it is possible that they worked in shifts, ensuring that at least one priestess would be on duty at all times. There is, however, some evidence that all six priestesses could be absent from the temple on certain ritual occasions. They appear as a group on the altar frieze of the Ara Pacis Augustae in a procession that very likely depicts the annual sacrifice commemorating Augustus' return from Spain and Gaul in 13 BC (fig. 5.5) as well as on the Banqueting Vestals relief (fig. 5.4).[35] This visual evidence

---

straight through the foundations of the building, "providing a direct connection with the virgin earth that, as Ovid tells us (*Fast.* 6.249–460), represented the goddess herself" (Scott 2009: 21). For the identification of Vesta with *terra* (earth), see also Dion. Hal. *Ant. Rom.* 2.66.3. Although the temple contained no cult statue, there was evidently no prohibition against depicting Vesta; the goddess appears on coins and sculptural reliefs (see, for example, Figs. 5.6, 6.1). Cicero's (*De or.* 3.2.10) claim that the blood of the *pontifex maximus* Q. Mucius Scaevola (cos. 95 BC) had spattered a statue (*simulacrum*) of Vesta suggests that there was an image of the goddess in the precinct, though perhaps not in the temple itself.

[31] Dion. Hal. *Ant. Rom.* 2.64.5; Plut. *Num.* 9.5.

[32] See, for example, Dion. Hal. *Ant. Rom.* 2.67.5. For a more detailed discussion of the association between the flame and Vestal virginity, see chapter 4.

[33] Livy 28.11.6.

[34] Dion. Hal. *Ant. Rom.* 2.67.3; Plut. *Num.* 10.4.

[35] For a more detailed discussion of these reliefs, see chapter 5.

suggests that the Vestals may have had assistants who cared for the flame when the priestesses were required to be present at a public festival. Some assistants may have been *servi publici* (public slaves). Nearly every cult and priesthood at Rome employed *servi publici* as priestly assistants, and there is no reason to believe that the cult of Vesta was any different.[36] In fact, Tacitus reports that a *servus publicus* sheltered L. Calpurnius Piso Frugi Licinianus in his room inside the precinct of Vesta when he was attempting to escape Otho's assassins in AD 69.[37] Inscriptions from the imperial period record *fictores virginum Vestalium* (bakers of the Vestal Virgins), a servile position associated with the pontifical college as well.[38] According to Varro, "*fictores* were so called from *fingere* (to shape) the *liba* (sacrificial cakes)" (*fictores dicti a fingendis libis, Ling.* 7.44).[39] If the Vestals employed *fictores* to bake *liba*, they undoubtedly relied on *servi publici* to assist them with other activities as well, perhaps even with tending the hearth of Vesta. Given that men were not permitted to enter the Temple of Vesta or to handle the *sacra* kept within it, we should assume that some public slaves attached to the cult were women. Following the Roman victory at Aquae Sextiae in 102 BC, a number of married women among the captured Teutones reportedly begged Marius to hand them over to the Vestals as a gift, pledging to refrain from sexual intercourse.[40] Even if this story is a fiction, it may indicate that some slaves attached to the cult of Vesta were expected to remain chaste during their period of service. The Vestals themselves, of course, remained personally culpable when the flame went out.

Praying for Rome

A number of written sources reveal that the Vestals also prayed for the welfare of the Roman people as they ministered at the hearth of Vesta.[41] Pliny even records a belief in their ability to root fugitives to the spot by uttering a specific prayer, provided the runaway had not yet left the city.[42] In his speech on behalf of M. Fonteius, Cicero reminds the jury of the plight of the defendant's Vestal sister, Fonteia, "who has been, on behalf of you and of your children, occupied for so many years in propitiating the immortal gods" (*quae pro vobis liberisque vestris tot annos in dis immortalibus placandis occupata est, Font.* 46). Without her prayers (*preces*), he continues, "these things [i.e., all these things which we

---

[36] For *servi publici* as priestly attendants, see Halkin 1897: 48–70, 160–166; Eder 1980: 41–56; Fless 1995: 54–56; Weiß 2004: 135–58.

[37] Tac. *Hist.* 1.43. Although no slave quarters have been positively identified in the republican levels, much of the early precinct is obscured by additions made during the imperial period (Scott 2009: 30).

[38] *CIL* 6.786, 2134, with Eder 1980: 43–45.

[39] It is important to distinguish between sacrificial cakes (*liba*) and *mola salsa*, which was a loose mixture of *far* (spelt) and *muries* (salt).

[40] Val. Max. 6.1.ext.3.

[41] Among modern scholars only Saquete (2000: 46–48) discusses the Vestals' prayers in any detail. For a general discussion of prayer in Roman religion, see Appel 1909; Hickson 1993: 1–15.

[42] Plin. *H.N.* 28.13.

see around us] could not be preserved" (*haec salva esse non possent*, 48). Although Cicero's rhetorical aims may have led him to exaggerate this point, other authors confirm the basic premise of his argument. Horace, for instance, suggests that Vesta, wearied by the violence of the civil wars, is ignoring the petitions (*carmina*) of her Vestals.[43] Taken together, these sources suggest that the Vestals prayed regularly for the welfare (*salus*) of the Roman people, just as individual families prayed to the *Lares* and *Penates*, the guardian deities of the household, and to Vesta, who was thought to reside in the domestic hearth, in order to guarantee the flourishing of the family and the prosperity of the household.[44]

In general, public prayer at Rome was not spontaneous, nor was it left to the individual priest or priestess to frame the petition in his or her own words. Effective prayer depended upon the careful repetition of precise ritual formulae. The ancient sources tell us that these formulae were preserved in priestly books (*libris sacerdotum*, Gell. *N.A.* 13.23.1).[45] According to Pliny the Elder, when it was time for the officiant to pray, one attendant dictated the formula from a written document (*de scripto*, H.N. 28.3) while another listened carefully to catch any mistakes. The Vestals presumably maintained their own set of prayer books in order to facilitate regular prayer.[46] The responsibility to pray for the welfare of the Roman people, both inside the temple and at public festivals, where they would have had to speak publicly in front of an audience, underscores the Vestals' prominent role in civic life.

Tending the *Penus Vestae*

The Vestals were also responsible for guarding the *penus* (storeroom) in the *aedes Vestae* and the *sacra* (sacred objects) stored within it. According to Festus, this innermost place in the temple was surrounded by screens, presumably in order to shield the *sacra* from view (*locus intimus in aede Vestae tegetibus saeptus*, 296L). It contained the mysterious *pignora imperii* (pledges of empire), the most significant of which was the Palladium, a small statue of Pallas Athena believed to have been brought by Aeneas from Troy.[47]

Pliny the Elder reports that the Vestals also worshipped the god Fascinus in the form of a *fascinum* (phallus):

quamquam religione tutatur et fascinus, imperatorum quoque, non solum infantium, custos, qui deus inter sacra Romana a Vestalibus coli-

---

[43] Hor. *Carm.* 1.2.28.
[44] Cat. *Agr.* 143.2; Ov. *Fast.* 6.291–310. For household ritual and the household gods, see especially Harmon 1978; Orr 1978; Dubourdieu 1989: 63–120; Frölich 1991; Turcan 2000: 14–37; Schultz 2006b: 121–137; Bodel 2008.
[45] See also Cic. *Dom.* 140; Pliny H.N. 28.3.
[46] Though badly damaged, one of the Vestals on the altar relief of the Ara Pacis appears to be carrying tablets that may contain prayers along with directions for the ritual (fig. 5.5).
[47] Cic. *Scaur.* 48, *Phil.* 11.24; Livy 5.52.7, 26.27.14; Ov. *Fast.* 6.417–436; Dubourdieu 1989: 460–467.

tur, et currus triumphantium, sub his pendens, defendit medicus invid-
iae. (*H.N.* 28.7.39)

And yet the child is also under the divine protection of Fascinus, guardian not only of infants but also of generals. He is worshipped as a god by
the Vestals as part of the Roman rites, and hanging beneath the chariots
of triumphing generals, defends them from envy as if a physician.

Modern scholars have generally connected Pliny's claim to the myth of the birth
of Servius Tullius (or of Romulus in some versions), whose mother was allegedly impregnated by a phallus that appeared in the hearth fire.[48] They argue,
therefore, that Vesta (and by extension the Vestals themselves) symbolized the
generative power of the phallus.[49] Fertility cults in the ancient world were often
associated with virgin priestesses, who were regarded as powerful mediators "of
stored up, potential procreative power," as Mary Beard has written.[50] It should
be stressed, on the other hand, that the various sources for the birth of Servius
Tullius attribute his miraculous conception not to Vesta, but rather to the *Lar*,
the *genius*, or Vulcan, who personified the masculine, procreative aspects of
fire.[51] According to Ovid, moreover, Vesta's fire was understood to be pure and
sterile, neither putting out nor receiving any seed (*semina nulla remittit / nec
capit, Fast.* 6.293–4).[52] In fact, his etiology for the Vestalia in June suggests that
the festival was understood to celebrate Vesta's escape from the unwelcome sexual advances of the ithyphallic god Priapus.[53] Fascinus may have had a place
within the *aedes Vestae*, but he was presumably held at arm's length.

A close reading of Pliny's text suggests that the Vestals worshipped Fascinus
for his protective (rather then his procreative) power.[54] The Romans believed
that the *fascinum*, from *fas* (favorable), was an apotropaic charm against the
evil eye and other demonic forces. Pliny elsewhere reveals that *satyrica signa*,
by which he means images of phalli, were frequently placed on hearths as protection against the incantations of the envious (*invidentium effascinationes,
H.N.* 19.19.1). It stands to reason that the hearth of Vesta, the most important
hearth in the city of Rome, would be protected against the evil eye by a *fascinum* as well. The power of the *fascinum* to avert evil is fundamentally connected to its fertility, but it is not necessarily the case that the Vestals assumed

---

[48] For the birth of Servius Tullius, see Dion. Hal. *Ant. Rom.* 4.2.1–3; Ov. *Fast.* 6.627–634; Pliny *H.N.*
36.70, 204; Plut. *De fort. Rom.* 10. Plutarch (*Rom.* 2.3) assigns a very similar legend to the birth of Romulus and Remus.

[49] See especially Brelich 1949: 48–85; Hommel 1974; Beard 1980: 24; Beard, North, and Price 1998: 53;
Staples 1998: 148–149; Littlewood 2006: 80–81; Takács 2008: 80, 84–85.

[50] Beard 1980: 15; MacLachlan 2007: 4–6.

[51] For the distinction between the hearth fire of Vesta and the fire of Vulcan (elided by Beard 1980:
24–25), see Dumézil 1975: 61–77; Versnel 1993: 271–272.

[52] Ov. *Fast.* 6.291–294.

[53] See further below.

[54] Wildfang 2006: 17. The context of Pliny's reference to the god Fascinus is vital and often omitted in
modern scholarship.

this power through their worship of the god Fascinus. In fact, as we have seen in the preceding chapters, the ritual and ideological power of a Vestal priestess depended upon her absolute physical virginity. One could more readily argue that the Vestals embodied the inviolability of the Palladium. The Vestals honored the god Fascinus in their role as ritual guardians of Rome and of the sacred flame.

The *sacra* kept within the *penus* could be seen and handled by the Vestals alone.[55] Even the *pontifex maximus* L. Caecilius Metellus (cos. 251 BC), who caught a glimpse of the Palladium as he attempted to rescue the sacred objects from the burning temple in 241 BC, was allegedly stricken with blindness as a result.[56] As the Gauls descended upon the city in 390 BC, the Vestals consulted with the *flamen Quirinalis*, who may have been the most senior member of the pontifical college on hand, but it seems very likely that they removed the *sacra* from the temple, and perhaps from the nearby *regia* as well, and carried the objects to safety with their own hands.[57] During the civil wars in the thirties BC, the situation in the city became so perilous that the Vestals were forced to hide the *sacra* once again, this time on their own initiative.[58]

Ovid and Plutarch tell us that the *penus* and the objects within it had to be purified with water on a daily basis.[59] The mythical Vestals Rhea Silvia and Tarpeia both fetch water themselves, which suggests that Roman authors imagined (rightly or wrongly) that the priestesses, rather than their assistants, performed this ritual work.[60] The Vestals drew water from the spring of the Camenae, water nymphs whose grove (*lucus*) and spring (*fons*) was located on the Caelian Hill near the Porta Capena.[61] Plutarch reports that this spring watered the place where the *ancile* (shield of Mars) had fallen from heaven.[62] Like the *pignora imperii* in the *aedes Vestae*, the *ancile* and its eleven identical copies were regarded as talismans for the preservation of Rome. The *salii* (Salian priests) carried and beat the shields as they performed a ritual song and dance through the city at various times each year.[63] The water from the spring where the original *ancile* had been discovered also had protective powers, which may explain why the Vestals used it, rather than water from a source closer to the temple, such as the spring of Juturna, to purify the *pignora* and the *aedes Vestae*.

---

[55] Plut. *Cam.* 20.

[56] Cic. *Scaur.* 48; Livy *Per.* 19; Ov. *Fast.* 6.439–452; Dion. Hal. *Ant. Rom.* 2.66.4; Val. Max. 1.4.5; Pliny *H.N.* 7.141; Orosius 4.11.9; Dubourdieu 1989: 487–502.

[57] Livy tells us that L. Albinus saw the public priestesses (*sacerdotes publicas*, 5.40.8) as they ascended the Janiculum Hill carrying the *sacra* of the Roman people. See also Val. Max. 1.1.10; Dubourdieu 1989: 470–480.

[58] Cass. Dio 42.31.3.

[59] Ov. *Fast.* 3.11–12; Plut. *Num.* 13.2. For water as a purificatory substance, see especially Edlund-Berry 2006.

[60] Prop. 4.4.16 (Tarpeia); Ov. *Fast.* 3.11–12 (Rhea Silvia).

[61] Plut. *Num.* 13.2; Festus 152L. For the Fons Camenarum (Spring of the Camenae), see Richardson 1992: 63–64.

[62] Plut. *Num.* 13.1–5.

[63] See chapter 3 for the *salii* and their female counterparts, the *saliae*.

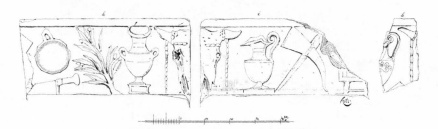

FIGURE 6.2. Surviving sections of the frieze of the Temple of Vesta (drawing after Jordan 1886, pl. 7).

According to Servius, the Vestals carried this water in a *futtile*, a special vessel designed to spill its contents when set down:

> nam futtile vas quoddam est lato ore, fundo angusto, quo utebantur in sacris Vestae, quia aqua ad sacra Vestae hausta in terra non ponitur, quod si fiat, piaculum est: unde excogitatum vas est, quod stare non posset, sed positum statim effunderetur. (ad *Aen.* 11.339)

> The *futtile* is a certain vessel with a wide mouth and a narrow base, which they use in the rites of Vesta, since water drawn for the rites of Vesta is not placed on the ground, because if this is done, it is a matter for expiation (*piaculum*). For this reason, a vessel was devised that could not stand up but would immediately spill when set down.

A large vase sitting on a square base on the entablature frieze of the *aedes Vestae* has been identified as the *futtile* (fig. 6.2).[64] The Vestals presumably used this vessel to carry the water that they needed to produce *mola salsa* as well.

Preparing *Mola Salsa*

The Vestals were responsible for preparing *mola salsa*, the mixture of ground *far* (spelt) and salt that priests and priestesses sprinkled on the backs of sacrificial victims at every public sacrifice in the city of Rome.[65] The author of the Servius Auctus commentary on Vergil's *Eclogues* provides the fullest description of the process:

> Virgines Vestales tres maximae ex nonis Maiis ad pridie idus Maias alternis diebus spicas adoreas in corbibus messuariis ponunt easque spicas ipsae virgines torrent, pinsunt, molunt atque ita molitum condunt. (8.82)

---

[64] La Follette 2011/2012: 23. Siebert (1999: 55) and Caprioli (2007: 161) are more hesitant to identify the jug as the *futtile*, describing it instead as a *hydria* sitting on a square base. Even so, Siebert (1999: 55) emphasizes that the jug is not in contact with the ground, which suggests that it could contain water suitable for use in the rites of Vesta.

[65] Festus 97L.

The three senior Vestal Virgins from the day after the Nones of May to the day before the Ides of May, on alternate days, place heads of grain in harvest baskets, and these heads the virgins themselves toast, pound, and grind, and then store what has been ground in this way.

This passage stresses that the Vestals (*ipsae virgines*), not their ritual assistants, performed the various tasks necessary to prepare *mola salsa*. They gathered the grain themselves on alternate days using a *corbis* (basket) and then processed what they had harvested.[66] Spelt is a husked wheat, which means that the grains cannot be detached from the husk by threshing, but must instead be roasted and then pounded with a mortar and pestle.[67] The process is labor intensive but absolutely critical for both practical and religious reasons: according to Pliny, the Romans believed that only roasted *far* could be offered to the gods.[68]

Once the three eldest Vestals had roasted and ground the *far*, they mixed it with "baked salt and hard salt" (*sale cocto et sale duro*, Serv. ad *Ecl.* 8.82) at the Vestalia in June, the *ludi Romani* in September and the Lupercalia in February. Festus describes the preparation of this salt, known as *muries*, in a passage based on Veranius, a late republican authority on the pontifical law:

> muries est, quemadmodum Veranius docet, ea quae fit ex sali sordido, in pila pisato, et in ollam fictilem coniecto, ibique operto gypsatoque et in furno percocto; cui virgines Vestales serra ferrea secto, et in seriam coniecto, quae est intus in aede Vestae in penu exteriore, aquam iugem, vel quamlibet, praeterquam quae per fistulas venit, addunt, atque ea demum in sacrificiis utuntur. (152L)

> *Muries* is, as Veranius teaches, that which is made from unrefined salt when it has been crushed in a mortar, put into an earthen jar, and there covered with gypsum and cooked thoroughly in an oven; to this, after it has been cut with an iron saw and put into an earthen vessel, which is within the Temple of Vesta in the outer *penus*, the Vestal Virgins add continually flowing water, however much (is needed), except that which comes through pipes, and finally they use it in sacrifices.

The Vestals first ground unrefined salt with a mortar and pestle, then baked it in a gypsum-covered clay pot, cut it with an iron *serra* (saw) and stored it in an earthen vessel known as the *seria*. At the appropriate moment, they mixed in water collected from a spring to create a brine that was added to the ground *far* in order to produce *mola salsa*.

---

[66] The Vestals gathered grain on alternate days beginning "*ex nonis Maiis*," by which the Servius Auctus commentator must mean the day after the Nones of May (May 8), rather than the Nones itself (May 7), and ending on the day before the Ides (May 14).

[67] Pliny *H.N.* 18.61, 97.

[68] Pliny *H.N.* 18.8.

The Vestals may have carried out their roasting, pounding, and baking in the House of the Vestals, where space was set aside for ritual activities that were not suited to the confined space inside the temple.[69] They stored the final product in the "outer storeroom" (*penus exterior*).[70] This second *penus*, which was associated with the preservation of specially prepared ritual substances, paralleled the household storeroom, just as the hearth in the temple corresponded to the private hearth in each Roman home. Just as the private *Penates* protected the household *penus*, moreover, the *Penates publici* protected the public *penus* in the precinct of Vesta.[71] While the matron of the house and her daughters prepared and stored the bread that sustained the family and the grain necessary to worship the household gods, the Vestals roasted the *far* that was used in the community's religious rites.[72] The *penus exterior* presumably held other ritual substances as well, including perhaps the ashes of the calves sacrificed at the Fordicidia and the blood of the October Horse, which the Vestals combined with bean stalks to produce the *suffimen* (cleansing agent) distributed at the Parilia in late April.[73] This ritual work was of great importance to civic life in ancient Rome.

Every public sacrifice in the city of Rome required *mola salsa*, and thus every public sacrifice originated in the sanctuary of Vesta where this substance was prepared and stored.[74] After offering a preliminary libation, the official in charge would have sprinkled the victim with *mola salsa*, poured a little wine on its brow, and run the knife along its back.[75] This series of gestures simultaneously purified the victim and transferred it to the possession of the deity concerned.[76] The centralization of this process suggests that Roman ritual practices were more systematic than they might appear at first glance. Although the gender, age, and species of each victim varied depending upon the specific ritual context, every animal was purified and dedicated in the same manner and with the same ritual substance. *Mola salsa*, and by extension the Vestals who had manufactured it, unified an otherwise disparate and seemingly chaotic collection of religious rites. As Ariadne Staples has written, because the Vestals belonged to and represented

---

[69] Though it is tempting to associate the preparation of *mola salsa* with the oven and mill discovered in two of the rooms in the southeastern corner of the complex, these were likely used to prepare the food eaten by the Vestals and their slaves (Coarelli 1994: 100).

[70] Although Festus implies that the *penus exterior* was located in the temple proper, Scott (2009: 31, n. 34) argues (persuasively, I think) that it must have been located elsewhere within the sanctuary.

[71] For the relationship between the *Penates publici* and Vesta, see especially Cic. *Cat.* 4.18; Cic. *Dom.* 144; Cic. *Har. resp.* 12; Cic. *Nat. D.* 2.67; Ov. *Met.* 15.864; Tac. *Ann.* 15.41.1; Serv. Auct. ad *Aen.* 2.296; Dubourdieu 1989: 453–520.

[72] Pliny *H.N.* 18.107.

[73] Dubourdieu 1989: 455–456.

[74] Festus 97L, with Scheid 1990: 335–336. It is not known whether the flame for each public sacrifice was ignited at the hearth of Vesta, though this would strengthen the symbolism.

[75] It is important to distinguish *mola salsa*, a loose mixture of salt and *far*, from sacrificial cakes (e.g., *libum*, *strues*, or *fertum*), which could be offered on their own or as a preliminary offering before an animal sacrifice.

[76] Cic. *Div.* 2.37; Tib. 1.5.14; Plin. *H.N.* 31.89; Festus 97, 124L; Serv. ad *Aen.* 2.133; Serv. Auct. ad *Aen.* 4.57.

the Roman community, *mola salsa* served "to make every sacrifice, however, exclusive in other respects, nevertheless representative of the collectivity."[77]

As others have noted, however, the timing of the initial ritual is perplexing. The Servius Auctus commentator claims that the Vestals harvested *far* beginning on the day after the Nones of May. According to Varro, however, the normal harvest season for *far* fell between the summer solstice and the rise of the Canicula (Dog Star), that is, from June 24 to July 26.[78] If the Vestals harvested in early May, the grain that they gathered was premature by over a month, maybe even two. Modern attempts to explain this chronological discrepancy by hypothesizing a symbolic association between unripe grain and the *lemures*, the wandering spirits of the prematurely deceased who were appeased at the Lemuria, a purification rite celebrated on the intervening days, are less than convincing.[79] The *far* gathered by the Vestals was turned into *mola salsa*, not offered to the *lemures* at the Lemuria. It seems more plausible to assume with Mario Torelli that the Vestals harvested the grain early in the expectation of a plentiful harvest in the weeks to come.[80] Their *mola salsa* constituted a true sacrifice of first fruits at every animal sacrifice performed during the following year.

The chronological problem may, on the other hand, have a calendrical rather than a ritual explanation. It is a puzzling feature of the Roman festival calendar that even after the Julian reforms in 45 BC, certain agricultural rites remained stranded at the wrong time of the year.[81] The Opiconsivia, for instance, which was evidently a harvest festival, fell at the end of August, a month or more after the end of the true harvest season. Under the pre-Julian calendar, the disjunction between civil and natural time was often far more pronounced.[82] The Romans did have a way to circumvent the inadequacies of their calendar. The Sementivae (Seed-Sowing Festival), for example, was one of the *feriae conceptivae*, movable feasts that did not have a fixed day on the calendar but were celebrated on dates set annually by the *rex sacrorum*.[83] Most rituals, including the harvest of *far* in early May, remained tied to specific dates on the civil calendar.

The lack of harmony between natural and civil time raises important questions about the way in which agricultural festivals, including the ritual harvest performed by the Vestals in early May, were experienced during the late republican period in particular. The large number of agricultural rites in the festival

[77] Staples 1998: 154.
[78] Varro *Rust.* 1.32. Pliny places the harvest in July (*H.N.* 18.295–298), while Columella says that in temperate places and along the coast, the harvest took place between July 15 and August 1 (*Rust.* 11.2.53–54). Studies of modern Italian agriculture indicate that the wheat harvest in the vicinity of Rome generally takes place around June 13, which could indicate that these authors are writing for a Northern Italian audience (Broughton 1936: 355).
[79] See, for example, Nagy 1985.
[80] Torelli 1997: 166–168.
[81] For the Roman calendar, see Michels 1967; Rüpke 1995; Feeney 2007. Roman authors were keenly aware of the difference between "the division made by nature" (*naturale discrimen*), as Varro calls it, and "the names of the days as given by the city" (*civilia vocabula dierum*, *Ling.* 6.12).
[82] Feeney 2007: 193–194.
[83] Varro *Ling.* 6.13, 28; Ov. *Fast.* 1.657–662; Macrob. *Sat.* 1.15.12.

calendar indicates that early Roman religion addressed the activities and anxieties of the peasant farmer. As the city became more urbanized, however, many of these festivals acquired new emphases. Mary Beard has argued that the festival calendar offered city-dwelling Romans of the late Republic one important way of "imaging Rome" by presenting "a picture of Romanness—linking the past with the present, and bringing together apparently diverse aspects of the Roman religious and cultural tradition. In a sense, the ritual calendar as a whole can be seen as a conceptual pageant of Rome and of what it was to be Roman."[84] Festivals like the Parilia, for example, which coincided with the traditional date for the foundation of Rome, were interpreted and experienced in light of the historical circumstances of their origin, rather than their primitive agricultural "meaning." In this way, Beard argues, the festivals remained relevant to the sophisticated urban culture of the late Republic.

The experience of producing *mola salsa* and the meaning of the ritual itself must have changed over time as well. When the Vestals harvested immature *far* in the weeks before the natural harvest time, their ritual work was largely symbolic. Both the harvest and the second phase in the process, during which the three eldest Vestals toasted, pounded and ground the *far*, helped to "image" Rome and a particular aspect of Romanness. *Far* is one of the oldest types of grain cultivated in Italy.[85] Although the Romans grew a wide variety of grains in order to avoid the perils of dependence on a single crop, *far* held a central position in Roman conceptions of their agricultural and alimentary history.[86] Roman authors frequently assert that *far* provided the basis of their ancestors' diet. It was also essential to a wide variety of religious rites. The Vestals' harvest of *far* and their production of *mola salsa* created a sense of continuity with the past and symbolized the antiquity of the city and its rituals.

Annual Public Festivals

The written sources tell us that the Vestals participated in annual public rites falling in nearly every month of the festival calendar. In fact, we hear more about their ritual responsibilities than about those of nearly any other priest at Rome, a circumstance that reflects ancient interest in their activities.[87] Even so, many of their obligations remain uncertain thanks to the uneven nature of the ancient sources. Ovid's *Fasti*, our most comprehensive written source for the festival calendar, covers only the months from January to June, which means that details about rites falling in the second half of the year must be pieced

---

[84] Beard 1987: 281.

[85] According to Pliny (*H.N.* 18.83), *far* was the first grain cultivated by the ancient Latins, who used it to make *puls* (porridge), not bread. See also Dion. Hal. *Ant. Rom.* 2.25.2; Pliny *H.N.* 18.62.

[86] Purcell 2003: 332.

[87] As noted by Beard, North, and Price 1998: 51.

together from less complete sources. It is clear, in any case, that the Vestals were occupied throughout the year with a complex and varied ritual program. In what follows, I treat the Vestals' obligations in chronological order, beginning in March with the rites surrounding the New Year. I organize the material in this way primarily to emphasize the Vestals' consistent public presence throughout the year, but also to avoid the reductionism of a scheme in which the rituals are classified according to type or "meaning," as many fulfilled more than one function.

The First of March

In early Rome, the new year began on March 1. Although the civil calendar eventually adopted January 1 as New Year's Day, religious rites associated with the beginning of the year remained fixed in their original place.[88] Indeed, Ovid suggests that the first of March, when spring was just beginning, was the "natural" day to begin the new year.[89] This was also the day of the Matronalia, when married women worshipped Juno Lucina, a goddess of childbirth, and husbands and wives prayed for one another. The first of March marked a fresh beginning for both human and agricultural fertility. In a ritual symbolic of this period of renewal, the laurel garlands that had adorned the houses of the *flamines* and the *rex* and *regina sacrorum*, the curial buildings, and the *aedes Vestae* throughout the previous year were replaced with fresh branches.[90] The Vestals also extinguished the fire on the hearth in the Temple of Vesta and kindled it anew.[91] This was the only time when it was permissible for the flame to be extinguished. Paul the Deacon describes the method used by the Vestals to obtain a new flame when the fire burned out through neglect, and it seems reasonable to suppose that they employed the same technique on New Year's Day:

> quibus mos erat tabulam felicis materiae tamdiu terebrare, quousque exceptum ignem cribro aeneo virgo in aedem ferret. (94L)

> It was the custom for them to drill a board of favorable wood until a virgin might carry the flame thus obtained into the temple with a bronze sieve.

Creating fire by friction requires great skill and considerable physical pressure, but there is no reason to doubt that the Vestals performed this task themselves.[92] The basic technique described by Paul involves spinning a drill against the bottom of a hole in a hearth board. The resulting friction produces heat and fine

---

[88] The consuls first took office on January 1 in 153 BC (Livy *Per.* 47).
[89] Ov. *Fast.* 1.149–151, with Feeney 2007: 204–205.
[90] Macrob. *Sat.* 1.12.6.
[91] Ov. *Fast.* 3.143–144; Macrob. *Sat.* 1.12.6; Festus (Paulus) 94L.
[92] For a practical explanation of the hand drill method of making fire, see Kidder 2001.

sawdust, known as char, which must reach eight hundred degrees Fahrenheit before it begins to smolder. Once the Vestal had created a flame, she carried it into the *aedes* in a bronze sieve (*cribrum*).

The renewal of the flame was highly symbolic. Robert Parker has written that the rekindling of the communal flame on the public hearth of a Greek city "was the most potent renewal a Greek community could undergo, since, lodged in the individual hearths of houses and the collective hearth of the city, fire was the symbolic middle point around which the life of the group revolved."[93] In Rome, where the flame of Vesta symbolized the inviolability of the city and its empire, the rekindling of the flame must have been particularly charged. The fresh laurel branches on the temple and the revitalized flame on the hearth ensured that the city would continue to flourish and gain strength in the new year.

The Fordicidia

The next public rites in which the Vestals participated were those of the Fordicidia on April 15. Thanks to Ovid's description in the *Fasti*, we may identify the role of the Vestals in this festival with some precision. The primary ritual was the parallel sacrifice of a pregnant cow to Tellus on the Capitol and in each of the thirty *curiae* of Rome.[94] When the individual sacrifices were complete, the *virgo maxima*, the eldest Vestal, burned the remains of the calves in the fire of Vesta. It is very unlikely that the burning of the calves was regarded as a sacrificial act.[95] Since the calf must have been dead when the *virgo maxima* received it, she did not slaughter it in the manner of a sacrificial victim. Moreover, the entire calf was burned on the altar, not just certain parts of the animal in accordance with traditional sacrificial practice. The *virgo maxima*'s role at the Fordicidia belonged to a secondary phase of the ritual. The ashes of the calves, together with beanstalks and blood from the tail of the October Horse, constituted the purificatory materials that she and the other Vestals distributed at the Parilia a few days later.[96] Given the symbolic significance of the hearth of Vesta and of the Vestals themselves, it is hardly surprising to find that the sacrifices of the individual *curiae* were brought together at the public hearth.

The Parilia

The rites of the Parilia occurred just under a week later on April 21. The Parilia coincided with the traditional day of Rome's foundation, and much of the ancient evidence associates the festival with the furrow ploughed by Romulus

---

[93] Parker 1996: 23.
[94] Ov. *Fast.* 4.629–640. For the *curiae*, ancient divisions of the people, see chapter 2.
[95] Wildfang 2001: 234, 2006: 24.
[96] Ov. *Fast.* 4.721–734.

to mark the *pomerium*, the sacred boundary of the city.[97] Many of the rituals, however, were evidently designed to purify and protect the flocks, and it is with these rites that the Vestals are associated.[98] Once again, the fullest description of the festival is found in Ovid's *Fasti*, where the poet even claims to have participated in the rituals.[99] Shepherds cleaned their sheepfolds and decorated them with garlands and fumigated their sheep with sulphur and fragrant plants. In the evening, the shepherd, and perhaps the sheep as well, had to pass through bonfires in what was evidently a boisterous and festive ceremony.[100]

According to Propertius, the festival had a rural and an urban component.[101] Some scholars speculate that the *suffimen* mentioned by Ovid was related to the urban festival, presumably because it originated at the hearth of Vesta:[102]

> i, pete virginea, populus, suffimen ab ara;
>   Vesta dabit, Vestae munere purus eris.
> sanguis equi suffimen erit vitulique favilla,
>   tertia res durae culmen inane fabae. (*Fast.* 4.731–734)

> Go, people, seek means of fumigation (*suffimen*) from the virgin's altar. Vesta will give them, with the gift of Vesta you will be purified. Those means of fumigation (*suffimen*) will be the blood of a horse and the ashes of a calf, the third thing will be the empty stalk of a hard bean.

Although Ovid does not mention the Vestals, the reference to Vesta and her altar imply that they were involved in the distribution of the *suffimen*. As we have seen, the Vestals had procured one element of this substance, the ashes of a calf (*vitulique favilla*), at the Fordicidia a few days earlier. They had preserved the second ingredient, the blood of a horse (*sanguis equi*), for even longer, having collected it at the previous year's October Horse.[103] The stalks of hard beans (*durae fabae*) may have been gathered in a ritual context as well, though we cannot be certain. The written sources do not explain why the Vestals preserved the blood of the October Horse and combined it with the remnants of another sacrifice for use in a third ritual. Even so, it is clear that the shared materials created a link between the three festivals and provided a sense of continuity across the seasons.[104] As the guardians of the public *penus*, where these materials were preserved and prepared for distribution to the Roman people, the Vestals played a vital role in guaranteeing the community's agricultural success.

---

[97] For the Parilia as Rome's birthday, see Prop. 4.4.73–80; Cic. *Div.* 2.98; Dion. Hal. *Ant. Rom.* 1.88.3; Vell. Pat. 1.8.4; Plut. *Rom.* 12.1; Beard 1987.

[98] Ovid (*Fast.* 783–848) offers several different explanations for the festival's origins and significance.

[99] Ov. *Fast.* 4.721–783. See also Prop. 4.4.73–80; Tib. 2.5.89; Cic. *Div.* 2.98; Varro *Ling.* 6.15; Dion. Hal. *Ant. Rom.* 1.88.3; Vell. Pat. 1.8.4; Plut. *Rom.* 12.1; Ath. 8.361; Festus (Paulus) 248L.

[100] Propertius refers to the drunken crowd (*ebria turba*, 4.4.78) leaping through the fires.

[101] Prop. 4.4.73–78.

[102] Beard, North, and Price 1998: 175.

[103] See below.

[104] Rüpke 2007b: 115.

The Argei

The Vestals also participated in the mysterious Argei festival.[105] Each year on the Ides of May they threw Argei, human shaped dolls made from rush straw, into the Tiber from the *pons Sublicius*, Rome's oldest bridge.[106] Dionysius of Halicarnassus provides one of the most detailed descriptions of this ritual, though his account raises almost as many questions as it answers:

> προθύσαντες ἱερὰ τὰ κατὰ τοὺς νόμους οἱ καλούμενοι ποντίφικες, ἱερέων οἱ διαφανέστατοι, καὶ σὺν αὐτοῖς αἱ τὸ ἀθάνατον πῦρ διαφυλάττουσαι παρθένοι στρατηγοί τε καὶ τῶν ἄλλων πολιτῶν οὓς παρεῖναι ταῖς ἱερουργίαις θέμις εἴδωλα μορφαῖς ἀνθρώπων εἰκασμένα, τριάκοντα τὸν ἀριθμὸν ἀπὸ τῆς ἱερᾶς γεφύρας βάλλουσιν εἰς τὸ ῥεῦμα τοῦ Τεβέριος, Ἀργείους αὐτὰ καλοῦντες. (*Ant. Rom.* 1.38.3)

> After offering the preliminary sacrifices mandated by custom, those called *pontifices*, the most conspicuous of the priests, and with them the virgins who guard the eternal flame, the praetors, and the other citizens permitted to be present at the rites, throw effigies made into the shape of men, thirty in number, from the sacred bridge into the current of the Tiber, calling them Argei.

According to Dionysius, the only author to depict the ritual as a collaborative effort, the *pontifices* offered a preliminary sacrifice before casting the Argei into the river with the assistance of the Vestals, the praetors, and a select group of Roman citizens. Plutarch implies that the *flaminica Dialis* was present as well, wearing a sad countenance (νενόμισται σκυθρωπάζειν, *Quaest. Rom.* 86 = *Mor.* 285a). Ovid and Paul's epitome of Festus, on the other hand, mention only the Vestals.[107] Dionysius' testimony may be accurate, though the significance of the grouping he describes is unclear.

Although Dionysius claims that there were thirty Argei, perhaps associating the festival with the thirty *curiae*, Varro tells us that there were twenty-seven effigies as well as twenty-seven *sacraria* (shrines) to which a procession was made on March 16 and 17.[108] Scholars have long speculated that the Romans deposited the Argei in the *sacraria* at this time. Ovid's wording, however, appears to contradict this assumption: *itur ad Argeos (qui sint, sua pagina dicet) / hac, si commemini, praeteritaque die* (The procession to the Argei (who they are, their own page will say) takes place on this day, if I remember, and the one

---

[105] Ov. *Fast.* 5.621–622; Plut. *Quaest. Rom.* 86 = *Mor.* 285a; Festus (Paulus) 14L.

[106] For the date of the festival, see Dion. Hal. *Ant. Rom.* 1.38.3, with Graf 2000: 94–95. For a discussion of the festival, see Holland 1961: 314–334; Harmon 1978; Nagy 1985; Porte 1986; Radke 1990; Ziolkowski 1998–1999; Graf 2000.

[107] Ov. *Fast.* 5.621–622; Festus (Paulus) 14L. Varro merely says that they were thrown "by the priests" (*a sacerdotibus, Ling.* 7.44).

[108] Varro *Ling.* 5.45–54; 7.44.

before, Ov. *Fast.* 3.791–2).[109] The rush dolls (*qui*) were already in their *sacraria* in March and may have received offerings at this time. This, at least, is what Livy implies.[110] Whether or not the Vestals participated in the *itur ad Argeos* is an open question, though their central role in the ceremony at the bridge suggests that they did.

The meaning of the Argei festival has been the subject of debate since antiquity. The ancient sources agree that the rush dolls replaced real humans, but are divided on the question of whether they represented the victims of a human sacrifice abolished by Hercules, or the bodies of the hero's Argive companions who hoped to be carried home by the waters of the Tiber.[111] Although some modern scholars have been willing to interpret the rite as a modified human sacrifice, these etiologies tell us more about ancient perceptions of the rite than they do about its historical origins.[112]

Most modern scholars agree with Plutarch, who describes the Argei as "the most important rite of purification" in the festival calendar (τὸν μέγιστον ποιοῦνται τῶν καθαρμῶν, *Quaest. Rom.* 86). In fact, the ceremony at the bridge may have been related to the Lemuria, a domestic festival celebrated by individual families on May 9, 11, and 13.[113] The Lemuria was designed to expel the *lemures*, the visiting spirits of prematurely dead ancestors. Perhaps the Argei represented and made visible the absent dead bodies of the *lemures* and any other spirits lurking throughout the city.[114] As Adam Ziolkowski has written, "The *sacraria* or, more precisely, the puppets deposited in them, would have acted as district vacuum-cleaners swallowing up ritual filth which eventually, like ordinary waste, ended up in the Tiber."[115]

The act of throwing objects into the Tiber was often related to cleansing and purification.[116] On the fifteenth of June, for instance, the *purgamina Vestae* (scourings of Vesta) were thrown into the Tiber, perhaps from the *pons Sublicius*.[117] A man who had killed his father was also cast into the river.[118] Such a monstrous being could not be buried within Roman territory because he might continue to pollute the community. Instead, he was thrown into the swiftly flowing Tiber. At the Argei, the Vestals sent the rush dolls off to sea by way of

---

[109] Radke 1990; Graf 2000: 99.

[110] Livy 1.21.

[111] For the idea that the effigies represented victims of human sacrifice, see Ov. *Fast.* 5.631; Dion. Hal. *Ant. Rom.* 1.38.2; Plut. *Quaest. Rom.* 32 = *Mor.* 272b–c; Festus 450–452L. For the idea that they represented the companions of Hercules, see Ov. *Fast.* 5.639–660; Macrob. *Sat.* 1.11.47

[112] See, for example, Fowler 1902: 115–119; Frazer 1929: 4, 74–79; Hallett 1970: 219–227.

[113] For the Lemuria, see Ov. *Fast.* 5.431–444.

[114] Frazer (1929: 4, 89–90) first proposed this explanation, though he later abandoned it in favor of one that saw the ritual as a human sacrifice. Recently, Ziolkowski (1998–1999) and Graf (2000) have revived the idea.

[115] Ziolkowski 1998–1999: 217.

[116] Graf 2000: 100.

[117] Varro *Ling.* 6.32; Ov. *Fast.* 6.227–228; Festus 310L. See further below.

[118] Cic. *Ros. Am.* 70–72.

the Tiber in order to purify Rome of any ritual impurities or malevolent spirits that might threaten the city.

The Vestalia

The Vestalia, Vesta's primary festival, was celebrated on June 9. The feast day and those surrounding it were characterized by three main activities involving the Vestals, professional bakers, and Roman *matronae* respectively. The ritual program, which appears rather incoherent at first glance, was united by the preparation of grain for ritual use and human consumption. On the day of the Vestalia, the three eldest Vestals prepared *mola salsa*.[119] Before considering why the Vestals performed this important ritual work on this day, however, I would like to examine the other components of the festival.

According to Ovid, the Vestalia was a day when bakers offered Vesta gifts of grain and honored her vital role in bread baking:

> fert missos Vestae pura patella cibos.
> ecce coronatis panis dependet asellis,
>   et velant scabras florida serta molas.
> sola prius furnis torrebant farra coloni
>   (et Fornacali sunt sua sacra deae):
> subpositum cineri panem focus ipse parabat,
>   strataque erat tepido tegula quassa solo.
> inde focum servat pistor dominamque focorum
>   et quae pumiceas versat asella molas. (*Fast.* 6.310–318)

A clean plate carries the food offered to Vesta. Look, loaves of bread hang from garlanded donkeys, and garlands of flowers wreath the rough millstones. Formerly farmers roasted only spelt (*far*) in their ovens (the goddess of ovens has her own rites); the hearth itself prepared the bread set under its ashes, and a broken tile was placed on the warm floor. And so the baker honors the hearth and the mistress of hearths, and the donkey that turns the millstones made of pumice.

Ovid's etiology reflects a common perception about Rome's alimentary history.[120] Romans in the late Republic believed that their ancestors had baked bread in a *testum,* a dome-shaped cover that could be placed directly on the hearth.[121] Although commercial bakers at Rome had long employed large bread ovens and worshipped the oven goddess Fornax at the Fornacalia in February, they

---

[119] Serv. Auct. ad *Ecl.* 8.82. See further above.

[120] As Gowers (1992) and Purcell (2003) have shown, food was an important tool of analysis employed by poets and moralists alike and was central to the story of moral progress and decline that appears in a variety of contexts.

[121] Seneca (*Epist. Mor.* 90.23) describes the same method and Cato (*Agr.* 74) even provides a recipe. For a discussion of Roman baking practices, see Frayn 1978; Cubberly 1995.

also celebrated the Vestalia in honor of this more ancient method of baking on the hearth itself.[122]

It is unclear what role, if any, the Vestals had in this portion of the Vestalia. Although some bakers may have brought their offerings to the *aedes Vestae*, where they were presumably received by the Vestals, most undoubtedly celebrated the festival at the hearth in their own bakeries. Material evidence confirms that some commercial bakeries placed special emphasis on the worship of Vesta. The *lararia* in several Pompeian bakeries depict Vesta alongside a donkey, including one in which she has displaced the *genius* as the central figure in the scene.[123] A marble altar dated to the early first century AD depicts Vesta accompanied by a donkey as well, clearly emphasizing her role as the patroness of bakers.[124] Although the provenance of the altar is not known, it was very likely commissioned for a private or semiprivate context, perhaps a bakery or the home of a baker. The so-called Baker's Relief of Vesta, dedicated in AD 144 by C. Pupius Firminus, quaestor of the *collegium pistorum* of Rome, depicts a similar scene, suggesting that bakers also worshipped Vesta communally.[125]

The third component of the Vestalia involved Rome's *matronae*. On the days surrounding the Vestalia (June 7 to June 14), the *penus Vestae* was open to married women, who visited the temple barefoot, if Ovid is to be believed (*huc pede matronam vidi descendere nudo*, *Fast.* 6.398).[126] These days were classified as *religiosi*, which made them unsuitable for weddings, military campaigns, and assemblies.[127] It is unclear what the women did when they entered the *penus*. Although Festus specifies that they visited the *penus* in the temple (*locus intimus in aede*, 296L), the *penus exterior*, which was more closely analogous to the domestic *penus*, seems a more logical object of their pilgrimage. Indeed, Carl Koch suggested that they received a small portion of mola salsa for use in the cult of Vesta at their own domestic hearths.[128] *Matronae* were responsible for baking bread and for keeping their own storerooms stocked with food and supplies for domestic sacrifices. In fact, unlike commercial bakers, a *matrona* wishing to make her own bread at home likely employed a *testum* to bake it on the hearth.[129] It seems reasonable to assume that they brought offerings as well.

Francesca Caprioli has proposed that the Vestalia is depicted on a fragmentary marble relief discovered in the house of Domitia Lucilla, the mother of

---

[122] For the Fornacalia, see Varro *Ling.* 6.13; Ov. *Fast.* 2.519–32, 6.313–314; Pliny *H.N.* 18.8; Plut. *Quaest. Rom.* 89 = *Mor.* 285d; Festus 73, 82, 298L.

[123] See, for example, Boyce 1937: Cat. Nos. 240, 313, 316 and 318.

[124] See Thompson 2005: 105–108, 188–189. For the association between Vesta and bakers, see also Prop. 4.1.21.

[125] See Thompson 2005: 146–154, 193.

[126] Festus 296L. The calendar of Philocalus records "VESTA APERIT" on June 7 and "VESTA CLUDITUR" on June 15 (Degrassi 1963: 249).

[127] Festus 296L.

[128] Koch 1958.

[129] Frayn 1978.

Marcus Aurelius.[130] On the first fragment, four partially preserved women bearing offerings process toward a small round building readily identified as the Temple of Vesta. While the door of the temple is clearly open in this first scene, it appears closed in the second fragment, which preserves only the podium and the lower portion of the temple. According to Caprioli's interpretation, the first fragment portrays a procession of matrons bringing offerings to the *penus Vestae* during the days surrounding the Vestalia (June 7 to 14). The second scene, on the other hand, represents the temple when it had been closed again at the conclusion of the festival on June 15. Despite its late date and private context, the relief may confirm that Rome's *matronae* did bring gifts to Vesta during the Vestalia.

The Vestalia complemented the Matralia on June 11, when *univirae* brought a cake baked in an earthen vessel (*testuacium*, Varro *Ling.* 5.106) to the temple of Mater Matuta in the Forum Boarium.[131] The women also led a slave girl into the temple (normally slaves were excluded) before driving her out, and then prayed for the children of their sisters.[132] A votive deposit from the seventh century BC contains models of sacrificial cakes and the remnants of an animal sacrifice, presumably offered by a priestess.[133] Mater Matuta is not well understood, but votive evidence suggests that she was a *kourotrophos* (child-nourishing) goddess and a protector of nursing mothers.[134] The Vestalia and the Matralia thus emphasized a *matrona*'s obligation to nourish her family by nursing her offspring and by preparing food for her husband and children as they continued to grow. The nurture of the family was an issue of immediate consequence not only to the security of the individual *domus* (elite household), but to the welfare of the civic community as well. Public cults such as Vesta and Mater Matuta consequently provided opportunities for *matronae* to address personal and civic success, maternal feeling, and the continuity of the state.

The Vestalia was also an ideal day on which to prepare *mola salsa*. The festival celebrated the hearth fire and its role in the transformation of raw grain into bread, a product fit for human consumption.[135] The ritual work performed by the Vestals on this day symbolized the production of bread.[136] It also produced a vital element of the Roman sacrificial economy. The Vestalia celebrated Vesta as the living flame and the facilitator of both these processes. Without the

[130] Caprioli 2007: 54–55, plate 14, 1–2.
[131] As suggested by Torelli 1997. For the Matralia, see also Ov. *Fast.* 6.473–562; Plut. *Cam.* 5.2, *Quaest. Rom.* 16 = *Mor.* 267d, 17 = *Mor.* 267e; Boëls-Janssen 1993: 341–371; Herbert-Brown 1994: 145–156 (on Ovid's account in the *Fasti*); Smith 2000; Takács 2008: 49–51.
[132] Ovid (*Fast.* 6.473–648) offers an etiology for the role of aunts when he equates Mater Matuta with Ino, the aunt of Dionysus, who nursed him after his mother's death, and tells us that the offerings commemorate the toasted cakes that she made when she arrived at the house of Carmenta.
[133] Smith 2000: 138–139.
[134] Boëls-Janssen 1993: 341–353. For the votive evidence, see Smith 2000, with bibliography.
[135] Wildfang 2006: 29.
[136] Torelli 1997.

hearth fire, civilized life as the Romans knew it could not have existed.[137] Vesta and her Vestals preserved the Roman community by guaranteeing the food supply and by facilitating the crucial act of sacrifice.

Q(uando) St(ercum) D(elatum) F(as)

The period of ritual activity surrounding the Vestalia culminated in a purification of the temple on June 15, a day marked on the calendars as Q.ST.D.F.[138] Varro helpfully expands this abbreviation and provides some context:

> dies qui vocatur "quando stercum delatum fas," ab eo appellatus, quod eo die ex aede Vestae stercus everritur et per Capitolinum clivum in locum defertur certum. (*Ling.* 6.32)

> The day that is called "when the *stercus* has been removed, it is permitted" was named for this reason, because on that day *stercus* is swept out from the Temple of Vesta and carried away along the *clivus Capitolinus* (the road leading up to the Capitoline Hill) to a certain place.

According to Varro, the abbreviation indicates that public business was permitted (*fas*) after the *stercus* from Vesta's temple had been removed. Festus agrees that on this day *stercus* was carried from the *aedes* "to an alley about halfway up the *clivus Capitolinus*, a place which is closed by the Porta Stercoraria" (*in angiportum medium fere clivi Capitolini, qui locus clauditur porta stercoraria*, 466L).[139]

In both literary and epigraphic contexts, *stercus* typically refers to human or animal waste.[140] It is unlikely, however, that there was ever any accumulation of solid waste in the *aedes Vestae*.[141] In this ritual context, the term likely describes refuse or trash of a less offensive variety. Ovid tells us that June 15 is the day "on which you, Tiber, send Vesta's sweepings (*purgamina*) through your Etrus-

---

[137] In fact, in his next vignette, Ovid emphasizes Vesta's role in preserving the city during the Gallic siege (*Fast.* 6.349–394). As Littlewood (2006: 121) writes, "because she is the goddess of the hearth, the place where primitive people traditionally baked their bread, Vesta is asked to be responsible for the miracle of creating the false impression that the Romans have plenty of food."

[138] The abbreviation Q.ST.D.F. appears in the *Fasti Antiates Maiores*, the only extant pre-Julian calendar, in the Augustan *Fasti Maffeiani*, and the *Fasti Venusini* from AD 34. In the *Fasti Tusculani*, the day is marked as Q.S.D.F. For a discussion of the evidence and the meaning of the abbreviation, see Keegan 2008.

[139] For the Clivus Capitolinus, the primary road leading up to the Capitoline Hill, see Wiseman 1993. For the Porta Stercoria, known only from Festus 466L, see Coarelli 1999a.

[140] Adams 1990: 234–237; Keegan 2008: 93–94. Keegan (2008: 95–96) cites two possible exceptions to this meaning (Cat. *Agr.* 33.4 and 37.2), "where Cato places *stercus* at the head of a list of plant varieties." Since both passages describe the production of compost, however, it is possible that *stercus* describes animal waste, rather than a type of plant, in this context as well. Cato advises farmers to make compost by mixing *stercus* with various organic materials, a process that is still used today to turn manure into fertilizer.

[141] Dumézil (1970: 317–318), therefore, interpreted the rite as a "fossilized" Indo-European ritual, "dating from a time before the existence of the city, when an encamped pastoral society had to cleanse the location of its sacred fire of the *stercus* of its herds."

can waters to the sea" (*haec est illa dies, qua tu purgamina Vestae, / Thybri per Etruscas in mare mittis aquas, Fast.* 6.713–714).[142] Perhaps anxious to avoid any confusion regarding the nature of the ritual, Ovid replaced *stercus* with *purgamina*, which may be translated literally as "that which is removed by cleansing."[143] The question of what kind of refuse was swept out from the temple, however, remains unanswered. Louise Holland suggested that the Vestals removed the offerings brought by the *matronae* in honor of the Vestalia.[144] Since gifts dedicated to the gods could not be summarily discarded, however, it seems more likely that the priestesses removed any dust and debris that had accumulated in the *aedes* during the visitation days. June 15 signaled an end to a period of unusual activity within the sanctuary and provided an opportunity for the Vestals to purify the *aedes* and the objects within it. The process made civic business *fas* again after the *dies religiosi* surrounding the Vestalia, which tends to underscore the significance of the festival and its importance to the civic life of the city.

The Consualia

The Vestals may have appeared at the Consualia of the god Consus on August 21. According to Tertullian, on the day of the festival, *virgines* (virgins) and the *flamen Quirinalis* offered a sacrifice at the subterranean altar of Consus, which was located at the first turning post in the Circus Maximus.[145] Dionysius of Halicarnassus mentions sacrifices as well, though without naming the officiants.[146] Modern scholars have long assumed that Tertullian's *virgines* were the Vestal Virgins, in which case the notice tends to support the notion that they sacrificed on behalf of the Roman people. As I argue in chapter 2, however, it is not absolutely certain that Tertullian is referring to the Vestals, rather than to citizen virgins who had an official role at the festival.[147] The traditional interpretation of the Consualia as a ritual for the protection of the newly stored harvest should probably be discarded as well, given that the subterranean altar was located beside a stream in the flood plain of the Tiber.[148] Whatever "original" meaning the Consualia had in the archaic period, the festival was understood primarily as a

---

[142] See also Ov. *Fast.* 6.227–228. In an effort to reconcile Ovid's account of the Vestalia with the one provided by Varro and Festus, Wissowa (1912: 160) suggested that some of the *stercus* was deposited along the *clivus Capitolinus* and the remainder dumped into the Tiber.

[143] *TLL* s.v. *purgamen* 1 (10.2.2674). Ovid also employs *purgamina* in book two of the *Fasti* when he derives February's name from *februa* (means of purification). In this context, the term *purgamina* must be translated instead as "that by which purification is completed" (*TLL* s.v. *purgamen* 2 (10.2.2675); Keegan 2008: 94–95).

[144] Holland 1961: 321.

[145] Tert. *Spect.* 5.7, quoted and discussed more fully in chapter 2.

[146] Dion. Hal. *Ant. Rom.* 2.31.2.

[147] See chapter 2.

[148] Green 2009, with chapter 2.

commemoration of the rape of the Sabine women during the late Republic and early principate.

The Opiconsivia

The Opiconsivia on August 25 was dedicated to Ops Consiva, the goddess of plentiful harvests.[149] Festus reports that the Romans equated Ops with the earth (*terra*) and worshipped her because she supplied the human race with all its resources (*omnes opes*, 202L). According to Varro, she was a Sabine deity whose cult had been introduced to Rome by Titus Tatius.[150] Other authors claim that she was the consort of Saturn and the mother of Jupiter, Juno, Ceres, Pluto, Neptune, and Vesta.[151] Access to her shrine (*sacrarium*) in the *regia* was evidently restricted to the Vestals and a public priest (*sacerdos publicus*), who attended her rites wearing the *suffibulum*, according to a provision recorded by Varro: "When he goes there, let him wear a *suffibulum*" (*is cum eat, suffibulum ut habeat, Ling.* 6.21). We should probably assume that Varro's *sacerdos publicus* is the *pontifex maximus*, who had his headquarters in the *regia*.[152] He also had a special relationship with the Vestals, and it is not surprising to find him performing rituals alongside these priestesses. It is rather unexpected, on the other hand, to learn that he wore a *suffibulum*, the same veil that the Vestals wore when they sacrificed.[153] Was he impersonating a Vestal or is there a problem with the text? Even if the passage is sound, and most assume that it is, the significance of the *pontifex*'s transvestism remains unclear.[154]

A fragmentary entry in the lexicon of Festus (supplemented by an abbreviated notice in Paul's epitome) implies that the festival of Ops Consiva included a sacrifice:

<praefericulum vas> aeneum sa<. . . . sine ansa patens summum, ve>lut pelvis, <quo ad sacrificia utebantur in sacra>rio Opis Co<nsivae. (292L)

A *praefericulum* is a broad bronze dish open on the top, without a handle, like a basin, which they used for sacrifices in the shrine of Ops Consiva.

Although the evidence is limited, the sacrifice may have been connected to the harvest and storage of the crops.[155] In fact, it has been proposed that the shrine of Ops Consiva was regarded as the *penus* (storeroom) of the *regia*, which was supposed to have been the palace of the legendary king Numa

---

[149] For a discussion of Ops, see Pouthier 1981. For the Opiconsivia, see Livy 39.22.4; Varro, *Ling.* 6.21; Festus 292L.
[150] Varro *Ling.* 5.74. See also Dion. Hal. *Ant. Rom.* 2.50.3.
[151] Ov. *Fast.* 6. 285–286.
[152] Wissowa 1912: 203.
[153] For the *suffibulum*, see Festus 474L, with chapter 5.
[154] Pouthier 1981: 60–61; Glinister 2011: 122–123.
[155] Pouthier 1981: 71–72; Wildfang 2001: 247–248, 2006: 30; Takács 2008: 56–57.

Pompilius.[156] As the custodians of the public *penus Vestae*, the Vestals were well suited to watch over a storeroom in the *regia* as well. Unfortunately, however, absolute certainty is impossible given the nature of our ancient evidence.

The October Horse

The Vestals also had a role in the rites of the October Horse. Each year on the Ides of October (October 15), a chariot race was held on the Campus Martius.[157] The right-hand horse of the victorious team was sacrificed, and the residents of the districts of the Subura and the Via Sacra fought for possession of the head. According to Timaeus (as quoted by Polybius) the horse was a war horse and was killed by a spear. These details have led some modern scholars to emphasize the militaristic aspect of the ritual and to connect it to the purification of the army at the Armilustrium on October 19.[158] Others argue that the October Horse was primarily an agricultural rite, pointing to the fact that the head of the sacrificed horse was decorated with cakes. Indeed, according to Paul the Deacon, "the sacrifice was made for the success of the crop" (*id sacrificium fiebat ob frugum eventum*, 246L).[159] These objects, of course, are not mutually exclusive, and it would be a mistake to place too much emphasis on either the military or the agricultural features of this rite.[160] The war horse and spear associate the ritual with Mars, who is in turn associated with agriculture in a prayer preserved by Cato the Elder, which invokes his assistance in warding off disease, destruction, and bad weather.[161] Military activity, moreover, helped to ensure a successful harvest by defending the crops against the enemy.

Paul's epitome of Festus claims that the tail of the October Horse was taken to the *regia*, where its blood was poured on the hearth.[162] We know from Ovid that the Vestals collected this blood and later combined it with beanstalks and the ashes of calves sacrificed at the Fordicidia to prepare the *suffimen* (cleansing agent) that they distributed to the people at the Parilia on April 21.[163] The protective function of the war horse presumably extended to the *suffimen* as well. Once again, the Vestals did not preside over the sacrifice proper, but rather received a part of the victim once it had already been killed. Their role in the festival was closely related to their oversight of the communal *penus*, where the blood was stored until the Parilia. The *penus Vestae* was clearly a focal point of Roman ritual practice, as were the priestesses who guarded it.

---

[156] As suggested by Scullard 1981: 181. For the identification of the *regia* with the palace of Numa, see Ov. *Fast.* 6.263; Tac. *Ann.* 15.41; Cass. Dio fr. 1.6.2; Plut. *Num.* 14; Festus 346–348, 439L.

[157] Plut. *Quaest. Rom.* 97 = *Mor.* 287a–b; Festus 190L.

[158] Pol. 12.4b.1. For the militaristic interpretation, see especially Wissowa 1912: 144–146; Dumézil 1970: 215–224. On the October Horse, see also Plut. *Quaest. Rom.* 97 = *Mor.* 287a–b; Festus (Paulus) 246L.

[159] For a summary of this view, see Fowler 1899: 243–250.

[160] As stressed by Scullard 1981: 193; Beard, North and Price 1998: 47–48.

[161] Cat. *Agr.* 141.

[162] Festus (Paulus) 246L.

[163] Ov. *Fast.* 4.721–734; Prop. 4.1.19, though see Dumézil 1970: 220–244. For the Parilia, see above.

The December Rites of Bona Dea

The Vestal Virgins also presided over the December rites of Bona Dea. The Good Goddess, "whose name men may not even know" (*cuius ne nomen quidem viros scire fas est*, Cic. *Har. resp.* 37), was a mysterious female deity from whose temple and ceremonies men were excluded categorically.[164] Her secret (*opertum*, Cic. *Parad.* 4.2.32) nocturnal rites were celebrated in early December at the home of a matron whose husband held *imperium*—that is, either a praetor or a consul.[165] The Roman tendency to assign important religious roles to senior magistrates evidently extended to their wives as well. Cicero's wife Terentia hosted the December rites during his consulship in 63 BC.[166] As we have seen, Caesar's second wife, Pompeia, presided over the most infamous celebration in the Bona Dea's history during his praetorship in 62 BC.[167] That the senate took the violation of that year's rites very seriously makes it difficult to sustain the argument that they should be regarded as marginal or insignificant.

On the day of the December festival, the hostess and her female slaves transformed the house in order to accommodate Bona Dea and her rites. All male members of the household were required to leave for the duration of the ceremony, and the *imagines* (ancestor masks) of male ancestors were covered.[168] According to Plutarch, the women then decorated the house with twigs and vines.[169] Myrtle, however, was banned; presumably because its power as an aphrodisiac was incongruous with the extreme modesty of the goddess.[170] A statue of Bona Dea, perhaps on loan from her temple on the Aventine, was also displayed in the house alongside a sacred serpent.[171]

Aside from the Vestal Virgins, the participants were all elite *matronae*.[172] At the climax of the evening, the Vestals sacrificed a *porca* (sow), a responsibility that offers the fullest confirmation of their ability to officiate over blood sacrifices.[173] The hostess then poured a libation of wine, though Plutarch and Macrobius affirm that the women called it milk and stored it in a covered vessel

---

[164] For the December rites of Bona Dea, see Brouwer 1989: 359–370; Versnel 1992, 1993: 228–288; Boëls-Janssen 1993: 429–468; Staples 1998: 13–51. For the cult of Bona Dea more generally, see also chapter 3.

[165] Cic. *Har. Resp.* 37.

[166] See chapter 7.

[167] For a fuller discussion of this episode, see chapter 4.

[168] For the exclusion of men from the rites, see especially Tib. 1.6.21–24; Prop. 4.9.53–60; Ov. *Ars. am.* 3.637–638, *Fast.* 5.153; Festus 348–350L; Lactant. *Div. inst.* 3.20.3–4; Macrob. *Sat.* 1.12.26.

[169] Plut. *Quaest. Rom.* 20 = *Mor.* 268d–e.

[170] Plut. *Quaest. Rom.* 20 = *Mor.* 268d–e, with Brouwer 1989: 336–339.

[171] Plut. *Quaest. Rom.* 20 = *Mor.* 268d–e. For the significance of the serpent in the cult and mythology of Bona Dea, see Brouwer 1989: 340–348.

[172] In his introduction to the *In Clodium et Curionem*, the author of the Scholia Bobiensia calls the women "high born ladies" (*matronas honestissimas*).

[173] Cic. *Har. resp.* 12, 37; *Att.* 1.13.3. Plutarch (*Cic.* 19) claims that the matron of the household performed the sacrifice, but Cicero's testimony is likely more accurate, particularly since his wife Terentia hosted the rites in 63 BC (as emphasized by Wildfang 2006: 31).

known as a honey pot.[174] According to Cicero, the sacrifice was a public one offered "for the safety of the Roman people" (*pro salute populi Romani, Har. resp.* 12).[175] His repeated allegations that Clodius had committed adultery with Caesar's wife Pompeia on a *pulvinar* (ritual couch) suggest that it included a *lectisternium*, an ancient kind of sacrifice in which a ritual meal was laid out on a table for the god.[176] Following the sacrifice proper, the women feasted, drank wine (under the name of milk), and enjoyed music and dancing.[177]

The ceremony is generally regarded as a fertility rite. In many ways, it resembles the Greek Thesmophoria, which likewise involved secrecy and the sacrifice of a pig.[178] Since the prosperity of the community depended upon its human and agricultural fertility, it is not surprising that Cicero characterized the rite as one performed for the safety (*salus*) of the Roman people. The cult of Bona Dea thus accorded the wives of Rome's most powerful men an important role in Roman civic life. The festival also reveals a complex relationship between gender, social status, political power, public ritual, and the private space of the house. Despite the official character of the ceremony, it took place not in the Aventine sanctuary of Bona Dea, but rather in the home of a senior magistrate, whose domestic tranquility was disrupted in order to make room for the performance of a public rite. On the night of the December ceremony, the private house of the magistrate became a public space under the control of his wife, her peers, and the Vestal Virgins.

The Parentalia

As the ritual year drew to a close, the Vestals celebrated an important festival honoring the dead. The *dies parentales* (days for the commemoration of the dead) began on February 13 and culminated in the Feralia on February 21.[179] In contrast to the rites of the Lemuria in May, which were designed to propitiate malevolent spirits and to purify the city of their presence, the Parentalia was a period for remembering and honoring the family dead. Individuals and families gathered at tombs outside the city to make simple offerings to ancestors, parents, siblings, spouses, and even to children.[180] Ovid suggests wine, violets, grain sprinkled with salt, and garlands left on a clay tile in the middle of the road.[181] Individuals provided whatever gifts they could afford, and no official

[174] Plut. *Quaest. Rom.* 20 = *Mor.* 268d–e; Macrob. *Sat.* 1.12.23.
[175] Suetonius calls the rites public (*publicas caerimonias, Iul.* 6.3), and Cassius Dio tells us that they were performed "on behalf of the people" (ὑπὲρ τοῦ δήμου, 37.35.4).
[176] Cic. *Har. resp.* 8, *Pis.* 95, *Mil.* 27.72, with Brouwer 1989: 366.
[177] Plut. *Quaest. Rom.* 20 = *Mor.* 268d–e; Juv. *Sat.* 2.82–90, 6.325–345; Macrob. *Sat.* 1.12.23. The presence of musical entertainment may be inferred from the fact that Clodius chose to disguise himself as a female musician (Plut. *Cic.* 28).
[178] See especially Versnel 1992, 1993: 228–288.
[179] For the Parentalia, see especially Varro *Ling.* 6.13; Ov. *Fast.* 2.533–570; Festus 75L; Dolansky 2011b.
[180] For the range of kin honored at the Parentalia, see Dolansky 2011b: 129–131.
[181] Ov. *Fast.* 2.533–542.

priestly involvement was necessary. The emphasis was on simplicity, rather than ostentatious gifts.

According to the fourth-century AD calendar of Philocalus, a Vestal Virgin made an offering to the dead (*virgo Vestalis parentat*) on the first day of the Parentalia.[182] The brevity of the entry and the lack of secure literary evidence for the role of the Vestals at the festival leaves many questions unresolved.[183] It seems unlikely that an individual Vestal's sacrifice to her own ancestors would warrant mention on the calendar of Philocalus.[184] The notation more likely indicates that one of the Vestals, presumably the *virgo maxima*, made an offering to all deceased Vestals, or even to all Roman dead on behalf of the community as a whole, perhaps to ensure that ancestors with no surviving descendants would be honored during the Parentalia.[185] The Vestals' unique position outside of the traditional family structure undoubtedly rendered them particularly well suited to make such an offering to dead who were not their own blood ancestors.[186]

Non-Annual Public Rites

In addition to their duties at annual public festivals, the Vestals had an important role in other non-annual cyclical rites and in rituals performed in times of great social or political crisis. Lucan, for instance, includes a "band of Vestals" (*vestalemque chorum*, 1.597) in the procession of public priests who circled the *pomerium* in a doomed *lustratio urbis* (purification of the city) as Caesar marched on Rome in 49 BC. Lucan's *lustratio*, which was allegedly performed on the recommendation of an Etruscan *vates* (seer), is almost certainly fictional. Nonetheless, it suggests that the Vestals could be imagined as participants in a ritual of this kind. The *lustratio*, which involved a procession around the area or group to be purified, was used in a variety of circumstances.[187] In addition to the annual *amburbium* (city circuit), a *lustratio* could also be performed as a "crisis rite" to expiate prodigies.[188] The Vestals may have participated regularly in *lustrationes* of both types, which could explain why they appear in the poetic procession of Lucan's *Bellum civile*.

---

[182] *CIL* I² p. 254.

[183] Prudentius (*C. Symm.* 2.1107–1108), a Christian poet of the late fourth century AD, mentions a sacrifice made by the Vestals to the spirits of the dead. Salzman (1990: 160) and Dolansky (2011b: 128–129) identify this sacrifice with the Parentalia.

[184] This is not to say that Vestals did not honor their own ancestors at the Parentalia (they almost certainly did), simply that a Vestal's personal observation of the rites would not appear on an official festival calendar.

[185] For other suggestions, see Mommsen *CIL* I² p. 309 (Tarpeia); Latte 1960: 111 (the ancestors of Rome's kings); Wildfang 2001: 227–230 (all deceased Vestals). Saquete (2000: 52, 59) assigns the sacrifice to the *virgo maxima*, while Porte (2001: 122) inexplicably argues that she watched while the *pontifex maximus* presided.

[186] For the legal status of the Vestal Virgins, see chapter 4.

[187] For lustral rites in general, see Baudy 1998.

[188] Rüpke 2012b: 308.

In fact, Tacitus reveals that the Vestals played a prominent role in the *lustratio* performed at the site of the Temple of Jupiter on June 21, AD 70. Accompanied by boys and girls with both parents living (*cum pueris puellisque patrimis matrimisque*), the Vestals sprinkled the area with water drawn from fountains and streams (*aqua e fontibus amnibusque hausta perluere*, *Hist.* 4.53) before the praetor and a *pontifex* performed a *suovetaurilia*, a lustral procession and sacrifice of a pig (*sus*), sheep (*ovis*), and bull (*taurus*). Like the "crisis rite" described by Lucan, the lustration of the Capitol was necessary in order to expiate the terrible fire that had destroyed the temple when Vespasian's men seized the hill during the civil war in the previous year.[189] Here, however, it is the Vestals, accompanied by *patrimi et matrimi*, rather than the *pontifices*, who sprinkle the site of the temple with water, a function that accords well with their responsibility to purify the common hearth of the Roman people with water on a daily basis. Their prominent role in the ceremony, moreover, underscores their central role in public cult at Rome. Although absolute certainty is impossible, it seems reasonable to assume that the Vestals participated in other historical *lustrationes* as well.

Learning and Teaching the *Sacra*

In the fall of 1883, excavators working in the House of the Vestals unearthed a marble statue base dating to the middle of the fourth century AD. The base once supported the image of a Vestal Virgin whose subsequent *damnatio memoriae* resulted in the partial obliteration of her name and identity.[190] Before her disgrace, this nameless Vestal had risen to the rank of *virgo maxima*. According to the inscription on her statue base, she had distinguished herself not only by her chastity and purity, but also by her "extraordinary learning" in the ritual sphere (*in sacris religionibusque doctrinae mirabilis*, CIL 6.32422). These words of praise are remarkable, particularly for what they suggest about the transmission of religious knowledge in the ancient world. Historians have long stressed that Rome lacked a formal system of religious education.[191] Technical handbooks were not a significant feature of Roman religion, nor were there sacred texts or doctrines that might require careful explication.[192] Only the *pontifices*, who interpreted and applied ritual regulations, and the *haruspices*, who trained in the Etruscan art of divination, are acknowledged to have possessed something resembling specialized ritual "knowledge." The average priest or priestess, on the other hand, is figured simply as a "practitioner." As John Scheid has commented

---

[189] For the fire on the Capitol, see Tac. *Hist.* 3.72.
[190] Lanciani (1888: 171) proposed that the Vestal in question was none other than Claudia, a priestess who reportedly converted to Christianity (Prudent. *Perist.* 2.527–528).
[191] See, for instance, Guittard 2012: 63.
[192] Rüpke 2007b: 131–132.

in a recent article, priests, "we are told . . . resembled grocers and clerks rather than holy men."[193] This approach to Roman priesthood is deeply flawed. Even in the absence of an institutionalized system for religious education, priests routinely used and transmitted specialized knowledge related to their ritual activities.[194]

The written sources confirm that the transmission of religious knowledge was central to life in the Vestal order. Valerius Maximus, for instance, describes a young Vestal as the pupil (*discipula*) of the chief Vestal Aemelia.[195] Dionysius of Halicarnassus reports that a Vestal's thirty-year career was divided into three distinct stages, each defined by a different responsibility. "During the first ten years," he writes, "their duty was to learn their functions, in the second ten to perform them, and during the remaining ten to teach others" (ἐν ᾧ δέκα μὲν ἔτη μανθάνειν αὐτὰς ἔδει, δέκα δ᾽ ἐπιτελεῖν τὰ ἱερά, τὰ δὲ λοιπὰ δέκα διδάσκειν ἑτέρας, *Ant. Rom.* 2.67.2). Plutarch records a similar distribution of ritual tasks.[196] Epigraphic evidence from later periods tends to confirm the existence of a formal progression from novice to senior Vestal. An inscription honoring the third-century AD *virgo maxima* Flavia Publicia, for instance, praises her "scrupulous care for the religious rites that she has displayed through all the grades of her priesthood with praiseworthy conduct" (*religiosam curam sacrorum quam per omnes gradus sacerdotii laudabili administratione operatur*, *CIL* 6.32414).[197]

Dionysius and Plutarch, however, appear to be mistaken in their belief that only Vestals in the middle stage actively participated in religious rituals.[198] As we have seen, certain rites required the presence of the *virgo maxima*, the eldest Vestal, while others, such as the preparation of *mola salsa*, included the eldest three. Furthermore, all six Vestals appear on the Ara Pacis Augustae arranged according to age, as the differences in height makes clear, with the youngest on the far right and the *virgo maxima*, the senior Vestal on the left.[199] The first four priestesses, moving from right to left, each carry ritual implements, including a spherical incense jar, a *simpulum*, and tablets containing prayers and instructions for the ritual.[200] Vestals at every stage of their career are actively engaged in the performance of the sacrifice. Dionysius and Plutarch also fail to take into account the likelihood that most Vestals would choose to remain in the order beyond the required number of years.[201]

---

[193] Scheid 2006: 15.
[194] Scheid 2006.
[195] Val. Max. 1.1.7.
[196] Plut. *Num.* 10.1.
[197] See also *CIL* 6.2135.
[198] Wildfang 2001: 253–254. As Wissowa (1912: 508, n. 5) rightly emphasizes, the division of a Vestal's period of service into three equal parts is "a fiction" (*eine Erfindung*).
[199] Moretti 1948: 280–281, though see Ryberg 1955: 42.
[200] Ryberg 1955: 41–42.
[201] The Vestal Occia served for fifty-seven years (Tac. *Ann.* 2.86).

Seneca alludes to a more fluid division of responsibility within the Vestal order in his *De otio* (*On Leisure*):

> hoc quod dico in duas dividam partes: primum, ut possit aliquis vel a prima aetate contemplation veritatis totum se tradere, rationem vivendi quaerere atque exercere secreto; deinde, ut possit hoc aliquis emeritis iam stipendiis, profligatae aetatis, iure optimo facere et ad alios acutissimo animo referre, virginum Vestalium more, quae annis inter officia divisis discunt facere sacra et cum didicerunt docent. (2.1–2)

> I shall divide what I have to say into two parts: firstly, that even from a very young age it is possible for a man to surrender himself entirely to the contemplation of truth, to seek a method for living, and to train himself in private. Secondly, that a man has a perfect right to do this when he has obtained release from public service and his life is nearly completed, and to pass it on to others while his mind is sharpest, according to the custom of the Vestal Virgins, who, their years of service divided between duties, learn to perform the sacred rites, and, once they have learned them, teach.

In this fascinating passage, the Vestals illustrate the ideal relationship between the enlightened Stoic *senex* and his pupil. Seneca clearly respected the Vestals and found in their pedagogical model an apt metaphor for his own situation as an aging statesman on the verge of retirement. Despite the obvious differences between the content of their pedagogies, Vestals and Stoics alike had a role in training the next generation of priestesses and philosophers.

In addition to revealing that the Vestals first learned and later taught a special set of skills, these ancient testimonia suggest that the priestesses exercised some autonomy within their sphere of influence. Senior Vestals handed down religious traditions with little intervention from the *pontifex maximus*, who may have been just as ill-informed about the details of their ritual program as was the average Roman on the street. This is not to say that the rites were secret, though some, including those performed in honor of Bona Dea, certainly were. It seems logical to assume, however, that the Vestals acquired and transmitted vital practical knowledge from which outsiders were excluded.

Consider, for instance, the description of the procedure for producing *muries* quoted in full above. Veranius, a contemporary of Varro and the author of several treatises on pontifical and augural rituals, presumably found his information in the pontifical archives.[202] Any attempt to follow this text as a recipe, however, would end in disaster. How long did the salt need to be baked? How much continually flowing water was needed to achieve the correct consistency? Like many cherished family recipes, crucial details are missing from this description, details that could be gleaned only through observation and hands on

---

[202] For the methods of antiquarian authors, see the introduction.

experience.[203] Young Vestals learned to make *muries*, to tend the eternal flame, and to offer the appropriate sacrifices not from the *pontifex maximus*, but rather from those with the requisite practical expertise: senior Vestals who had themselves been trained by their predecessors in the order. Indeed, priestesses could presumably answer questions such as, "why do we sprinkle the heads of sacrificial victims with *mola salsa*," or, "why do we offer a pig at the December festival of Bona Dea." Their answers may not have accorded perfectly with those given by antiquarian authors like Veranius, but it seems likely that a thriving oral tradition existed among female ritual specialists in Rome.

New Ritual Activities in the Age of Augustus

Like many things in Rome, the role of the Vestals underwent significant changes during the early principate. Augustus in particular cultivated a close relationship with Vesta and the Vestals throughout his public career.[204] Unable to join the priesthood or even to insert his wife Livia in his place, Augustus assigned to the Vestals new privileges and responsibilities that directly associated the order with the imperial family.[205] Perhaps the most striking example of this reconfiguration occurred in 12 BC, when the first *princeps* was finally elected *pontifex maximus*. Having lived comfortably in his house on the Palatine Hill for many years, Augustus was reluctant to leave it in order to take up residence in the *domus publica* (public house), the traditional home of the *pontifex maximus*. Instead, he donated this property to the Vestal priesthood, whose residence was located nearby, and established his house as the official home of the *pontifex maximus*. On April 28, Augustus founded a shrine to Vesta in a part of his residence that he had made public property. These two moves effectively redefined the position of the *pontifex maximus* and intensified the relationship between that religious office, the imperial household, and the goddess Vesta.[206] Although no archaeological evidence has been found to support the existence of a Palatine cult of Vesta, two reliefs depicting Vesta and the Vestals likely represent the new foundation.

The first of these, the so-called Sorrento Base, was unearthed in the early nineteenth century in the Roman ruins of Sorrento, the ancient city of Surrentum (fig. 5.6). All four sides of the base are decorated with figurative reliefs that

---

[203] For the role of oral tradition in religious education at Rome, see Scheid 2006, especially 14–15; Prescendi 2010.

[204] For Augustus' interest in Vesta and the Vestals, see especially Bömer 1987; Price 1996: 826; Grandazzi 1997: 167; Scott 2000; Mekacher 2006.

[205] For the privileges assigned to the Vestals, see chapter 4.

[206] Ov. *Fast.* 4.949–954. For the longstanding debate concerning the Palatine cult of Vesta, see Degrassi 1955; Guarducci 1964; Degrassi 1966–1967: 98–115; Kolbe 1966–1967: 101–103; Guarducci 1971; Fraschetti 1988: 949–965; Cappelli 1990; Fishwick 1993; Cecamore 1994–1995; Thompson 2005: 73–113.

illustrate various divine and mythical figures associated with the Palatine Hill and therefore with Augustus himself.[207] On the left side of Side A, five Vestals stand facing right toward the center of the scene. An expanse of drapery hangs between two Ionic columns and forms a curtain-like backdrop for the five Vestals, indicating an interior setting for the scene, in this case perhaps the house of Augustus.[208] On the right end of Side A, three additional figures appear in front of a similar architectural backdrop. Enthroned at the center is the goddess Vesta. To her left stands the sixth Vestal, perhaps the *virgo maxima*, who holds a small figurine that may represent the *Palladium* (or a copy) to be deposited in the new shrine.[209] To the right of Vesta, another veiled female figure likely represents Livia.[210] Behind these figures, the drapery gives way to reveal a small, circular building in the Ionic order. This building is very likely the new Palatine shrine of Vesta.[211]

The Palermo Relief depicts a similar scene (fig. 5.3). On the right side of the panel stands a fragmentary togate figure whose right forearm is extended over a small round altar. Although the upper portion of his body is missing, the figure has been identified as Augustus.[212] The *princeps* was likely shown presiding over the dedication of Vesta's new shrine. On the basis of this relief, it may even be possible to reconstruct a similar figure in the center of the damaged scene on the Sorrento Base. These two reliefs, presumably modeled on an original from Rome, affirmed the new relationship between the household of Augustus and the cult of Vesta. His house was no longer just one of many aristocratic residences on the Palatine. It had been transformed into a palace shared by three eternal gods (*aeternos tres . . . deos*, Ov. *Fast.* 4.954): Augustus, Vesta, and Apollo. The new shrine allowed Augustus to meld the public hearth of Vesta, with its implications for the welfare of the community and the continuity of the empire, with his own private hearth. The *princeps* (and his house) could now be understood to stand for the state.[213]

In the shifting religious landscape of the early principate, the Vestals themselves, whose virginity and legal isolation had long guaranteed their independence from any individual family within the community, also found themselves increasingly drawn into the circle of the imperial family. The priestesses were integrated into a series of new rituals designed to celebrate Augustus and his household.[214] The Vestals presumably participated in public vows undertaken for the health and safety of the emperor (*vota pro salute imperatoris*), but the

---

[207] For further discussion, with bibliography, see chapter 5.

[208] Rizzo 1932: 25–26; Ryberg 1955: 49.

[209] Ryberg 1955: 52; Thompson 2005: 77. Rizzo (1932: 47–49) and Guarducci (1971: 105–106) suggest Ceres instead.

[210] Ryberg 1955: 96; Thompson 2005: 95–99.

[211] Thompson 2005: 88.

[212] Cappelli 1990: 31.

[213] Beard, North, and Price 1998: 191.

[214] See especially Mekacher 2006: 70–76.

details are murky at best.[215] They celebrated the anniversary of Augustus' election as *pontifex maximus* on March 6, and perhaps other anniversaries as well, by offering incense at the hearth of Vesta.[216]

In the *Res Gestae Divi Augustae* (*Deeds of the Divine Augustus*), the first *princeps* records that the senate dedicated an altar to Fortuna Redux (Home-Bringing Fortune) in honor of his return from the East in 19 BC.[217] It ordered the *pontifices* and the Vestals to offer an annual sacrifice there on October 12 and named the day the Augustalia. Several years later, in 13 BC, the senate voted to erect an Ara Pacis Augustae (Altar of Augustan Peace) in the northern Campus Martius in honor of Augustus' return from Spain and Gaul. According to the *Res Gestae*, they also ordered the magistrates, priests, and Vestal Virgins to make a yearly sacrifice at the altar.[218] This annual sacrifice, described in most modern sources as the *anniversarium sacrificium*, was celebrated on January 30, the anniversary of the dedication of the Ara Pacis in 9 BC and, perhaps not coincidentally, Livia's birthday.[219]

The *anniversarium sacrificium* is likely the subject of the small figural frieze encircling the parapet of the altar (fig. 5.5). All six Vestals are depicted wearing their *suffibula* (sacrificial veils) and carrying various ritual implements, including a spherical incense jar, a *simpulum*, and tablets inscribed with prayers or directions for the ritual.[220] The *simpulum*, a ladle that allowed the officiant to taste the wine before he or she poured it on the head of the sacrificial victim, communicates the Vestals' membership in the *collegium pontificium*.[221] Even more importantly, it indicates that the Vestals were actively involved in the sacrifice proper.

The specific combination of victims present on the altar frieze—a sheep or ram, a steer, and a heifer—led Inez Scott Ryberg to suggest that an offering was made to Janus, Jupiter, and Pax respectively.[222] There are good reasons to believe that Jupiter and Janus received offerings alongside the altar's eponymous deity. When Augustus returned from Spain and Gaul in 13 BC, he dedicated the laurel from his *fasces* in the temple of Jupiter on the Capitol.[223] Although Janus was not associated with this particular homecoming, his temple gates were closed three times under Augustus, a gesture that symbolized the peace he had brought to the empire. The offerings to Jupiter and Janus thus recalled other rituals that the *princeps* had performed in proclaiming the *pax Augusta* (Augustan peace). The Vestals, alongside the magistrates and other priests, had

---

[215] For a discussion of the evidence, see Mekacher 2006: 70–71.
[216] Ov. *Fast.* 3.415–428.
[217] Aug. *R.G.* 11.
[218] Aug. *R.G.* 12.
[219] Ov. *Fast.* 1.709–722.
[220] Thompson 2005: 45.
[221] For the symbolism of the *simpulum*, see Siebert 1999: 47–51, 236–239.
[222] Ryberg 1955: 42–43. See also Thompson 2005: 49–52.
[223] Cass. Dio 54.25.

an important and highly visible role in the commemoration of the initial decla-
ration of this peace and the guarantee of its continuity.

The Vestals were placed in charge of the cult of the deified Livia as well,
though not until the reign of her grandson Claudius.[224] Following her death in
AD 29, the senate had moved to vote the first empress divine honors. Although
her cult had been widespread throughout the empire during her lifetime, this
new proposal would have officially recognized her divinity in Rome and established a temple and priestess in her honor, making Livia the first woman to
achieve the status of *diva* (goddess) in Rome itself. Tiberius refused to accept
the honor. Claudius, perhaps eager to enhance his own status, had new divine
honors voted to Livia on January 17, AD 42, the anniversary of her wedding
to Augustus.[225] He erected her statue in the temple of Augustus on the Palatine
and ordered that women should use her name in taking oaths. Claudius placed
the Vestals in charge of making the appropriate sacrifices. The decision to entrust the rites of Diva Augusta to the Vestals, rather than to a newly established
priestess, as the senate had originally proposed, is noteworthy. The Vestals certainly would have lent considerable prestige and legitimacy to the new cult. Although they continued to perform their traditional ritual obligations, they had
acquired a new function as intermediaries between the republican religious
system and the altered religious landscape of the principate.

Conclusion

Unlike most priests, who served only part-time and were engaged in other
public and private activities, the Vestals devoted themselves exclusively to their
ritual activities on a daily basis.[226] Most served for nearly their entire lives, taking office when they were no more than ten years old and remaining Vestals
until they died. Their obligations were exacting and included the performance
of an extensive ritual program and the maintaining of their virginity, both of
which prevented them from leading a normal family life. They were, in short,
religious professionals. The rites they performed were numerous and varied:
they addressed matters concerned with purification, agricultural fertility, the
production of bread, and, above all, the protection of the city.[227] The Vestals
carried out many of their activities within the sanctuary of Vesta, where they
guarded the eternal flame and the *pignora imperii*, which guaranteed the wellbeing of Rome and its empire. In time and space, the Vestals stood at the center of

[224] Cass. Dio 60.5.2, with Barrett 2002: 219–225.

[225] Cass. Dio 60.5.2.

[226] Cancik-Lindemaier 1996b: 138. A significant exception is the *flamen Dialis*, who is described as
"celebrating daily" (*cotidie feriatus*, Gell. *N.A.* 10.15.16, with chapter 5).

[227] In fact, Dionysius of Halicarnassus records a belief that the Romans increased the number of
priestesses from four to six "on account of the great number of sacred rites that they perform" (διὰ
πλῆρος τῶν ἱερουργιῶν ἅς ἐπιτελοῦσιν, *Ant. Rom.* 2.67.1). See also Plut. *Num.* 10.1.

religious life in the city. The temple anchored the ritual system at the city's public hearth, where the Vestals produced *mola salsa* and other ritual substances, while the priestesses themsleves, as Sarolta Takács writes, "were the constant element that linked festivals and bridged the months."[228] Other ritual obligations took them out of the temple and assigned them a prominent role on the public stage. Dressed in their distinctive costumes, they must have provided striking visual confirmation of the importance of priestesses to the security and success of the community.

[228] Takács 2008: 44.

CHAPTER SEVEN

The Vestal Virgins in Roman Politics

Tarpeia, the Vestal daughter of Sp. Tarpeius, earned her reputation as the arch-traitor of Roman history when she betrayed the city to Titus Tatius and the Sabines who were besieging Rome in retaliation for the rape of the Sabine women.[1] As a Vestal, Tarpeia's primary loyalty should have been to the city of Rome, whose boundaries she protected by guarding the hearth of Vesta and her own inviolate body. Instead, she flung open the gates and welcomed the enemy inside. While most versions tell us that Tarpeia lusted after the gold bracelets worn by the Sabines, Propertius turns her tale into a love story, a move that offers a fresh perspective on a Vestal's unique position in Roman society. Tormented by her longing for Tatius and by her equally powerful sense of duty to Rome, she laments her fate in a long monologue at the center of the poem:

> quantum ego sum Ausoniis crimen factura puellis,
> improba uirgineo lecta ministra foco!
> Pallados exstinctos si quis mirabitur ignis,
> ignoscat: lacrimis spargitur ara meis (4.4.43–6).

How great a crime I am about to commit for Italian girls, a shameless girl chosen to be a minister at a virgin's hearth! If anyone should wonder that the fires of Pallas have been extinguished, let him pardon me: the altar is sprinkled with my tears.

Propertius presents Tarpeia as a Vestal struggling to reconcile her private de-sire for Tatius with her public role as a Vestal. The poem is significant precisely because, as Tara Welch writes, "Tarpeia disagrees with the state's appropria-tion of her sexuality for its own benefit, and this is expressed in her desire to marry Tatius."[2] Propertius creates space for Tarpeia to voice her dissent, and this inversion of the traditional perspective throws into high relief the relentless

---

[1] Varro *Ling.* 5.41; Prop. 4.4; Livy 1.11.5–9; Dion. Hal. *Ant. Rom.* 2.38.1–40.3; Ov. *Met.* 14.776, *Fast.* 1.261–262; Val. Max. 9.6.1. Though only Varro and Propertius explicitly describe Tarpeia as a Vestal, other sources call her a virgin (Livy 1.11.5; Dion. Hal. *Ant. Rom.* 2.38.1; Val. Max. 9.6.1) and tell us that she encountered Tatius and the Sabines when she went outside of the city to collect water for the *sacra* (Livy 1.11.6; Val. Max. 9.6.1). Plutarch (*Num.* 10.1) also tells us that Numa selected a Vestal named Tar-peia, which indicates that there may have been variation in the tradition regarding the date and occasion of her treason. For a discussion of the sources for Tarpeia, see Welch 2005: 56–57.

[2] Welch 2005: 77.

demands that Rome placed upon the Vestals. Unlike other women, who were permitted to cultivate personal loyalties, the Vestals were expected to devote themselves entirely to the state.

Tarpeia is a legendary Vestal, but Cicero's speech on behalf of M. Fonteius, whose sister Fonteia was a member of the Vestal order, also suggests that the historical reality of life as a Vestal was often far more complicated than the ideal outlined in chapter 4.[3] Vestals were legally isolated from their birth families and set apart from the traditional structures of Roman society. Their unique legal status ensured that they belonged, above all, to the Roman people, whose hearth they guarded on a daily basis. In the *peroratio* of the *pro Fonteio*, however, Cicero warns the jury that if they convict Fonteius for extortion, the tears of the grief-stricken priestess will extinguish the eternal flame on the hearth of Vesta (*prospicite ne ille ignis aeternus . . . sacerdotis vestrae lacrimis exstinctus esse dicatur*, 47).[4] The legal provisions that sought to isolate Vestals from their families have quite clearly failed to achieve their objective in this case. Remarkably, Cicero places the onus for the potential calamity not on the Vestal, but rather on the members of the jury. In fact, he appeals to their emotions by emphasizing how vulnerable Fonteia will be without her brother, to whom she is uniquely bound:

> cui miserae quod praesidium, quod solacium reliquum est hoc amisso? nam ceterae feminae gignere ipsae sibi praesidia et habere domi fortunarum omnium socium participemque possunt; huic vero virgini quid est praeter fratrem quod aut iucundum aut carum esse possit? (*Font.* 47)

> What protection, what comfort is left to the poor woman, if this man is lost? Other women, for their part, can bear guardians for themselves, and have at home an ally and participant in all of life's fortunes. But for this virgin, what can be either dear or pleasant except her brother?

While other women acquire guardians through marriage and motherhood, Cicero argues, a Vestal must find protection (*praesidium*) and comfort (*solacium*) in her birth family alone. His emotional appeal depends upon the assumption that the jury will empathize with a Vestal who has remained loyal to her brother, even as she "has been, on behalf of you and of your children, occupied for so many years in propitiating the immortal gods" (*quae pro vobis liberisque vestris tot annos in dis immortalibus placandis occupata est*, *Font.* 46). In Cicero's *pro Fonteio*, there is a clear tension between the ideal of a Vestal whose primary loyalty is to the state and the more complicated reality of familial obligations.

Fonteia's grief (and Cicero's treatment of it) suggests that we need a more dynamic conceptualization of the historical processes that shaped the experi-

---

[3] For the circumstances of the trial, which likely took place in 69 BC, see Crawford 1984: 55–57, with further bibliography. For Fonteia's career as a Vestal, see Rüpke 2008: 695, No. 1733.

[4] For an analysis of Cicero's rhetorical strategy in the *peroratio* of the *pro Fonteio*, see especially North 2000: 360–364.

ences and behavior of individual Vestals.[5] While the preceding chapters have elucidated the role of the ideal Vestal as presented in our ancient sources, this approach tends to reduce her to a one-dimensional figure and fails to account for her competing obligations to state and to family. A prosopographical approach, on the other hand, reveals that some Vestals challenged the normative ideal by acting on behalf of family members in a variety of social and political contexts. Prosopography has its own disadvantages as a methodology, including the danger of falling for what Keith Hopkins has called "the Everest fallacy," by which he means "the tendency to illustrate a category by an example which is exceptional."[6] Such examples are often misleading because they may suggest, for example, that Cicero was a "typical" new man, which would be about as helpful as claiming that Mount Everest is a "typical" mountain. The Vestals under consideration in this chapter are undoubtedly exceptional, and it would be unwise to extrapolate too widely on the basis of their individual biographies. I am, however, interested in the "exceptional," since my goal in this chapter is to explore the gap that existed between the normative ideal of Vestal behavior and the reality of their lived experiences, rather than the ideal itself.[7]

This chapter considers the Vestals as independent actors who more or less successfully negotiated between their identity as public priestesses and their identity as daughters, sisters, and kinswomen. It argues that they played an important role in political life at Rome by investing in the careers of their male relatives. Moreover, it suggests that their prominence within the priestly community and the privileges associated with their office, including their unusual legal status, allowed the Vestals to press their political agendas in ways that other elite women could not. While the order as a whole maintained its reputation as an isolated and apolitical body at the heart of Rome's religious community, individual Vestals often forged vibrant public careers for themselves and for their family members.

The Triumph of Claudia

In the middle of the second century BC, Claudia, the daughter of Ap. Claudius Pulcher (cos. 143 BC), took advantage of her position as a Vestal to influence the outcome of a potentially explosive political situation. Claudia's father, who

---

[5] For a similar observation, see Cancik-Lindemaier 2010: 341.

[6] Hopkins 1983: 41.

[7] I have adopted an approach to the prosopographical evidence that is similar to the one Várhelyi (2010) applies to the religious activities of the senatorial elite in the imperial period. As Várhelyi notes, "a less static model of social interactions may allow us to read a variety of human discourses and actions that do not fully conform to social norms, while not excluding the possibility that some of these very same individuals followed established *mores* throughout most of their lives (2010: 10)." Though Bauman (1992) and Wildfang (2006) have examined many of the episodes under consideration in this section, their focus and conclusions differ from my own in many respects. Gallia 2015 covers some of the same material and adds important examples from the imperial period, but his arguments against the validity of the "normative ideal" are problematic (see chapter 4).

served as consul in 143 BC, won a victory over the Alpine Salassi in that year.[8] On his return to Rome, Claudius asked the senate for public funds to pay for a triumph, evidently presuming that the honor itself would be awarded.[9] The senate, however, refused his request, citing the heavy losses he had sustained during the campaign.[10] One late source claims that Claudius had killed five thousand Salassi, the minimum number required for a triumph, but had lost just as many of his own men.[11] The consul was undeterred. Although the relevant portion of the *Fasti triumphales* is missing, the literary sources indicate that he celebrated an unsanctioned triumph at his own expense.[12]

Unable to thwart the consul by withholding official sanction, Claudius' opponents were forced to act more directly. One tribune attempted to forcibly remove the consul from his chariot and was prevented from doing so only by the intervention of Claudius' Vestal daughter. Valerius Maximus describes the scene with characteristic flair: [13]

> quae, cum patrem suum triumphantem e curru violenta tribuni plebis manu detrahi animadvertisset, mira celeritate utrisque se interponendo amplissimam potestatem inimicitiis accensam depulit. igitur alterum triumphum pater in Capitolium, alterum filia in aedem Vestae duxit, nec discerni potuit utri plus laudis tribueretur, cui victoria an cui pietas comes aderat. (Val. Max. 5.4.6)

> When she observed her father at his triumph being dragged from his chariot by the violent hand of a tribune of the plebs, she held off his excessive power, which had been inflamed by hostility, by interposing herself between the two with marvelous speed. The father thus led one triumph to the Capitol while the daughter led another to the Temple of Vesta, nor could it be determined which of the two should receive more praise, the one who had victory as a companion or the one whom piety (*pietas*) accompanied.

Claudia evidently intervened just as the situation threatened to devolve into violence and protected her father by means of her *sacrosanctitas* (sacrosanctity) as a Vestal.[14]

---

[8] Livy *Per.* 53; Cass. Dio fr. 74.

[9] Cass. Dio fr. 74. The ancient sources indicate that the senate had the power to award triumphs and to allocate public money to pay for them (see, for example, Pol. 6.15.7–8; Livy 3.63.9–10; Dion. Hal. *Ant. Rom.* 3.22.2, with Brennan 1996: 316; Pittenger 2008: 35–37).

[10] Oros. 5.4.7.

[11] Oros. 5.4.7.

[12] Orosius specifies that Claudius paid for the triumph with his own money (*usus privatis sumptibus*, 5.4.7).

[13] See also Cic. *Cael.* 34. According to Suetonius, Claudia intervened at her brother's triumph (*Tib.* 2), but this may be an error rather than an alternative version of the event (Rüpke 2008: 609, n. 2, No. 1152). Although Mueller (2002: 54–55) suggests that Claudia actually led a procession to the *aedes Vestae*, the parallel is more likely to be metaphorical.

[14] Scholars have generally assumed that the tribune was attempting to interpose his veto (Bauman 1992: 47; Flower 2002b: 164; Wildfang 2006: 92). Indeed, Suetonius claims that Claudia accompanied her brother (an alternative to the more common tradition) "so that it would not be permissible (*fas*) for

FIGURE 7.1. Denarius of C. Clodius Vestalis showing Flora on the obverse (left) and the Vestal Virgin Claudia on the reverse (right), 41 BC. (*RRC* 512/2). Inv. No. R.9271, British Museum. Photo © Trustees of the British Museum.

Claudia's actions appear quite unprecedented.[15] She employed her personal inviolability to secure a triumph for her father, inserting herself directly into the public spectacle and enabling her father to contravene accepted political behavior by triumphing without the approval of the senate or the people. Despite this affront to *mos maiorum* (ancestral custom) and the tribune's attempt to intercede, ancient authors evidently accepted Claudius' triumph as legitimate, thanks in large part, no doubt, to the support offered by his Vestal daughter.[16] The episode illustrates how a Vestal might use the privileges of her office in an unorthodox manner in support of a family member's political agenda.

Claudia's actions on behalf of her father also reveal the inherent tension in the Vestals' position in Roman society. As we have seen, the Vestals appear to have been deliberately isolated from their families, both legally and physically,

---

any of the tribunes to veto or interrupt [his triumph]" (*ne vetare aut intercedere fas cuiquam tribunorum esset, Tib.* 2). As Brennan (1996: 319) has noted, however, this is not strictly accurate. Claudius had bypassed the senate and the popular assembly, the two bodies that had the power to authorize a triumph in this period, and therefore had not given the tribune an opportunity to use his veto. Instead, the tribune was forced to resort to violence, "a desperate act—prompted by the frustration of having nothing to veto" (Brennan 1996: 319). For Vestal *sacrosanctitas*, see chapter 4.

[15] Flower 2002b: 164.

[16] All the sources indicate that the triumph was successfully completed, and the *vir triumphalis* of Macrob. *Sat.* 3.14.14 likely refers to Ap. Claudius (Brennan 1996: 331, n. 25). Although Claudius lacked senatorial or popular approval for his triumph, Brennan (1996: 319) has suggested that he may have convinced the college of augurs to issue a *decretum* allowing him to keep his military auspices within the *pomerium* on the day of the triumph. Claudius' father, C. Claudius Pulcher (cos. 177 BC), had been an augur for twenty-eight years (Livy 33.44.3, 45.44.3), and Claudius may already have been a member of the college by this year. This theory adds a further layer to the picture of how priestly powers could be manipulated for political purposes.

in order to guarantee their ability to symbolize the entire community.[17] We might, therefore, expect Claudia to be criticized for her overt intrusion into political life on behalf of her father. Instead, she is praised for her achievement and idealized as a paragon of female virtue.[18] Valerius Maximus even suggests that her *exemplum* may constitute a "stronger and more courageous" (*valentius et animosius*, 5.4.6) display of filial *pietas* than that displayed by any son. Claudia also features as a model Roman in a well-known passage from Cicero's *pro Caelio*, where the orator admonishes the infamous Clodia for failing to imitate the example set by her illustrious ancestor.[19] Claudia was even commemorated on a coin minted by C. Clodius Vestalis, a relatively unknown figure who served as moneyer in 41 BC (fig. 7.1).[20] On the reverse of a coin featuring Flora on the obverse, she is shown seated, holding a sacrificial vessel with her hair bound by the characteristic *infula* and *vittae*. Although Clodius chose not to depict the triumph itself, the portrait was very likely enough to evoke the scene in the mind of the viewer. The ancient sources thus indicate that by the late Republic, Claudia's filial piety had overshadowed her role in assisting Claudius' blatant disregard for the senate and the *mos maiorum*.

Licinia's Shrine to Bona Dea

The afterlife of Claudia's intervention into Roman political life suggests that the Romans could accept a Vestal who maintained close ties to her family. Individual Vestals sometimes challenged social norms, even as the order as a whole worked to uphold the prevailing ideology. In fact, further evidence suggests that Claudia's allegiance to her father was far from exceptional. Loyalty to familial interests emerges as an important trend in the political activities of republican Vestals. In 123 BC, just twenty years after Claudia used her *sacrosanctitas* to secure a triumph for her father, the Vestal Licinia dedicated an altar and a small shrine at the Aventine temple of Bona Dea.[21] The dedication, which included an inscription identifying Licinia as the benefactor, advertised her wealth and status within the community. It also became a political issue almost immediately. The urban praetor, Sex. Julius Caesar (pr. 123 BC), challenged Licinia's right to

---

[17] On this point, see above.

[18] Flower 2002b: 164; Pittenger 2008: 48. The sources are more ambivalent about Claudius' determination to triumph at all costs. Dio (fr. 74), for instance, claims that his decision to attack the Salassi was motivated by jealousy for his colleague, M. Claudius Metellus. Even so, the scandal apparently did not impede Claudius' subsequent political career. He served as censor in 136 BC (Cass. Dio fr. 81; Festus 360L), appointed himself *princeps senatus* (Plut. *Ti. Gracch.* 4.1), and served on the Gracchan land commission (Cic. *Leg. Agr.* 2.31; Vell. Pat. 2.2.3; Val. Max. 7.2.6; Plut. *Ti. Gracch.* 13.1; App. *B Civ.* 1.13, 18–19).

[19] Cic. *Cael.* 34. Clodia was the daughter of Ap. Claudius Pulcher (cos. 79 BC), the sister of P. Clodius Pulcher (tr. pl. 58 BC), and the niece of the Vestal Claudia.

[20] *RRC* 512/1–2, with chapter 5.

[21] See Cic. *Dom.* 137, quoted below. For Licinia's career, see Rüpke 2008: 765, No. 2219.

make a dedication without the permission of the people.[22] The senate referred the issue to the pontifical college, which made the following pronouncement quoted by Cicero in the *De domo sua*:

QUOD IN LOCO PUBLICO LICINIA CAII FILIA INIUSSU POPULI DEDICASSET, SACRUM NON VIDERIER. (136)

That which Licinia, daughter of Gaius, had consecrated in a public place without the people's consent did not seem a valid consecration.

On the basis of this ruling by the *pontifices*, the senate ordered Caesar to remove Licinia's inscription and, presumably, her shrine as well.

The circumstances surrounding Licinia's failed dedication raise a number of important questions. That the urban praetor chose to challenge the legitimacy of the shrine suggests that it was understood as a political statement. Licinia made her dedication during a period of renewed conflict between the *optimates* and the *populares* over control of religious authority at Rome.[23] In particular, the two groups disagreed over whether new members of the priestly colleges should be coopted by existing members or elected in the assembly.[24] Licinia's decision to set up a shrine without the formal consent of the people has thus been read as a public assertion of her belief that the priestly community should not be subject to decisions of the assembly.[25]

Richard Bauman, who places Licinia firmly in the conservative camp, acknowledges that there are a number of difficulties with this interpretation.[26] The filiation in Scaevola's ruling suggests that Licinia was the daughter of C. Licinius Crassus (tr. pl. 145 BC), who as tribune had attempted to pass a law requiring vacancies in the major priestly colleges to be filled by a popular vote.[27] If, therefore, Licinia intended to reaffirm the authority of the priestly hierarchy vis à vis the assembly, she would have done so in direct opposition to her father and his political program. Such independence on the part of a Vestal is not inconceivable. Some Vestals, including Claudia and Fonteia, continued to demonstrate filial piety, even after legal ties to their birth families had been

[22] Licinia had evidently violated the terms of a *lex Papiria* forbidding the dedication of an *aedis* (shrine), *terra* (piece of property), or *ara* (altar) without the permission of the people. For the terms of the *lex*, passed sometime between 174 BC and 154 BC, see Cic. *Dom.* 127–128, with Johnson 2007: 167. See also Gai. *Inst.* 2.3–8, with Rives 2011. Bauman (1992: 52–53) overemphasizes Licinia's gender in his analysis of this episode. The legitimacy of her dedication was questioned not because she was a woman, but rather because she had made it without the consent of the people.

[23] For a discussion of the religious and political struggles in this period, see especially Rawson 1974.

[24] The issue was eventually decided by the *lex Domitia* of 104 BC, on which see North 1990b, 2011.

[25] See, for example, Bauman 1992: 52–53. Wildfang (2006: 93) has modified his thesis slightly, arguing that Licinia "was attempting to demonstrate that her actions as a Vestal, and thus implicitly her order's power, were not subjected to the dictates of the people."

[26] Bauman 1992: 53.

[27] For Licinia's parentage, see Münzer 1920: 243; Bauman 1992: 53; Rüpke 2008: 765, No. 2219. For the failed *lex Licinia*, see Cic. *Amic.* 25, *Brut.* 21, *Nat. D.* 3.2.

formally dissolved. Others, by contrast, might have forged independent political identities. How can we be certain?

The location where Licinia chose to dedicate her shrine suggests that her political views were aligned closely with those of *popularis* magistrates like her father. According to Ovid, the Aventine sanctuary of Bona Dea sat just below the *saxum*, the place where Remus had taken his auspices during the infamous contest with his brother Romulus.[28] Remus appears to have emerged as the founder of the plebeian cause during the period of the Licinio-Sextian revolution, when plebeians first gained access to the consulship.[29] His observation point on the Aventine Hill was likewise associated with the struggle for political equality. It was the traditional site of the second secession in 449 BC, when the plebs withdrew from the city to protest the tyranny of the second board of *decemviri* and the outrageous behavior of Ap. Claudius.[30] The Aventine was also home to a number of sanctuaries with plebeian associations, including the Temple of Ceres, where the plebeian aediles kept their records.[31] Though the Temple of Bona Dea was the site of a festival celebrated by elite *matronae*, its healing cult attracted a diverse group of predominantly plebeian worshippers.[32] Licinia's high profile devotion to the cult may have been calculated to advertise her solidarity with the *populares* and their efforts to transfer the power of selecting new priests to the people.

We should, therefore, reevaluate the long-held view among scholars that Licinia intended to express her optimate sentiments when she dedicated the shrine without the approval of the people. In fact, she may have taken her cue from contemporary popular politicians, who often used religious dedications to make a political point. During this period, several *popularis* tribunes attempted to dedicate the property of their patrician opponents to the gods.[33] In each case, the *pontifices* nullified the dedication because the tribune had not received the explicit consent of the people. If even popular leaning politicians bypassed the assembly on occasion, we should not assume that Licinia intended to snub the people when she failed to seek their permission to make her dedication.

Any interpretation of the evidence lies open to a number of valid criticisms. Perhaps, for example, Licinia had simply been healed of some infirmity after visiting Bona Dea's shrine on the Aventine. While her reasons may be ulti-

---

[28] Ov. *Fast.* 5.148–154.
[29] See especially Wiseman 1995.
[30] Livy 3.50.10.
[31] Livy 3.55.13.
[32] For a discussion of the evidence for the social status of Bona Dea worshippers, see Brouwer 1989 and chapter 3.
[33] In 131 BC, the tribune C. Antinius Labeo attempted to dedicate the property of Q. Metellus (cens. 131 BC), who had ejected him from the senate (Cic. *Dom.* 123). In 70 BC, the property of the censor Cn. Lentulus Clodianus was the subject of a similar dedication by an unnamed tribune (Cic. *Dom.* 124). Cicero (*Dom.* 124) implies that these were not isolated incidents. Livy (43.16.10) reports a similar conflict as early as 169 BC involving Ti. Sempronius Gracchus and C. Claudius. For a discussion of these episodes, see Rawson 1974: 196.

mately irrecoverable, the urban praetor's hostile reaction suggests that he saw the dedication as politically motivated. In my view, Licinia's decision to erect a shrine at a site closely associated with the plebs seems deliberately calculated to communicate her sympathy with the *popularis* cause. The issue of how new priests should be chosen may have been particularly important to Licinia, given her father's legislative efforts. While she could not follow in her father's footsteps as *tribunus plebis*, she could still attempt to influence public opinion by dedicating a shrine to Bona Dea on the Aventine.[34]

Licinia Campaigns for Murena

The Vestals were also embroiled in several high-profile political scandals in the sixties BC, including a heavily contested consular election and the infamous Catilinarian Conspiracy. In 63 BC, another Vestal named Licinia offered her reserved seat at the gladiatorial games to her relative, L. Licinius Murena (cos. 62 BC), who was campaigning for the consulship of 62 BC.[35] If the Vestals sat together, as they did during the principate, then the sight of Murena seated among the members of the order must have made for a particularly striking tableau.[36] The gesture communicated Licinia's political preferences to the large crowd at the games and was presumably calculated to enhance her kinsman's candidacy. Licinia was certainly not the first Roman woman to campaign for a political candidate, but her status as a Vestal did give her a more visible platform from which to express her views.[37]

Murena's bid for the consulship was successful, but by late November he faced prosecution for electoral malpractice (*ambitus*).[38] The benefit he had derived from Licinia's favor was apparently among the charges leveled against him. Although the details are unclear, Cicero, who spoke in defense of the consul-elect, argued that neither Murena nor Licinia had done anything wrong:

> nec si virgo Vestalis, huius propinqua et necessaria, locum suum gladiatorium concessit huic, non et illa pie fecit et hic a culpa est remotus. (*Mur.* 73)

[34] It should be noted that if Licinia did affiliate herself with the popular cause, this did not protect her from prosecution for *incestum* by L. Cassius Longinus Ravilla (cos. 127 BC) in 113 BC. For the political implications of this infamous case, see Gruen 1968: 127–129.

[35] Cic. *Mur.* 73, quoted below. For Licinia's career, see Rüpke 2008: 765, No. 2218. The same Licinia was accused of *incestum* in 70 BC when the frequent visits of her relative M. Licinius Crassus (cos. 70 BC) aroused suspicion of impropriety (Plut. *Crass.* 1.2). The pair escaped conviction when they were able to prove that they had been discussing the sale of a piece of Licinia's property.

[36] Rawson 2006: 329.

[37] See, for example, Savunen's (1995) study of electoral inscriptions from Pompeii, which demonstrates that even though women could not vote in elections, they actively campaigned for their favorite candidates. It is unlikely that Pompeian women were alone in their political activity.

[38] The accusation of electoral misconduct was brought by Ser. Sulpicius Rufus (cos. 51 BC), an unsuccessful competitor for the consulship of 62 BC. Murena was tried under the new *lex Tullia de ambitu*, which placed Cicero in an awkward position as he defended the consul-elect.

If a Vestal Virgin, a relative and close friend, gave this man her place at the gladiatorial games, she acted dutifully (*pie*) and he is free from guilt.

Cicero emphasizes the close personal relationship between Licinia and Murena in an effort to characterize the Vestal's gesture as an act of *pietas*, rather than as an illegitimate political favor. In spite of this rhetorical sleight of hand, Licinia's motivations seem perfectly clear. Like other Vestals before her, she sought to advance the political career of a male relative by utilizing the privileges associated with her priesthood. Her decision to offer Murena her seat at the games was both an act of familial piety and an expression of her political affiliation. While the prosecution undoubtedly criticized Licinia for intervening in the consular elections, it is unlikely that the trial had any lasting effect on her public reputation. Murena was ultimately acquitted of the charge of electoral misconduct and went on to serve as consul in 62 BC.

The Vestals and the Catilinarian Conspiracy

While Ser. Sulpicius Rufus (cos. 51 BC) and his supporters fought the outcome of the election of 63 BC in the courts, another unsuccessful candidate, L. Sergius Catilina (pr. 68 BC), plotted to overthrow the Republic with violence. Just a few weeks after he had successfully defended Murena, Cicero found himself in possession of definitive evidence against several leading Catilinarians. The conspirators were arrested on December 3, 63 BC and confessed their role in the plot, but the senate failed to reach a decision regarding their fate. That night, as Cicero deliberated his next move at the house of a close friend, his wife Terentia hosted the nocturnal rites of Bona Dea.[39] The current political crisis must have loomed large in the minds of the *matronae* in attendance on that particular evening. Already experiencing a mixture of relief and apprehension, the women's emotions were further excited by an unexpected omen. Plutarch describes the scene in his biography of Cicero:

> ταῦτα τοῦ Κικέρωνος διαπ οροῦντος, γίνεταί τι ταῖς γυναιξὶ σημεῖον θυούσαις. ὁ γὰρ βωμός, ἤδη τοῦ πυρὸς κατακεκοιμῆσθαι δοκοῦντος, ἐκ τῆς τέφρας καὶ τῶν κατακεκαυμένων φλοιῶν φλόγα πολλὴν ἀνῆκε καὶ λαμπράν. ὑφ' ἧς αἱ μὲν ἄλλαι διεπτοήθησαν, αἱ δ' ἱεραὶ παρθένοι τὴν τοῦ Κικέρωνος γυναῖκα Τερεντίαν ἐκέλευσαν ᾗ τάχος χωρεῖν πρὸς τὸν ἄνδρα καὶ κελεύειν, οἷς ἔγνωκεν ἐγχειρεῖν ὑπὲρ τῆς πατρίδος, ὡς μέγα πρός τε σωτηρίαν καὶ δόξαν αὐτῷ τῆς θεοῦ φῶς διδούσης. (Plut. *Cic.* 20.1–2)

> A sign was given to the women who were sacrificing. For the altar, although the fire seemed to have gone out already, sent forth from the ashes

---

[39] Plut. *Cic.* 19.3. For the December rites of Bona Dea, see chapter 6.

and burnt remnants a great and brilliant flame. The rest of the women were terrified at this, but the sacred virgins urged Terentia, the wife of Cicero, to go with haste to her husband and tell him to carry out what he had in mind on behalf of the country, since the goddess was giving him a great light to safety and glory.[40]

The "omen," and the Vestals' interpretation of it, undoubtedly made a strong impression on the assembled matrons, who could reasonably be expected to report the event to their husbands.[41] At a meeting of the senate on December 5, Cicero threw his weight behind a recommendation that the conspirators be put to death and, after a heated debate, the senate voted to support this motion.[42]

Cicero was certainly under pressure to justify his execution of the Catilinarians at a later date, but it is unnecessary to assume that he invented the omen after the fact.[43] Responsibility for organizing the portent very likely rested with Terentia and her half-sister Fabia, who was a Vestal Virgin and must have been present on the night in question. The sisters may have been close.[44] We know, for instance, that Terentia fled to the House of the Vestals in 58 BC, when a mob loyal to P. Clodius Pulcher (tr. pl. 58 BC) looted and burned Cicero's home on the Palatine. It is not difficult to imagine that Terentia and her sister coordinated the miraculous flame on the altar. In fact, immediately following the passage cited above, Plutarch provides an assessment of Terentia's character, underscoring her reputation for taking an active interest in her husband's political career, before claiming, "and she made these things known to him and incited him against the conspirators," (ταῦτά τε πρὸς αὐτὸν ἔφρασε καὶ παρώξυνεν ἐπὶ τοὺς ἄνδρας, *Cic.* 20.3). Susan Treggiari has even suggested that the author of the anonymous *Invectiva in Ciceronem* (*Invective Against Cicero*) may have had this incident in mind when he accused Terentia of engaging in sacrilege and perjury (*sacrilega ac periuriis*, 2).[45] While the ancient sources focus on Terentia's ambition, the Vestals, who oversaw the rites and performed the actual sacrifice, must have been complicit in staging the "omen."[46] Even more importantly,

---

[40] See also Cass. Dio 37.35.4.

[41] Although Cicero does not refer to the omen in the published version of the speech that he delivered in the senate on December 5 (*Cat.* 4), the senators in attendance had likely heard the news from their wives. In contrast to the cult on the Aventine, the nocturnal rites of the Bona Dea were an exclusively elite affair (Brouwer 1989: 256, 268).

[42] Sall. *Cat.* 50.3–53.1; Plut. *Cic.* 20.4–21.5; Cass. Dio 37.35.4–36.3.

[43] As Brouwer (1989: 263) notes, "It must be admitted that this token of divine approval appeared at the most convenient moment for Cicero, particularly in view of the amount of criticism of his mode of action afterwards. This does not imply that no "miracle" took place during this particular night, but one wonders whether Cicero's contemporaries attached the same value as he did himself to this miracle, one which came in very handy for him."

[44] Admittedly, as Treggiari (2007: 30–31) emphasizes, Cicero never mentions Fabia or the possibility of exploiting her position as a Vestal in his letters.

[45] Treggiari 2007: 44–45.

[46] Although Plutarch claims that the matron of the household performed the sacrifice, Cicero (*Har. resp.* 37; *Att.* 1.13.3) and Asconius (*Mil.* 43) both specify that it was offered by the Vestals. The testimony of Cicero, whose wife once hosted the rites, seems more reliable. For a fuller discussion of this issue, see chapter 6.

without the interpretation that Fabia and her colleagues allegedly provided, the incident may have received little credence among the *matronae* in attendance. On the night of December 3, 63 BC, the Vestals appear to have taken advantage of their role at a public sacrifice in order to orchestrate a portent. They then relied upon their prestige and credibility as religious officials to interpret the sign and to to influence the course of events in the midst of a political crisis.[47]

The Vestals and Julius Caesar

Thus far I have outlined how individual Vestals exploited the prestige and resources of their priesthood on behalf of family members in a variety of social and political contexts. On at least one occasion, however, they acted collectively and on behalf of a fellow priest. In 82 BC, the Vestals petitioned Rome's new dictator, L. Cornelius Sulla (cos. 88, 80 BC), to pardon his fellow patrician, C. Julius Caesar (cos. 59 BC). Caesar's name had been added to the list of the proscribed when he refused to divorce his wife Cornelia, the daughter of Sulla's bitter enemy, L. Cornelius Cinna (cos. 86, 85, 84 BC).[48] According to Suetonius, several prominent Sullans attempted to secure his pardon, including C. Aurelius Cotta (cos. 75 BC), a cousin of Caesar's mother, Aurelia, and Mam. Aemilius Lepidus Livianus (cos. 77 BC), a more distant maternal relation.[49] Sulla finally relented, but only after the Vestals joined these men in pleading for the young patrician's life.[50]

Scholars have often wondered what arguments were made on Caesar's behalf, and why Sulla accepted them.[51] Suetonius makes it plain that he did so unwillingly. When faced with the persistent demands of his own supporters and those of the Vestal Virgins, however, he evidently felt that he had little choice. An equally fascinating question concerns the factors that motivated the Vestals to intercede at this time of exceptional political violence. The traditional view has been that they took action because they shared Caesar's political sympathies and sought to oppose Sulla by saving a victim of his horrific proscriptions.[52] There are a number of difficulties with this position. First, thousands of

---

[47] Fabia may have had her own reasons for inciting the public against Catiline, with whom she had been accused of committing *incestum* in 73 BC.

[48] Vell. Pat. 2.41.2; Plut. *Caes.* 1.1–3, with chapter 1.

[49] Münzer first elucidated Caesar's relationship to these men (1920: 312–313, 326).

[50] Suet. *Iul.* 1.2: *Donec per virgines Vestales perque Mamercum Aemilium et Aurelium Cottam propinquos et adfines suos veniam impetravit* (He at length obtained a pardon through the intercession of the Vestal virgins, and Mamercus Aemilius and Aurelius Cotta, his near relatives).

[51] For a discussion of modern scholarship on this question, see Ridley 2000.

[52] Rawson 1974: 211. Unfortunately, we know very little about the political sympathies of the Vestals who were active in the late eighties BC. Fonteia, who entered the college by 91 BC at the latest, was the daughter of a Marian family (Rawson 1974: 211; Rüpke 2008: 695, No. 1733). Perpennia, initiated around 100 BC, also belonged to a relatively new political family that had sided with Marius and Cinna during the civil war (Rawson 1974: 211; Rüpke 2008: 830, No. 2642). Terentia's sister Fabia, on the other

Sulla's political enemies were put to death during the proscriptions, and there is no evidence that the Vestals made an attempt to bring the widespread violence to an end. Second, Caesar was a very young man from a relatively insignificant family.[53] Why would the Vestals choose to intervene on his behalf while other more prominent men were hunted down and brutally murdered?

The episode is fully intelligible only if we assume that the Vestals were motivated to act on behalf of a priestly colleague. Marius and Cinna had appointed Caesar to replace L. Cornelius Merula (cos. suff. 87 BC) as *flamen Dialis* in late 87 BC or very early in 86 BC.[54] Even if Caesar had not been fully inaugurated by the time Sulla returned to Rome in 82 BC —though it is very likely that he had been—his status as *flamen Dialis* designate (*destinatus*, Suet. *Iul.* 1.1) was evidently enough to prompt the Vestals to intervene.[55] The Vestals and the *flamen Dialis* were colleagues in the extended pontifical college and presumably enjoyed a close relationship with Caesar's wife, Cornelia, who may have played a decisive role in persuading the women to join the embassy to Sulla. The Vestals and the *flaminica Dialis* cooperated with one another on a variety of ritual occasions, including the Argei festival in May and the Vestalia in early June.[56] Other formal occasions, including pontifical banquets, provided ample opportunity for members of the college to create and solidify social bonds.[57] Perhaps as a result of interactions such as these, the Vestals stepped forward and petitioned Sulla to spare the *flamen Dialis*. The dictator's decision to listen to their plea underscores the influence they wielded even in times of great social and political turmoil. It may also suggest that he attributed their action to their loyalty to the state and its religious officials, rather than to a particular political stance.

Political Vestals during the Triumviral Period

The Vestals remained influential in Roman politics during the triumviral period and the early principate.[58] While we no longer hear about the political activities of individual Vestals, the order continues to appear in the historical record as a group. According to Cassius Dio, the Vestals prayed over the sacrifices in 40 BC in an effort to staunch the flow of slaves fleeing Italy to join Sex. Pompeius

---

hand, was likely from a patrician family, though it is difficult to determine where their political sympathies lay (Rüpke 2008: 672, No. 1577). Arruntia may also have joined the order by this year, but she would have been very young and almost certainly would not have participated in the embassy to Sulla (Rüpke 2008: 545, No. 722).

[53] Meier 1996: 86. For a survey of the political fortunes of the Julii Caesares in the republican period, see Badian 2009: 12–16.

[54] Vell. Pat. 2.43.1; Suet. *Iul.* 1.1.

[55] For the question of Caesar's inauguration, see also chapter 1.

[56] Gell. *N.A.* 10.15.30 (Argei); Ov. *Fast.* 6.227–234 (Vestalia).

[57] See chapter 6.

[58] Indeed, the prestige of the Vestal priesthood increased markedly under Augustus, who gave them new legal privileges and religious responsibilities (see chapters 4 and 6).

Magnus in Sicily (τοσοῦτοι γὰρ δὴ ηὐτομόλουν ὥστε καὶ τὰς ἀειπαρθένους καθ᾽ ἱερῶν εὔξασθαι ἐπισχεθῆναί σφων τὰς αὐτομολίας, 48.19.4). Though Dio reveals no further details, it is possible, perhaps even probable, that the Vestals acted on their own initiative.[59]

During the chaotic triumviral period, the Vestals were entrusted with the care of important legal documents, valuables, and even money.[60] The practice of depositing valuables and documents in temples was well established in the republican period.[61] Although it was equally common to give copies to friends, potentially contentious documents were typically deposited in a temple in order to ensure that the proper legal authority would have access to a legitimate copy.[62] Individual Romans may have regarded the Vestals as suitable custodians of their valuables for a variety of reasons. Their organization into a college of six members ensured that even if one priestess died, others would remain to care for the objects that had been deposited with them. The Vestals were also very closely attached to their temple, as they lived in the House of the Vestals within the same complex as the Temple of Vesta in the Forum. Furthermore, depositors might reasonably expect that the personal *sacrosanctitas* of the Vestals would guarantee the safety of any document left in their care. As we shall see, however, this was not always the case.

According to Suetonius, Caesar gave his will to the *virgo maxima*, the chief of the Vestal Virgins, who released it after his death in 44 BC.[63] A copy of the Pact of Misenum, a treaty signed in 39 BC by Sex. Pompeius and the members of the second triumvirate, was also sent to the Vestals for safe-keeping.[64] Perhaps the most infamous document entrusted to the Vestals, however, was the will of M. Antonius (cos. 44 BC). Octavian seized this document in 32 BC during his propaganda campaign against the *triumvir*, who was then living in Egypt with Cleopatra.[65] Plutarch describes the sequence of events as follows:

ἀπέκειντο δ᾽ αὗται παρὰ ταῖς Ἑστιάσι παρθένοις, καὶ Καίσαρος αἰτοῦντος οὐκ ἔδωκαν· εἰ δὲ βούλοιτο λαμβάνειν, ἐλθεῖν αὐτὸν ἐκέλευον. ἔλαβεν οὖν ἐλθών. (Plut. *Ant.* 58.3)

This will was on deposit with the Vestal Virgins, who refused to give it up when Caesar demanded it. But if he wished to take it, they advised him to come and do so. And so he went and took it.

---

[59] For a different interpretation of this episode, see Mekacher 2006: 69.
[60] For a brief discussion of the evidence, see Mekacher 2006: 42.
[61] For a discussion of the evidence, see Vidal 1965.
[62] Vidal 1965: 550–553, 560–563. The Temple of Castor was frequently used as a depository, though the Temple of Vesta was also popular during the triumviral period. According to Vidal (1965: 572), the temples of foreign deities such as Isis or Cybele were never used as depositories for valuables. This may indicate that Romans did not trust foreign deities as much as native Roman gods, or perhaps more importantly that they did not trust the priests of foreign cults, who were often foreign as well.
[63] Suet. *Iul.* 83.1.
[64] App. *B Civ.* 5.73; Cass. Dio. 48.37.1.
[65] For Octavian's propaganda campaign against Antony, see Osgood 2006: 353–357.

The seizure of Antony's will was the second violation of this kind since the creation of the triumvirate. According to Plutarch, the *triumviri* had confiscated money on deposit with the Vestals during the height of the proscriptions. In fact, Cassius Dio says that the violence and instability in the city prompted the Vestals to remove the sacred objects (ἱερά) from the Temple of Vesta.[66] Octavian's violation of the sanctity of the temple should certainly be viewed within the context of the excesses of the triumviral period.[67]

The Vestals' reply to Octavian's audacious request, however, suggests that they may have been sympathetic to his cause. Although they refused to surrender the will, which would have violated their pledge to protect it, they offered their tacit approval to its removal by inviting Octavian to enter the sanctuary in order to take it himself. If Plutarch's sources are correct, it must be acknowledged that the Vestals contributed to the manipulation of public opinion during the run-up to the final civil war.[68] The contents of the will bolstered Octavian's effort to depict Antony as a slave to Cleopatra who had lost touch with traditional Roman values. Plutarch tells us that Octavian read aloud in the senate particularly incriminating passages, including Antony's desire to be buried in Alexandria beside Cleopatra, "even if he should die in Rome" (κἂν ἐν Ῥώμῃ τελευτήσῃ, Plut. *Ant.* 58.4).[69] This shocking revelation, coupled with other damning testimony, was evidently enough to persuade the senate to declare war on Cleopatra.[70]

Historians have long debated the authenticity of the provisions contained in the document produced by Octavian.[71] Whether or not the publicized version was a forgery, there can be little doubt that Antony had deposited his will with the Vestals, otherwise Octavian would never have risked the censure he undoubtedly faced for admitting that he had removed it from their care. In any case, the fact that the document had been in their possession was apparently enough to guarantee its authenticity to the senate.[72] Antony's decision to entrust his will to the Vestals suggests that he had faith in their integrity and impartiality, an impressive testament to their importance in Roman society.

[66] Cass. Dio 42.31.3.

[67] Vidal (1965: 559) has suggested that after the death of Caesar, the Vestals were often entrusted with money and valuable documents because of the state of political unrest and insecurity in Rome. This episode demonstrates that no location was completely safe.

[68] Wildfang 2006: 100. As Crook (1957: 37, n. 13) has noted, however, the Vestals "are not likely to have been unanimously in collusion with Octavian." Once again, Plutarch's habit of referring to the Vestals as an undifferentiated group may be misleading.

[69] Plut. *Ant.* 58.6.

[70] Plut. *Ant.* 58–60.

[71] Syme (1939: 282), for instance, called the will "An opportune discovery—so opportune that forgery might be suspected, though the provisions of the will do not perhaps utterly pass belief." For arguments against the authenticity of the will, see Crook 1957, 1989. In favor of its authenticity, see Johnson 1978. Sirianni (1984) suggests that only some of the provisions were invented by Octavian.

[72] As Johnson stresses (1978: 496), none of the ancient sources indicate that there were suspicions about the will's authenticity.

Despite this unseemly episode in 32 BC, Augustus deposited the final version of his own will with the Vestals in AD 13, a decision that may have been guided by the close relationship he had cultivated with the order throughout his principate.[73] According to Tacitus and Suetonius, the Vestals themselves brought the will into a meeting of the senate where it was opened and read aloud, a gesture that undoubtedly contributed to the solemnity of the whole affair.[74] The Vestals had also been entrusted with several testamentary annexes written in Augustus' own hand.[75] These included detailed instructions for his funeral, an account of his achievements (the *Res Gestae Divi Augusti*), an assessment of the resources of the empire, and his famous admonition "to keep the empire within its present boundaries" (*coercendi intra terminos imperii*, Tac. *Ann.* 1.11). The *Res Gestae* in particular was critical to Augustus' efforts to shape his legacy and remains central to our perception of his principate. Prior to its publication, the text was in the care not of Livia or Tiberius, but of the Vestal Virgins.

Conclusion

The position of the Vestals in Roman society was unparalleled. They enjoyed a degree of respect and deference that was afforded to no woman outside their order before the principate of Augustus. Indeed, the exceptional nature of their status can be inferred from the fact that the public position of Livia, the wife of Augustus and first empress of Rome, and Octavia, his sister, was often closely modeled on that of the Vestals. Despite pressure to place the community first, individual Vestals used the prestige and privileges of their office to advance their own political agendas by defending and promoting the interests of relatives and other close associates. Like other elite Roman women, some Vestals were evidently quite loyal to their family members and willing to employ creative strategies to ensure their political success. These priestesses challenged the norms of their order and intervened in public life, often with spectacular results. Our ancient sources indicate that the Romans generally tolerated such behavior, though not without exception. Admittedly, the examples in this chapter may not be entirely representative. Claudia and Licinia were remembered precisely because Vestals did not normally behave in this way. Many priestesses may have lived relatively unobtrusive lives, abiding by the ideal and refraining from exercising their influence on behalf of family members. It seems very

[73] Tac. *Ann.* 1.8.1; Suet. *Aug.* 101.1; Cass. Dio 56.32.1. For Augustus' relationship to the Vestals, see above.
[74] Tac. Ann. 1.8.1; Suet. *Aug.* 101.1. Dio (56.32.1), on the other hand, says that Tiberius retrieved the testament from the Vestals and brought it to the senate himself.
[75] Suet. *Aug.* 101.1, 4; Tac. *Ann.* 1.11; Cass. Dio 56.33.1. See also Swan 2004: 314–315, with further bibliography.

likely, however, that these stories represent just the tip of the iceberg. At the very least, the ancient evidence demonstrates that we cannot treat the Vestals as socially constructed ciphers without any individual agency.[76] These women were adept social actors who understood how to use their position and its privileges to their advantage.

[76] The unintended consequence of Beard 1980; Staples 1998; Parker 2004.

Conclusion

The *pontifex* C. Aurelius Cotta (cos. 75 BC), who serves as the Academic spokesman in Cicero's *De natura deorum*, a dialogue concerning "the nature of the gods" written in 45 BC during the period of Caesar's dictatorship, provides the following classification of Roman religion:

> Cumque omnis populi Romani religio in sacra et in auspicia divisa sit, tertium adiunctum sit, si quid praedictionis causa ex portentis et monstris Sibyllae interpretes haruspicesve monuerunt. (3.5)

> As a whole, the religion of the Roman people is divided into ritual (*sacra*) and auspices (*auspicia*)—a third additional heading being the warnings produced concerning the future from portents and prodigies by the interpreters of the Sibyl [i.e., the *quindecemviri sacris faciundis*] and the *haruspices*.

However imperfectly this division reflects the complex religious landscape of ancient Rome, it provides a useful framework for a discussion of Roman priestesses. Cotta sets ritual action (*sacra*) opposite a range of strategies for consulting the gods, often grouped under the broad rubric "divination" in modern scholarship.[1] What were the ideological underpinnings of this division, and what do they reveal about the nature of priesthood in republican Rome?

Like all religious ritual, divinatory activities were widely distributed among the priestly, political, and military officials in ancient Rome. While the *auspicia* were the special concern of the college of augurs, the business of taking the auspices fell to the individual magistrate, who consulted the will of the gods at certain fixed moments in the exercise of his office. In fact, decisions about how to interpret and act upon signs from the gods often entailed cooperation among different groups of officials. The *quindecemviri* and the *haruspices*, for instance, could comment upon prodigies and recommend expiatory rites only if the senate asked them to do so. Despite the multiplicity of officials concerned with divination, a stark division along gender lines persisted. There were no female *haruspices* or *quindecemviri*, and women, who could not hold political office or lead an army on campaign, were never permitted to take the aus-

---

[1] For a general overview, see North 1990a.

pices.[2] Ascertaining the will of the gods was an integral part of the political process in republican Rome, and so it is not surprising to find the Romans unwilling to grant women such influence over the conduct of public business.

The exclusion of women from divinatory activities contrasts sharply with their authority to perform rituals (*sacra*) that ensured the welfare of the city and citizenry of Rome. In fact, the ancient evidence suggests that official religious service was the one area of public life in which Roman women assumed roles of equal legitimacy and comparable status to those of men. Although the specific ritual context was often different, priestesses performed many of the same religious rituals as male priests, as well as others unique to their specific priestly roles, and they did so in an official capacity.

As argued in the introduction, recovering female sacrificial capacity is an important step in writing the history of Rome's priestesses. At the same time, we risk constructing too narrow a view of their role if we define sacrifice, especially animal sacrifice, as "the central defining ritual of civic religious activity."[3] As the evidence considered in this book demonstrates, the search for a single "priestly" act is ultimately misguided. In addition to animal sacrifice, Roman priests and priestesses performed a wide variety of rituals. Prayer, for instance, was central to the practice of Roman religion. The Vestals tended the eternal flame on the hearth of Vesta and prepared *mola salsa*, the salted grain needed for the consecration of sacrificial victims. The Vestals and the *flaminica Dialis* also participated in important purification rituals, including the mysterious Argei festival. The *sallii* (and perhaps the *saliae* as well) danced through the city in celebratory processions in the month of March. The *antistites* of Bona Dea prepared herbal remedies in the temple pharmacy. Indeed, as Jörg Rüpke has written, the votive gift, despite its ubiquity, may be an "overrated element of ritual action."[4]

As Rüpke has stressed in his recent study of religion in republican Rome, "The complex topographic and calendrical structure of Roman religion necessitated a large number of priesthoods and agents that were coordinated rather than subordinated."[5] Religious officials could be individual men or women, members of a board of peers, or part of a two-person priestly couple.[6] In light of this remarkable variety, any single definition of the Roman "priest" must be abandoned in favor of one that emphasizes diversity and cooperation between officials. All religious activity, moreover, was tied to a precise social context, and so seemingly identical rituals took on different meanings depending upon the setting and the officiant.[7] Each priest and magistrate possessed the

---

[2] In the private sphere, of course, women could and did interpret dreams and omens; some even worked as professional diviners (see, for example, Plaut. *Mil.* 691–693).

[3] Beard, North, and Price 1998: 297.

[4] Rüpke 2007b: 100.

[5] Rüpke 2012c: 37.

[6] As stressed by Schultz 2006b: 16, 81.

[7] Scheid 1993: 55.

authority to perform only those rites assigned to his or her particular office. The Roman "priest," according to this interpretation, was defined by his or her institutional position, rather than by the type of ritual he or she carried out in a given situation. Public priests and priestesses were tasked with performing a specific ritual program on behalf of the community (or a subset of the whole).

Roman priesthood differs sharply from the Roman Catholic priesthood in this respect, to take just one relatively familiar counterexample. The Catholic church operates according to a strict functional hierarchy. Within that hierarchy, however, the authority to perform the Liturgy of the Eucharist may be multiplied exponentially without the ritual itself being fundamentally altered. Regardless of whether the Mass is celebrated by the pope at Saint Peter's in Vatican City, or by the parish priest at Saint Louis in Waco, Texas, the central sacrifice achieves the same purpose. This was only rarely the case in ancient Rome. With the exception of the major priestly colleges, whose members generally had the same ritual capacities, priests were not interchangeable. Rituals differed, not only according to scale and location, but also according to the deity addressed, the victim employed, the cast of support personnel, and the competence of the presiding official.

Priestly competence was constructed and expressed in different ways. The *sacerdos Cereris*, a Greek woman from southern Italy, was made a Roman citizen so that she could pray and sacrifice on behalf of citizens (*pro civibus*) "with the frame of mind of a native and a citizen" (*mente domestica et civili*, Cic. *Balb.* 55). The foreignness of the priestesses of Magna Mater, on the other hand, was preserved as thoroughly as possible. The Vestals were legally isolated from their birth families so that they could represent the entire community at the hearth of Vesta. Married priests like the *flamen* and *flaminica Dialis* held their office jointly so that they could perform complementary rites. Civic and marital status, therefore, worked together with gender to determine access to priestly office in ancient Rome.

Roman priestesses, moreover, could be relatively independent ritual actors. The ancient evidence shows that, like their male colleagues, they possessed "the knowledge of giving the gods their due" (*scientia colendorum deorum*, Cic. *Nat. D.* 1.116).[8] The Vestals, for instance, could advise the *pontifices* and the senate on matters related to their sphere of influence, as they did following the so-called Bona Dea scandal in 62 B.C. Older Vestals were also responsible for teaching the *sacra* to new initiates, who would in turn impart the traditions they had received to the next generation. The *sacerdos Cereris* was selected for her Greek *scientia*. In literature, priestesses are depicted as respected and knowledgeable women who understand and even influence sacred regulations within the cults they serve. Ovid's *flaminica Dialis*, for example, appears as a repository

---

[8] For a discussion of male priests as "specialists," see Marquardt 1885: 219–220; Wissowa 1912: 501; Beard 1990; Scheid 1993; Rüpke 1996.

of religious knowledge related to women's lives, particularly the days on which marriage ought to be avoided. Valeria, the first priestess of Fortuna Muliebris, is credited with instituting a rule prohibiting any woman who was not a *univira* from adorning the goddess's cult statue. All of this suggests that priestesses enjoyed a degree of autonomy and authority over the *sacra* entrusted to their care. Women were not simply tools of the male priestly hierarchy, but rather ritual agents in their own right.

The idea that women attained a more prominent role in society during and after the Hannibalic War has become axiomatic among scholars of Roman history. The evidence presented in this study, however, suggests that women had been an important part of civic religion from an early date. The Vestals, the *flaminicae*, the *regina sacrorum*, the curial priestesses, and the *saliae* all belong to what Fay Glinister has described as the "archaic religious complex," a constellation of offices that may have been in place long before Rome became a Republic.[9] Many of the same offices are also attested in Latium.[10] Roman women certainly exercised greater autonomy during the last two centuries of the Republic, but priestesses had been operating in the public sphere from the very beginning.

Admittedly, women who participated in civic cult were required to comply with the limitations imposed by traditional gender roles. Priesthoods filled by women reflect the fundamental organizing principles of Roman gender ideology: the *virgo* (virgin), the *matrona* (married woman), and the *univira* (one-man woman). The Vestals were career virgins. Like Verginia, whose silence in Livy's text underscores her status as an object of exchange between men, their sexuality was not their own.[11] A Vestal's inviolate body was a metaphor for the welfare of the city; every citizen had an interest in her absolute physical virginity. The structure of the flaminate of Jupiter and other priesthoods like it also underscores the gender asymmetry of Roman society. The *flaminica Dialis* was figured as a model *univira*. She had to be in the *manus* of her husband. Her signature saffron-colored veil, the *flammeum*, served as a symbol of marital fidelity and was consequently worn by the bride on her wedding day. Ritual practices and religious institutions reinforced certain restrictive notions of female identity, helping to produce "good" daughters, wives, and mothers. At the same time, Roman priestesses demonstrated that proper behavior for a woman entailed ritual action on behalf of the community.

[9] Glinister 2011: 111, 132.

[10] A *flamen Dialis* is attested at Lavinium (*CIL* 14.4176), Lanuvium (*ILS* 6196), and Tibur (*CIL* 14.3586), a *flamen Martialis* at Lavinium (*CIL* 14.4176), Lanuvium (*ILS* 6200), and Aricia (*CIL* 14.2169), and a *rex sacrorum* at Lanuvium (*CIL* 14.2089), Lenola (*AEpigr* 1952, 157), Bovilllae (*CIL* 14.2413), Formiae (*AEpigr* 1995, 279), and Tusculum (*CIL* 14.2634). Several of these cities also had *salii, saliae,* and Vestal Virgins. They may have imported these priesthoods from Rome, but it is also possible that Rome adopted them from their neighbors, or simply that the "archaic religious complex" was part of a common culture in early Latium (Beard, North, and Price 1998: 323; Delgado Delgado 2005: 122).

[11] Livy 3.44–58.

This study has shown that material remains that is capable of reshaping our understanding of women's religious activities. Priestly service offered women opportunities for leadership, prestige, and even, on occasion, authority, all in the name of maintaining the *pax deorum*. Some priestesses served cults that were restricted to women, but many men and women served the gods together. This principle applied at the level of household, local, and citywide cult. The *saliae virgines*, the female counterparts of the *salii*, demonstrate that cooperation between the genders was not limited to husbands and wives. In fact, in his symbolic picture of Rome's permanence and his own poetic immortality, Horace links the *pontifex* and the Vestal, and he positions both on the Capitol. In cults operating within the public sphere, women were neither marginal nor incidental. Rather, they served as indispensable participants in a fundamentally cooperative endeavor.

BIBLIOGRAPHY

Journal titles are abbreviated according to the conventions in *L'Année Philologique*.

Adams, J. N. 1990. *The Latin Sexual Vocabulary*. London.

Albanese, B. 1969. "Il 'trinoctium' del flamen Dialis." *SDHI* 35: 73–98.

Albertson, F. C. 1990. "The Basilica Aemilia Frieze: Religion and Politics in Late Republican Rome." *Latomus* 49: 801–815.

Altheim, F. 1938. *A History of Roman Religion*. Translated by H. Mattingly. London.

Alton, E. H., D.E.W. Wormell and E. Courtney. 1973. "Problems in Ovid's *Fasti*." *CQ* 23: 144–151.

Ando, C. 2008. *The Matter of the Gods: Religion and the Roman Empire*. Berkeley.

———. 2009. "Evidence and Orthopraxy." Review article of John Scheid, *Quand faire, c'est croire. Les rites sacrificiels des Romains*, Paris: Aubier, 2005. *JRS* 99: 171–181.

André, J. 1949. *Étude sur les termes de couleur dans la langue latine*. Paris.

———. 1964. "Arbor felix, arbor infelix," in *Hommages à Jean Bayet*, edited by M. Renard and R. Schilling, 35–46. Brussels.

Appel, G. 1909. *De Romanorum precationibus*. Giessen.

Aron, G. 1904. *Études sur la condition juridique des prêtres à Rome. Les vestales et le flamine de Jupiter*. Paris.

Badian, E. 1961. Review of *Caesar. Der Politiker und Staatsmann. Sechste, bearbeitete und erweiterte Auflage*, by M. Gelzer. *Gnomon* 33: 597–600.

———. 1990. Review of *Caesar*, by C. Meier. *Gnomon* 62: 22–39.

———. 2009. "From the Iulii to Caesar," in *A Companion to Julius Caesar*, edited by M. Griffin, 11–22. Malden.

Bagnall, R. S. and B. W. Frier. 1994. *The Demography of Roman Egypt*. Cambridge.

Barney, S. A., J. A. Beach, and O. Berghof, with the collaboration of M. Hall. 2006. *The Etymologies of Isidore of Seville*. Cambridge.

Barrett, A. A. 2002. *Livia: First Lady of Imperial Rome*. New Haven.

Bartman, E. 1999. *Portraits of Livia: Imaging the Imperial Woman in Augustan Rome*. Cambridge.

———. 2001. "Hair and the Artifice of Roman Female Adornment." *AJA* 105: 1–25.

Baschirotto, S. 2012. "Vesta and the Vestals, Protectors of Rome," in Demeter, Isis, Vesta, and Cybele: Studies in Greek and Roman Religion in Honour of Giulia Sfameni Gasparro, edited by A. Mastrocinque and C. G. Scibona, 165–181. Stuttgart.

Bätz, A. 2012. *Sacrae virgines. Studien zum religiösen und gesellschaftlichen Status der Vestalinnen*. Paderborn.

Baudy, D. 1998. *Römische Umgangsriten. Eine ethologische Untersuchung der Funktion von Wiederholung für religiöses Verhalten*. Berlin.

Bauman, R. A. 1981. "Tribunician Sacrosanctity in 44, 36 and 35 BC." *RhM* 124: 166–183.

———. 1992. *Women and Politics in Ancient Rome*. London.

Beard, M. 1980. "The Sexual Status of Vestal Virgins." *JRS* 70: 12–27.

———. 1987. "A Complex of Times: No More Sheep on Romulus' Birthday." *PCPhS* 33: 1–15.

———. 1990. "Priesthood in the Roman Republic," in *Pagan Priests: Religion and Power in the Ancient World*, edited by M. Beard and J. North, 17–48. Ithaca.

———. 1994. "The Roman and the Foreign: The Cult of the "Great Mother" in Imperial Rome," in *Shamanism, History, and the State*, edited by N. Thomas and C. Humphrey, 164–190. Ann Arbor.

———. 1995. "Re-reading Vestal Virginity," in *Women in Antiquity: New Assessments*, edited by R. Hawley and B. Levick, 166–177. New York.

———. 1998. "Documenting Roman Religion," in *La mémoire perdue. Recherches sur l'administration romaine*, edited by C. Moatti, 75–101. Rome.

———. 2004. "Writing Ritual: The Triumph of Ovid," in Rituals in Ink, edited by A. Barchiesi, J. Rüpke, and S. Stephens, 115–126. Stuttgart.

———. 2007. *The Roman Triumph*. Cambridge.

Beard, M. and J. North. 1990. *Pagan Priests: Religion and Power in the Ancient World*. Ithaca.

Beard, M., J. North, and S. Price. 1998. *Religions of Rome*. 2 volumes. Cambridge.

Bell, C. 1997. *Ritual: Perspectives and Dimensions*. New York.

Bendlin, A. 2000. "Looking Beyond the Civic Compromise: Religious Pluralism in Late Republican Rome," in *Religion in Archaic and Republican Rome and Italy: Evidence and Experience*, edited by E. Bispham and C. Smith, 115–125. Edinburgh.

———. 2001. "Rituals or Beliefs? 'Religion' and the Religious Life of Rome (W. Mary Beard, John A. North, Simon R. F. Price, *Religions of Rome*; J.A. North, *Roman Religion*)." *SCI* 20: 191–208.

———. 2002. "Mundus Cereris: Eine kultische Institution zwischen Mythos und Realität," in *Epitomē tes oikoumenēs: Studien zur römischen Religion in Antike und Gegenwart*, edited by C. Auffarth and J. Rüpke, 37–73. Stuttgart.

———. 2008. "Rex sacrorum." *BNP* 12: 515–517.

———. 2010. "Volcanus." *BNP* 15: 496–498.

Bendlin, A., et al. 1993. "Priesthoods in Mediterranean Religions: Review article of *Pagan Priests: Religion and Power in the Ancient World*, edited by M. Beard and J. North." *Numen* 40: 82–94.

Bernstein, F. 1997. "Verständnis- und Entwicklungsstufen der archaischen Consualia. Römisches Substrat und griechische Überlagerung." *Hermes* 125: 413–446.

Besnier, M. 1902. L'Ile Tibérine dans l'antiquité. Paris.

Billows, R. 1993. "The Religious Procession of the Ara Pacis Augustae: Augustus' *Supplicatio* in 13 BC." *JRA* 6: 80–92.

Blundell, S. 1995. *Women in Ancient Greece*. Cambridge.

Blundell, S. and M. Williamson, eds. 1998. *The Sacred and the Feminine in Ancient Greece*. New York.

Boak, A.E.R. 1916. "The *Magistri* of Campania and Delos." *CPh* 11: 25–45.

Boatwright, M. T. 2011. "Women and Gender in the Forum Romanum." *TAPA* 141: 105–141.

Bodel, J. 2000. "Dealing with the Dead: Undertakers, Executioners and Potter's Fields in Ancient Rome," in *Death and Disease in the Ancient City*, edited by V. M. Hope and E. Marshall, 128–151. London.

———. 2008. "Cicero's Minerva, *Penates*, and the Mother of the *Lares*: An Outline of Roman Domestic Religion," in *Household and Family Religion in Antiquity*, edited by J. Bodel and S. M. Olyan, 248–275. Malden.

Bodel, J. and S. M. Olyan, eds. 2008. Household and Family Religion in Antiquity. Malden.

Boels, N. 1973. "Le statut religieux de la *flaminica Dialis*." *REL* 51: 77–100.

Boëls-Janssen, N. 1989. "La prêtresse aux trois voiles." *REL* 67: 117–133.

———. 1991. "Flaminica cincta. A propos de la couronne rituelle de l'épouse de flamine de Jupiter." *REL* 69: 32–50.

———. 1993. *La vie religieuse des matrones dans la Rome archaïque*. Rome.

———. 1996. "L'interdit des *bis nuptae* dans les cultes matronaux: sens et formulation." *REL* 74: 47–66.

———. 2008. "Le double mythe de la Bona Dea," in *Epiphania: études orientales, grecques et latines offertes à Aline Pourkier*, edited by E. Oudot and F. Poli, 273–295. Paris.

Böhm, S. 2003. "Gottesdienst im antiken Rom. Reine Männersache?," in *Geschlechter-differenz, Ritual und Religion*, edited by E. Klinger, S. Böhm, and T. Franz, 79–103. Würzburg.

Bömer, F. 1987. "Wie ist Augustus mit Vesta verwandt?" *Gymnasium* 94: 525–528.

Bonanno, A. 1979. "Paris, Pelops, Hieron II or a Roman Flamen?" *MÉFRA* 91: 343–353.

Bonfante, L. 1981. "Etruscan Couples and their Aristocratic Society," in *Reflections of Women in Antiquity*, edited by H. P. Foley, 323–343. New York.

———. 1994. "Introduction," in *The World of Roman Costume*, edited by J. L. Sebesta and L. Bonfante, 3–10. Madison.

———. 2003. *Etruscan Dress*. Updated edition. Baltimore.

———. 2009. "Ritual Dress," in *Votives, Places and Rituals in Etruscan Religion: Studies in Honor of Jean MacIntosh Turfa*, edited by M. Gleba and H. Becker, 183–191. Leiden.

Bonfante-Warren, L. 1973. "Roman Costumes: A Glossary, and Some Etruscan Derivations." *ANRW* 1.4: 584–614.

Bonjour, M. 1975. "Les personnages féminins et la terre natale dans l'épisode de Coriolanus (Liv., 2, 40)." *REL* 53: 157–181.

Borgna, E. 1993. "Ancile e arma ancilia. Considerazioni intorno allo scudo dei Salii." *Ostraka* 2: 9–42.

Borkowski, A. 1994. *Textbook on Roman Law*. London.

Botsford, G. W. 1909. *The Roman Assemblies from their Origin to the End of the Republic*. New York.

Bouché-Leclercq, A. 1871. *Les pontifes de l'ancienne Rome*. Paris.

Bowersock, G. 1990. "The Pontificate of Augustus," in *Between Republic and Empire: Interpretations of Augustus and His Principate*, edited by K. Raaflaub and M. Toher, 380–394. Berkeley.

Boyce, G. K. 1937. *Corpus of the Lararia of Pompeii. MAAR* 14. Rome.

Bradley, K. R. 1991a. *Discovering the Roman Family*. Oxford.

————. 1991b. "Remarriage and the Structure of the Upper-Class Roman Family," in *Marriage, Divorce, and Children in Ancient Rome*, edited by B. Rawson, 79–98. Oxford.

Bradley, M. and K. Stow, eds. 2012. *Rome, pollution, and propriety: dirt, disease, and hygiene in the eternal city from antiquity to modernity*. Cambridge.

Brelich, A. 1949. *Vesta*. Zurich.

Bremmer, J. N. 1987a. "Romulus, Remus and the Foundation of Rome," in *Roman Myth and Mythography*, edited by J. N. Bremmer and N. M. Horsfall, 25–48. London.

————. 1987b. "The Old Women of Ancient Greece," in *Sexual Asymmetry: Studies in Ancient Society*, edited by J. Blok and P. Mason, 191–213. Amsterdam.

————. 1993. "Three Roman Aetiological Myths," in *Mythos in mythenloser Gesellschaft: das Paradigma Roms*, edited by F. Graf, 158–174. Stuttgart.

————. 1998. "'Religion,' 'Ritual' and the Opposition of 'Sacred vs. Profane,'" in *Ansichten griechischer Rituale: Geburtstag-Symposium für Walter Burkert*, edited by F. Graf, 9–32. Stuttgart.

Brennan, T. C. 1996. "Triumphus in Monte Albano," in *Transitions to Empire: Essays in Greco-Roman History, 360–146 BC in honor of E. Badian*, edited by R. W. Wallace and E. M. Harris, 315–137. Norman.

————. 2000. *The Praetorship in the Roman Republic*. 2 volumes. Oxford.

Briquel, D. 2003. "Augures." *BNP* 2: 339–341.

Broughton, A. L. 1936. "The Menologia Rustica." *CPh* 31: 353–356.

Broughton, T.R.S. 1951. *The Magistrates of the Roman Republic*. 2 vols. New York.

Brouwer, H.H.J. 1989. *Bona Dea: The Sources and a Description of the Cult*. Leiden.

Brouwers, A. 1933. "A propos de la formule de la "captio" des Vestales." *Revue belge de philologie et d'histoire* 12: 1080–1082.

Bruhl, A. 1953. *Liber pater: Origines et expansion du culte dionysiaque à Rome et dans le monde romain*. Paris.

Brumfield, A. C. 1981. *The Attic Festivals of Demeter and their Relationship to the Agricultural Year*. New York.

Brunt, P. A. 1971. *Italian Manpower, 225 BC–AD 14*. Oxford.

Buckland, W. W. 1963. A Textbook of Roman Law from Augustus to Justinian. Revised by P. Stein. 3rd edition. Cambridge.

Burkert, W. 1985. *Greek Religion: Archaic and Classical*. Translated by John Raffar. Oxford.

Butler, J. 1990. *Gender Trouble: Feminism and the Subversion of Identity*. New York.

Butler, M. and W. Paisley. 1980. "Coordinated-Career Couples: Convergence and Divergence," in *Dual-Career Couples*, edited by F. Pepitone-Rockwell, 207–228. Beverly Hills.

Cameron, A. 1966. "The Date and Identity of Macrobius." *JRS* 56: 25–38.

————. 2010. "The Date of the Scholia Vetustiora on Juvenal." *CQ* 60: 569–576.

————. 2011. *The Last Pagans of Rome*. Oxford.

Cancik-Lindemaier, H. 1990. "Kultische Privilegierung und gesellschaftliche Realität: Ein Beitrag zur Sozialgeschichte der Virgines Vestae." *Saeculum* 41: 1–16.

————. 1996a. "Der Diskurs Religion im Senatsbeschluss über die Bacchanalia von 186 v. Chr. Und bei Livius," in *Geschichte-Tradition-Reflexion. Festschrift M. Hengel*, vol. 2, edited by H. Cancik, H. Lichtenberger, and P. Schäfer, 77–96. Tübingen.

————. 1996b. "Priestly and Female Roles in Roman Religion: The *virgines Vestae.*" *Hyperboreus* 2: 138–150.

————. 2010. "Vestals." *BNP* 15: 340–342.

Cappelli, R. 1990. "Augusto e il culto di Vesta sul Palatino." *BdArch* 1–2: 29–33.

Caprioli, F. 2007. *Vesta Aeterna: l'Aedes Vestae e la sua decorazione architettonica.* Rome.

Carandini, A. 1997. *La nascita di Roma: Dei, lari, eroi, uomini all'alba di una civiltà.* 2 volumes. Turin.

Catalano, P. 1960. *Contributi allo Studio del Diritto Augurale.* Turin.

Cecamore, C. 1994–1995. "Apollo e Vesta sul Palatino fra Augusto e Vespasiano." *BullCom* 96: 9–32.

Champeaux, J. 1982. *Fortuna: Recherches sur le culte de la Fortune à Rome et dans le monde romain des origines à la mort de César I: Fortuna dans la religion archaïque.* Rome.

Champlin, E. 1991. *Final Judgments: Duty and Emotion in Roman Wills, 200 BC–AD 250.* Berkeley.

Chandler, T. 2012. "Seneca, *On Leisure.*" *Colloquy* 23: 214–22.

Chioffi, L. 1993. "Bona Dea Subsaxana." *LTUR* I: 200–201.

Cichorius, C. 1922. *Römische Studien.* Leipzig.

Cirilli, R. 1913. *Les prêtres danseurs de Rome: étude sur la corporation sacerdotale des Saliens.* Paris.

Clark, E. A. 2004. "Engendering the Study of Religion," in *The Future of the Study of Religion: Proceedings of Congress 2000,* edited by S. Jakelić and L. Pearson, 217–242. Leiden.

Clarke, J. 2003. *Imagery of Colour & Shining in Catullus, Propertius & Horace.* New York.

Clarke, J. R. 2003. *Art in the Lives of Ordinary Romans: Visual Representation and Non-Elite Viewers in Italy, 100 BC–AD 315.* Berkeley.

Cleland, L., M. Harlow and L. Llewellyn-Jones. 2005. *The Clothed Body in the Ancient World.* Oxford.

Coarelli, F. 1983. *Il Foro Romano. 1: Il period arcaico.* Rome.

————. 1994. *Roma.* Milan.

————. 1995. "Flora, Templum (In Colle)." *LTUR* 2: 254.

————. 1999a. "Porta Stercoraria." *LTUR* 4: 115–116.

————. 1999b. "Quirinus, Aedes." *LTUR* 4: 185–187.

————. 2007. *Rome and Environs: An Archaeological Guide.* Translated by J. J. Clauss and D. P. Harmon. Illustrations adapted by J. A. Clauss and P. A. MacKay. Berkeley.

Colantoni, E. 2012. "Polarities in Religious Life: Male/Female in the Roman World." *ThesCRA* 8: 270–282.

Conlin, D. A. 1997. *The Artists of the Ara Pacis: The Process of Hellenization in Roman Relief Sculpture.* Chapel Hill.

Connelly, J. B. 2007. *Portrait of a Priestess: Women and Ritual in Ancient Greece.* Princeton.

Cooper, K. 1996. *The Virgin and the Bride: Idealized Womanhood in Late Antiquity.* Cambridge.

Corbett, P. E. 1930. *The Roman Law of Marriage.* Oxford.

Cornell, T. J. 1975. "Aeneas and the Twins: The Development of the Roman Foundation Legend." *PCPhS* 21: 1–32.

———. 1981. "Some Observations on the *Crimen Incesti*," in *Le délit religieux dans la cité antique. Actes de la table ronde de Rome (6–7 avril 1978)*, edited by M. Torelli, 27–37. Rome.

———. 1995. *The Beginnings of Rome: Italy and Rome from the Bronze Age to the Punic Wars (c. 1000–264 BC)*. New York.

———, ed. 2013. *The Fragments of the Roman Historians*. 3 volumes. Oxford.

Crawford, J. W. 1984. *M. Tullius Cicero: The Lost and Unpublished Orations*. Göttingen.

Crawford, M. H. 1974. *Roman Republican Coinage*. 2 volumes. Cambridge.

Crook, J. 1957. "A Legal Point about Mark Antony's Will." *JRS* 47: 36–38.

———. 1967. "Patria Potestas." *CQ* 17: 113–122.

———. 1989. "A Negative Point about Mark Antony's Will." *AC* 58: 221–223.

Croom, A. T. 2002. *Roman Clothing and Fashion*. Charleston.

Cubberly, A. 1995. "Bread-baking in Ancient Italy: *clibanus* and *sub testu* in the Roman World," in *Food in Antiquity*, edited by J. Wilkins, D. Harvey and M. Dobson, 55–68. Exeter.

Culham, P. 1982. "The *Lex Oppia*." *Latomus* 41: 786–793.

———. 1990. "Decentering the Text: The Case of Ovid." *Helios* 17: 161–170.

———. 2004. "Women in the Roman Republic," in *The Cambridge Companion to the Roman Republic*, edited by H. I. Flower, 139–159. Cambridge.

Curti, E. 2000. "From Concordia to the Quirinal: Notes on Religion and Politics in Mid Republican/Hellenistic Rome," in *Religion in Archaic and Republican Rome and Italy: Evidence and Experience*, edited by E. Bispham and C. Smith, 77–91. Edinburgh.

Cyrino, M. S. 1998. "Heroes in D(u)ress: Transvestism and Power in the Myths of Herakles and Achilles." *Arethusa* 31: 207–241.

D'Arms, J. H. 1981. *Commerce and Social Standing in Ancient Rome*. Cambridge.

———. 2004. "The Culinary Reality of Roman Upper-Class Convivia: Integrating Texts and Images." *Comparative Studies in Society and History* 46: 428–450.

de Cazanove, O. 1987. "'Exesto.' L'incapaicité sacrificielle des femmes à Rome (à propos de Plutarque *Quaest. Rom.* 85)." *Phoenix* 41: 159–173.

Degrassi, A. 1955. "Esistette sul Palatino un tempio di Vesta?" *MDAI(R)* 62: 144–154.

———. 1963. *Inscriptiones Italiae XIII: Fasti et Elogia, Fasc. II: Fasti Anni Numani et Iuliani*. Rome.

———. 1966–1967. "La dimora di Augusto sul Palatino e la base di Sorrento." *RendPontAcc* 39: 77–116.

Delgado Delgado, J. A. 2005. "Priests of Italy and the Latin provinces." *ThesCRA* 5: 116–139.

de Ligt, L. 1993. *Fairs and Markets in the Roman Empire: Economic and Social Aspects of Trade in a Pre Industrial Society*. Amsterdam.

Demougin, S. 1988. *L'ordre équestre sous les Julio-Claudiens*. Rome.

De Robertis, F. M. 1963. *Lavoro e lavoratori nel mondo romano*. Bari.

Detienne, M. 1989. "The violence of well-born ladies: women in the Thesmophoria," in *The Cuisine of Sacrifice Among the Greeks*, edited by M. Detienne and J.-P. Vernant, 129–147. Translated by P. Wissing. Chicago.

Dickie, M. 2001. *Magic and Magicians in the Greco-Roman World*. New York.

Dillon, M. 2002. *Girls and Women in Classical Greek Religion*. New York.

Dixon, J. 2014. "Dressing the Adulteress," in *Greek and Roman Textiles and Dress: An Interdisciplinary Anthology*, edited by M. Harlow and M.-L. Nosch, 298–305. Philadelphia.

Dixon, S. 1983. "A Family Business: Women's Role in Patronage and Politics at Rome 80–44 BC." *C&M* 34: 91–112.

———. 1985. "The Marriage Alliance in the Roman Elite." *Journal of Family History* 10: 353–378.

———. 1998. *The Roman Mother*. Norman.

———. 2001. *Reading Roman Women: Sources, Genres, and Real Life*. London.

———. 2007. *Cornelia, Mother of the Gracchi*. New York.

Dolansky, F. 2011a. "Celebrating the Saturnalia: Religious Ritual and Domestic Life," in *A Companion to Families in the Greek and Roman Worlds*, edited by B. Rawson, 488–503. Chichester.

———. 2011b. "Honouring the Family Dead on the Parentalia: Ceremony, Spectacle, and Memory." *Phoenix* 65: 125–157.

———. 2011c. "Reconsidering the Matronalia and Women's Rites." *CW* 104: 191–209.

Dorcey, P. 1989. "The Role of Women in the Cult of Silvanus." *Numen* 36: 143–155.

Douglas, M. 1966. *Purity and Danger*. London.

———. 1970. *Natural Symbols*. New York.

Dragendorff, H. 1896. "Die Amtstracht der Vestalinnen." *RhM* 51: 281–302.

Drine, A. 1994. "Cérès, les *Cereres* et les *sacerdotes magnae* en Afrique: quelques témoignages épigraphiques et littéraires (Tertullien)," in *L'Afrique, la Gaule, la Religion à l'époque romaine. Mélanges à la mémoire de Marcel Le Glay*, edited by Y. Le Bohec, 174–184. Brussels.

Dubourdieu, A. 1989. *Les origines et le développement du culte des Pénates à Rome*. Rome.

———. 2008. "Quirinus." *BNP* 12: 359–360.

Dumézil, G. 1935. *Flamen-Brahman*. Paris.

———. 1963. "QII 18, *Te, amata capio*." *REL* 41: 89–91.

———. 1970. *Archaic Roman Religion*. 2 volumes. Translated by P. Krapp. Chicago.

———. 1975. *Fêtes romaines d'été et d'automne*. Paris.

Dunbabin, K.M.D. 2003. *The Roman Banquet: Images of Conviviality*. Cambridge.

Dyck, A. R. 1996. *A Commentary on Cicero, De Officiis*. Ann Arbor.

Eckstein, A. M. 1982. "Human Sacrifice and Fear of Military Disaster in Republican Rome." *AJAH* 7: 69–95.

Eder, W. 1980. *Servitus publica. Untersuchungen zur Entstehung, Entwicklung und Funktion der öffentlichen Sklaverei in Rom*. Wiesbaden.

Edgeworth, R. J. 1992. *The Colors of the Aeneid*. New York.

Edlund-Berry, I. E. M. 1994. "Whether Goddess, Priestess or Worshipper: Considerations of Female Deities and Cults in Roman Religion," in *Opus Mixtum: Essays in Ancient Art and Society*, edited by B. Alroth, 25–33. Stockholm.

———. 2006. "Hot, Cold, or Smelly: The Power of Sacred Water in Roman Religion, 400–100 B.C," in *Religion in Republican Italy*, edited by C. E. Schultz and P. B. Harvey, 162–180. Cambridge.

Edmondson, J. and A. Keith. 2008. *Roman Dress and the Fabrics of Roman Culture*. Toronto.

Eitrem, S. 1923. "G. Gracchus und die Furien." *Philologus* 78: 183–187.

Elvers, K.-L. 2005. "Laenas." *BNP* 7: 168.

Erdkamp, P. 2005. *The Grain Market in the Roman Empire: A Social, Political, and Economic Study*. Cambridge.

Ernout, A. and A. Meillet. 1959. *Dictionnaire étymologique de la langue latine*. 4th edition. Paris.

Estienne, S. 2005a. "Définitions." *ThesCRA* 5: 67–68.

———. 2005b. "Prêtres des subdivisions du peuple romain." *ThesCRA* 5: 110–112.

———. 2005c. "Saliens (*Salii Palatini, Salii Collini*)." *ThesCRA* 5: 85–87.

Fantham, E. 1998. *Ovid Fasti Book IV*. Cambridge.

———. 2002. "The *Fasti* as a Source for Women's Participation in Roman Cult," in *Ovid's Fasti*, edited by G. Herbert-Brown, 23–46. Oxford.

———. 2008. "Covering the Head at Rome: Ritual and Gender," in *Roman Dress and the Fabrics of Roman Culture*, edited by J. Edmondson and A. Keith, 158–171. Toronto.

Feeney, D. 1998. *Literature and Religion at Rome*. Cambridge.

———. 2004. "Interpreting Sacrificial Ritual in Roman Poetry: Disciplines and their Models," in *Rituals in Ink*, edited by A. Barchiesi, J. Rüpke and S. Stephens, 9–29. Stuttgart.

———. 2007. *Caesar's Calendar: Ancient Time and the Beginnings of History*. Berkeley.

Feeney, D. and J. T. Katz. 2006. "Review of *The World of Roman Song: From Ritualized Speech to Social Order*, by T. Habinek." *JRS* 96: 240–242.

Feig Vishnia, Rachel. 1996. *State, Society and Popular Leaders in Mid-Republican Rome 241–167 BC*. New York.

Felletti Maj, B. M. 1977. *La tradizione italica nell'arte romana*. Rome.

Finley, M. I. 1973. *The Ancient Economy*. London.

Fishwick, D. 1966. "The *Cannophori* and the March Festival of Magna Mater." *TAPA* 97: 193–202.

———. 1993. "A Temple of Vesta on the Palatine?" *Antiquitas* 18: 51–57.

Flemming, R. 2007. "Festus and the Role of Women in Roman Religion," in *Verrius, Festus & Paul: Lexicography, Scholarship and Society*, edited by F. Glinister and C. Woods, with J. A. North and M. H. Crawford, 87–108. London.

Fless, F. 1995. *Opferdiener und Kultmusiker auf stadtrömischen historischen Reliefs: Untersuchungen zur Ikonographie, Funktion und Benennung*. Mainz.

Flory, M. B. 1996. "The Symbolism of Laurel in Cameo Portraits of Livia." *MAAR*: 43–68.

Flower, H. I. 1996. *Ancestor Masks and Aristocratic Power in Roman Culture*. Oxford.

———. 2002a. "Rereading the *Senatus Consultum de Bacchanalibus* of 186 BC: Gender Roles in the Roman Middle Republic," in *Oikistes: Studies in Constitutions, Colonies, and Military Power in the Ancient World*, edited by V. B. Gorman and E. W. Robinson, 79–98. Leiden.

———. 2002b. "Were Women ever 'Ancestors' in Republican Rome?," in *Images of Ancestors*, edited by J. Munk Højte, Aarhus Studies in Mediterranean Antiquity 5, 157–182. Aarhus.

———. 2008. "Remembering and Forgetting Temple Destruction: the Destruction of the Temple of Jupiter Optimus Maximus in 83 BC," in *Antiquity in Antiquity: Jewish and Christian Pasts in the Greco-Roman World*, edited by G. Gardner and K. L. Osterloh, 74–92. Tübingen.

Forbis, E. P. 1990. "Women's Public Image in Italian Honorary Inscriptions." *AJPh* 111: 493–512.

Forsythe, G. 2005. *A Critical History of Early Rome: From Prehistory to the First Punic War*. Berkeley.

Foss, P. 1997. "Watchful *Lares*: Roman Household Organization and the Rituals of Cooking and Eating," in *Domestic Space in the Roman World: Pompeii and Beyond*, edited by R. Laurence and A. Wallace-Hadrill, 196–218. Portsmouth.

Fowler, W. W. 1895. "Was the Flaminica Dialis Priestess of Juno?" *CR* 9: 474–476.

———. 1899. *The Roman Festivals of the Period of the Republic*. London.

———. 1902. "Dr. Wissowa on the Argei." *CR* 16: 115–119.

Foxhall, L. 2013. *Studying Gender in Classical Antiquity*. Cambridge.

Fraschetti, A. 1984. "La sepolutura delle vestali e la città," in *Du châtiment dans la cité: Supplices corporels et peine de mort dans le monde antique*, CEFR 79, 97–128. Rome.

———. 1988. "'Cognata numina:' Culti della città e cult della casa del principe in epoca augustea." *StudStor* 29: 941–965.

Frayn, J. M. 1978. "Home-baking in Roman Italy." *Antiquity* 52: 28–33.

———. 1993. *Markets and Fairs in Roman Italy: Their Social and Economic Importance from the Second Century B.C. to the Third Century A.D.* Oxford.

Frazer, J. G. 1885. "The Prytaneum, the Temple of Vesta, the Vestals, Perpetual Fires." *Journal of Philology* 14: 145–172.

———. 1929. *The Fasti of Ovid*. 4 volumes. London.

Frederiksen, M. W. 1959. "Republican Capua: A Social and Economic Study." *PBSR* 27: 80–130.

———. 1984. *Campania*. Edited by N. Purcell. London.

Freier, H. 1963. *Caput Velare*. Diss. Universität Tübingen. Tübingen.

Frei-Stolba, R. 1998. "Flavia Publicia, virgo Vestalis maxima. Zu den Inschriften des Atrium Vestae," in *Imperium Romanum: Studien zu Geschichte und Rezeption. Festschrift für Karl Christ zum 75. Geburtstag*, 233–251. Stuttgart.

Frier, B. W. 1999. *Libri Annales Pontificum Maximorum: The Origins of the Annalistic Tradition*. 2nd edition. Ann Arbor.

Fröhlich, T. 1991. *Lararien und Fasadenbilder in den Vesuvustädten*. Mainz.

Fullerton, M. D. 1990. *The Archaistic Style in Roman Statuary*. Leiden.

Fulminante, F. 2014. *The Urbanisation of Rome and Latium Vetus*. Cambridge.

Gabba, E. 1991. *Dionysius and the History of Archaic Rome*. Berkeley.

Gagé, J. 1963. *Matronalia*. Brussels.

Gallia, A. B. 2012. *Remembering the Roman Republic: Culture, Politics and History under the Principate*. Cambridge.

———. 2014. "The Vestal Habit." *CPh* 109: 222–240.

———. 2015. "Vestal Virgins and their Families." *ClaAnt* 34: 74–120.

Gardner, J. 1986. *Women in Roman Law and Society*. Bloomington.

———. 1998. *Family and* Familia *in Roman Law and Life*. Oxford.

Garland, R. 1984. "Religious Authority in Archaic and Classical Athens." *ABSA* 79: 75–123.

———. 1990. *The Greek Way of Life*. Ithaca.

Gaspar, V. 2011. "Status and Gender in the Priesthood of Ceres in Roman North Africa," in *Priests and State in the Roman World*, edited by J. H. Richardson and F. Santangelo, 471–500. Stuttgart.

———. 2012. *Sacerdotes piae: Priestesses and other female cult officials in the western part of the Roman Empire from the first century B.C. until the third century A.D.* Diss. University of Amsterdam. Amsterdam.

Gelzer, M. 1968. *Caesar: Politician and Statesman*. Translated by P. Needham. Cambridge.

Giacobello, F. 2008. *Larari pompeiani: Iconografia e culto dei Lari in ambito domestico*. Milan.

Giannecchini, G. 1980–1981. "Seni crines." *AFLPer* 4: 91–92.

Giannelli, G. 1913. *Il sacerdozio delle vestali romane*. Florence.

Giovannini, M. J. 1981. "Woman: A Dominant Symbol Within the Cultural System of a Sicilian Town." *Man* 16: 408–426.

Girard, P. F. 1911. *Manuel elémentaire de droit romain*. 5th edition. Paris.

Giuliano, A. 1953. "Fuit apud Segestanos ex aere Dianae simulacrum." *ArchCl* 5: 48–54.

Gizewski, C. 2005. "Lictor." *BNP* 7: 543–544.

Gladigow, B. 1970. "Condictio und Inauguratio. Ein Beitrag zur römischen Sakralverfassung." *Hermes* 98: 369–379.

———. 1972. "Die sakralen Funktionen der Liktoren. Zum Problem von institutioneller Macht und sakraler Präsentation." *ANRW* 1.2: 295–314.

Glinister, F. 2007. "Constructing the Past," in *Verrius, Festus, & Paul: Lexicography, Scholarship and Society*, edited by F. Glinister and C. Woods, with J. A. North and M. H. Crawford, 11–32. London.

———. 2011. "Bring on the Dancing Girls," in *Priests and State in the Roman World*, edited by J. H. Richardson and F. Santangelo, 107–136. Stuttgart.

Glinster, F. and C. Woods, eds., with J. A. North and M. H. Crawford. 2007. *Verrius, Festus, & Paul: Lexicography, Scholarship and Society*. London.

Goff, B. 2004. *Citizen Bacchae: Women's Ritual Practice in Ancient Greece*. Berkeley.

Golden, M. and P. Toohey, eds. 2011. *A Cultural History of Sexuality, Volume 1: A Cultural History of Sexuality in the Classical World*. New York.

Goldman, N. 1994. "Roman Footwear," in *The World of Roman Costume*, edited by J. L. Sebesta and L. Bonfante, 101–129. Madison.

Goold, G. P. 1970. "Servius and the Helen Episode." *HSCPh* 74: 101–168.

Gordon, R. 1990. "From Republic to Principate: Priesthood, Religion, and Ideology," in *Pagan Priests*, edited by M. Beard and J. North, 179–198. Ithaca.

Gordon, R. and J. Reynolds. 2003. "Roman Inscriptions 1995–2000." *JRS* 93: 212–294.

Gowers, E. 1993. *The Loaded Table: Representations of Food in Roman Literature*. Oxford.

Gradel, I. 2002. *Emperor Worship and Roman Religion*. Oxford.

Graf, F. 2000. "The rite of the Argei–once again." *MH* 57: 94–103.

———. 2002. "Aedituus." *BNP* 1: 170.

———. 2003. "Carmentis." *BNP* 2: 1114.

———. 2004. "Flora." *BNP* 5: 466.

Graillot, H. 1912. Le culte de Cybèle, mere des dieux, à Rome et dans l'Empire romain. Paris.

Grandazzi, A. 1997. *The Foundations of Rome*. Translated by J. M. Todd. Ithaca.

Granino Cecere, M. G. 2003. "Vestali non di Roma." *SEL* 20: 67–80

Gras, M. 1983. "Vin et société à Rome et dans le Latium à l'époque archaïque," in *Modes de contacts et processus de transformation dans les sociétés anciennes*, 1067–1075. CEFR(A) 67. Rome.

Green, C.M.C. 2007. *Roman Religion and the Cult of Diana at Aricia*. Cambridge.

———. 2009. "The Gods in the Circus," in *New Perspectives on Etruria and Early Rome, in Honor of R. D. De Puma*, edited by S. Bell and H. Nagy, 56–78. Madison.

———. 2010. "Holding the Line: Women, Ritual and the Protection of Rome," in *Women and Gender in Ancient Religions: Interdisciplinary Approaches*, edited by S. P. Ahearne-Kroll, P. A. Holloway, and J. A. Kelhoffer, 279–295. Tübingen.

Grieve, L. 1985. "Livy 40.51.9 and the Centuriate Assembly." *CQ* 35.2: 417–429.

Gruen, E. S. 1968. *Roman Politics and the Criminal Courts, 149–78 BC*. Cambridge.

———. 1990. *Studies in Greek Culture and Roman Policy*. Leiden.

Guarducci, M. 1964. "Vesta sul Palatino." *RM* 71: 158–169.

———. 1971. "Enea e Vesta." *RM* 78: 73–118.

Guittard, C. 2012. "*Etrusca Disciplina*: How Was it Possible to Learn about Etruscan Religion in Ancient Rome," in *Religious Education in Pre-Modern Europe*, edited by I. Tanaseanu-Döbler and M. Döbler, 63–75. Leiden.

Guizzi, F. 1968. *Aspetti giuridici del sacerdozio romano: Il sacerdozio di Vesta*. Naples.

Habinek, T. 2005. *The World of Roman Song: From Ritualized Speech to Social Order*. Baltimore.

Halkin, L. 1897. *Les esclaves publics chez les Romains*. Brussels.

Hall, E. 1988. "When Did the Trojans Turn into Phrygians? Alcaeus 42.15." *ZPE* 73: 15–18.

———. 1989. *Inventing the Barbarian: Greek Self-Definition through Tragedy*. Oxford.

Hallett, J. P. 1970. ""Over Troubled Waters": The Meaning of the Title *Pontifex*." *TAPA* 101: 219–227.

———. 1984. *Fathers and Daughters in Roman Society*. Princeton.

———. 1989. "Woman as *Same* and *Other* in the Classical Roman Elite." *Helios* 16: 59–78.

Hannestad, N. 1994. *Tradition in Late Antique Sculpture: Conservation, Modernization, Production*. Aarhus.

Hänninen, M.-L. 1999a. "The Dream of Caecilia Metella," in *Female Networks and the Public Sphere in Roman Society*, edited by P. Setälä and L. Savunen, 29–38. Rome.

———. 1999b. "Juno Regina and the Roman Matrons," in *Female Networks and the Public Sphere in Roman Society*, edited by P. Setälä and L. Savunen, 39–52. Rome.

Harlow, M, ed. 2010. "Betrothal, Mid-Late Childhood and the Life Course," in *Ancient Marriage in Myth and Reality*, edited by L. Larsson Lovén and A. Stömberg, 56–77. Newcastle upon Tyne.

———. 2012. *Dress and Identity*. Birmingham.

Harlow, M. and R. Laurence. 2002. *Growing Up and Growing Old in Ancient Rome: A Life Course Approach*. New York.

Harlow, M. and M.-L. Nosch, eds. 2014. *Greek and Roman Textiles and Dress: An Interdisciplinary Anthology*. Philadelphia.

Harmon, D. P. 1978. "The Public Festivals of Rome." *ANRW* 2.16.2: 1440–1468.

Headlam, J. W. 1933. *Election by Lot at Athens*. 2nd edition. Cambridge.

Helbig, W. 1880. "Über den Pileus der alten Italiker." *Sitzungsberichte der philosophisch-philologischen und historischen Classe der K.B. Akademie der Wissenschaft zu München* 1.4: 487–554.

Hemelrijk, E. A. 1999. *Matrona Docta: Educated Women in the Roman Elite from Cornelia to Julia Domna*. New York.

———. 2005. "Priestesses of the Imperial Cult in the Latin West: Titles and Function." *AC* 74: 137–170.

———. 2006. "Priestesses of the Imperial Cult in the Latin West: Benefactions and Public Honour." *AC* 75: 85–117.

———. 2007. "Local Empresses: Priestesses of the Imperial Cult in the Cities of the Latin West." *Phoenix* 61: 318–349.

———. 2009. "Women and Sacrifice in the Roman Empire," in *Ritual Dynamics and Religious Change in the Roman Empire*, edited by O. Hekster, S. Schmidt-Hofner, and C. Witschel, 253–267. Leiden.

Henry, M. and S. L. James. 2012. "Woman, City, State: Theories, Ideologies, and Concepts in the Archaic and Classical Periods," in *A Companion to Women in the Ancient World*, edited by S. L. James and S. Dillon, 84–95. Malden.

Herbert-Brown, G. 1994. *Ovid and the Fasti: An Historical Study.* Oxford.

Hersch, K. K. 2010. *The Roman Wedding: Ritual and Meaning in Antiquity.* Cambridge.

Hersh, C. and A. Walker. 1984. "The Mesagne Hoard." *American Numismatic Society Museum Notes* 29: 103–134.

Heskel, J. 1994. "Cicero as Evidence for Attitudes to Dress in the Late Republic," in *The World of Roman Costume*, edited by J. L. Sebesta and L. Bonfante, 133–145. Madison.

Heyob, S. K. 1975. *The Cult of Isis among Women in the Graeco-Roman World.* Leiden.

Hickson, F. V. 1993. *Roman Prayer Language: Livy and the Aeneid of Vergil.* Stuttgart.

Hillard, T. 1989. "Republican Politics, Women and the Evidence." *Helios* 16: 165–182.

———. 1992. "On the Stage, Behind the Curtain: Images of Politically Active Women in the Late Roman Republic," in *Stereotypes of Women in Power: Historical Perspectives and Revisionist Views*, edited by B. Garlick, S. Dixon, and P. Allen, 37–64. New York.

Hinz, V. 1998. *Der Kult von Demeter und Kore auf Sizilien und in der Magna Graecia.* Wiesbaden.

Hirschmann, V. E. 2004. "Methodische Überlegungen zu Frauen in antiken Vereinen," in *Roman Rule and Civic Life: Local and Regional Perspectives*, edited by L. de Ligt, E. A. Hemelrijk, and H. S. Singor, 401–414. Amsterdam.

Holford-Strevens, L. 2005. *Aulus Gellius: An Antonine Scholar and his Achievement.* 2nd edition. Oxford.

———. 2015. "Varro in Gellius and Late Antiquity," in *Varro Varius: The Polymath of the Roman World*, edited by D. J. Butterfield, 143–160. Cambridge.

Holland, L. 2011. "Family Nomenclature and Same-Name Divinities in Roman Religion and Mythology." *CW* 104: 211–226.

———. 2012a. "Aedituus," in *The Encyclopedia of Ancient History*, edited by R. S. Bagnall, K. Brodersen, C. B. Champion, A. Erskine, and S. R. Huebner, 114–115. Malden.

———. 2012b. "Women and Roman Religion," in *A Companion to Women in the Ancient World*, edited by S. L. James and S. Dillon, 104–114. Malden.

Holland, L. A. 1953. "Septimontium or Saeptimontium?" *TAPA* 84: 16–34.

———. 1961. *Janus and the Bridge.* Philadelphia.

Hollywood, A. 2004. "Agency and Evidence in Feminist Studies of Religion: A Response to Elizabeth Clark," in *The Future of the Study of Religion: Proceedings of Congress 2000*, edited by S. Jakelić and L. Pearson, 243–249. Leiden.

Hommel, H. 1972. "Vesta und die frührömische Religion." *ANRW* 1.2: 397–420.

Hopkins, M. K. 1965. "The Age of Roman Girls at Marriage." *Population Studies* 18: 309–327.

———. 1983. *Death and Renewal Volume 2: Sociological Studies in Roman History.* Cambridge.

Horster, M. 2007. "Living on Religion: Professionals and Personnel," in *A Companion to Roman Religion*, edited by J. Rüpke, 331–341. Malden.

Huet, V. 2012. "Le voile du sacrifiant à Rome sur les reliefs romains: une norme?," in *Vêtements antiques. S'habiller, se déshabiller dans les mondes anciens*, edited by F. Gherchanoc and V. Huet, 47–62. Arles.

———. 2015. "Watching Rituals," in *A Companion to the Archaeology of Religion in the Ancient World*, edited by R. Raja and J. Rüpke, 144–154. Malden.

Humphrey, J. H. 1986. *Roman Circuses: Arenas for Chariot Racing.* London.

Hünemörder, C. 2003. "Beans." *BNP* 2: 565.

Iacopi, I. 1974. *L'antiquarium Forense.* Rome.

Isayev, E. 2011. "Just the Right Amount of Priestly Foreignness," in *Priests and State in the Roman World*, edited by J. H. Richardson and F. Santangelo, 373–390. Stuttgart.

Janan, M. 1998. "Refashioning Hercules: Propertius 4.9." *Helios* 25: 65–77.

Jeanmaire, H. 1951. *Dionysos. Histoire du culte de Bacchus.* Paris.

Jocelyn, H. D. 1989. "Romulus and the *di genitales* (Ennius, *Annales* 110–111 Skutsch)," in *Studies in Latin Literature and its Tradition in Honour of C. O. Brink*, edited by J. Diggle, J. B. Hall, and H. D. Jocelyn, 39–65. Cambridge.

Johansson, L. 2010. "The Roman Wedding and the Household Gods: The Genius and the Lares and Their Different Roles in the Rituals of Marriage," in *Ancient Marriage in Myth and Reality*, edited by L. Larsson Lovén and A. Stömberg, 136–147. Newcastle upon Tyne.

———. 2011. "The Pompeian *Lararium* as a Symbol of Commemoration: A Study of Roman Domestic Cult and Its Role as a Link to the Past," in *In Memoriam: Commemoration, Communal Memory and Gender Values in the Ancient Graeco-Roman World*, edited by H. Whittaker, 144–156. Cambridge.

Johnson, J. R. 1978. "The Authenticity and Validity of Antony's Will." *AC* 47: 494–503.

Johnson, M. J. 2007. *The Pontifical Law of the Roman Republic.* Diss. Rutgers, The State University of New Jersey. New Brunswick.

Johnson, P. J. 1997. "Ovid's Livia in Exile." *CW* 90: 403–420.

Jones, J. W. 1961. "Allegorical Interpretations in Servius." *CJ* 56: 217–26.

Jordan, H. 1886. *Der Tempel der Vesta und das Haus der Vestalinnen.* Berlin.

Joshel, S. R. 1992a. "The Body Female and the Body Politic: Livy's Lucretia and Verginia," in *Pornography and Representation in Greece and Rome*, edited by A. Richlin, 112–130. Oxford.

———. 1992b. *Work, Identity, and Legal Status at Rome: A Study of the Occupational Inscriptions.* Norman.

Jucker, H. 1961. "Bildnisbüste einer Vestalin." *RM* 68: 93–113.

Kaltsas, N. and A. Shapiro, eds. 2008. *Worshipping Women: Ritual and Reality in Classical Athens.* New York.

Kaster, R. A. 1980. "Macrobius and Servius: *Verecundia* and the Grammarian's Function." *HSCPh* 84: 219–262.

———. 1988. *Guardians of Language: The Grammarian and Society in Late Antiquity.* Berkeley.

———. 1995. *C. Suetonius Tranquillus: De Grammaticis et Rhetoribus.* Oxford.

————. 2010. "Scholarship," in *The Oxford Handbook of Roman Studies*, edited by A. Barchiesi and W. Scheidel, 492–504. Oxford.

Keaney, A. M. 1991. "Three Sabine Nomina: Clausus, Cōnsus, *Fisus." *Glotta* 69: 202–214.

Keegan, P. 2008. "Q(uando) St(ercus) D(elatum) F(as): What was Removed from the Temple of Vesta?" *NECJ* 35: 91–97.

Kelly, J. 1984. *Women, History, and Theory: The Essays of Joan Kelly*. Chicago.

Ker, J. 2010. "*Nundinae*: The Culture of the Roman Week." *Phoenix* 64: 360–385.

Kidder, N. 2001. "Fire," in *Primitive Technology: A Book of Earth Skills*, edited by D. Wescott, 36–37. Layton.

Kilpatrick, R. S. 2002. "The Early Augustan "Aldobrandini Wedding" Fresco: A Quatercentenary Reappraisal (1601–2001)." *MAAR* 47: 19–32.

Kleiner, D.E.E. 1992. *Roman Sculpture*. New Haven.

Klose, A. 1910. *Römische Priesterfasten*. Breslau.

Koch, C. 1949. "*Patrimi et matrimi*." *RE* 18.3: 2250–2252.

————. 1958. "Vesta." *RE* 2.16: 1717–1776.

Kolbe, H.-G. 1966–1967. "Noch einmal Vesta auf dem Palatin." *RM* 73–74: 101–104.

Koschaker, P. 1937. "Le mariage dans l'ancien droit romain." *RD* 16: 746–749.

Kraemer, R. S. 1979. "Ecstasy and Possession: The Attraction of Women to the Cult of Dionysius." *HThR* 72: 55–80.

————. 1992. *Her Share of the Blessings: Women's Religions among Pagans, Jews and Christians in the Greco-Roman World*. New York.

————. 2011. *Unreliable Witnesses: Religion, Gender, and History in the Greco-Roman Mediterranean*. Oxford.

Kroppenberg, I. 2010. "Law, Religion, and Constitution of the Vestal Virgins." *Law and Literature* 22: 418–439.

Kübler, B. 1901a. "Curia." *RE* 4.2: 1814–1826.

————. 1901b. "Curio (2)." *RE* 4.2: 1836–1838.

Lacey, W. K. 1986. "Patria Potestas," in *The Family in Ancient Rome*, edited by B. Rawson, 121–144. Ithaca.

La Follette, L. 1994. "The Costume of the Roman Bride," in *The World of Roman Costume*, edited by J. L. Sebesta and L. Bonfante, 54–64. Madison.

————. 2011. "Se parer en Vestale: un travail de funambule?," in *Parures et artifices: le corps exposé dans l'Antiquité*, edited by L. Bodiou, F. Gherchanoc, V. Huet, V. Mehl, 155–171. Paris.

————. 2011/2012. "Parsing Piety: The Sacred Still Life in Roman Relief Sculpture." *MAAR* 56/57: 15–35.

La Follette, L. and R. Wallace. 1993. "Latin *Seni Crines* and the Hair Style of Roman Brides." *Syllecta Classica*: 4: 1–6.

Lambert, S. D. 1993. *The Phratries of Attica*. Ann Arbor.

Lambrechts, P. 1946. "Consus et l'enlèvement des Sabines." *AC* 15: 61–82.

Lanciani, R. 1888. *Ancient Rome in the Light of New Discoveries*. Boston.

Langlands, R. 2006. *Sexual Morality in Ancient Rome*. Cambridge.

La Rocca, E. 1992. "Ara reditus Claudii. Linguaggio figurative e simbologia nell'età di Claudio," in *La storia, la letteratura e l'arte a Roma*, 61–121. Mantova.

————. 1994. "Arcus et arae Claudii," in *Die Regierungszeit des Kaiser Claudius*, 267–292. Mainz.

Latham, J. 2012. ""Fabulous Clap-Trap": Roman Masculinity, the Cult of Magna Mater, and Literary Constructions of the *galli* at Rome from the Late Republic to Late Antiquity." *JR* 92: 84–122.

Latte, K. 1960. *Römische Religionsgeschichte*. Munich.

Lattimore, R. 1962. *Themes in Greek and Latin Epitaphs*. Urbana.

Leach, E. W. 2007. "Claudia Quinta (*Pro Caelio* 34) and an altar to Magna Mater." *Dictynna* 4. Retrieved January 27, 2014 from http://dictynna.revues.org/157.

Le Bonniec, H. 1958. *Le culte de Cérès à Rome. Des origines à la fin de la République*. Paris.

———. 1969. *P. Ovidius Naso: Fastorum Liber Secundus*. Paris.

Lefkowitz, M. R. 1983. "Wives and Husbands." *G&R* 30: 31–47.

Lelis, A. A., W. A. Percy and B. C. Verstraete. 2003. *The Age of Marriage in Ancient Rome*. Lewiston.

Lennon, J. 2012. "Pollution, religion and society in the Roman world," in *Rome, Pollution, and Propriety: Dirt, Disease and Hygiene in the Eternal City from Antiquity to Modernity*, edited by M. Bradley with K. Stow, 43–58. Cambridge.

Leone, M. 1976. "Il Problema del Flaminato di Cesare," in *Studi di Storia Antica Offerti dagli Allievi a Eugenio Manni*, 193–212. Rome.

Lerner, G. 1986. *The Creation of Patriarchy*. Oxford.

Levene, D. S. 1993. *Religion in Livy*. Leiden.

Levine, M. M. 1995. "The Gendered Grammar of Ancient Mediterranean Hair," in *Off With Her Head! The Denial of Women's Identity in Myth, Religion, and Culture*, edited by H. Eilberg-Schwartz and W. Doniger, 76–130. Berkeley.

Levin-Richardson, S. 2013. "*Fututa sum hic:* Female Subjectivity and Agency in Pompeian Sexual Graffiti." *CJ* 108: 319–345.

Lhommé, M.-K. 2007. "Varron et Verrius au 2ème siècle après Jésus-Christ," in *Verrius, Festus, & Paul: Lexicography, Scholarship, and Society*, edited by F. Glinister and C. Woods, with J. A. North and M. H. Crawford, 33–47. London.

Lightman, M. and W. Zeisel. 1977. "Univira: An Example of Continuity and Change in Roman Society." *ChHist* 46: 19–32.

Lincoln, B. 1981. *Emerging from the Chrysalis: Rituals of Women's Initiation*. Cambridge.

Linderski, J. 1972. "The Aedileship of Favonius, Curio the Younger and Cicero's Election to the Augurate." *HSPh* 76: 181–200.

———. 1986. "The Augural Law." *ANRW* 2.16.3: 2146–2312.

———. 2005. "Religious Aspects of the Conflict of the Orders: The Case of *confarreatio*," in *Social Struggles in Archaic Rome*, edited by K. A. Raaflaub, 223–238. 2nd edition. Malden.

Lindheim, S. H. 1998. "Hercules Cross-Dressed, Hercules Undressed: Unmasking the Construction of the Propertian *Amator* in Elegy 4.9." *AJPh* 119: 43–66.

Lindner, M.M.M. 1995. *The Vestal Virgins and their Imperial Patrons: Sculptures and Inscriptions from the Atrium Vestae in the Roman Forum*. Diss. The University of Michigan. Ann Arbor.

———. 2015. *Portraits of the Vestal Virgins, Priestesses of Ancient Rome*. Ann Arbor.

Lindsay, H. 2000. "Death Pollution and Funerals in Rome," in *Death and Disease in the Ancient City*, edited by V. M. Hope and E. Marshall, 152–173. London.

Lintott, A. 1965. "*Trinundinum*." *CQ* 15: 281–285.

———. 1999. *The Constitution of the Roman Republic*. Oxford.

Liou-Gille, B. 1999. "César, 'Flamen Dialis Destinatus.'" *REA* 101: 433–459.

———. 2006. "Femmes-guerrières. Les Romains se sont-ils intéressés aux Amazones et à leurs légendes?" *Euphrosyne* 34: 51–64.

Lipka, M. 2009. *Roman Gods: A Conceptual Approach*. Leiden.

Littlewood, R. J. 2006. *A Commentary on Ovid, Fasti, Book 6*. Oxford.

Liu, J. 2009. *Collegia Centonariorum: The Guilds of Textile Dealers in the Roman West*. Leiden.

Lloyd, R. B. 1961. "Republican Authors in Servius and the Scholia Danielis." *HSCPh* 65: 291–341.

Lott, J. B. 2004. *The Neighborhoods of Augustan Rome*. Cambridge.

Lovisi, C. 1998. "Vestale, *incestus* et juridiction pontificale sous la République romaine." *MEFR* 110: 699–735.

Lyons, D. 2007. "The Scandal of Women's Ritual," in *Finding Persephone: Women's Rituals in the Ancient Mediterranean*, edited by M. Parca and A. Tzanetou, 29–51. Bloomington.

MacBain, B. 1982. *Prodigy and Expiation: A Study in Religion and Politics in Republican Rome*. Brussels.

MacLachlan, B. 2007. "Introduction," in *Virginity Revisited: Configurations of the Unpossessed Body*, edited by B. MacLachlan and J. Fletcher, 3–12. Toronto.

MacMullen, R. 1970. "Market Days in the Roman Empire." *Phoenix* 24: 333–341.

Mæhle, I. 2008. "Female Cult in the Struggle of the Orders," in *Religion and Society: Rituals, Resources and Identity in the Ancient Graeco-Roman World*, edited by A. H. Rasmussen and S. W. Rasmussen, 61–69. Rome.

Magi, F. 1945. *I rilievi flavi del palazzo della Cancelleria*. Rome.

Mantle, I. C. 2002. "The Roles of Children in Roman Religion." *G&R* 49: 85–106.

Marco Simón, F. 1996. *Flamen Dialis: El sacerdote de Júpiter en el religión romana*. Madrid.

Marquardt, J. 1885. *Römische Staatsverwaltung*. 3 volumes. 2nd edition. Leipzig.

Martens, M. 2015. "Communal Dining: Making Things Happen," in *A Companion to the Archaeology of Religion in the Ancient World*, edited by R. Raja and J. Rüpke, 167–180. Malden.

Martini, M. C. 1997a. "Carattere e struttura del sacerdozio delle Vestali: un approccio storico religioso. Prima parte." *Latomus* 56: 246–263.

———. 1997b. "Carattere e struttura del sacerdozio delle Vestali: un approccio storico religioso. Seconda parte." *Latomus* 56: 477–503.

———. 2004. *Le vestali: Un sacerdozio delle funzionale al 'cosmo' romano*. Brussels.

Maslakov, G. 1983. "The Roman Antiquarian Tradition in Late Antiquity," in *History and Historians in Late Antiquity*, edited by B. Croke and A. M. Emmett, 100–106. Sydney.

Masséglia, J. 2015. *Body Language in Hellenistic Art and Society*. Oxford.

Mastrocinque, A. 2014. *Bona Dea and the Cults of Roman Women*. Stuttgart.

McGinn, T.A.J. 1998. *Prostitution, Sexuality, and the Law in Ancient Rome*. Oxford.

McManus, B. F. 1997. *Classics and Feminism: Gendering the Classics*. New York.

Meier, C. 1995. *Caesar*. Translated by D. McLintock. London.

Mekacher, N. 2006. *Die vestalischen Jungfrauen in der römischen Kaiserzeit*. Weisbaden.

Mekacher, N. and F. Van Haeperen. 2003. "Le choix des Vestales, miroir d'une société en évolution (IIIème s. a.C.–Ier s. p.C.)." *RHR* 220: 63–80.

Merlin, A. 1906. *L'Aventin dans l'antiquité*. Paris.

Michels, A. K. 1967. *The Calendar of the Roman Republic*. Princeton.

Middleton, J. H. 1886. "The Temple and Atrium of Vesta and the Regia." *Archaeologia* 49: 391–423.

Miller, J. F. 1982. "Callimachus and the Augustan Aetiological Elegy." *ANRW* 2.30.1: 371–417.

Milnor, K. 2005. *Gender, Domesticity, and the Age of Augustus: Inventing Private Life*. Oxford.

Mitchell, R. E. 1990. *Patricians and Plebeians: The Origins of the Roman State*. Ithaca.

———. 2005. "The Definition of *patres* and *plebs*: An End to the Struggle of the Orders," in *Social Struggles in Archaic Rome: New Perspectives on the Struggle of the Orders*, edited by K. A. Raaflaub, 128–167. 2nd edition. Malden.

Moede, K. 2007. "Reliefs, Public and Private," in *A Companion to Roman Religion*, edited by J. Rüpke, 164–175. Malden.

Momigliano, A. 1963. "An Interim Report on the Origins of Rome." *JRS* 53: 95–121.

Mommsen, T. 1864–1879. *Römische Forschungen*. 2 volumes. Berlin.

———. 1870. "Die Erzählung von Cn. Marcius Coriolanus." *Hermes* 4: 1–26.

———. 1887–1888. *Römisches Staatsrecht*. 3 volumes. Leipzig.

———. 1899. *Römisches Strafrecht*. Leipzig.

Moreau, P. 1982. «*Clodiana Religio*». *Un procès politique en 61 av. J.C.* Paris.

Moretti, G. 1948. *Ara Pacis Augustae*. Rome.

Morgan, M. G. 1974. "Priests and Physical Fitness." *CQ* 24: 137–141.

Moyle, J. B. 1912. *Imperatoris Iustiniani Institutionum libri quattuor*. 2 volumes. Oxford.

Mueller, H.-F. 2002. *Roman Religion in Valerius Maximus*. New York.

Müller, F.G.J.M. 1994. *The Aldobrandini Wedding*. Amsterdam.

Münzer, F. 1920. *Römische Adelsparteien und Adelsfamilien*. Stuttgart.

———. 1937. "Die römischen Vestalinnen bis zur Kaiserzeit." *Philologus* 92: 47–67, 199–222.

———. 1999. *Roman Aristocratic Parties and Families*. Translated by T. Ridley. Baltimore.

Mustakallio, K. 1990. "Some Aspects of the Story of Coriolanus and the Women Behind the Cult of Fortuna Muliebris," in *Roman Eastern Policy and Other Studies in Roman History*, edited by H. Solin and M. Kajava, 125–131. Helsinki.

———. 1992. "The '*crimen incesti*' of the Vestal Virgins and the Prodigious Pestilence," in *Crudelitas: The Politics of Cruelty in the Ancient and Medieval World*, edited by T. Viljamaa, A. Timonen, and C. Krötzl, 56–62. Helsinki.

———. 2007. "The Changing Role of the Vestal Virgins," in *Public Roles and Personal Status: Men and Women in Antiquity*, edited by L. Larsson Lovén and A. Strömberg, 185–203. Sävedalen.

———. 2010. "Creating Roman Identity: Exemplary Marriages. Roman Model Marriages in the Sacral and Historical Sphere," in *Ancient Marriage in Myth and Reality*, edited by L. Larsson Lovén and A. Strömberg, 12–24. Newcastle upon Tyne.

Mustonen, P. 2010. *Flaminica Dialiksen uskonnollinen rooli Rooman tasavalta- ja keisariajalla*. M.A. thesis, University of Tampere. Tampere.

Mucznik, S. 1999. "Roman Priestesses: The Case of Metilia Acte." *Assaph* 4: 61–78.

Nagy, B. 1985. "The Argei Puzzle." *AJAH* 10: 1–27.

Nelson, J. L. 1990. "The Problematic in the Private." *Social History* 15: 355–364.

Néraudau, J.-P. 1984. *Être Enfant à Rome*. Paris.

Niccolini, G. 1934. *I fasti dei tribuni della plebe*. Milan.

Nicholas, B. 1962. *An Introduction to Roman Law*. Oxford.

Nicolet, C. 1980. *The World of the Citizen in Republican Rome*. Translated by P. S. Falla. London.

Nilsson, M. P. 1957. *The Dionysiac Mysteries of the Hellenistic and Roman Age*. Lund.

Nixon, L. 1995. "The Cults of Demeter and Kore," in *Women in Antiquity: New Assessments*, edited by R. Hawley and B. Levick, 75–96. New York.

Noailles, P. 1936. "Les rites nuptiaux gentilices et la *confarreatio*." *RD* 15: 401–417.

Noonan, J. D. 1990. "Livy 1.9.6: The Rape at the Consualia." *CW* 83: 493–501.

North, H. F. 2000. "*Lacrimae Virginis Vestalis*," in *Rome and Her Monuments: Essays on the City and Literature of Rome in Honor of Katherine A. Geffcken*, edited by S. K. Dickison and J. P. Hallett, 357–367. Wauconda.

North, J. A. 1979. "Religious Toleration in Republican Rome." *PCPhS* 25: 85–103.

———. 1986. "Religion and Politics, from Republic to Principate." *JRS* 76: 251–258.

———. 1989. "Religion in Republican Rome." *CAH*² 7.2: 573–624.

———. 1990a. "Diviners and Divination at Rome," in *Pagan Priests: Religion and Power in the Ancient World*, edited by M. Beard and J. North, 51–71. Ithaca.

———. 1990b. "Family Strategy and Priesthood in the Late Republic," in *Parenté et stratégies familiales dans l'antiquité romaine*, edited by J. Andreau and H. Bruhns, 527–543. Rome.

———. 1998. "The Books of the *Pontifices*," in *La mémoire perdue. Recherches sur l'administration romaine*, edited by C. Moatti, 45–63. Rome.

———. 2000. *Roman Religion*. Oxford.

———. 2007. "Why Does Festus Quote What He Quotes?," in *Verrius, Festus, & Paul: Lexicography, Scholarship and Society*, edited by F. Glinister and C. Woods, with J. A. North and M. H. Crawford 49–68. London.

———. 2012. "Priests (Greek and Roman)," in *The Oxford Classical Dictionary*, edited by S. Hornblower and A. Spawforth with assistance from E. Eidinow, 1209–1210. 4th edition. Oxford.

———. 2014. "The Limits of the "Religious" in the Late Roman Republic." *History of Religions* 53: 225–245.

Oakley, S. P. 1998. *A Commentary on Livy, Books VI–X. Volume I: Introduction and Book VI*. Oxford.

Ogilvie, R. M. 1965. *A Commentary on Livy, Books I–V*. Oxford.

Olson, K. 2002. "*Matrona* and Whore: The Clothing of Women in Roman Antiquity." *Fashion Theory* 6.4: 387–420.

———. 2008. *Dress and the Roman Woman: Self-presentation and Society*. New York.

Oppermann, M. 1985. *Römische Kaiserreliefs*. Leipzig.

Orlin, E. M. 1997. *Temples, Religion and Politics in the Roman Republic*. Leiden.

———. 2002. "Foreign Cults in Republican Rome: Rethinking the Pomerial Rule." *MAAR* 47: 1–18.

———. 2010. *Foreign Cults in Rome: Creating a Roman Empire*. Oxford.

Orr, D. G. 1978. "Roman Domestic Religion: The Evidence of the Household Shrines." *ANRW* 2.16.2: 1557–1591.

Ortner, S. B. 1978. "The Virgin and the State." *Feminist Studies* 4: 19–35.

Osborne, R. 1993. "Women and Sacrifice in Classical Greece." *CQ* 43: 392–405.

Osgood, J. 2006. *Caesar's Legacy: Civil War and the Emergence of the Roman Empire.* Cambridge.

Oswald, R. and M. Haase. 2010. "Wedding Customs and Rituals." *BNP* 15: 605–612.

Pailler, J.-M. 1987. "Les matrones romaines et les empoisonnements criminels sous la République." *CRAI* 131: 111–128.

———. 1988. *Bacchanalia. La répression de 186 av. J.-C. à Rome et en Italie: vestiges, images, tradition.* Rome.

———. 1995. "Marginales et exemplaires. Remarques sur quelques aspects du rôle religieux des femmes dans la Rome républicaine." *Clio* 2: 41–60.

Palmer, R.E.A. 1969. *The King and the Comitium.* Wiesbaden.

———. 1970. *The Archaic Community of the Romans.* Cambridge.

———. 1972. "Ivy and Jupiter's Priest," in *Homenaje a Antonio Tovar*, 341–348. Madrid.

Palombi, D. 1995a. "Domus Flaminia." *LTUR* 2: 100.

———. 1995b. "Genius Publicus/Populi Romani." *LTUR* 2: 365–368.

Papanek, H. 1973. "Men, Women, and Work: Reflections on the Two-Person Career." *American Journal of Sociology* 78: 852–872.

Papi, E. 1995. "Flora, Aedes." *LTUR* 2: 253–254.

Parca, M. and A. Tzanetou, eds. 2007. *Finding Persephone: Women's Rituals in the Ancient Mediterranean.* Bloomington.

Parke, H. W. 1977. *Festivals of the Athenians.* London.

Parker, H. 2004. "Why Were the Vestals Virgins? Or the Chastity of Women and the Safety of the Roman State." *AJPh* 125.4: 563–601.

Parker, R. 1996. *Miasma: Pollution and Purification in Early Greek Religion.* 2nd edition. Oxford.

Parkin, T. G. 1992. *Demography and Roman Society.* Baltimore.

Pearce, T.E.V. 1974. "The Role of the Wife as *Custos* in Ancient Rome." *Eranos.* 72: 16–33.

Peruzzi, E. 1995. "La sacerdotessa di Corfinio." *PP* 50: 5–15.

Peterson, R. 1919. *The Cults of Campania.* 2 volumes. Rome.

Phillips, C. R. III. 2008. "Robigalia." *BNP* 12: 656–657.

Piccaluga, G. 1964. "Bona Dea. Due contribute all'interpretazione del suo culto." *SMSR* 36: 195–237.

Pichon, R. 1912. "Le rôle religieux des femmes dans l'ancienne Rome." *Annales du musée Guimet* 39: 77–135.

Picozzi, M. G. 1990. "Statua di Vestale, restaurata come Musa," in *Catalogo della Galleria Colonna in Roma, Sculture*, edited by F. Carinici, L. Musso, H. Keutner, and M. G. Picozzi, 157–162. Rome.

Piganiol, A. 1923. *Recherches sur les jeux romains.* Strasbourg.

Pittenger, M.R.P. 2008. *Contested Triumphs: Politics, Pageantry, and Performance in Livy's Republican Rome.* Berkeley.

Platner, S. B. 1929. *A Topographical Dictionary of Ancient Rome.* Completed and revised by T. Ashby. London.

Pley, J. 1911. *De lanae in antiquorum ritibus usu.* Giessen.

Pomeroy, S. 1975. *Goddesses, Whores, Wives, and Slaves: Women in Classical Antiquity.* New York.

Porte, D. 1981. "Romulus-Quirinus, prince et dieu, dieu des princes." *ANRW* 2.17.1: 300–342.

———. 1986. "La noyade rituelle des homes de jonc," in *Beiträge zur Altitalischen Geistesgeschichte. Festschrift Gerhard Radke zum 18. Februar 1984*, edited by R. Altheim-Stiehl and M. Rosenbach, 193–211. Münster.

———. 1989. *Les donneurs de sacré: le prêtre à Rome*. Paris.

———. 2001. *Fêtes romaines antiques*. Paris.

———. 2007. *Les donneurs de sacré: le prêtre à Rome*. 2nd edition. Paris.

Pötscher, W. 1968. "Flamen dialis." *Mnemosyne* 4: 215–240.

Poucet, J. 1985. *Les origines de Rome. Tradition et histoire*. Brussels.

Pouthier, P. 1981. *Ops et la conception divine de l'abondance dans la religion romaine jusqu'à la mort d'Auguste*. Rome.

Prescendi, F. 2005. "Liber, Liberalia." *BNP* 7: 485–486.

———. 2007. *Décrire et comprendre le sacrifice. Les réflexions des Romains sur leur proper religion à partir de la littérature antiquaire*. Stuttgart.

———. 2010. "Children and the Transmission of Religious Knowledge," in *Children, Memory and Family Identity in Roman Culture*, edited by V. Dasen and T. Späth, 73–94. New York.

Preuner, A. 1864. *Hestia-Vesta*. Tübingen.

Price, S. 1996. "The Place of Religion: Rome in the Early Empire." *CAH*[2] 10: 812–847.

Purcell, N. 1983. "The *Apparitores*: A Study in Social Mobility." *PBSR* 51: 125–173.

———. 2003. "The Way We Used to Eat: Diet, Community, and History at Rome." *AJPh* 124: 329–358.

Raaflaub, K. A. 2005. *Social Struggles in Archaic Rome: New Perspectives on the Conflict of the Orders*. 2nd edition. Malden.

Radke, G. 1965. *Die Götter Altitaliens*. Münster.

———. 1972. "Acca Larentia und die fratres Arvales. Ein Stück römisch-sabinischer Frühgeschichte." *ANRW* 1.2: 421–441.

———. 1981. "Die *dei Penates* und Vesta in Rom." *ANRW* 2.17.1: 343–373.

———. 1990. "Gibt es Antworten auf die 'Argeerfrage'?" *Latomus* 49: 5–19.

Raepsaet-Charlier, M.-Th. 1984. "L'origine sociale des Vestales sous le Haut-Empire," in *MNHMH Georges A. Petropoulos*, edited by P. D. Dimakis, 235–270. Athens.

Rapoport, R. and R. N. Rapoport. 1969. "The Dual Career Family: A Variant Pattern and Social Change." *Human Relations* 22: 3–30.

Rawson, B. 2006. "Finding Roman Women," in *A Companion to the Roman Republic*, edited by N. Rosenstein and R. Morstein-Marx, 324–341. Malden.

Rawson, E. 1972. "Cicero the Historian and Cicero the Antiquarian." *JRS* 62: 33–45.

———. 1974. "Religion and Politics in the Late Second Century BC at Rome." *Phoenix* 28: 193–212.

———. 1978. "The Introduction of Logical Organisation in Roman Prose Literature." *PBSR* 46: 12–34.

———. 1985. *Intellectual Life in the Late Roman Republic*. Baltimore.

———. 1987. "*Discrimina Ordinum*: The *Lex Julia Theatralis*." *PBSR* 55: 83–114.

Rehak, P. 2002. "Imag(in)ing a Women's World in Prehistoric Greece: The Frescoes from Xeste 3 at Akrotiri," in *Among Women: From the Homosocial to the Homoerotic in the Ancient World*, edited by N. Rabinowitz and L. Auanger, 34–59. Austin.

Richard, J-C. 1978. *Les origines de la plèbe romaine. Essai sur la formation du dualisme patricio-plébéien.* Rome.

Richardson, J. H. 2011. "The Vestal Virgins and the Use of the *Annales Maximi*," in *Priests and State in the Roman World*, edited by J. H. Richardson and F. Santangelo, 91–106. Stuttgart.

Richardson, L. 1992. *A New Topographical Dictionary of Ancient Rome.* Baltimore.

Richlin, A. 1997. "Carrying Water in a Sieve: Class and the Body in Roman Women's Religion," in *Women and Goddess Traditions: In Antiquity and Today*, edited by K. L. King, 330–374. Minneapolis.

———. 2014. *Arguments with Silence: Writing the History of Roman Women.* Ann Arbor.

Riddle, J. M. 1992. *Contraception and Abortion from the Ancient World to the Renaissance.* Cambridge.

Ridley, R. T. 2000. "The Dictator's Mistake: Caesar's Escape from Sulla." *Historia* 49: 211–229.

Rives, J. B. 1992. "The *Iuno Feminae* in Roman Society." *EMC* 11: 33–49.

———. 1995. *Religion and Authority in Roman Carthage from Augustus to Constantine.* Oxford.

———. 2008. "Sacerdos." *BNP* 12: 824–825.

———. 2011. "Control of the Sacred in Roman Law," in *Law and Religion in the Roman Republic*, edited by O. Tellegen-Couperus, 165–180. Leiden.

———. 2013. "Women and Animal Sacrifice in Public Life," in *Women and the Roman City in the Latin West*, edited by E. Hemelrijk and G. Woolf, 129–146. Leiden.

Rizzo, G. E. 1932. "La base di Sorrento." *BullCom* 60: 1–109.

Robinson, M. 2003. "Festivals, Fools and the *Fasti*: The *Quirinalia* and the *Feriae Stultorum* (Ovid, *Fast.* II 475–532)." *Aevum(ant)* 3: 690–721.

———. 2011. *Ovid Fasti Book 2: Edited with Introduction and Commentary.* Oxford.

Roccos, L. J. 1995. "The Kanephoros and Her Festival Mantle in Greek Art." *AJA* 99: 641–666.

Roller, L. E. 1999. *In Search of God the Mother: The Cult of Anatolian Cybele.* Berkeley.

Roller, M. B. 2004. "Exemplarity in Roman Culture: The Case of Horatius Cocles and Cloelia." *CPh* 99: 1–56.

———. 2006. *Dining Posture in Ancient Rome: Bodies, Values, and Status.* Princeton.

Rose, C. B. 1997. *Dynastic Commemoration and Imperial Portraiture in the Julio-Claudian Period.* Cambridge.

Rose, H. J. 1926. "De Virginibus Vestalibus." *Mnemosyne* 54: 440–448.

———. 1924. *The Roman Questions of Plutarch.* New York.

———. 1949. "*Mana* in Greece and Rome." *HThR* 42: 155–174.

———. 1959. *Religion in Greece and Rome.* New York.

Rosenstein, N. 1995. "Sorting out the Lot in Republican Rome." *AJPh* 116: 43–75.

Rossbach, A. 1853. *Untersuchungen über die römische Ehe.* Stuttgart.

Rossetto, P. C. 1993. "Consus, Ara." *LTUR* 1: 322.

Rossini, O. 2009. *Ara Pacis.* Rome.

Rotondi, G. 1962. *Leges publicae populi romani. Elenco cronologico con una introduzione sull'attivita legislative dei comizi romani.* Hildesheim.

Rüpke, J. 1990. *Domi militia. Die religiöse Konstruktion des Krieges in Rom.* Stuttgart.

———. 1995. *Kalender und Öffentlichkeit: die Geschichte der Repräsentation und religiösen Qualifikation von Zeit in Rom.* Berlin.

———. 1996. "Controllers and Professionals: Analyzing Religious Specialists." *Numen* 43: 241–262.

———. 2004. "Acta aut agenda: Relations of Script and Performance," in *Rituals in Ink*, edited by A. Barchiesi, J. Rüpke, and S. Stephens, 23–43. Stuttgart.

———. 2005. *Fasti sacerdotum : die Mitglieder der Priesterschaften und das sakrale Funktionspersonal römischer, griechischer, orientalischer und jüdisch-christlicher Kulte in der Stadt Rom von 300 v. Chr. bis 499 n. Chr.* 3 volumes. Stuttgart.

———. 2006. "Religion in the *lex Ursonensis*," in *Religion and Law in Classical and Christian Rome*, edited by C. Ando and J. Rüpke, 34–46. Stuttgart.

———, ed. 2007a. *A Companion to Roman Religion*. Malden.

———. 2007b. *Religion of the Romans*. Translated by R. Gordon. Malden.

———. 2007c. *Römische Priester in der Antike: Ein biographisches Lexicon*. Stuttgart.

———. 2008. *Fasti Sacerdotum: A Prosopography of Pagan, Jewish and Christian Religious Officials in the City of Rome, 300 BC to AD 499*. Translated by D. Richardson. Oxford.

———. 2011. *The Roman Calendar from Numa to Constantine: Time, History and the Fasti*. Translated by D.M.B. Richardson. Malden.

———. 2012a. "*Flamines, Salii*, and the Priestesses of Vesta: Individual Decision and Differences of Social Order in Late Republican Roman Priesthoods," in *Demeter, Isis, Vesta, and Cybele: Studies in Greek and Roman Religion in Honour of Giulia Sfameni Gasparro*, edited by A. Mastrocinque and C. Giuffrè Scibona, 183–194. Stuttgart.

———. 2012b. "Public and Publicity: Long-Term Changes in Religious Festivals during the Roman Republic," in *Greek and Roman Festivals: Content, Meaning, and Practice*, edited by J.R. Brandt and J.W. Iddeng, 305–322. Oxford.

———. 2012c. *Religion in Republican Rome: Rationalization and Ritual Change*. Philadelphia.

Russell, D. A. 1973. *Plutarch*. London.

Ryberg, I. S. 1949. "The Procession of the Ara Pacis." *MAAR* 19: 79–101.

———. 1955. *Rites of the State Religion in Roman Art. MAAR* 22. Rome.

Saller, R. 1987. "Men's Age at Marriage and Its Consequences for the Roman Family." *CPh* 82: 21–34.

———. 1994. *Patriarchy, Property and Death in the Roman Family*. Cambridge.

Sallman, K. 2010. "Varro [2]." *BNP* 15: 209–226.

Salzman, M. 1990. *On Roman Time*. Berkeley.

Santinelli, I. 1902. "Alcune questioni attinenti ai riti delle vergini Vestali. Vesta aperit." *RFIC* 30: 255–269.

———. 1904. "La condizione giuridica delle Vestali." *RFIC* 32: 63–82.

Saquete, J. C. 2000. *Las vírgines Vestales: un sacerdocio femenino de la religión pública romana*. Madrid.

Savunen, L. 1995. "Women and Elections in Pompeii," in *Women in Antiquity: New Assessments*, edited by R. Hawley and B. Levick, 194–206. New York.

Schäfer, T. 1980. "Zur Ikonographie der Salier" *JDAI* 95: 342–373.

Scheid, J. 1984. "Le prêtre et le magistrat," in *Des ordres à Rome*, edited by C. Nicolet, 243–80. Paris.

———. 1985. *Religion et piété à Rome*. Paris.

———. 1986. "Le flamine de Jupiter, les Vestales et le général triomphant. Variations romaines sur le thème de la figuration des dieux." *Le temps de la réfexion* 7: 213–230.

————. 1991. "D'indispensables étrangères. Les rôles religieux des femmes à Rome," in *Histoire des Femmes en Occident 1: L'Antiquité*, edited by P. Schmitt Pantel, 405–437. Rome.

————. 1992a. "Le prêtre," in *L'homme romain*, edited by A. Giardina, 71–106. Paris.

————. 1992b. "Myth, Cult and Reality in Ovid's Fasti." *PCPhS* 38: 118–133.

————. 1992c. "The Religious Roles of Roman Women," in *A History of Women in the West*, volume 1: *From Ancient Goddesses to Christian Saints*, edited by P.S. Pantel. Translated by A. Goldhammer, 377–408. Cambridge.

————. 1993. "The Priest," in *The Romans*, edited by A. Giardina, 55–84. Translated by L. G. Cochrane. Chicago.

————. 1995. "*Graeco Ritu*: A Typically Roman Way of Honoring the Gods." *HSCPh* 97: 15–31.

————. 1998. *Commentarii fratrum arvalium qui supersunt*. Rome.

————. 1999. "Auguste et le grand pontificat: politique et droit sacré au début du Principat." *RD* 77: 1–19.

————. 2003. *An Introduction to Roman Religion*. Bloomington.

————. 2005a. "Augustus and Roman Religion: Continuity, Conservatism, and Innovation," in *The Cambridge Companion to the Age of Augustus*, K. Galinsky, ed. Cambridge.

————. 2005b. "Consualia." *BNP* 2: 744–746.

————. 2005c. "Manger avec les dieux: partage sacrificiel et commensalité dans la Rome antique," in *La cuisine et l'autel*, edited by S. Georgoudi, R. Piettre, and F. Schmitt, 273–287. Turnhout.

————. 2005d. *Quand faire, c'est croire. Les rites sacrificiels des Romains*. Paris.

————. 2006. "Oral and written tradition in the formation of sacred law in Rome," in *Religion and Law in Classical and Christian Rome*, edited by C. Ando and J. Rüpke, 14–33. Stuttgart.

————. 2007. "Sacrifices for Gods and Ancestors," in *A Companion to Roman Religion*, edited by J. Rüpke, 263–272. Malden.

Scheid, J. and M. G. Granino Cecere. 1999. "Les sacerdoces publics équestres," in *L'ordre équestre. Histoire d'une aristocratie (IIe siècle av. J.-C.-IIIe siècle ap. J.-C.)*, edited by S. Demougin, H. Devijver and M.-T. Raepsaet-Charlier, 79–189. *CEFR* 257. Rome.

Scheidel, W. 2007. "Roman Funerary Commemoration and the Age at First Marriage." *CPh* 102: 389–402.

Schilling, R. 1954. *La Religion romaine de Vénus depuis les origines jusqu'au temps d'Auguste*. Paris.

Scholz, U. W. 1970. *Studien zum altitalischen und altrömischen Marskult und Marsmythos*. Heidelberg.

————. 1993. "Consus und *Consualia*," in *Religio Graeco Romana. Festschrift für W. Pötscher*, edited by J. Dalfen, G. Petersmann, and F. F. Schwarz, 195–213. Graz.

Schultz, C. E. 2000. "Modern Prejudice and Ancient Praxis: Female Worship of Hercules at Rome." *ZPE* 133: 291–297.

————. 2006a. "Juno Sospita and Roman Insecurity in the Social War," in *Religion in Republican Italy*, edited by C. E. Schultz and P. B. Harvey, 207–227. Cambridge.

————. 2006b. *Women's Religious Activity in the Roman Republic*. Chapel Hill.

————. 2007. "*Sanctissima Femina*: Social Categorization and Women's Religious Experience in the Roman Republic," in *Finding Persephone: Women's Rituals in the Ancient Mediterranean*, edited by M. Parca and A. Tzanetou, 92–113. Bloomington.

————. 2010. "The Romans and Ritual Murder." *Journal of the American Academy of Religion* 78: 516–541.

————. 2012. "On the burial of unchaste Vestal Virgins," in *Rome, Pollution, and Propriety: Dirt, Disease and Hygiene in the Eternal City from Antiquity to Modernity*, edited by M. Bradley with K. Stow, 122–135. Cambridge.

Schwartz, S. R. 2006. *The Rabbi's Wife: The Rebbetzin in American Jewish Life*. New York.

Scott, J. 1986. "Gender: A Useful Category of Historical Analysis." *AHR* 91: 1053–1075.

————. 2012. "Gender: Still a Useful Category of Analysis?" *Diogenes* 225: 7–14.

Scott, R. T. 1999. "Regia." *LTUR* 4: 189–192.

————. 2000. "*Vestae Aedem Petitam*? Vesta in the Empire," in *Rome and her Monuments: Essays on the City and Literature of Rome in Honor of Katherine A. Geffcken*, edited by S. K. Dickison and J. P. Hallet, 173–191. Wauconda.

————. 2009. "The Excavations," in *Excavations in the Area Sacra of Vesta (1987–1996)*, edited by R. T. Scott, 1–81. Ann Arbor.

Scullard, H. H. 1981. *Festivals and Ceremonies of the Roman Republic*. Ithaca.

Seaby, H. A. 1967. *Roman Silver Coins Vol. 1: The Republic to Augustus*. 2nd edition. London.

Sebesta, J. L. 1994a. "Symbolism in the Costume of the Roman Woman," in *The World of Roman Costume*, edited by J. L. Sebesta and L. Bonfante, 46–53. Madison.

————. 1994b. "*Tunica Ralla, Tunica Spissa*: The Colors and Textiles of Roman Costume," in *The World of Roman Costume*, edited by J. L. Sebesta and L. Bonfante, 65–76. Madison.

————. 1997. "Women's Costume and Feminine Civic Morality in Augustan Rome." *Gender & History* 9.3: 529–541.

————. 2005. "The *toga praetexta* of Roman Children and Praetextate Garments," in *The Clothed Body in the Ancient World*, edited by L. Cleland, M. Harlow and L. Llewellyn-Jones, 113–120. Oxford.

Sebesta, J. L. and L. Bonfante, eds. 1994. *The World of Roman Costume*. Madison.

Sensi, L. 1980–1. "Ornatus e status sociale dell donne romane." *ALFPer* 18: 55–102.

Shackleton Bailey, D. R. 1965. *Cicero's Letters to Atticus Volume I: 68–59 BC, 1–45 (Books I and II)*. Cambridge.

Shaw, B. D. 1981. "Rural Markets in North Africa and the Political Economy of the Roman Empire." *AntAfr* 17: 37–83.

————. 1987. "The Age of Roman Girls at Marriage: Some Reconsiderations." *JRS* 77: 30–46.

Sherwin-White, A. N. 1973. *Roman Citizenship*. 2nd edition. Oxford.

Siebert, A. V. 1995. "Quellenanalytische Bemerkungen zu Haartracht und Kopfschmuck römischer Priesterinnen." *Boreas* 18: 78–83.

————. 1999. *Instrumenta Sacra: Untersuchungen zu römischen Opfer-, Kult- und Priestergeräten*. Berlin.

————. 2005. "Immolation." *BNP* 6: 744–746.

Simon, E. 1968. *Ara Pacis Augustae*. Greenwich.

————. 1983. *Festivals of Attica: An Archaeological Commentary*. Madison.

Sirianni, F. A. 1984. "Was Antony's Will Partially Forged?" *AC* 53: 236–241.

Sissa, G. 1990. *Greek Virginity*. Translated by A. Goldhamer. Cambridge.

Smith, C. 2000. "Worshipping Mater Matuta: Ritual and Context," in *Religion in Archaic and Republican Rome and Italy: Evidence and Experience*, edited by E. Bispham and C. Smith. Edinburgh.

———. 2006. *The Roman Clan: The Gens from Ancient Ideology to Modern Anthropology.* Cambridge.

Spaeth, B. S. 1990. "The Goddess Ceres and the Death of Tiberius Gracchus." *Historia* 39: 182–195.

———. 1996. *The Roman Goddess Ceres.* Austin.

Spickermann, W. 1994. "Priesterinnen im römischen Gallien, Germanien und den Alpenprovinzen (1.-3. Jahrhundert n. Chr.)." *Historia* 43: 189–240.

Staples, A. 1998. *From Good Goddess to Vestal Virgins: Sex and Category in Roman Religion.* New York.

Starr, R. T. 1997. "Aeneas as the *Flamen Dialis*? Vergil's *Aeneid* and the Servian Exegetical Tradition." *Vergilius* 43: 63–70.

Stephens, J. 2008. "Ancient Roman Hairdressing: On (Hair)pins and Needles." *JRA* 21: 111–132.

———. 2013, January 4. *Vestal Hairdressing: Recreating the "Seni Crines."* Retrieved August 29, 2013, from https://www.youtube.com/watch?v=eA9JYWh1r7U.

———. 2013, February 9. *The Tutulus Hairstyle: Ancient Roman Hairdressing.* Retrieved August 29, 2013, from https://www.youtube.com/watch?v=83V38YbkQJs.

Šterbenc Erker, D. 2013. *Religiöse Rollen römischer Frauen in "griechischen" Ritualen.* Stuttgart.

Stevenson, A. J. 1993. *Aulus Gellius and Roman Antiquarian Writing.* Diss. King's College London. London.

———. 2004. "Gellius and the Roman Antiquarian Tradition," in *The Worlds of Aulus Gellius*, edited by L. Holford-Strevens and A. Vardi, 118–155. Oxford.

Summers, K. 1996. "Lucretius' Roman Cybele," in *Cybele, Attis and Related Cults: Essays in Memory of M. J. Vermaseren*, edited by E. N. Lane, 337–365. Leiden.

Sumner, G. V. 1973. *The Orators in Cicero's Brutus: Prosopography and Chronology.* Toronto.

Swan, P. M. 2004. *The Augustan Succession: An Historical Commentary on Cassius Dio's Roman History Books 55–56 (9 B.C.–A.D. 14).* New York.

Sydenham, E. A. 1952. *The Coinage of the Roman Republic.* London.

Syme, R. 1939. *The Roman Revolution.* Oxford.

———. 1944. Review of *Caesar. Der Politiker und Staatsmann*, by M. Gelzer. *JRS* 34: 92–103.

Szemler, G. J. 1972. *The Priests of the Roman Republic: A Study of Interactions Between Priesthoods and Magistracies.* Brussels.

———. 1978. "Pontifex." *RE* suppl. 15: 331–396.

———. 1986. "Priesthoods and Priestly Careers in Ancient Rome." *ANRW* 2.16.3: 2314–2331.

Takács, S. A. 1995. *Isis and Sarapis in the Roman World.* Leiden.

———. 2000. "Politics and Religion in the Bacchanalian Affair of 186 B.C.E." *HSPh* 100: 301–310.

———. 2008. *Vestal Virgins, Sibyls, and Matrons: Women in Roman Religion.* Austin.

Talbert, R.J.A. 1984. *The Senate of Imperial Rome.* Princeton.

Tansey, P. 2000. "The Inauguration of Lentulus Niger." *AJPh* 121: 237–258.

Tatum, W. J. 1999. *The Patrician Tribune: Publius Clodius Pulcher.* Chapel Hill.

Taylor, L. R. 1941. "Caesar's Early Career." *CPh* 36: 113–132.

———. 1942a. "Caesar's Colleagues in the Pontifical College." *AJPh* 63: 385–412.

———. 1942b. "The Election of the Pontifex Maximus in the Late Republic." *CPh* 37: 421–424.

———. 1966. *Roman Voting Assemblies from the Hannibalic War to the Dictatorship of Caesar*. Ann Arbor.

Thilo, G. and H. Hagen, eds. 1881–1902. *Servii grammatici qui feruntur in Vergilii carmina Commentarii*. 3 volumes. Leipzig.

Thomas, G. 1984. "Magna Mater and Attis." *ANRW* 2.17.3: 1499–1535.

Thomas, Y. 1982. "Droit domestique et droit politique à Rome." *MEFRA* 58: 527–580.

Thompson, J. E. 2005. *Images of Vesta and the Vestal Virgins in Roman State Religion and Imperial Policy of the First and Second Centuries AD*. Diss. Yale University. New Haven.

Thompson, L. J. 2010. *The Role of the Vestal Virgins in Roman Civic Religion: A Structuralist Study of the Crimen Incesti*. Lewiston.

Tierney, J. J. 1947. "The *Senatus Consultum de Bacchanalibus*." *Proceedings of the Royal Irish Academy* 51: 89–117.

Torelli. 1984. *Lavinio e Roma: Riti iniziatici e matrimonio tra archeologia e storia*. Rome.

———. 1982. *Typology and Structure of Roman Historical Reliefs*. Ann Arbor.

———. 1997. "Il culto romano di Mater Matuta." *MNIR* 56: 165–176.

Tramonti, S. 1989. "Neptunalia e Consualia: A proposito di Ausonio, *Ecl.* 23, 29." *RSA* 19: 107–22.

Treggiari, S. 1969. *Roman Freedmen During the Late Republic*. Oxford.

———. 1980. "Urban Labour in Rome: *Mercenarii* and *Tabernarii*," in *Non-Slave Labour in the Greco-Roman World*, edited by P. Garnsey, 48–64. Cambridge.

———. 1984. "Digna Condicio: Betrothals in the Roman Upper Class." *EMC* 3: 419–451.

———. 1991. *Roman Marriage: Iusti Coniuges from the Time of Cicero to the Time of Ulpian*. Oxford.

———. 1994. "Putting the Bride to Bed." *EMC* 38: 311–331.

———. 1996a. "Divorce Roman Style: How Easy and How Frequent Was It?," in *Marriage, Divorce and Children in Ancient Rome*, edited by B. Rawson, 31–46. Oxford.

———. 1996b. "Social Status and Social Legislation." *CAH²* X: 873–904.

———. 2007. *Terentia, Tullia and Publilia: The Women of Cicero's Family*. New York.

Trimble, J. 2011. *Women and Visual Replication in Roman Imperial Art and Culture*. Cambridge.

Turcan, R. 2000. *The Gods of Ancient Rome: Religion in Everyday Life from Archaic to Imperial Times*. Translated by A. Neville. New York.

Turner, V. 1967. *The Forest of Symbols*. Ithaca.

Tyrell, R. Y. and L. C. Purser. 1904. *The Correspondence of M. Tullius Cicero*. 3rd edition. London.

Tzanetou, A. 2007. "Ritual and Gender: Critical Perspectives," in *Finding Persephone: Women's Rituals in the Ancient Mediterranean*, edited by M. Parca and A. Tzanetou, 3–26. Bloomington.

Vaahtera, J. 2001. *Roman Augural Lore in Greek Historiography*. Stuttgart.

Vahlen, I. 1871. *M. Tullii Ciceronis De Legibus libri*. Berlin.

Van Buren, A. W. 1934. "New Items from Rome." *AJA* 38: 479–481.

Van Deman, E. B. 1908. "The Value of the Vestal Statues as Originals." *AJA* 12: 324–342.

Vanggaard, J. H. 1988. *The Flamen: A Study in the History and Sociology of Roman Religion.* Copenhagen.

Van Haeperen, F. 2002. *Le collège pontifical (3ème s.a. C.-4ème s.p. C.). Contribution à l'étude de la religion publique romaine.* Brussels.

Várhelyi, Z. 2010. *The Religion of Senators in the Roman Empire: Power and the Beyond.* Cambridge.

Vermaseren, M. J. 1977. *Cybele and Attis: The Myth and the Cult.* London.

Versnel, H. S. 1992. "The Festival for Bona Dea and the Thesmophoria." *G&R* 39: 31–55.

———. 1993. *Inconsistencies in Greek and Roman Religion 2. Transition and Reversal in Myth and Ritual.* Leiden.

Vidal, H. 1965. "Le dépôt in aede." *Revue historique de droit français et étranger* 43: 545–587.

Vuolanto, V. 2012. "Faith and Religion," in *A Cultural History of Childhood and Family in Antiquity,* edited by M. Harlow and R. Laurence, 133–151. Oxford.

Wagenvoort, H. 1956. *Studies in Roman Literature, Culture, and Religion.* Leiden.

———. 1980. *Pietas.* Leiden.

Wallace-Hadrill, A. 1983. *Suetonius. The Scholar and His Caesars.* London.

———. 1996. "Engendering the Roman House," in *I, Claudia: Women in Ancient Rome,* edited by D.E.E. Kleiner and S. B. Matheson, 104–115. New Haven.

———. 1998. "*Mutatio Morum*: The Idea of a Cultural Revolution," in *The Roman Cultural Revolution,* edited by T. Habinek and A. Schiesaro, 3–22. Cambridge.

Ward, R. B. 1998. "The Public Priestesses of Pompeii," in *The Early Church in its Context. Essays in Honor of Everett Ferguson,* edited by A. J. Malherbe, F. W. Norris, and J. W. Thompson, 318–334. Leiden.

Wardman, A. 1982. *Religion and Statecraft among the Romans.* London.

Warrior, V. M. 2006. *Roman Religion.* Cambridge.

Watson, A. 1967. *The Law of Persons in the Later Roman Republic.* Oxford.

———. 1971. *The Law of Succession in the Later Roman Republic.* Oxford.

Weiß, A. 2004. *Sklave der Stadt: Untersuchungen zur öffentlichen Sklaverei in den Städten des römischen Reiches.* Stuttgart.

Welch, T.S. 2005. *The Elegiac Cityscape: Propertius and the Meaning of Roman Monuments.* Columbus.

Wessner, P. 1928. "Macrobius." *RE* 14.1: 170–198.

White, K. D. 1970. *Roman Farming.* Ithaca.

Wild, J. P. 1970. *Textile Manufacture in the Northern Roman Provinces.* Cambridge.

Wildfang, R. L. 1999. "The Vestal Virgins' Ritual Function in Roman Religion." *C&M* 50: 227–234.

———. 2001. "The Vestals and Annual Public Rites," *C&M* 52: 223–255.

———. 2006. *Rome's Vestal Virgins: A Study of Rome's Vestal Priestesses in the Late Republic and Early Empire.* New York.

Williams, G. W. 1958. "Some Aspects of Roman Marriage Ceremonies and Ideals." *JRS* 48: 16–29.

Willrich, H. 1911. *Livia.* Leipzig.

Wilson, S. G. 1996. "Voluntary Associations: An Overview," in *Voluntary Associations in the Graeco-Roman World,* edited by J. S. Kloppenborg and S. G. Wilson, 1–15. New York.

Winkler, J. J. 1990. "The Laughter of the Oppressed," in *The Constraints of Desire: The Anthropology of Sex and Gender in Ancient Greece*, edited by J. J. Winkler, 188–209. New York.

Wiseman, T. P. 1982. "Philodemus 26.3 G-P." *CQ* 32: 475–476.

———. 1993. "Clivus Capitolinus." *LTUR* 1: 280–283.

———. 1995. *Remus: A Roman Myth*. Cambridge.

Wissowa, G. 1912. *Religion und Kultus der Römer*. 2nd edition. Munich.

———. 1923–1924. "Vestalinnenfrevel." *Archiv für Religionswissenschaft* 22: 201–214.

Wood, S. 1978. "Alcestis on Roman Sarcophagi." *AJA* 82: 499–510.

———. 1999. *Imperial Women: A Study in Public Images*, 40 B.C.–A.D. 68. Leiden.

Woods, C. 2007. "A Contribution to the King's Library: Paul the Deacon's Epitome and Its Carolingian Context," in *Verrius, Festus, & Paul: Lexicography, Scholarship, and Society*, edited by F. Glinister and C. Woods, with J. A. North and M. H. Crawford, 109–135. London.

Worsfold, T. C. 1934. *The History of the Vestal Virgins of Rome*. London.

Zehnacker, H. 1973. *Moneta: recherches sur l'organisation et l'art des émissions monétaires de la République romaine : (289–331 av. J.-C.)*. 2 volumes. Rome.

Zeitlin, F. I. 1982. "Cultic Models of the Female: Rites of Dionysus and Demeter." *Arethusa* 15: 129–157.

Ziegler, K. 1969. "Magna Mater oder Mater Magna?," in *Hommages à Marcel Renard*, edited by J. Bibauw. Brussels.

Zimmermann, T. and R. Frei-Stolba. 1998. "Les prêtesses campaniennes sous l'empire romain," in *Femmes et vie publique dans l'antiquité gréco-romaine*, edited by R. Frei-Stolba and M. Corbier, 91–116. Lausanne.

Ziolkowski, A. 1992. *The Temples of Mid-Republican Rome and their Historical and Topographical Context*. Rome.

———. 1998–1999. "Ritual Cleaning-up of the City: From the Lupercalia to the Argei." *AncSoc* 29: 191–218.

INDEX

Priestesses and other religious officials are listed by Latin title. Where Latin titles are unattested or otherwise uncertain, officials are listed by deity or community served.